D0204243

SIN AND CONFESSION
ON THE EVE OF THE REFORMATION

The Heavenly Road. Illustration from Stephen Lanzkranna,
Himmelstrass. im latin genant Scala celi. Johann Otmar:
Augsburg, 1510. Courtesy of the British Museum.

Sin and Confession on the Eve of the Reformation

Thomas N. Tentler

Princeton University Press
Princeton, New Jersey

COPYRIGHT © 1977 BY PRINCETON UNIVERSITY PRESS
PUBLISHED BY PRINCETON UNIVERSITY PRESS, PRINCETON, NEW JERSEY
IN THE UNITED KINGDOM: PRINCETON UNIVERSITY PRESS,
GUILDFORD, SURREY

ALL RIGHTS RESERVED

LIBRARY OF CONGRESS CATALOGING IN PUBLICATION DATA WILL
BE FOUND ON THE LAST PRINTED PAGE OF THIS BOOK

THIS BOOK HAS BEEN COMPOSED IN LINOTYPE JANSON

PRINTED IN THE UNITED STATES OF AMERICA
BY PRINCETON UNIVERSITY PRESS, PRINCETON, NEW JERSEY

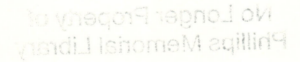

To Leslie, Kate, Justin, and Sarah

Contents

Preface

This is a study of a religious institution. It explains, in language as free from theological technicalities as possible, the ordinary teaching about sin, guilt, and forgiveness in the decades before the Reformation. At the same time it describes what was required of all Christians who had attained the age of reason and who sought justification through ecclesiastical penance. It emphasizes attitudes and habits more than theological concepts, in an effort to explain the social and psychological impact of the institution that, in the sixteenth century, Protestant reformers vehemently attacked and Catholic counter-reformers just as vehemently defended. In other words, this study attempts to portray the institution that tormented Luther and outraged Calvin so that we can understand why religious men and women might respond to that institution with anguish and anger. But it also tries to explain the strength of sacramental confession so that we can understand why religious men and women might need it and want to keep it.

A little over seventy years ago Henry C. Lea published his detailed and scholarly *History of Auricular Confession*. Why, then, is a study of sacramental confession before the Reformation warranted? I think the answers to that question are important, not only to justify my efforts, but also to clarify how I have proceeded and what I have tried to do.

Lea was an energetic and reliable researcher who seldom made factual mistakes. Nevertheless, in the seventy years since he wrote, there has been a wealth of investigation of subjects that Lea dealt with, or only touched on, or ignored completely—subjects that are essential to understanding the theory and practice of confession. Historians such as Nikolaus Paulus, Franz Falk, Johannes Dietterle, Bernhard Poschmann, Peter Browe, Paul Anciaux, Amédée Teetaert, Ludwig Hödl, Benjamin Nelson, Leonard Boyle, Josef Ziegler, Pierre Michaud-Quantin, and John T. Noonan—to name only some of those who have written on confession or directly related subjects—have revised and corrected the intellectual and institutional history of penance. Bibliographical research and intellectual biographies have supplemented narrower investigations of the power of the keys, the nature of contrition, sexual and economic morality, excommunication, the obligations to confess and make restitution, and a host of other problems. And while this scholarship does not entirely supersede Lea, it inevitably changes our understanding of the institution.

An even more compelling reason for a new treatment of Lea's subject, however, is one of method. Lea offers an abundance of accurate information; but his research techniques and his obvious bias limit the usefulness of his work. Any study of the magnitude of the *History of Auricular Confession* must be selective, but Lea's selectivity is especially vitiating. Even when he cites such important authors as Jean Gerson, Sylvester Prierias, or Antoninus of Florence, Lea does not convey any sense of coherency in their thought. The grand chronological sweep of the work obscures the relationship between institutional developments and other phases of ecclesiastical and social history. But Lea's most serious flaw is his anticlerical motivation, which accounts for many of the shortcomings in his selectivity, and which forces a contemporary reader to use the *History of Auricular Confession* only as a reference work and not as a work of historical interpretation. Lea wanted to demonstrate that the Roman clergy were depraved, their moral doctrine degenerate, and their teaching on confession confused. He was scandalized by their frank discussions of sexual morality. He was horrified by a laxity that he saw threatening all civilized institutions, including private property. For Lea the whole science of casuistry—the systematic application of general norms to particular cases—was not essential to ethics, but rather a sophistry that directly undermined ethics. Thus for all his erudition, Lea remained a "whig" critic whose goal was to amass evidence of inconsistency, hypocrisy, and turpitude. While he was fascinated by the mechanical operation of the institution and the details of its evolution, he never tried to analyze the ways in which auricular confession served the social and psychological needs of Western Christendom. That a fundamentally different approach is now possible is also owing to a vast body of sociological and psychological knowledge. Freud, Weber, Durkheim, Talcott Parsons, and R. K. Merton influence this study, and make possible an interpretation different from Lea's, at least as significantly as the intellectual and institutional historians listed above.

I began this study with an intention wholly different from Lea's, but almost as single-minded. I wanted to show that the late medieval Sacrament of Penance contained a theology of consolation, a logical and formidable system, answering the same questions Luther and Calvin were later to raise. I expected to find the popularization of a set of theological opinions making it clear to medieval Christians why confession and absolution comprised the safe, easy, and certain way to justification. Then I hoped to represent this tight intellectual system as medieval Catholicism's entry into the sixteenth century competition for souls—a competition in which systematically different theologies of consolation gave their own answers to the same questions.

The results were not quite so simple. Sometimes pastoral authorities disagreed on basic issues, and sometimes they seemed uninterested in issues related to consolation. The persistence of old books and ideas precluded any easy judgment on the triumph of a single system of consolation at the end of the middle ages. Characteristic assumptions and preoccupations concerning penance were consistent only within a broad frame of reference: they certainly could not be reduced to the neat and narrow theology of assurance I had set out to find. Perhaps the most important realization of all was that this institution continued to perform, as it had throughout its long and varied history, the function of discipline or social control. Or perhaps it would be more accurate to say that it became apparent that discipline could not be ignored, that the cure of anxiety could not be examined separately. Sacramental confession was designed to cause guilt as well as cure guilt, and it no longer seemed fruitful to try to analyze one without the other. Reformation issues—legalism, scrupulosity, human effort, certainty of forgiveness, grace and freedom, the power of the keys, and the role of Christ—remained as guides to this study. But I tried to gather and interpret evidence so that the system I described would faithfully represent the expressed interests and implicit goals of those authorities whose ideas and writings governed sacramental confession from the advent of printing until the beginning of the Reformation. Thus I have tried to describe an institution performing positive social functions. My judgments on the institution represent an attempt to evaluate its effectiveness in performing these functions.

As a functioning institution, sacramental confession sometimes appears diffuse and disorganized. But I have tried to integrate all of its elements—the actual behavior of confessing, the clichés and commonplaces used to teach doctrine, terse theological definitions and abstract theological speculations, moral regulations, the rhetoric of comfort, disapproval, and terrorization, and analysis of emotions and legalistic complications—and depict an institutional rather than an intellectual coherency. In short, I have used anything relevant to the theory and practice of confession that would take it from the level of theological abstraction and help explain it in terms of human experience.

The sources I have used come primarily from an ecclesiastical establishment. They are books and manuals written by the people who ran the church—or who spoke for those who ran the church—and who tried to get people to conform to the standards embodied in the ecclesiastical institutions over which they presided. Consequently the evidence in this study is, in one sense, indirect, because it represents the point of view of these religious authorities and observers of society. Examination of late medieval literature for popular manifestations of religiosity, repentance, or even doctrines of penance lies beyond the scope of this book, as does the attempt to determine the frequency of the reception of the sacraments. I have used but have not emphasized statistics on attendance at confession because, as I have argued below, these data have a limited value as indicators of the effectiveness of sacramental confession. Similarly, I have not tried to amass anecdotes about confessors and penitents.

Nevertheless, the evidence I have used has the virtues of being abundant and, within its recognized limitations, reliable. The men who told priests how to run confession were considered experts, with special knowledge about penitents, confessors, and confessing. They were authorities in every sense of the word. They may sometimes have been mistaken about what actually went on in the hearts of individual Christians or even whole classes of the faithful; but they knew what they wanted to go on in Christian hearts, and their expertise and power were devoted to achieving those goals. Similar qualifications can be claimed for preachers and devotional writers, who may have misjudged the piety or pliability of their audiences, but who leave no room for doubt about what they tried to make their audiences feel about contrition, confession, satisfaction, and absolution. Of course no one can know what went on in individual confessions. Indeed, we cannot even find direct evidence on how often and how carefully penitents used lists of sins to prepare for confession—to take but one example of the material at our disposal. Nevertheless, this literature reproduces lists of sins with such consistency and assurance that one is forced to conclude that such lists both reflect and determine attitudes toward sin.

Thus while I cannot prove the importance of confession quantitatively or demonstrate directly the theological conceptions of the Christian community at large, I can say a great deal about the teachings that religious authorities wanted the Christian community to believe and put into practice. I can point to important consistencies in the teaching contained in a voluminous and varied literature, which emanated from all kinds of clerical authorities, which was published in every part of Europe, and which responded directly to the needs of the pastoral clergy. A clergy trained by this literature, directly or indirectly, could in turn instruct those in their spiritual care. It would be ridiculous to suppose that all Christians who had achieved the age of discretion conformed to the standards and obligations they were taught. The literature itself contains the evidence that this was not the case, that Christians were ignorant, impenitent, sinful, and downright unconcerned. What could be less surprising? It is not contradictory to assert, however, that the institution represented in this literature was a powerful force in late medieval religious experience. Clerical authorities tried to ensure that their subjects were instructed about sin and forgiveness in the ways set down in this literature; and it would have been impractical and self-defeating for preachers of repentance and authors of summas and manuals of confession to appeal to ideas and expectations that were novel, irrelevant, or unintelligible. For everything about this literature, as I have argued below, attests to its practicality. It is the practicality of men who understood the inherent power of the system placed at the disposal of every rank of ecclesiastical authority, from itinerant mendicants and simple curates to the papacy itself.

By deliberate choice, this study concentrates almost entirely on the theologian's *culpa*, the psychologist's guilt: how they are incurred, used, and cured. That choice means that I have ignored many other medieval religious beliefs and practices, which certainly disciplined and consoled. I have focused on a theology and experience of guilt and absolution—a religion of individual, internal purification. Consequently, I neglect vast areas of medieval religious experience, such as the canon law court, the cult of the saints, and public rituals of expiation and celebration, all of which performed the same functions as sacramental confession. Even within penance, I have only touched on the theory or practice of indulgences, satisfaction, and purgatory. These areas of medieval religious experience represent, in a sense, rivals to the system of guilt and absolution I have described. When a medieval community depends for protection and comfort on the invocation of special saints, it seeks consolations other than those of the keys. When fines, excommunication, or public humiliation are involved in religious sanctions, it is, as it were, an admission that the inner sanctions are not enough. And when the horrors of purgatory are preached, and sinners urged to take up a harder regime of penitential exercises, or take advantage of indulgences, the simplicity of control by guilt and comfort by absolution is belied. And these are only examples of the areas I have excluded from this study. I do not pretend to portray the only system of discipline and consolation, but one system of discipline and consolation. Social historians are well aware of how potent these rival systems could be. But I could not, on the basis of my evidence, weigh them against each other in concrete historical cases. I have not even explained how they are rivals, with alternative modes of organizing religious belief and action and with different means of achieving the discipline and consolation of the community. I have only done what the evidence justifies: I have described a complex but coherent system of religious belief and practice performing vital social functions.

The Introduction to this study begins with a brief and schematic survey of the history of forgiveness of sins in the Western church. I have identified for the institutions of forgiveness two social and psychological functions—discipline (or social control) and consolation (or cure of anxiety)—and I have rephrased the history of penance in terms of those functions. The rest of the study is likewise organized around discipline and consolation. The historical introduction, therefore, establishes a continuity between the institutions of penance in the ancient, early medieval, high medieval, and pre-Reformation church. This functional analysis also helps avoid theological polemics, because it employs a more neutral terminology than has been generally used by historians, even in this century. Of course we cannot remove theology from religious history, and I have not tried to do so. But I have tried to redefine theological issues so that they can be seen as more than the intellectual concerns of professional academics. The term "sacramental confession" has been used instead of "Sacrament of Penance" in order to focus attention on the whole institutional structure, not just its theology. Thus I have tried not to evaluate doctrine and practice according to the standards of apostolic, evangelical, traditional, Pauline, Augustinian, or any other truth. Rather, the focus is on an institution performing social functions, which provide the most useful standards for evaluating it. Since several historians have objected to the term "social control," I should also explain that I do not consider it original or controversial to show that social control was a function of sacramental confession. I consider that observation a truism. This study attempts to make a contribution by showing how sacramental confession was an integrated system of social control.

The second section of the Introduction discusses the primary sources on which the study is based: the printed literature expressly devoted to teaching pre-Reformation Christians about sin and forgiveness. I have tried to give some idea of the popularity, purpose, and organization of these books, so that they can be better appreciated as agents for affecting attitudes and behavior. History of theology would have addressed itself to the unraveling of the opinions of the schools in this literature; it would have looked for doctrinal development and filiations, and organized the discussion chronologically. History of ideas, on the other hand, is more concerned with the influence than the parentage or classification of ideas. Certainly it is useful to know the source of a doctrine to interpret it properly and even to determine its influence; but it is most important to try to discover what ideas gained currency, were promulgated in laws, used as didactic commonplaces, established as binding obligations, and popularized in nonprofessional language. In this enterprise, the printing history of a book is more important than the fidelity of its author to a theological school. For that reason I have selected those books I thought most representative of the range of belief before the Reformation in continental Europe: France, Germany, Switzerland, and the Netherlands. I have limited myself to printed works in German, French, and Latin (including the works of Italian authors that circulated in the north), and emphasized, as I explain in this section, the most frequently published books, which I assume were the most widely used and influential. But I have also selected works for special consideration because they provide valuable insights into the problems of late fifteenth and early sixteenth century confession.*

The rest of the work, the major part, describes how sacramental confession was defined and how it operated. It begins with a section discussing the most ordinary problems of confession: why and when a penitent must confess; how the penitent and confessor are supposed to act in confession; and what makes a good confession and a bad one. The purpose of this section on practice is to describe as accurately as possible the actual behavior of confessing; to summarize the commonplace standards for, and attitudes toward, sacramental forgiveness; and to relate these basic characteristics of the institution to its social functions.

The next section analyzes what religious authorities meant by sin. First, a general discussion explains what medieval and Reformation critics referred to when they attacked the detailed categorization of sins and complex treatment of moral cases. The dangers of scrupulosity are an important issue here. But I have suggested that the completeness of medieval treatments of sin had a positive intention best understood in relation to social control. At the same time, I have argued that the need to help anxious penitents imposed limits on this form of discipline because of the fear that excessive severity would make compliance impossible.

Following this general discussion of sin is a detailed examination of one kind of penitent and one kind of sin: the sexual transgressions of married people. The purpose of this examination is to make as explicit as possible the consequences of moral principles for actual behavior. It is especially in the discussion of sexual sins that my decision to emphasize the language of the sources rather than summarize their conclusions is most apparent. The reason for this decision should also be most apparent here. For it should become clear from the language I have quoted that medieval religious authorities were not neutral on sin, especially sexual sin. I have not tried to determine, or even speculate on, the

---

* To exclude the religious literature of Great Britain, Iberia, and Italy on the grounds that these lands had no true Reformation in the sixteenth century may seem strained, but I needed some principle of selection and this one seemed the least arbitrary. I excluded Dutch, Scandinavian, and Eastern European literature because I needed to limit my sources and because I cannot read those languages.

xviii

extent to which the values revealed here are the property of the clergy alone or of medieval culture in general. I have assumed, nevertheless, that ordinary methods of textual analysis are sufficient to explain the meaning of these authors' rhetoric. And to understand this literature's attempts to persuade and control, we must pay attention to the language in which human acts are described, justified, and condemned. The words authorities choose can be more significant than the stands they take.

There are a number of arguments for choosing the sexual sins of married people as the subject to explore in detail. First, as I have noted in the chapter itself, explicit concern and detailed analysis on the part of those who wrote on confession prove that they themselves considered this one of the most basic moral issues. Second, pronouncements on the sexual conduct of marriage were directed at one of the largest "classes" of Christians, and often dealt with this behavior in frank and threatening ways. Third, excellent studies of the sexual ethics of the period—the most prominent of which are by Peter Browe, John T. Noonan, Josef Ziegler, Leopold Brandl, Michael Müller, Heinrich Klomps, Dennis Doherty, and Josef Fuchs—provide an expert and scholarly guide to the topic. Finally and most importantly, the moral teaching about and interrogation into the sexual conduct of married people is a critical aspect of the relationship between celibate confessors and their lay penitents. To evaluate that relationship, certain questions are naturally suggested. What sexual behavior do confessors try to control? How do they interrogate and judge married penitents? Can confessors bridge obvious gaps in experience and deal realistically with the problems of married people? The answers to such questions carry implications for the system of discipline beyond the conduct of marriage. For the control of sexual behavior has remained to this day a cornerstone of the whole disciplinary structure of the Roman Catholic Church. It is in that context—of the fundamental role of sexual morality in the total system of social control—that we must interpret the bitter conflicts in the fifteenth and sixteenth centuries over vows of celibacy and the canon law doctrine of marriage. That is also the context in which debates over the value of confessing secret sins were to be waged. And underlying such conflicts is a basic fact: a celibate male clergy exercised control over a married laity through sacramental confession. One might justifiably invoke here the language of class conflict.

xix

It is appropriate at this point, however, to stress that sacramental confession is a system of discipline and consolation that is universally binding. From one perspective—an essential one— clergy and laity confront each other in an unequal power relationship. The clergy hold the keys. The laity submit. Nevertheless, from another perspective—an equally essential one—both clergy and laity are subject to the same system of social control and are confined to the same means for the cure of anxiety. Indeed, the clergy are subject in even more restrictive ways. If they are rulers, they are also subjects. If they exercise control, they are also most decidedly controlled. Thus while our focus is on the class of married people—because of their numbers and because they were subject to unmarried people—we should not forget that the clergy were the class most frequently and strictly disciplined through sacramental confession. No conspiracy existed to tyrannize over the laity. On the contrary, the strength of the system resides in its universality, which means that those in power are explicitly subject to its regulations. The medieval clergy, like the laity, may be accused of hypocrisy individually, but not corporately.

The last section discusses theories of how sacramental confession works to forgive sins. It tries to represent simply, yet accurately, the range of theological explanations in the literature as a whole. At the same time, it avoids complex investigations of the opinions of theological schools and instead stresses the variety and practical relevance of these ideas for discipline and consolation. Even the rather technical discussions of the *ornatus anime*, the *obex*, and attrition and contrition attempt to answer practical questions: How might theology affect personal security about forgiveness? What might penitents have experienced in this institution had they understood and followed these teachings? That is also the purpose of the regrettably brief section dealing with legalistic restrictions on the power of absolution. Those who looked to sacramental confession for consolation had to understand that it was administered according to ecclesiastical law; and it seemed fitting to end the description of the way the sacrament works with a review of the legalistic restrictions that removed penitents from the comforts of a universalistic theological system and returned them to the harsher realities of legal control. Here, as elsewhere, the late medieval institution projects a complicated image. Yet it is one that must be grasped as a whole if one is to appreciate the social role of ecclesiastical forgiveness and the place of penitents in it.

Recent study of late medieval and Renaissance religion has revealed much about the intellectual origins of the Reformation. The work of Walter Dress, Paul Vignaux, Stephen Ozment, Heiko Oberman, and Charles Trinkaus, to mention only a few, has demonstrated the inseparable relationship between the reformers and their philosophical and theological predecessors. But the Reformation involved institutions as well as ideas, churches as well as theologies. It was a European revolution— perhaps the first in Western history—in which conflicting systems of belief provided the ideological basis for social and institutional change. This study hopes to illuminate one part of that revolution: the interplay between ideas and action that comprises the institution of sacramental confession. In this institution, where theology, law, and life converge, where theories of grace and rules for conduct work together to discipline and console, we place ourselves in touch with one of the most sensitive and critical religious experiences of faithful Christians before the Reformation.

Acknowledgments

The Rackham School of Graduate Studies of the University of Michigan was the principal source of support for research on this book; the Department of History of the University of Michigan, and its chairman at that time, William B. Willcox, generously arranged my teaching schedule so that I could have an uninterrupted year of study; and a National Endowment for the Humanities Younger Humanist Fellowship supported a project, part of which has been incorporated into chapters ii and vi. Without the assistance of Rackham, my department, and the National Endowment for the Humanities, this book would not have been possible. I am grateful to the staff of the British Museum, especially the North Library, and most especially Dennis Rhodes, for helping to make my research in early printed books a pleasure. My typist, Dorothy Foster, and my research assistant, Mary Beechy Pfeiffer, were superb, and I thank them.

In the long course of research and writing, a number of people have contributed ideas that have saved me time and embarrassment or have changed my understanding of the subject. Most important among these has been my wife, Leslie Woodcock Tentler. Sylvia Thrupp, Gerald Strauss, Joseph J. Tiziani, Lionel Tiger, Emmanuel LeRoy Ladurie, Richard Soloway, and Natalie Zemon Davis are some of those who would probably be astonished to learn that casual remarks of theirs helped my research or influenced the argument of the following pages. I hope they will not be shocked to discover the use to which I put their ideas.

Many friends and colleagues have given their time generously to reading and criticizing this manuscript. Raymond Grew, David Bien, Bradford Perkins, Jacob Price, Lionel Rothrug, C. S. Chang, Stephen Tonsor, William B. Willcox, and Sylvia Thrupp, who read an earlier and shorter version of this manuscript, offered encouragement and helpful suggestions for revision. I owe special thanks to Bill Willcox for his meticulous and unerring stylistic criticisms of that draft. I am most deeply grateful to those who read the manuscript in its later and longer form: Elisabeth A. R. Brown, Vladimir Dedijer, Marvin Becker, Steven Ozment, William Courtenay, and Charles Trinkaus. Their careful and honest responses helped me more than an acknowledgment can convey. I hope I have satisfied some of their objections.

Finally, I want to acknowledge particular debts to Myron Gilmore and Charles Trinkaus. I began the dissertation, out of which this study grew, years ago under Professor Gilmore. Only a small part of that research appears here; but the problems I have continued to investigate were defined then, and I remember with gratitude his tolerant guidance. More recently, Charles Trinkaus has prodded, disagreed with, and supported me as one would want a colleague and friend to do. My debt to him is indeed great.

Part One

Introduction

CHAPTER I

THE HISTORICAL BACKGROUND

ROM the earliest centuries of the church there has been some kind of ecclesiastical ritual to restore baptized Christians who have committed serious sins, fallen from grace, and forfeited their right to full participation in the body of the faithful. There is, moreover, a rough continuity between the institutions of forgiveness in the early church and those that were known on the eve of the Reformation. Throughout the history of this ritual of forgiveness four substantive elements persist, even though they receive varying emphasis from century to century. First, to be forgiven, sinners have always been required to feel sorrow at having lapsed. Second, they have consistently made some kind of explicit confession of their sins or sinfulness. Third, they have assumed, or had imposed on them, some kind of penitential exercises. And fourth, they have participated in an ecclesiastical ritual performed with the aid of priests who pronounce penitents absolved from sin or reconciled with the communion of believers. But to identify these four general elements of the forgiveness of sins leaves many theological and more historical questions unanswered. And in a summary as general as the one just described, we must admit at the outset that vastly different regimes develop through the centuries as one of these elements is emphasized, or penalties vary, or restrictions change. Nevertheless, it is useful to place the theory and practice of the forgiveness of sins on the eve of the Reformation against its historical background, and to see, in very broad outline, how the penitential institutions of the Roman Catholic Church had developed in these four areas from Christian antiquity to the high middle ages, when they took the form they have retained until the present.[1]

[1] The following general summary ignores exceptions (for example, penance in the Eastern Church), and does not try to settle controversies in the history of dogma. Principal authorities for this survey are E. Amann and A. Michel, "Pénitence," *Dictionnaire de théologie catholique* (Paris, 1909–1950), 12[1], 722–1050 (hereafter cited as *DTC*); Bernhard Poschmann, *Die abendländische Kirchenbusse im Ausgang des christlichen Altertums*, Münchener Studien

THE HISTORICAL BACKGROUND

Canonical Penance

A formal system of forgiveness of serious sins and reconciliation with the body of the faithful began to emerge in the middle
of the second century and developed into "canonical" penance,
which ruled until the middle of the seventh. Its most striking feature is its extreme severity. To begin with, it was completely public. Exclusion from the body of the faithful was public. The
avowal of sin and the penitential exercises imposed on the penitent before his readmission to the church were to be performed
in public. And public too was the ceremony of reconciliation.
Furthermore, for some sins (adultery, murder, and idolatry)
reconciliation was allowed only gradually and with reluctance.
And finally, as Ambrose was later to put it, "There is only one
penance, just as there is only one baptism."[2] This public admis-

---

zur historischen Theologie, ed. by E. Eichmann et al., no. 7 (Munich, 1928);
idem, *Die abendländische Kirchenbusse im frühen Mittelalter*, Breslauer
Studien zur historischen Theologie, ed. by F. X. Seppelt et al., vol. 16
(Breslau, 1930); idem, *Penance and the Anointing of the Sick*, tr. and rev. by
Francis Courtney, The Herder History of Dogma (Freiburg and London,
1964); Amédée Teetaert, *La Confession aux laïques dans l'église latine depuis
le VIIIe jusqu'au XVIe siècle*, Universitas Catholica Lovaniensis. Disserta-
tiones ad gradum magistri in Facultate Theologica vel in Facultate Iuris
Canonici . . . , ser. 2, vol. 17 (Paris, Wetteren, and Bruges, 1926); and Oscar
D. Watkins, *A History of Penance*, 2 vols. (London, 1920). See Amann,
"Pénitence," *DTC*, 12¹, 748ff., Watkins, *History of Penance*, I, 50, 57 69–
72, 191–196, 466–496. Excellent studies of the early scholastic period are
Paul Anciaux, *La Théologie du sacrement de pénitence au XIIe siècle*, Uni-
versitas Catholica Lovaniensis. Dissertationes ad gradum magistri in Facultate
Theologica vel in Facultate Iuris Canonici . . . , ser. 2, vol. 41 (Louvain and
Gembloux, 1949); and Ludwig Hödl, *Die Geschichte der scholastischen
Literatur und der Theologie der Schlüsselgewalt*, vol. 1: . . . *bis zur Summa
Aurea*, Beiträge zur Geschichte der Philosophie und Theologie zur Mittel-
alters, vol. 38, part 4 (Münster i. W., 1960).

  [2] Amann, "Pénitence," *DTC*, 12¹, 773ff., 777, 805; St. Ambrose, *De poenitentia*, II, 10, 95 in J. P. Migne, ed., *Patrologiae cursus completus*. . . .
Series latina (Paris, 1844–1890; hereafter cited as *PL*), 16, 520. Arthur Darby
Nock has noted that the creation of some ritual of forgiveness was entirely
predictable: "The practice of open confession of sins mentioned by James
v. 16 . . . is a natural concomitant of such Church discipline as we see exemplified in St. Paul's First Epistle to the Corinthians. Its development, *inevitable from the moment it was discovered that people sinned after baptism*,
was completed later" (*Early Gentile Christianity and Its Hellenistic Back-*

4

sion of guilt, exclusion from the body of the faithful, performance of arduous penitential exercises, and reconciliation with the body of the faithful was allowed a Christian only once.

It is true, moreoever, that in the first two centuries of the church forgiveness of sins was less prominent than expulsion for sins. Perhaps in these early days, when Christianity was confined to zealous and selective communities, there was less need for an easily available ritual for restoring sinners. But especially as a result of the Decian persecution in the third century, and with the extensive conversions of the subsequent era of peace and official recognition in 311, the need became pressing. The abundance of documents on the system of canonical penance of the Western church in the fourth and fifth centuries is itself evidence that this necessity was recognized and that formal penance was widely practiced. The public character persisted. In Rome, a formal ceremony, including the laying on of hands, signified the sinner's entrance into an order of penitents, a third class of Christians distinct from catechumens and faithful. These penitents performed private exercises, such as almsgiving and fasting, as well as public humiliation, and were received back into the community by a ceremony of reconciliation in which there was, again, the laying on of hands. But once reconciled, the penitent had to live with severe disabilities. The restored penitent was forbidden admission to the clergy; he could not contract marriage; if he was already married he could not enjoy his conjugal rights; he was not to engage too actively in worldly affairs; and, above all, he was not to perform military service.[3] In the next two centuries these features continued to dominate practice. Without pretending that there was uniformity everywhere, we can nevertheless discern a general pattern of reconciliation in the West from the middle of the fifth to the middle of the seventh century. It was still harsh. Entrance into the order of penitents was still formalized, and might even include tonsure along with the donning of hair shirt and ashes. Exclusion from the body of the faith-

---

ground [New York, 1964], 86 [italics added]). The teaching and practice of St. John Chrysostom and the church of Antioch in the second half of the fourth century are an apparent exception to the ancient severity: see Watkins, *History of Penance*, I, 328ff., 475–476.

[3] Amann, "Pénitence," *DTC*, 12¹, 789–805, 834. Watkins, *History of Penance*, I, 412, 422–429, 460–465, 482–483.

ful for Lent, which had become the normal time of penance, might be in a monastery or in a special part of the church building. The disabilities remained, and nonreiteration of penance was still the rule. If a penitent did not fulfill his penitential duties, he might at death be given the viaticum, but some would deny him, even in that final hour, the laying on of hands, the symbol of reconciliation.[4]

Penance at Death

But these first centuries of the medieval church witnessed a profound change in the practice and conception of penance. The extreme severity of the discipline, with its disabling consequences, perhaps inevitably led Christians to defer penance until the last possible moment. Evidently the faithful, weak but prudent, were applying a kind of utilitarian calculation to the losses and gains of the serious decision to undertake penance; and the logical solution for all but the truly ascetic was to wait until the imminence of death. Arduous penitential exercises obviously could not be required of a dying man, and his exclusion from economic, military, and marital life would be similarly irrelevant. But formal reconciliation was still possible, and Pope Leo the Great directed that dying Christians be reconciled without the imposition of penitential exercises.

The very existence of deathbed penance makes it clear that, at least by the pontificate of St. Leo in the fifth century, the ceremony of reconciliation was more than disciplinary and purported to mean more than reconciliation with the authority of the church. If penance was important to receive at death, it must have been because it signified some kind of divine as well as ecclesiastical forgiveness. And despite the absence of ascetic works of satisfaction, and although there was a special formula for reconciliation at death, deathbed penance meant substantially the

[4] Amann, "Pénitence," *DTC*, 12[1], 813, 832–833. Watkins, *History of Penance*, I, 275, 495; II, 522–523, 566–568, 580. To mitigate the impression of uniformity of practice in the early centuries, however, see Cyrille Vogel, *La Discipline pénitentielle en Gaule des origines à la fin du VIIe siècle* (Paris, 1952), 21ff. Poschmann, *Kirchenbusse im Ausgang des christlichen Altertums*, 65–67, speaks of Leo I's relaxations by which penitents were advised to desist from litigation and business, but not forbidden. The ban on military service and sexual intercourse remained, however.

6

same thing as normal canonical penance: for example, if the sick person recovered, the usual disabilities remained.[5]

Thus two contrary practices had developed: *doing* penance and *receiving* penance. Some zealous pastors urged their flocks to do penance, and, faced with a recalcitrant laity who were waiting to receive penance at the end and yet were not staying away from the communion, they preached before the great feasts to arouse contrition and amendment. Others, however, were prudently circumspect: in the early sixth century two church councils in Gaul actually demanded that young Christians delay penance until they achieved some maturity.[6] The problem of deferring penance had been introduced into the life of the early church and it was to continue to be vitally significant through the period of the Reformation. Indeed, the two fundamental and conflicting opinions were expressed already in the fifth century. On the one hand, St. Leo insisted with peremptory simplicity that

[5] Amann, "Pénitence," *DTC*, 12¹, 833. Cf. Vogel, *La Discipline pénitentielle*, 24–25, 29, 35–36, 47ff., 116ff. Vogel sees St. Augustine as a proponent of the divine significance of ecclesiastical penance: "Enfin—et on risque là une hypothèse—l'influence de S. Augustin, sensible surtout dans la province arlésienne, inclinait ses disciples à l'indulgence la plus grande." If grace is efficacious apart from our merits, Vogel continues, then nothing can hinder its action, even *in extremis*. Thus Vogel emphasizes an opposite tendency in Augustine; cites Leo I (see below, n. 7 and text) as a supporter of the validity of late repentance; and then goes on to show its currency in popular religion: "Dans la croyance populaire, le fidèle qui avait reçu la pénitence était sûr de son salut. C'est ce qu'atteste une inscription d'Aix de 492: HIC IN PACE QVIESCIT/ADIVTOR QVI POST/ACCEPTAM PAENITENTIAM/MIGRAVIT AD DOMINVM. . . . La formule *migravit ad Dominum post acceptam paenitentiam* équivaut très exactement à celle qui est employée de nos jours: *muni des sacrements de l'Eglise*" (ibid., 50–51). Karl Rahner, "Forgotten Truths," *Theological Investigations*, vol. 2, *Man in the Church* (Baltimore, 1963), 164–165, argues that the refusal of the intercessory prayers (the *Misereatur* and the *Indulgentiam*) "constitutes the gravest rebuff imaginable to a sinner by the Church," and he cites James 5:16, the *Didache*, and Tertullian in addition to the other Fathers in general. The Emperor Theodosius thought that Ambrose's excommunication had divine significance too; see Watkins, *History of Penance*, I, 436–437. There is, of course, more evidence for this belief. For the important developments in the practice of penance at death during and after the Decian persecutions, see Watkins, *History of Penance*, I, 176ff., and especially 198–201, 207, 238; on penance for the dying, ibid., 421, 447–449, 465, 481–482.

[6] Amann, "Pénitence," *DTC*, 12¹, 835–836; Vogel, *La Discipline pénitentielle*, 117–118. Vogel thinks it was forbidden before about thirty-five years of age. Cf. Watkins, *History of Penance*, II, 555–556, 562.

this great comfort not be denied the dying: even though they could not fulfill the penitential exercises, they were to be reconciled. "No one," he urged, "is to be despaired of while he still lives in this body."[7] On the other hand, St. Augustine preached with impressive eloquence against the practice as unsafe, and his sermon, which became one of the most widely quoted sources for those who wanted early repentance, is a sensitive discussion of the moral and theological problems of deathbed sacraments.

Augustine's sermon begins by exhorting penitents to show their sincerity by changing their lives, and this, he charges, is incompatible with the practice of living sinfully and postponing penance to the end. The sinner must change his life while he lives, while he is healthy. Does he expect to be reconciled as he begins to die? "We have known many who have expired expecting to be reconciled," Augustine admits, but he can only express his fears. He is sure that the baptized man who lives well without committing serious sin—who is not sinless but nevertheless is guilty only of those daily, unavoidable sins forgiven simply by the petition in the Lord's Prayer—will go to a peaceful and happy life after death. If, however, a baptized Christian falls seriously, he can be restored through sincere penance, which begins with the honest admission, "I have sinned." If that man lives well after penance, he too will be saved. Receiving penance at death is another matter:

> But if someone poised in the last necessity of his illness wants to receive penance, and receives it, and is immediately reconciled and dies, I confess to you that we do not deny to that man what he seeks, but we do not presume that he has made a good end. I do not presume: I do not deceive you, but I do not presume. The faithful man living well leaves here sure. The man who is baptized in that hour, leaves here sure. A man who has done penance and been reconciled while he is healthy and afterwards has lived well, leaves here sure. But a man who does penance at the end and is reconciled, whether he leaves here sure, I am not sure.

When he is sure, Augustine continues, he gives assurance; but in this case he can only give penance, not assurance. He will not say

---

[7] The relevant texts of Leo are conveniently collected by Watkins, *History of Penance*, I, 371ff. Popes Innocent I and Coelestinus I both accepted deathbed reconciliation before Leo; ibid., 370–371, 416ff.

whether the man who is reconciled at the end is damned or saved; he will only say that he does not know and cannot promise. "Do you wish to free yourself from doubt? Do penance while you are healthy." You can be sure of the sincerity of such a penance because you do it while it is still possible to sin. But if you do penance when you no longer are able to sin, it is more a case of the sins abandoning you than of your abandoning the sins. Once again he reiterates his uncertainty. If he knew for certain that it was not helpful, then he would not even give it. If he knew it was useful, he would not admonish and terrify. It has to be one or the other but he is not sure which it is. His conclusion is simple: "Therefore, leave the uncertain and take up the certain."[8]

The conflicting opinions of Leo and Augustine were assured of an enduring place in the debate on this subject in the twelfth century when they were included in Gratian's *Decretum* and the *Sentences* of Peter Lombard. And despite immense changes in the form of penitential institutions, their words would continue to be profoundly relevant to Christians of succeeding centuries.

The Penitentials

By the end of the sixth century, in Ireland, another system of forgiveness existed that would eventually turn into the private penance of the high middle ages. It was based on the penitentials, short manuals that classified sins and told a priest what penance he should impose for a specific sin. This penitential "tariff" was the central feature of these works, but later more detailed and discursive manuals developed, which even advised priests on how to conduct confession. The system reached the Continent around 600, where its spread was greatly furthered by the Anglo-Saxon missionary monks. Its popularity was undoubtedly based on some striking contrasts with the old system: canonical penance was thoroughly public, whereas the penitentials instituted a system that was essentially private, between a priest and an in-

---

[8] St. Augustine, Sermo 393, "De poenitentibus," *PL*, 39, 1713–1715. His language is scholastic as he defines two mutually exclusive possibilities: "Nam si scirem tibi nihil prodesse, non tibi darem. Item si scirem tibi prodesse, non te admonerem, non te terrerem. Duae sunt: aut ignoscitur tibi aut non ignoscitur; quid horum tibi futurum sit nescio. Ergo dimitte incertum, tene certum" (ibid., 1715). What Augustine calls "certain," later writers will call "safe." A divine significance for ecclesiastical penance is implicit in Augustine's exposition here.

dividual penitent. Penance was now privately imposed, for although it required, like canonical penance, denial of the sacraments for the duration of Lent, there was no longer a formal entrance into an order of penitents. Nor in this new system was there a solemn and public reconciliation. Penitents had other inestimable advantages as well. The forgiveness offered under the penitentials left no harsh disabilities. In addition, it was reiterable; and it could be used frequently not only for grave sins but also for less serious offenses. The added benefit that, unlike canonical penance, the penitentials provided a way of restoration open to the clergy must also have contributed to their success.[9] For they did succeed, and by the middle of the tenth century this momentous reformation of religious sentiment and institutions had been won.

Despite the open clash between these systems, however, they were fundamentally similar. The great contrast exists not between canonical penance and the penitentials, but between both of them and the system of private penance that was to rule the church from the twelfth and thirteenth centuries to the present. In the first place, there is a direct continuity from the canonical regime to the penitentials in the old practice of receiving penance at death. Augustine deplored it, but deathbed repentance even in his day was a fact and a decisive one. For here the distinctive public features of canonical penance became mere formalities: entrance into an order of penitents could have little meaning, and reconciliation followed almost immediately after the avowal of sins. Thus canonical penance received at death was already a kind of private penance. Second, both systems contain the four principal parts of the ecclesiastical way to forgiveness. Avowal of sinfulness was far more detailed in the penitentials but essential to both. Both also recognized that penance requires an expression of sorrow or a change of heart. Inner sorrow was important enough in canonical penance to admit a contrite penitent to reconciliation in the last hour, even according to Augustine; similarly, it is clear that sorrow was critical for the penitentials, since it was normal to restore the penitent to full enjoyment of the

[9] Amann, "Pénitence," *DTC*, 12¹, 846–847, 849–855, 857. Watkins thinks that the idea of a mathematical correspondence between sin and punishment is contained as early as A.D. 100 in *The Shepherd of Hermas* (*History of Penance*, I, 62, 63); for the clash between the two, see *History of Penance*, II, 790ff. and n. 13.

sacraments of the church before the long periods of penance were completed. Also indispensable for both was ecclesiastical participation, by a bishop in canonical penance and a simple priest under the penitentials. Third, and most important of all, both emphasized an inordinately rigorous schedule of penitential exercises.[10]

The *Roman Penitential* may serve as a model of this rigor. Its penalties are not unusual, and even if in some cases they provided for redemption of fasts by money payments (that is, by alms), and even if the definition of fasting is often doubtful (it was not seven days a week), nevertheless, the sheer length of the penance proves its harshness, especially when we consider what was thought permissible in succeeding centuries. If a cleric is guilty of homicide, the *Roman Penitential* begins, "he shall do penance for ten years, three of these are bread and water"; for the same crime a layman gets seven years with three on bread and water. A cleric whose adultery results in childbirth will do penance for seven years, but if it is without issue and not notorious, then he need only do penance for three years, one of them on bread and water. Sins of sexual desire—if, it seems, they entail an overt proposition—are also taxed:

11. If any cleric lusts after a woman and is not able to commit the act because the woman will not comply, he shall do penance for half a year on bread and water and for a whole year abstain from wine and meat.

15. If anyone wishes to commit adultery and cannot, that is, is not accepted, he shall do penance for forty days.

Perjury is penalized with three to seven years' penance; serious theft, five to seven; and usury, three years (one on bread and water). The *Roman Penitential* deals similarly with magic (causing death or conjuring up storms), assault and battery, idolatry, and abortion. Sacrileges owing to neglect are punished in terms of days; bestiality can be worth twenty-five years if the offender is over thirty.[11] No matter what definition of fasting is used,

---

[10] Amann, "Pénitence," *DTC*, 12^1 858–861; cf. Watkins, *History of Penance*, II, 707ff., 757–758, 764–769.

[11] John Thomas McNeill and Helena M. Gamer, *Medieval Handbooks of Penance: A Translation of the Principal Libri Poenitentiales and Selections from Related Documents*, Columbia Records of Civilization: Sources and Studies, No. 29 (New York, 1965; reprint of 1938 edn.), 217–234. For the

therefore, it is a harsh system; and modern authors who talk about the decline of discipline have only thought about this system in relation to the canonical penance that had gone before it. For if we call the penitentials "lax," what words will describe the discipline of the high middle ages?

Thus in both systems the ecclesiastical authorities insisted that proper performance entailed long periods of asceticism, worship, and charity. Renunciation of the world for the rest of one's life under the canons; fasts, abstinences, and almsgivings of years' duration under the penitentials: these rigors were essential to both systems, theologically and psychologically. Here lies the greatest similarity among all the ideas of forgiveness from the Fathers to the Carolingian Reformers: all felt that forgiveness rested most securely on works of expiation.

The Functions of Ecclesiastical Penance

These penitential institutions, developed in the first centuries of the ancient and medieval church, performed social functions. They existed first of all to insure discipline, to exercise control. In ecclesiastical or theological terms this discipline insured the purity of those who associated in the mystical body of Christ and received, on the great feasts, the consecrated Body of Christ. In secular terms, these institutions worked to enforce or maintain obedience to a society. The willing recourse to excommunication; the public nature of exclusion, retribution, and reconciliation; concentration on the most serious crimes against marriage, property, and life; and the punitive nature of the system's sanctions: all of these harsh characteristics point to the prominent role played by the church in the maintenance of social order. In the early centuries, under canonical penance, it preserved order in a highly restricted local community, which expected strict obedi-

---

sake of simplicity I have retained the old title of *Roman Penitential*. For the meaning of the fast, see ibid., 31, 120; Hermann Joseph Schmitz, *Die Bussbücher und die Bussdisciplin der Kirche, nach handschriftlichen Quellen dargestellt* (Mainz, Düsseldorf, 1898), 1, 250, 314–316; Henry C. Lea, *A History of Auricular Confession and Indulgences in the Latin Church*, 3 vols. (Philadelphia, 1896), II, 119–123; Robert of Flamborough, *Liber Poenitentialis. A Critical Edition with Introduction and Notes*, ed. by J. J. Francis Firth, Pontifical Institute of Medieval Studies, Studies and Texts, 18 (Toronto, 1971), V, xiv, 352, pp. 274–275.

ence to its rules and, when there were failures, gave only one difficult chance for readmission to full privileges in that group. But even under the penitentials, when there was a chance for repetitions of forgiveness, the idea of social control is evident in the legalistic tariffing that imposed heavier sentences on the more serious antisocial sins, and whose penalties, in any case, were themselves severe deterrents. Throughout both there was a determination to readmit to society someone who had been made to understand the gravity of crimes and was not prone to recidivism. The first function of ecclesiastical penance then is discipline, or social control. The penitent was accepted by society and in turn was expected to accept and conform to society's rules.

The second function is directed more to the individual: it is the cure of a guilty conscience. It is most striking in that dramatic exception to normal canonical penance, the reception of penance on the deathbed. In this ritual the function of giving psychological comfort is self-evident. While preaching against such repentance, Augustine described it as a search for security (a security not easily available to Christians before the advent of private, reiterated penance). If the first function is social control, the second is reconciliation with the self and with those social norms that the penitent has internalized. Its purest and simplest formulation is in the language of religion: "How do I know my sins are forgiven me?"

Consolation and discipline, then, are our major themes. They provide a functional continuity, in addition to the substantive continuity of the requirement of sorrow, the avowal of sin, the performance of penitential acts, and the pronouncement of absolution or reconciliation. And we must emphasize here that simply to have eliminated discipline would have made consolation impossible, not more effective. In addition, although we can understand consolation psychologically as the cure of anxiety, we must obviously begin by explaining theological problems: the operation of grace and the cooperation of the will; the causality of the sacrament and the power of the priest; the role of fear and love; the function of jurisdiction; the definition of necessity. All these theological elements will be examined so that we can find out what in this practice offered or hindered assurance. God's mercy figures prominently even in the thought of the ancient church, which judged most sins to be outside the realm of ecclesiastical penance and reconciliation and hence delivered them over to His direct forgiveness. But the *institutional practice* of the ancient and early medieval church did not try to comfort the penitent solely by assuring him he could rely on God's mercy. Membership in the community of the church was too important and there was obviously too much human effort involved in reconciliation with that church to lead us to that fideistic interpretation. The distinctive feature of this ancient and early medieval consolation lies elsewhere, and when we turn from abstractions and ask the simple question for both canonical penance and the penitentials —how does the sinner know he is forgiven?—the answer lies in the principal activity they demand.

One knows he is forgiven because he is willing to perform the overwhelming penitential exercises demanded by the church. The consolation of this system lies in its difficulty. There could hardly be a more convincing test of sincerity than the willing and faithful endurance of either of these ascetic regimes. Thus such great differences as existed between these early systems— one was public, the other private; one was offered once and the other was reiterable—become less overwhelming. The sixth century Council of Toledo denounced as an execrable abuse the practice of going to a priest for forgiveness whenever a Christian had committed a serious sin. But the canonical penance they upheld, with its single opportunity for forgiveness, was basically similar to that system of frequent penance that would spread in the next century from the British Isles all over Europe. To the council, frequent confession was a sign of lamentable laxity. Later, Carolingian reformers continued to object to so faint-hearted an innovation, and they successfully prolonged the life of public penance for notorious public sins. Nevertheless, those who innovated and those who resisted all lived with the same social consciousness in the same ecclesiastical world; to them only the ascetic seemed efficacious.[12] The sinner had to prove his sincerity through asceticism for the benefit of his spiritual superiors,

[12] Amann, "Pénitence," *DTC*, 12^1, 837–840, 872–883. Text and translation of the Council of Toledo's remonstrance in Watkins, *History of Penance*, II, 337, 519, 567. Jean Laporte, ed., *Le Pénitentiel de saint Colomban. Introduction et édition critique*, Monumenta Christiana Selecta, ed. by J. C. Didier, vol. 4 (Tournai, Paris, Rome, and New York, 1958), 67–72, discusses the severity of the practice of the period, and concludes concerning the document that he has edited: "La sévérité de ce Pénitentiel qui stupéfie parfois, doit être appréciée d'après l'esprit étroitement rigoriste de l'Eglise d'alors, et les châtiments barbares de l'authorité civile." McNeill and Gamer, *Medieval Handbooks*, 44–46, also emphasize the severity of the penitentials and, at

and above all for himself. Martin Luther himself recognized this. With historical insight, and with a profound sensitivity to the problems of suffering and certitude, he makes in the Ninety-five Theses a characteristically definite judgment of penance in the ancient church:

12. In former days canonical penances were imposed before, not after, absolution—as tests of true contrition.[13]

To pass this institutionalized test was, for both systems, the peculiar source of consolation.

---

the same time, their important psychological functions. McNeill has also stressed the psychological function of both early forms of penance in *The Celtic Penitentials and Their Influence on Continental Christianity*, Chicago University Dissertation in Church History (Paris, 1923), 182: "Something of a supernatural meaning may have been attached to penance even by the early church. Reconciliation, restoration to communion by the imposition of hands, partook of the nature of the later absolution and gave the restored penitent a feeling of security which he could not possess while under the discipline. No doubt under the Celtic system the completion of the penance brought a similar sense of relief. Here the lack of any formal reconciliation was a natural result of the fact that excommunication had not taken place. The acceptance of a penitential duty after confession itself constituted an important step toward complete reunion with the church. . . ."

[13] Martin Luther, "Disputatio pro declaratione virtutis indulgentiarum," *D. Martin Luthers Werke. Kritsche Gesamtausgabe* (Weimar, 1883–) I, 233 (hereafter cited as *WA*): "12. Olim pene canonice non post, sed ante absolutionem imponebantur tanquam tentamenta vere contritionis." Luther rejected the scholastic theory of satisfaction for sin and indicates here a very different meaning for penitential exercises in the ancient church. The word *satisfactio*, however, was used to describe penitential exercises as early as Cyprian: Watkins, *History of Penance*, I, 158, 214–215. Poschmann, *Kirchenbusse im Ausgang des christlichen Altertums*, 303–304, goes so far as to admit that the personal performance of penitential acts was so emphasized in the earlier period that the sacramental quality of the church's intervention was seriously neglected: "Was die dogmatische Auffassung von der Wirksamkeit der Busse angeht, so ist es kennzeichnend für die altchristliche Busslehre überhaupt, dass sie die Kraft der persönlichen Bussleistung stark in der Vordergrund rückt auf Kosten der kirklichen Schlüsselgewalt. Am meisten wird noch Augustinus dem sakramentalen Faktor gerecht mit seiner Lehre, dass die Rekonziliation die Eingliederung in die organische Lebensgemeinschaft mit der allein das Heil vermittelnden Kirche bewirkt. Leo I betont wenigstens scharf die Unerlässlichkeit der kirchlichen Vermittlung. Dagegen tritt der sakramentale Faktor vollständing zurück bei den semipelagianisch [!] beeinflussten gallischen Theologen. . . . Aber auch sonst ist in den Predigten und Belehrungen über die Busse von der Bedeutung der priesterlichen Lösegewalt nur wenig die Rede." Cf. ibid., pp. 71–88, and above, n. 5.

The Development of Private Penance

Once the system of private confession had been established, there remained several important developments before the institution of the late middle ages emerged with its characteristic definitions, practices, and unresolved problems. Between the ninth and the thirteenth centuries four changes occurred in the theology and practice of this sacrament: (1) penances were lightened and made arbitrary; (2) contrition became the essential element for the penitent and pushed penitential exercises into a subservient position;[14] (3) private confession, already accepted as a necessary part of the forgiveness of sins, was declared universally obligatory by the Fourth Lateran Council of 1215; and (4) the meaning of the priest's role was more carefully defined and its importance in the process of forgiveness radically enhanced. The groundwork for these changes was laid by such great theologians as Abelard, Peter Lombard, Thomas Aquinas, and Duns Scotus. But none of them, not even Aquinas, succeeded in giving a definitive explanation of the Sacrament of Penance. Moreover, the balance between these four elements was constantly shifting. Nevertheless, before we examine the literature on forgiveness circulating in the half century before the Reformation, before we describe the prevalent teaching and attitudes of the late fifteenth and early sixteenth centuries, we must sketch in broad outlines these four important changes. For by the thirteenth century, theologians had delineated the major problems that would concern speculative and practical writers on penance at the end of the middle ages.

PENANCES BECOME LIGHTER AND ARBITRARY

Already in the twelfth century the authority of Gratian was lent to the opinion that penances are arbitrary—that is, that they

---

[14] In a sense this is confirmed by the willingness of Leo to dispense with penitential exercises *in articulo mortis*: and also by the fact that the person who does penance according to the penitentials is reconciled at Eastertime, and thus is considered forgiven even though his penance may continue for years after he resumes taking communion. Nevertheless, as long as penance remained as burdensome as under the penitential canons, it must be considered the most prominent element in the institutional system, if not from a purely logical or dogmatic view, as least from the point of view of those who had to perform its arduous tasks.

16

might be decided by the priest and were not dictated by a written, fixed tariff. This principle had even been recognized by Burchard of Worms in the preceding century.[15] The *Liber Poenitentialis* of Gratian's contemporary, Alain de Lille, offered its own commentary on the laxity that was appearing in their age. In the primitive church, Alain explained, penances were harsh to dissuade people from sinning; but as the church grew, it became necessary to lighten penances lest they become more harmful than medicinal. "For then human nature was stronger than it is now for bearing the burdens of penance; and that is why penance must be moderated." As a substitute for the fasts and vigils that some cannot endure, Alain suggested offerings, prayers, and pilgrimages. Writing at the beginning of the thirteenth century, Robert of Flamborough was in substantial agreement with his predecessor. Robert lamented that one could hardly find anyone in his day willing to perform the full austerity prescribed by the penitential canons; and when one considers that the normal tariff for each mortal sin was seven years of fairly difficult fasting and abstinence, one can hardly be surprised. Robert advised under these circumstances a kind of progressive bargaining with the penitent; the priest was to diminish the penance bit by bit until he found the penitent willing to accept it, so that (hopefully and presumably) something of the original letter of the law remained. Yet Robert also insisted that as long as the penitent intended to stop sinning, he should not be dismissed without any penance at all (which would have meant refusal of sacramental forgiveness) lest he be forced into despair and damnation.[16]

In Robert of Flamborough and Alain de Lille, then, we detect a certain severity in the ideal of penance: the harsh rule of the penitential canons had not been completely forgotten. Indeed, it

[15] Pierre Michaud-Quantin, *Sommes de casuistique et manuels de confession au moyen âge (XII-XVI siècles)*, Analecta Mediaevalia Namurcensia, 13 (Louvain, Lille, and Montreal, 1962), 15–16. Asia Minor knew a graded penance in the fourth century, and there is evidence that the bishops were given discretionary powers there to depart from the letter of the canon. But the voices upholding the letter of the ancient penances persisted in the eleventh century. Burchard reflects northern Europe's accommodation to the "laxity" of the penitentials. Peter Damiani expresses dissatisfaction with his customary vehemence; see Watkins, *History of Penance*, I, 325; II, 739ff.

[16] Michel, "Pénitence," *DTC*, 12¹, 926–927; Alain de Lille, *Liber poenitentialis*, *PL*, 210, 293; Robert of Flamborough, *Liber poenitentialis*, V, xii-xvi, pp. 273–277.

would still be remembered, particularly by canonists, in the late fourteenth and early fifteenth century; and this memory was to be preserved when these fourteenth and fifteenth century works were published in the decades before the Reformation. Nevertheless, the consistent trend was toward mitigation. In later ages even the rigorists introduced so many reasons for departing from the rules of the canons that they virtually acceded to the principle that penances are arbitrary—that they were to be decided according to the judgment of the priest and, it is important to add, according to the willingness of the penitent to perform them.

The capitulation to a milder regime by Raymond of Peñaforte shows that even the legal mind had come to accept the change in the thirteenth century. Raymond defended arbitrary penances, but he still tried to give as a guide the general rule that capital sins such as adultery, perjury, fornication, or homicide were to be given seven years' penance. He had to admit, however, that this was only a norm, and that penances should be lengthened or shortened according to circumstances. Some, Raymond tells us, argued that the discretion of the priest extended only to the decision as to how he would depart from the canons. Others argued that the choice was completely his, without, it seems, reference to the canons. It is clear that Raymond liked the first alternative, but could not honestly endorse it.[17] Whatever he preferred, however, the canons were becoming increasingly irrelevant. And persistent reference in the fourteenth and fifteenth centuries to the harsher norms of the canons does not mean, as we shall see later, that anyone was actually doing arduous penances.

Thus "satisfaction"—expiatory acts of charity and self-denial —lost the preeminence it had enjoyed in the early church and its de-emphasis corresponded to other fundamental changes in the institutions of the forgiveness of sins. After penances had become lighter and arbitrary, the answer to the question, "How do I know I am forgiven?" had to be found elsewhere than in the willing performance of penitential exercises.

CONTRITION

In the place of penitential works of satisfaction, theologians of the twelfth and thirteenth centuries accepted contrition as the principal part of the forgiveness of sins. Indeed, as soon as the

[17] Amédée Teetaert, "La Doctrine pénitentielle de saint Raymond de Penyafort, O.P.," *Analecta Sacra Tarraconensia*, 4 (1928), 45-47.

church accepted deathbed repentance, it implied that internal sorrow could substitute in some sense for outward penance in ecclesiastical reconciliation. As early as the tenth century, moreover, there were authorities who exalted contrition and explicitly reversed the order of values: they argued that deathbed repentance was acceptable because of the acknowledged superiority of contrition over satisfaction. As soon as theologians could argue on such an assumption, they were already well on the way to changing the source of assurance that one is forgiven. Nevertheless, the elaboration and popularization of the idea that contrition is the principal part of penance—that pardon comes from sorrow proceeding from the love of God—belongs to the twelfth not the tenth century, and its foremost proponent was none other than Abelard. Abelard's teaching was then taken up by such influential authorities as Hugh of St. Victor, Alain de Lille, Gratian, and, most important of all for the history of dogma, Peter Lombard.[18]

But if contrition is the principal part of the Sacrament of Penance, is there any need for confession? What does the priest do? Was it not possible, even logical, to conclude that the telling of sins and the intervention of the priest had become superfluous, that the forgiveness of sins was purely a matter between the contrite man and a forgiving God? There were pronounced tendencies in that direction in medieval theology, and they created tensions that remained until the time of Luther. But the practice, theory, and law of the church did not move in this antisacramental and antisacerdotal direction. Indeed, the thirteenth century church, while still accepting the primacy of contrition in the sacramental process of the justification of the individual Christian, conferred on the confession of sins to the priest a more impelling necessity than ever before in the decree *Omnis utriusque sexus*; and the theologies of Thomas Aquinas and Duns Scotus explained the priest's power of absolution so that the intervention of the priest in the forgiveness of sins became more intelligible and important than it had ever been before.

[18] Teetaert, *La Confession aux laïques*, 86–87; idem, "La Doctrine . . . de saint Raymond," 8. Anciaux, *La Théologie*, 67ff., 176ff., 463ff.; Hödl, *Geschichte der scholastischen Literatur*, vol. 1, 376–377 and references. Hödl finds three theologians—Gilbert de la Porré, Simon of Tournai, and Radulphus Ardens—who argue that God alone forgives and that contrition is not the cause but the sign (like forgiveness, *given* to man) of forgiveness.

THE YEARLY NECESSITY OF CONFESSION

Confession of sins was thought necessary long before theologians began to talk about the primacy of contrition in the forgiveness of sins; and the hierarchical church was not likely to give up confession no matter what logic might seem to demand. Most important, the habit of confessing to priests was an old one. In addition, a variety of theological rationales existed. In the Carolingian age Alcuin had gathered together scriptural texts that were to become classic in the proof of the divine origin and necessity of confession to priests. Alcuin's line of argument—confession was mandatory because it was divine and apostolic—would remain the simplest and most important defense of the need to tell sins to priests. Other justifications were sought, however, and in the ninth and tenth centuries a curious alternative was proposed. Instead of stressing divine institution, some theologians asserted that the chief virtue of confession derived from the shame it engendered when the penitent was forced to tell his sins to another man. The historical origins of the idea are evident: to explain the substantial lightening of works of satisfaction they saw in contemporary discipline, they simply concluded that shame made confession itself a work of satisfaction. Thus the necessity of confession was related directly and decisively to the psychology of the old discipline. A church in transition still liked the idea of penitential exercises; confession was held to be one, a work of satisfaction judged necessary and effective in the remission of sins.[19]

Despite theological justifications and the weight of traditional observance, however, doubts about the necessity of confession to a priest could be real. In the twelfth century Gratian accepted the argument that confession was a work of satisfaction because of its shame; but at the same time he refused to decide between the conflicting authorities he cited on whether a contrite man had to confess to a priest; and Gratian's doubt was itself a potent authority against necessity. Peter Lombard, on the other hand, was not so hesitant as Gratian, and he shows how the force of tradition prevailed. For although the *Sentences* follows Abelard's lead in exalting contrition, and although it became a source for

[19] Teetaert, *La Confession aux laïques*, 68–70; idem, "La Doctrine . . . de saint Raymond," 4–5; Hödl, *Geschichte der scholastischen Literatur*, vol. 1, 378–379, and passim.

all future theologians who would do the same, even at the expense of sacerdotal power, Peter Lombard nevertheless decided that it was necessary to salvation to confess to a priest if one had the chance.[20] The service Peter Lombard performs for confession is profound. For in the midst of the theology of contrition, confession to a priest is upheld, if not logically, at least emphatically.

Practice, however, prevailed over any authority, doubts, or contradictions. The necessity of confession of all serious sins before communion had long been established. It was customary, as innumerable episcopal decrees attest, for bishops to command confession to a priest at least once, or even three times, a year. In the twelfth century Richard of St. Victor flatly condemned as guilty of sacrilege anyone who went to communion without going to confession, no matter how much contrition he might feel.[21] Clearly there was a healthy tradition of confession to a priest that would militate against any theoretical attempt to undermine the custom. And the relationship of this observance to the function of social control is obvious.

It is important to keep these attitudes and this legislation in mind when one evaluates the great decree of the Fourth Lateran Council of 1215, *Omnis utriusque sexus*, which commanded yearly confession. It has often been seen by historians as a radical turning point. H. C. Lea called it "perhaps the most important legislative act in the history of the Church." In more pejorative language, its effects have been summarized as a victory for pure legalism: "Nothing remained to prevent confession from being dealt with as a purely juridical thing," according to Dietterle; and he added simply, "confession was no longer a religious but only a legal act."[22]

[20] Amann, "Pénitence," *DTC*, 12^1, 902, 936; Hödl, *Geschichte der scholastischen Literatur*, vol. 1, 81, 156, 190ff. For other evidence on the frequency and necessity of confession, see Watkins, *History of Penance*, II, 742ff., and especially 747–748.

[21] Peter Browe, "Die Pflichtbeichte im Mittelalter," *ZkTh*, 57 (1933), 340–341; idem, "Die Kommunionvorbereitung im Mittelalter," *ZkTh*, 56 (1932), 386–387.

[22] H. C. Lea, *History of Auricular Confession*, I, 230; Johannes Dietterle, "Die Summae confessorum (sive de casibus conscientiae)—von ihren Anfängen an bis zu Silvester Prierias—unter besonderer Berücksichtigung ihrer Bestimmungen über den Ablass," *ZKG*, 24 (1903), 374. Text of *Omnis utriusque sexus* in Watkins, *History of Penance*, II, 733–734, 748–749; and Charles Joseph Hefele and H. Leclerq, *Histoire des conciles*, 8 vols. (Paris, 1907–1916), 5^2, 1350–1351.

Now in these judgments there is some danger of exaggeration. This act of the pontificate of Innocent III, which required all Christians to confess their sins once a year to their own priest under pain of excommunication, did not break with tradition in either theory or practice. It was not the first legal act to require confession to the priest and it can in no sense be said to have invented the necessity of confession. Nevertheless it was momentous; and even if it was originally designed as a disciplinary canon to allow pastors to know their parishioners and watch for heresy, its effects were in fact broader. For the requirement of yearly confession now had the authority of Pope and council, who had prescribed powerful religious sanctions to back it up. Consequently, the sacramental character of penance was emphasized and canonists and theologians, in explaining this decree, were forced to specify more carefully the power of the priest who pronounces absolution on the penitent. By the end of the century all the canonists and theologians agreed that sacramental confession was obligatory, divinely instituted, and necessary (if not in fact, at least in desire) for the remission of sins, even when the major part of them at the same time held that contrition was the most important and effective part of the Sacrament of Penance.[23]

THE POWER OF THE PRIEST'S ABSOLUTION

Theologians looked at these developments in law and practice—the decline of penitential exercises, the exaltation of contrition, and the declaration of yearly obligation in the universal church—and tried to clarify the meaning of the Sacrament of Penance. Accordingly, they developed three main ways to explain what the priest does, and they represented three different estimates of his power. Those who continued in the tradition of Peter Lombard gave him very little to do. Those who followed St. Thomas tried to combine the contrition of the penitent and the action of the priest in a causal unity that produced grace, and

[23] Michel, "Pénitence," *DTC*, 12[1], 950. Teetaert, *La Confession aux laïques*, 360, 460–463; Anciaux, *La Théologie*, 164ff., 491ff. Thus Poschmann, *Kirchenbusse im frühen Mittelalter*, 232; "Seit dem Jahre 800 wird von den Gläubigen durch Diözesan gesetze verlangt, dass sie jährlich einmal oder gar dreimal dem Priester die Sünden beichten und von ihm die Rekonziliation erbitten. Das 4. Laterankonzil erhebt die Sitte zu einem allgemeinem, streng verpflichtenden Kirchengebot."

thus made the priest logically indispensable. Those who followed Duns Scotus gave the priest the greatest importance, and, starting from the indispensability established by St. Thomas, they stressed the priest's role to such an extent that some of them could speak of "the sacrament of absolution." These three solutions, to which we now turn, determined the major theological choices available to the practical literature on forgiveness at the end of the middle ages.

Even after the declaration, in 1215, of the obligation of confession to a priest, the predominant opinion before St. Thomas gave almost all causal effectiveness in the remission of guilt to the contrition of the penitent. According to this opinion, the absolution of the priest did nothing more than declare that God had already forgiven the *guilt* of the contrite man. The priest was said to "show" this forgiveness. Guilt, of course, was the most serious consequence of sin: it was the condition of divine disfavor that meant the sinner had fallen from grace, lost heaven and become liable to eternal punishment. Aside from the guilt of sin, however, which these theologians held was forgiven directly by God through divinely infused contrition, there was also thought to be a temporal punishment due to sin, to be expiated ultimately in purgatory. But this bill of suffering could also be paid in part or in full on earth by doing satisfaction, that is, works of prayer, self-denial, and charity. Furthermore, the most effective satisfaction was the penance the priest imposed in confession. The school of thought that gave the priest only a declaratory role in the remission of *the guilt of sin*, tended to emphasize the priest's role in remitting the *temporal punishment due to sin*. By the priest's prayers the admittedly inadequate works of the penitent would be placed in relationship to the merits of Christ and consequently (and only in consequence of that relationship) be worthwhile in diminishing the suffering owed for sin. In addition, these theologians gave to the priest the function of freeing the penitent from the obligation to confess and of reconciling the penitent with the church. In terms of the most important part of the forgiveness of sins—the remission of guilt, which constitutes justification and saves the Christian from Hell—the priest does not, however, play an integral role. Some of these theologians, it is true, suggested a more important role for the priest, one that would eventually become of critical significance: in those cases where the penitent's sorrow was not yet adequate (because he had not yet been given sufficient grace to awaken his love of God), the priest in confession was thought in some way to help raise this inadequate sorrow to adequate or perfect contrition. But there were many unresolved problems in this view and in general the priest was thought to have only a declaratory role, with justification emanating from contrition alone, even though these same authors accepted the obligatory nature and even divine institution of confession to the priest.[24]

The thought of St. Thomas is at once a cautious and yet fundamental departure from the contritionist thinking of Peter Lombard. Although Thomas remained faithful throughout to the main emphasis of the *Sentences* on the preeminent role of contrition in the remission of guilt, at the same time he explained the priest's absolution in such a way that it became indispensable to justification, even for the perfectly contrite penitent. For the priest's words, "I absolve you," were, in the language of Thomas's scholasticism, the form of the sacrament. Pronounced in the indicative mood, the absolution works to cause grace just as the words of the baptismal formula produce grace in connection with the water. Only the absolution of the priest, St. Thomas argued, can apply the passion of Christ to the forgiveness of the guilt of sins. Thus, even though in the normal course of events the penitent becomes contrite and forgiven *before* he goes to confession and actually hears the words of absolution, that contrition is effective only by virtue of the power of the priest's absolution to relate the sinner's sorrow to the Atonement. In a less usual case, it is possible for a penitent to go to confession thinking he is contrite without actually being fully contrite. In this case he is said to be "attrite" or to have "attrition," which is imperfect and inadequate sorrow. In such a case the absolution gives the added grace that the attrite man lacks and thus, in this exceptional circumstance, justifies him. In this second case, the benefits and the role of the priest's absolution are easier to understand; and it was along these lines that future development of the theology of penance would run. But on balance, St. Thomas remained a "contritionist." He insisted, as Peter Lombard had insisted, that the way to forgiveness was for the penitent to be perfectly sorry for his sins, and then confess them.

St. Thomas did not spend a great deal of time exploring the

[24] Michel "Pénitence," *DTC*, 12¹, 970. Watkins finds the declaratory function of the priest in Gregory the Great (*History of Penance*, II, 568ff.).

nature of that perfect sorrow: he did not meticulously define the proper motives of contrition or distinguish it psychologically from imperfect contrition. Indeed, he explicitly warned against examining the reasons for sorrow, "because a man cannot easily measure his own emotions." And it is of immense practical importance that he drew back from the attempt to establish rigid and exalted standards for contrition. Thus he judged sorrow to be adequate even if a penitent was displeased with his sins only because he found them repugnant, and not because he had reached that higher level of sorrow, displeasure at sin primarily because it is an offense against God. Moreover, he was even willing to believe that the simple desire for salvation was akin to charity and hence a worthy element in the disposition of the penitent. In short, although he was a contritionist, the authority of the Angelic Doctor could not be associated with the rigorists of later ages who wanted to define, and define severely, the motives and qualities of perfect sorrow.

His most important contribution, however, was his insistence that contrition does not produce forgiveness apart from the sacramental absolution of the priest, no matter in what sequence contrition and absolution occur. As Poschmann has summed it up: "The great and epoch-making achievement of Aquinas' teaching on penance was the integration of the sacrament in the process of justification, and consequently the proof that it was an indispensable cause of the forgiveness of sins."[25] In achieving this integration, St. Thomas merely treated the efficacy of the Sacrament of Penance consistently with his general sacramental theory. In scholastic language, the sacraments produced grace not from the work of the person receiving them—as would be the case if contrition were the efficient cause of forgiveness—but from the actual performance of the sacrament itself. The first way (called *ex opere operantis*, that is, from the work of the worker or the recipient) emphasizes the disposition and effort of the penitent, even when theologians, anxious to avoid Pelagianism, declare love or sorrow to be infused by God. The second

[25] This summary of the thought of St. Thomas follows Poschmann, *Penance and . . . Anointing*, 169–174. An excellent summary of the position of Thomas Aquinas on indicative absolution—and its background—is Ludwig Ott, "Das Opusculum des hl. Thomas von Aquin *De forma absolutionis* in dogmengeschichtlicher Betrachtung," in Martin Grabmann and K. Hoffmann, eds., *Festschrift Eduard Eichmann* (Paderborn, 1940), 99–135.

25

way (called *ex opere operato*, that is, from the work worked or performed, or from the work itself) also requires the proper disposition of the penitent—he could not be drunk, asleep, joking, or, in this case, dissimulating sorrow or the intention to stop sinning—but it emphasizes the automatic power of the sacramental sign. By explaining the Sacrament of Penance in terms of its efficacy "from the work worked," St. Thomas had made clearer than any theologian before him why it was necessary to receive the absolution of the priest.

But for clarity, nothing could surpass the thought of Duns Scotus, who represents the culmination of the explanation of the sacrament's efficacy "from the work worked." Scotist theology firmly established the role of the priest and the benefits of his absolution in bold and precise language.

According to Duns Scotus there are two ways to justification. First there is perfect contrition, which includes the intention to confess but which obtains the forgiveness of God before confession and not, as in the theory of Aquinas, by virtue of the priest's absolution. But where Aquinas had thought of contrition as the normal way to forgiveness, Duns thought of it as exceptional, a way for saints capable of extraordinary devotion and sorrow. The second and usual way to forgiveness or justification for Duns is within the Sacrament of Penance. Here attrition—an imperfect sorrow that must exclude all intention of sinning but can legitimately begin in fear of punishment—is a sufficient disposition for the penitent. It is the power of the sacrament that makes up for the deficiencies in the sinner who is only attrite, and the sacrament works infallibly so long as the penitent does not place an obstacle to its effectiveness.

St. Thomas too had used the idea that the sacrament was effective so long as no obstacle was placed in its path, and by obstacle, both he and Duns meant an intentional fraud by which one dissimulated the desire to confess and amend. But St. Thomas had remained faithful to the thought of Peter Lombard. Contrition for him was normal and indispensable, and attrition was acceptable only when the penitent was mistaken about the nature of his own sorrow. Not to be contrite and to know it and still confess would, for St. Thomas, have been a case of willful dissimulation, invalidating the sacrament. For Duns, however, perfect contrition is not necessary. Contrition, confession, and satisfaction do not even belong to the essence of the sacrament. On the contrary, the essence of the Scotist Sacrament of Penance is the absolution of the priest; and although imperfect contrition, confession, and satisfaction are necessary for the sacrament to forgive sins, the overwhelming emphasis in this conception is on the power of the words of forgiveness—the external sign—pronounced by the priest. As Duns defines it:

> Penance is the absolution of a penitent man, done by certain words that are pronounced with the proper intention by a priest having jurisdiction, efficaciously signifying by divine institution the absolution of the soul from sin.[26]

In sum, the Scotist doctrine made forgiveness easier. And most important for our purposes, it made it easier to know you were forgiven. The requirements demanded of the penitent were less exacting, and there was less occasion for him to doubt that he had met them. Forgiveness and security flowed from "the work worked."

[26] Michel, "Pénitence," *DTC*, 12¹, 1027–1029; Teetaert, *La Confession aux laïques*, 393. "Poenitentia est absolutio hominis poenitentis, facta certis verbis, cum debita intentione, prolatis a sacerdote, jurisdictionem habente ex institutione divina, efficaciter significantibus absolutionem animae a peccato." Duns Scotus, *Quaestiones in quartum librum sententiarum*, dis. 14, q. 4, 2, *Opera omnia*, vol. 18 (Paris, 1894), p. 139. Duns also dramatically rejects the traditional designation of three parts—contrition, confession, and satisfaction—as the essence of the sacrament so that he can underscore again the *ex opere operato* efficacy grounded in priestly absolution: "De poenitentiae Sacramento dico, quod ista tria nullo modo sunt partes ejus, quia, ut dictum est. dist. 14 poenitentia [sic] Sacramentum est illa absolutio Sacramentalis facta certis, etc. Hujus autem nulla pars est contritio, quae est quoddam spirituale in anima, necque confessio, quia nihil est ipsius sententiae Sacerdotis, sed actus rei accusantis se; neque satisfactio, sed sequitur illam absolutionem sacramentalem. Haec tamen tria ad Sacramentum Poenitentiae ad hoc, ut digne recipiatur, requiruntur, vel praevia, vel sequentia . . ." ibid., dis. 16, q. 1, *Opera*, 18:421.

CHAPTER II

THE LITERATURE OF THE FORGIVENESS OF SINS

EVELOPMENTS in theology and ecclesiastical legislation concerning the forgiveness of sins naturally
evoked a literary response. It was necessary to integrate changing ideas and habits into the values of a
Christian culture, and it was imperative that ecclesiastical authority disseminate practical instruction on private, auricular confession.

One of the most striking features of this response is the variety
of literary forms discussing the Sacrament of Penance. Theologians universally treated problems of confession and forgiveness when they commented on Book IV of the *Sentences* of Peter
Lombard, and their conclusions reached far beyond the confines
of the academic world. Canon lawyers explicated *Omnis utriusque sexus* as this legislation further complicated ecclesiastical
jurisdiction and became a practical concern of clerical authorities. Purely devotional literature too is filled with commonplace
legal and theological ideas about sin, sorrow, confession, absolution, and penance.

From saints' legends and collections of prayers to commentaries on the Penitential Psalms, the need to talk about forgiveness in terms of the institution of confession is evident. The sheer
variety of literature delving into the Sacrament of Penance—by
preachers of piety as well as professional theologians—proves its
intellectual significance. But any discussion of the literature of
the forgiveness of sins must give first place to the specialized
works of pastoral care designed to instruct confessors and thereby reach their penitents as well. This literature comprises the
summas and manuals for confessors, and its astonishing popularity in the first century and a half of printing is incontestable
evidence of the importance of the Sacrament of Penance and the
practical usefulness of the books that told confessors and, in rare
instances, penitents how this institution ought to work.[1]

---

[1] Michaud-Quantin, *Sommes de casuistique*, has an invaluable list of manuals and summas, with an indication of their publication history, in his index,

To understand the forgiveness of sins in the decades before the Reformation, we must first realize that if the published literature formed people's opinions and influenced practice, then we must examine what was actually published. It is not a question of looking only at fifteenth and early sixteenth century authors or late medieval theological development. We must rather look at the books that were printed, sold, and, we must assume, read. Of

---

pp. [113–121]. In establishing frequency of publication, I have tried to err on the side of underestimation. I have used Michaud-Quantin, the short-title catalogs of the British Museum, the general catalogs of the British Museum and the Bibliothèque Nationale, and the following standard bibliographical aids: Ludwig Hain, *Repertorium bibliographicum in quo libri omnes ab arte typographica inventa usque ad annum MD typis expressi ordine alphabetico vel simpliciter enumerantur vel adcuratius recensentur*, 2 vols. (Stuttgart, 1826–1838), cited as Hain; Walter Arthur Copinger, *Supplement to Hain's Repertorium bibliographicum*, 2 parts in 3 vols. (London, 1895–1902), cited as Copinger; Dietrich Reichling, *Appendices ad Hainii-Copingeri Repertorium bibliographicum*, 7 vols. (Munich, 1905–1911), cited as Reichling; *Gesamtkatalog der Wiegendrucke*, 7 vols. ("Abano" to "Eigenschaften"), (Leipzig, 1925–1938; reprint, New York, 1968), cited as *GKW*; British Museum, Department of Printed Books, *Catalogue of Books Printed in the XVth Century Now in the British Museum*, 10 vols. (London, 1908–1971), cited as *BMC XVth*; Marinus Frederick A. G. Campbell *Annales de la typographie néerlandaise au XVe siècle*, with 4 *Suppléments* (The Hague, 1874–1890) cited as Campbell; Maria E. Kronenberg, *Campbell's Annales . . . Contributions to a New Edition* (The Hague 1956), and, idem, "More Contributions to a New Campbell Edition," *Het Boek*, 36 (1964), 129–139, both cited as Kronenberg; L. Hellinga and W. Hellinga, "Additions and Notes to Campbell's *Annales* and *GW*," *Beiträge zur Inkunabelkunde*, ser. 3, no. 1 (1965), 76–86; Marie Pellechet, *Catalogue général des incunables des bibliothèques publiques de France*, 26 vols., reprint (Nendeln, Liechtenstein, 1970), cited as Pell.; Frederick R. Goff, *Incunabula in American Libraries, A Third Census . . .* (New York, 1964), cited as Goff; *Bibliotheca Catholica Neerlandica, Impressa 1500–1727* (The Hague, 1954), cited as *BCN*; Robert A. Peddie, *Conspectus incunabulorum*, Pt. I (A-B); Pt. II (C-G) (London, 1910–1914); Jean Dagens, *Bibliographie chronologique de la littérature de spiritualité et de ses sources, 1501–1610* (Paris, 1952), cited as Dagens. See also Johannes Geffken, *Der Bildercatechismus des funfzehnten Jahrhunderts und die catechetischen Hauptstücke in dieser Zeit bis auf Luther* (Leipzig, 1855); and Charlotte Zimmermann, *Die deutsche Beichte vom 9 Jahrhundert bis zur Reformation*, University of Leipzig Dissertation (Weida i. Thür., 1934). For the importance of printing in early modern European history, see Lucien Febvre and Henri-Jean Martin, *L'Apparition du livre*, L'Evolution de l'humanité, vol. 49 (Paris, 1958), esp. pp. 376–496; Elizabeth Eisenstein, "L'Avènement de l'imprimerie et la Réforme. Une Nouvelle approche au problème du démembrement de la chrétienté occidentale," *Annales: économies, sociétés, civilisations*, 26, no. 6 (November-December, 1971), 1355–1382 (with references to other literature on the subject).

course it is relevant and crucial to know that a certain author lived and wrote about penance in the last years of the fifteenth century or the first decades of the sixteenth. Contemporaries are important because they were contemporary. And when an author refers to modern opinions as if they were better, that fact too is indispensable to our understanding of the vital issues. If theology develops coherently and basic solutions become increasingly acceptable, that is worth noting.

But it would be wrong to think that the teaching church and its literature was evolving consistently a single theory of the forgiveness of sins. As we shall see, this literature reveals a wide range of attitudes and ideas about sin and forgiveness. No particular scholastic doctrine reigned supreme on the eve of the Reformation. New answers were proposed for old questions, but that does not mean that they became the most popular answers. For the early history of printing reveals one thing clearly: although some books for confessors were advertised as modern, and were successful apparently because they were modern, the longevity of some very old manuals and encyclopedic summaries proves that many of the purchasing public cared not at all for the latest word. Indeed, for some printers and for a portion of their market it was clearly the other way around—the best books were the old books. In addition, it should be no surprise to anyone familiar with the medieval intellectual tradition to learn that the modernity of later authorities was grounded solidly in opinions that derived from thirteenth or fourteenth century theologians. Thomas Aquinas, Duns Scotus, Albert the Great, Petrus de Palude, and above all Jean Gerson are some of the great names invoked to decide a case of conscience or describe the action of grace and the power of the priest. To be sure, there was plenty in the work of these theologians on which to build a new synthesis that could be called different and even modern. But at the end of the middle ages, as at the beginning, there was no desire for novelty. Outside of the special literature for confessors, in devotional works, for example, old notions and authorities are especially prominent. Yet even for the specialized literature one often finds no apparent sense that there even was a latest word. Thus the fourteenth century curate Guido de Monte Rocherii and the early fifteenth century canonist Andreas de Escobar enjoy an enduring popularity; before the Reformation their books sold in the thousands, and their audience did not mind it that they might be out of date.

Such a public had little sense of history. It is perhaps only a slight exaggeration to say that to readers at the end of the fifteenth century Guido de Monte Rocherii was a contemporary.

The relevant literature, therefore, is not what was modern but what was published. Furthermore, although the summas and manuals for confessors are obviously the most authoritative kinds of sources, other books appeared in print that formed opinion about forgiveness and consolation and therefore shed light on our study. The people who bought these books wanted to find out what a sin was, how it was to be confessed, why and when it was forgiven. They might consult a whole variety of literature, which will be sampled in the following study in an attempt to describe the range of opinion on these questions in the decades before the Reformation.

Summas for Confessors

The most important works on cases of conscience and the Sacrament of Penance are long, broad in scope, and detailed in their discussions. Most of these big books belong to an identifiable genre, the *Summa confessorum* or *Summa de casibus conscientiae*, whose originator was Raymond of Peñaforte, the Catalan doctor of canon law who compiled his summa between 1220 and 1245. It is in the tradition started by Raymond that a sense of progressive development of doctrine is most apparent, and this development undoubtedly explains why Raymond's summa—known as the *Raymundina*—was not published in the fifteenth or sixteenth century.[2] The opinions of the *Raymundina* remain of historical interest, however, even in the special task of defining re-

---

[2] On the genre see Thomas N. Tentler, "The Summa for Confessors as an Instrument of Social Control," in Charles Trinkaus, ed., *Pursuit of Holiness* (Leiden, 1974), 105–109; Leonard E. Boyle, "The Summa for Confessors as a Genre and Its Religious Intent," ibid., 126–127; and Thomas N. Tentler, "Response and *Retractatio*," ibid., 131–134. I have rejected notices of an edition of Raymond's *Summa* (Paris, 1500), in Hain (12567, 13711) as does Johann Friedrich von Schulte, *Die Geschichte der Quellen und Literatur des Canonischen Rechts von Gratian bis auf die Gegenwart*, 3 vols. (Stuttgart, 1875–1880), II, 410–411. Von Schulte notes the paucity of manuscripts of the *Raymundina* from the fifteenth century. All citations of *Raymundina* are to Raymond of Peñaforte, *Summa sancti Raymundi de Peniafort . . . de poenitentia et matrimonio cum glossis Ioannis de Friburgo* [i.e., William of Rennes] (Rome, 1603; reprint, Farnborough, England, 1967).

31

ligious sentiment on the eve of the Reformation. For although Raymond's direct influence declined in the fourteenth century, he remained the prestigious initiator of a genre intensely respectful and conscious of its past. Thus it is the best starting point for studying this more academic branch of the literature.

The *Raymundina*'s organization tells us something about the human problems that gave rise to this genre. It is in four books. The first deals with sins against God, and the second with sins against one's neighbor. Book Three takes up the priesthood, its ordination and functions, and includes a long section expressly on the Sacrament of Penance. This section on the Sacrament of Penance, about one-tenth of the first three books, corresponds in subject matter to the manuals of penance that preceded the *Raymundina*. Book Four, which was added later, is a complete treatise on marriage. Each of the four books is divided into chapters and sections, and the organization is plainly based on legal, pedagogical ideas; for the purpose is not only to provide a summary, but also a useful handbook. Yet the *Raymundina* is, above all, a summary of accepted ideas. As the editors of the Roman edition of 1603 admiringly note, no one could justly accuse Raymond of originality: "Rarely or never does he rely on his own authority or judgment; for he thought novelties and unique opinions ought perpetually to be avoided like the plague." The principle of organization by summarizing cases and opinions, however, was formative. In the fourteenth century Astesanus of Asti cited the *Raymundina* more than St. Thomas or St. Bonaventure, and even in the sixteenth century Sylvester Prierias referred back to him. Within ten years the *Raymundina* was glossed by another Dominican, William of Rennes, and most of the vast number of manuscripts that circulated from that time on contained both Raymond's text and William's gloss.[3]

The *Raymundina* and its successors are summas in the true sense of the word. They try to include all the best teaching of moral and sacramental theology, and in this attempt succeeding summas reflect the polemics and intellectual change of the later middle ages. That there were such changes, and that they were apparent and important to medieval canonists and theologians,

---

[3] Dietterle, "Die Summae confessorum," *ZKG*, 24 (1903), 530–545; Teetaert, *La Confession aux laïques*, 354ff.; idem, "La Doctrine pénitentielle de saint Raymond de Penyafort, O.P.," *Analecta Sacra Tarraconensia*, 4 (1928), 121–182; Michaud-Quantin, *Sommes de casuistique*, 9–11, 34–43.

is obvious; otherwise there would have been no need for William of Rennes to comment on the *Raymundina*, or for subsequent authors to go beyond the *Raymundina* and its gloss. It seems equally evident that the forces evoking new summas and new opinions were more than academic disputes. Change in medieval society and the practical experience of confessors made new books both necessary and profitable. Indeed, convincing evidence that practical needs and experience were determinants in this process is a striking innovation: by the second half of the thirteenth century Monaldus de Capo d'Istria, a Franciscan, had organized the contents of his summa alphabetically so that it is a veritable encyclopedia. The advantages of this encyclopedic form to a confessor who wanted to consult a problem in a hurry —"irregularity," "excommunication," "usury," "conjugal debt," and the like—is obvious. Thus the practical orientation of the genre is symbolized by this organizational innovation; and it is equally significant that it became customary to provide an alphabetical index for those summas that were divided into books.

To study the opinion of the church on the eve of the Reformation, however, it is important to consider not the pioneers but the most popular printed books. The *Raymundina* is less important than its successors, therefore, because even though parts of it were copied into later books, it was not itself published until the seventeenth century. The *Monaldina* is a similar case. It was never printed in the fifteenth century, and we know of only one edition in the sixteenth, in which its Lyons printer, acutely aware of his competition and probably fearful of a publishing failure, advertised on the title page that although it was not as long as some of the others, "nevertheless in its goodness and subtlety it is not unequal to the summa of lord Antoninus, brother Angelus, Astesanus, and all the rest." It is understandable that the influence of the legalistic *Monaldina* remained limited. A modern historian's judgment that when it was published in 1516 it had "only antiquarian interest," appears justified, because its rivals were more in touch with confessors who needed theological as well as legal guidance. On the other hand, we have convincing evidence of the importance of completeness, and a kind of modernity, in the comparative popularity of the *Summa Pisanella* of Bartholomaeus de Sancto Concordio, and its direct successor, the *Supplementum* (that is, the "supplement" to the *Pisanella*) of Nicolaus de Ausimo. Both were written in the fourteenth century and both rely on canon law more than theology. But the *Supplementum*, which includes the text of the *Pisanella*, is more detailed, offering new citations and, in some cases, different solutions. Consequently, the *Supplementum* enjoyed greater popularity both in manuscripts and in early printed books.[4]

If we take publishing success as a partial guide, certain books are more important. Of the summas for confessors, the *Raymundina*, *Monaldina*, and *Pisanella* are examples of less important works. In addition to the *Supplementum*, the older summas that retain the greatest prestige and thus seem worthy of serious attention are the *Summa confessorum* by the Dominican John of Freiburg, written at the very end of the thirteenth century, and the *Astesana* by the Franciscan Astesanus of Asti, which dates from the first part of the fourteenth. The two whose popularity was unsurpassed, however, are the summas of the Franciscan Angelus de Clavasio and the Dominican Sylvester Prierias Mazzolini—the *Angelica* printed for the first time in 1486, and the *Sylvestrina* in 1514.[5]

Some idea of the popularity of summas for confessors is revealing. John of Freiburg's *Summa* survived not only in many manuscript copies but also came to be published three times in the fifteenth and once in the sixteenth century. It is frequently cited in manuals and summas; and the prologue of the *Summa rudium*, in singling it out for special praise, says that Pope John XXI exclaimed after reading it: "I consider the brother who compiled this summa one of the best persons in the whole church—and I have learned many things from him." In addition, the work of Berthold of Freiburg, which was long known simply as a German translation of the *Summa confessorum* by "Brother Berthold," is really a reworking of John of Freiburg's material. Seven different printers published this vernacular summa in no fewer than eleven editions in the fifteenth century and one in the early

[4] Joannes Mondaldus di Capo d'Istria, *Summa in vtroque iure* (Lyon, 1516), hereafter cited as *Monaldina*; Nicolaus de Ausimo, *Supplementum summae pisanellae* (L. Wild: Venice, 1489); Dietterle, "Die Summae confessorum," *ZKG*, 25 (1904), 248–252; 27 (1906), 183, 187; Michaud-Quantin, *Sommes de casuistique*, 42, 60–64.

[5] Astesanus de Ast, *Summa de casibus conscientiae* (Lyon, 1519), hereafter cited as *Astesana*; Angelus [Carletus] de Clavasio, *Summa angelica* ([M. Havard]: Lyon, 1500), cited as *Angelica*; Sylvester Prierias Mazzolini, *Summa summarum, que Sylvestrina dicitur* (Bologna, 1515), cited as *Sylvestrina*.

sixteenth.[6] Similarly, the *Astesana* was printed ten times in incunabular editions and once in the sixteenth century.[7] And twenty-nine incunabular editions are known of Nicolaus de Ausimo's *Supplementum.*[8]

But the two greatest successes were the *Angelica* and the *Sylvestrina.* The *Angelica* saw at least twenty-four incunabular editions, and they represent the major printing areas of Europe—there were, for example, six in Venice, seven in Nuremberg and Strasbourg, and seven in Lyons. It was printed at least nineteen times between 1501 and 1520, and in Venice alone it was published in the second half of the century four times. Perhaps the *Angelica*'s most illustrious moment occurred in December of 1520 when—along with books by Johann Eck, some canon law, and the papal bull of excommunication—it was solemnly and publicly burned by Martin Luther.[9]

The *Sylvestrina* provided the most serious competition for the *Angelica,* and indeed, in the latter half of the sixteenth century the Dominican seems to have outsold the Franciscan by a substantial margin. The *Sylvestrina* was first published in Italy, and

[6] Johannes von Freiburg, *Summa confessorum* (Lyon, 1518); Berthold von Freiburg, *Summa Joannis, deutsch* (J. Bämler: Augsburg, 1472); *Summa rudium* (Reutlingen, 1487), "Prologus," A2a: "Est etiam quadam liber qui vocatur summa Johannis Friburgensis maior Vel summa confessorum compilata per Reverendum lectorem conventus Friburgensis in brisgaudio ordinis supradicti [i.e., Dominican] tante autoritatis quod dominus papa Johannes XXIX [sic] qui fuit subtilis indagator iuris cum memoratam summam perlegeret dixit fratrem qui istam summam collegit reputo unam esse de melioribus personis totius ecclesie a quo etiam multa recepi." Leonard E. Boyle's study of John of Freiburg' *Summa confessorum* demonstrates an influence that far exceeds that claimed here for the work: see *Addendum to Bibliography.* Editions of the *Summa confessorum*: Hain, 7365–7366; Copinger, 2583; British Museum (Koeberger: [Nuremberg], 1518). See also Dietterle, "Die Summae confessorum," *ZKG,* 25 (1904), 255–259; 26 (1905), 67–70; Michaud-Quantin, *Sommes de casuistique,* 43–48; Rudolf Stanka, *Die Summa des Berthold von Freiburg. Eine rechtsgeschichtliche Untersuchung,* Theologische Studien der "Österreichischen Leo-Gesellschaft, 36 (Vienna, 1937), p. 189. Adam Petri published Berthold's summa (Basel, 1518), and a brief extract for merchants was translated into French (Hain, 7378).

[7] Dietterle, "Die Summae confessorum," *ZKG,* 26 (1905), 350–353; Michaud-Quantin, *Sommes de casuistique,* 57–60. The sixteenth-century edition (Guenard [Pinet]: Lyon, 1519) is in the British Museum.

[8] Hain, 2149–2172; Copinger, 784–787; Reichling, 825.

[9] Dietterle, *ZKG,* 27 (1906), 296–302; Michaud-Quantin, *Sommes de casuistique,* 99–101; Dagens, p. 27; *GKW,* 1923–1946.

it appears, oddly enough, that there was only one German edition, which came out in Strasbourg in 1518. Outside of Germany, however, its popularity with publishers was immense, and numerous editions appeared in Antwerp, Lyons, and Venice. Perhaps much of its later popularity was owing to the reputation of Sylvester as an implacable foe of Luther. But one suspects that a good part of its success came from the confidence that permeates the work, for Sylvester is even here the polemicist, forcefully asserting his own solutions and pronouncing those of his rivals inferior. On the Franciscans he is especially hard—the *Rosella*, *Supplementum*, and, above all, the *Angelica* itself. One example of unusual asperity occurs when Sylvester attacks the *Angelica*'s judgment on whether one may invoke demons to get rid of demons. Almost everyone forbids it, Sylvester notes, but not the audacious *Angelica*:

> Indeed the *Summa Angelica*—bold and dangerous in its habit of deciding—says this is licit. . . . But this opinion is abominable [*nefanda*], and the occasion of infinite sins, and grossly contributing to the expansion of the kingdom of the devil.[10]

Despite this frank opposition, however, the *Sylvestrina* has much in common with the *Angelica*. They both show an unusual degree of originality. Indeed, as far as the limitations of the form allow, they are both stamped with the individuality of their authors. Moreover, both exemplify a humane tendency in pastoral theology, which occasionally appears in their liking for some opinion of Duns Scotus or Albert the Great, as well as in their general preference for theology over canon law. Thus in his introduction Angelus asserts his determination to eschew legalism and follow the best theologians. He intends to be moderate as he declares himself in favor of more flexible attitudes toward cases of conscience:

> Nothing has been said here that I have not thought to be in agreement with justice and truth, especially in *the forum of conscience*, which I have judged more in need of satisfaction than the forum of contentions; and for that reason I have *not*

---

[10] Dietterle, "Die Summae confessorum," *ZKG*, 28 (1907), 416–420; Michaud-Quantin, *Sommes de casuistique*, 101–103; *Sylvestrina*, "Maleficium," q. 8.

followed at times the common opinion of the doctors, *especially of the canonists and legists,* because it did not seem to me to conform to *the truth of theology and conscience.*

Nevertheless, he humbly assures us that he submits his opinions "to be corrected" by "the judgment of Holy Mother Church or anyone of greater wisdom." Angelus was no radical, then, but he, like many others concerned with moral theology and the forum of conscience, recognized that there were dangers in excessive legalism. Sylvester also saw those dangers. And surely this awareness helps explain why the *Angelica* and *Sylvestrina* appealed to the world of the late middle ages and Reformation.[11]

Two other big books on confession deserve special attention: the *Manipulus curatorum* by Guido de Monte Rocherii, a fourteenth century curate from Teruel, near Madrid; and the *Confessionale* of Godescalc Rosemondt, a Dutch churchman, a humanist of sorts, contemporary of Luther and Erasmus. Neither is called a summa, but because of the broad scope of the moral and theological questions they raise, and because of the detail in which they discuss their subject, they occupy a middle ground between the summas and the manuals.

The *Manipulus curatorum* seems closely related to the family of summas, if only because whole sections—especially those discussing such legal technicalities as impediments to marriage—derive from, indeed plagiarize, the *Raymundina.* But plagiarism was no sin, and in other places Guido shows an independent spirit—for example, he takes up the difficult and complex theory of the "adornment of the soul," a theological eccentricity that will enter into our discussion of how penance works forgiveness. Whatever our judgment on the intrinsic merits of the *Manipulus curatorum,* it was popular. More than ninety incunabular editions were published, one of them in far-off London. Its popularity held up in the sixteenth century too, for it was published in, among other places, Paris in 1504, 1505, 1516, and 1523; London in 1508 and

[11] *Angelica,* "Prologus": "Et quamvis in ea [Angelus's summa] nihil sit dictum quod non arbitratus fuerim conuenire iusticie et veritati: presertim in foro conscientie: cui satisfaciendum magis censui quam ad forum contentiosum propterea non sum secutus aliquando communem opinionem doctorum presertim canonistarum et legistarum: quia conscientali et theologice veritati non mihi visa fuit conuenire. Tamen iudicio sancte matris ecclesie et cuiuslibet melius sapientis corrigendam submitto."

1509; Venice in 1515, 1543, and 1566; and in Louvain in 1553 and Antwerp in 1555.[12]

Godescalc Rosemondt's *Confessionale* is not organized like the summas, but its 576 octavo pages seem to warrant discussing it along with them. It first appeared in 1518, was printed three more times by 1525, and once again in 1554. The *Confessionale* was closely related, moreover, to his vernacular book on confession, which was printed four times in 1517 and 1518 by Henri Eckert van Homberch of Antwerp. But it is not merely the circulation of this book that commands our attention. For here is a theologian writing on the eve of Luther's break with Rome, a close friend of Adrian of Utrecht and a correspondent of Erasmus, who wrote to John à Lasco that he lamented, in the passing of Godescalc, "a man better than the common sort of theologians." Godescalc was an academic, a moral reformer, a popular writer, and a member of the ecclesiastical power elite. He was as much in places of influence as Guido had probably been out of them, but, in different ways, both of their books contribute to our understanding of problems of conscience and forgiveness in the pre-Reformation era.[13]

[12] Guido de Monte Rocherii, *Manipulus curatorum* (P. Levet: Paris, 1489/ 90); Michaud-Quantin, *Sommes de casuistique*, 11; Hugo Hurter, *Nomenclator litterarius theologiae catholicae theologos exhibitens aetate, natione disciplinis distinctos*, 5 vols., reprint (New York, 1962), II, 612; Cyr Ulysse Chevalier, *Répertoire des sources historiques du Moyen Age, Bio-Bibliographie*, rev. ed., reprint (New York, 1960), 2011; Hain, 8157–8214; Copinger, 2824–2850; Reichling, 205, 206, 546, 547, 931; Dagens, 30. Peddie, *Conspectus Incunabulorum*, II, 304–306, counts ninety-eight editions in the fifteenth century, and there are several editions after 1500 in the British Museum. The influence of the *Manipulus curatorum* in the diocese of Geneva—its recommendation by the bishop in the early fifteenth century, an appraisal of its strengths and limitations as a practical manual, and the importance of its availability in print—is discussed in Louis Binz, *Vie religieuse et réforme ecclésiastique dans le diocèse de Genève pendant le grand schisme et la crise conciliaire (1378–1450)*, vol. 1, "Mémoires et documents" publiés par la Société d'histoire et d'archéologie de Genève, vol. 46 (Geneva, 1973), 169–171, 345–352. Binz concludes judicieusement: "L'apparition de l'imprimerie a constitué un tournant décisif dans l'amélioration du niveau intellectuel du clergé . . . . Grâce à l'imprimerie, le monde ecclésiastique, jugé globalement et non sur une mince élite, parviendra en 1500 à un niveau culturel, encore bien faible à nos yeux modernes, mais jamais atteint jusqu'alors" (p. 352).

[13] Godescalc Rosemondt, *Confessionale* (Antwerp, 1518); William de Vreese, "Rosemondt, Godescalc," *Biographie nationale* (Brussels: L'Académie Royale des Sciences des Lettres et des Beaux-arts de Belgique, 1866–), vol. 20, 102–110.

In conclusion, if we consider only those books we have called summas for confessors, it would seem that there was a learned, primarily clerical audience that was sensitive to doctrinal development and wanted the latest opinion. They could buy the *Angelica* or *Sylvestrina* and get it. The persistence of the fourteenth century *Astesana* and *Supplementum*, or of John of Freiburg's thirteenth century summa and its German offspring, the *Summa of Brother Berthold*, cannot be said really to contradict this assertion, for their success was not comparable. If the summas for confessors reflect a desire to keep up with recent theological opinion, we may speculate that they were bought and used by more learned confessors who had a greater interest than their fellow clerics in what was new. Nevertheless, some older summas found a market; a book like the *Manipulus curatorum* remained immensely popular; and among the manuals it is clear that wide circulation was never the exclusive privilege of modern writers. Indeed, when we add to the summas the plethora of manuals of confession and devotional books that deal with repentance, confession, and consolation, the market for this literature reveals more than anything a desire to get any information at all to meet the needs of Christians bound by conscience and the law to be confident in the forgiveness of the institutional church.

Manuals of Confession and Pastoral Care

Two authors of the most extraordinary popularity head the list of those who wrote manuals for confession: St. Antoninus of Florence and Andreas de Escobar. Antoninus's *Confessionale—Defecerunt* (even if we count only one of its various forms) and Andreas's *Modus confitendi* are among the most frequently printed books in the fifteenth century.

The manual of St. Antoninus most often published begins, "Defecerunt scrutantes scrutinio . . ."; it is consequently known as the *Confessionale—Defecerunt*, and this is the version used in the present study. Taking all of St. Antoninus's manuals in Latin and Italian, we find over one hundred incunabular editions, and they were published in thirty-two different cities of Europe. Seventy-two of these printings represent one or another form of the *Confessionale—Defecerunt*, including translations into Italian and Spanish. The authority of Antoninus is well known, for all learned authors cited his casuistry. And the popularity of the

Confessionale—Defecerunt is entirely understandable: intelligent, succinct, and authoritative, written by a judge, archbishop, and member of the Dominician order, it was bound to succeed.[14]

The case of the *Modus confitendi*, however, is different. It is not a manual for confessors in the true sense because it neglects most of the practical questions necessary for a useful instruction on the conduct and powers of confession and absolution. It is rather a general confession designed to be read as an examination of conscience. It has none of the intellectual qualities of the *Confessionale—Defecerunt*; indeed, it has virtually no intellectual qualities whatsoever. Yet it corresponded to an apparent need for a handy list of sins with some brief thoughts on forgiveness and repentance. Eighty-six different printings in twenty-three different cities survive from the fifteenth century; and it achieved wider circulation by being included complete in Nicolaus de Saliceto's popular *Antidotarius anime*. Further possibilities of the influence of this kind of literature were revealed some years ago by the discovery of two condensed versions of the *Modus confitendi* (Andreas's original could fit on six leaves), both published in Cracow. One is an abbreviated Latin version, while the other is a one-page German epitome—a *Beichtzettel*—that may have been designed to be hung on the wall of a home or church. It is obvious that the chances of survival for one-page publications are small, and we can only wonder how many of this kind of brief instruction for confession have been lost. But the wide influence of the *Modus confitendi* is exemplified by this rare find, and it serves as further confirmation of what figures of publication already show.[15]

[14] Antoninus of Florence, *Summula confessionis* (Flach: Strasbourg, 1499), hereafter cited as *Confessionale—Defecerunt*; Hieronymus Wilms, "Das Confessionale 'Defecerunt' des hl. Antonin," *Divus Thomas*, 3d ser., 24 (1946), 99–108. Of the two versions of the *Confessionale—Defecerunt*, Wilms argues that the shorter is probably by Antoninus and precedes his summa, and that the longer, which includes interpolations from other works, may not have been put together by Antoninus. See Dietterle, "Die Summae confessorum," *ZKG*, 24 (1903), 362–363; Michaud-Quantin, *Sommes de casuistique*, 73–75; *GKW*, 2075–2177, and appendix, II, 779–781.

[15] Andreas de Escobar, *Modus confitendi . . . . Interrogationes . . . . Canones penitentiales . . . . Casus papales et episcopales* (Nuremberg, 1508); *GKW*, 1769–1855, and appendix, II, 777–778. There are also many editions of Nicolaus de Saliceto's *Antidotarius* (Hain, 14154–14172; Copinger, 5215–5218; Reichling, *HC* 14159–14160), including some published after 1500. For the

Given the popularity of the *Modus confitendi*, however, it is somewhat difficult to account for the failure of Andreas's full-length manual, the *Lumen confessorum*, to achieve comparable fame. In fact, the *Lumen confessorum* was never published under its right name (unless we count its appearance in the concluding words of one incunabule). But four separately titled segments were printed, and when they are put together, they almost correspond to the original manual. The most widely published part, *Interrogations and Teaching by Which a Priest Ought to Question His Penitent*, was printed at least forty-eight times in the fifteenth century.[16] One suspects that in choosing the *Modus confitendi* or the brief *Interrogations* from the *Lumen confessorum*, publishers and public were looking for something shorter and therefore cheaper. Andreas is a canonist pure and simple, with none of the sophistication of an Angelus de Clavasio or Sylvester Prierias Mazzolini. He is insensitive to theological and moral complexities and his works breathe the letter of the law. Perhaps if his writing had been in direct competition with the manuals of Antoninus of Florence—if, for example, the whole *Lumen confessorum* had been published—he would not have sold quite so well. Nevertheless, these are merely guesses; and we are bound to note that the name of Andreas de Escobar is extraordinarily prominent in the history of early printed books. In the pre-Reformation era thousands of copies of the *Modus con-*

Beichtzettel, see Joseph Fritz, "Zwei unbekannte Bearbeitungen des Modus confitendi von Andreas Hispanus," *Der Katholik*, 4th ser., 10 (1912), 57ff. For the medieval meaning of "general confession," see Michaud-Quantin, *Sommes de casuistique*, 71–72, 82 n. 12.

[16] *GKW*, 7292. The ending "Explicit Lumen confessorum" is in *GKW*, 7304, and correctly identifies the source. The British Museum has seven editions of Andreas's writings published between 1500 and 1519—[Rome? 1500?], [Paris? 1515?], (Nuremberg, 1506 and 1508), (Augsburg, 1507, 1513, and 1519)—whose contents include the *Interrogationes*, the *Canones penitentiales*, and the *Casus papales et episcopales*. Only Michaud-Quantin has drawn attention to the extensive publication of these excerpts from the *Lumen confessorum* (*Sommes de casuistique*, 71–72). Cf. Richard Stapper, "Das 'Lumen Confessorum' des Andreas Didaci," *Römische Quartalschrift für christliche Altherthumskunde und für Kirchengeschichte*, 11 (1897), 271–285; E. Delaruelle, E.-R. Labande, and Paul Ourliac, *L'Eglise au temps du grand schisme et de la crise conciliaire (1378–1449)*, in Augustin Fliche and Victor Martin, eds., *Histoire de l'église depuis les origines jusqu'à nos jours*, vol. 14² (Paris, 1964), 660–661.

fitendi and the *Interrogations* defined for people the types and kinds of sins.

Next to these giants of publication success, the circulation of the other manuals is diminutive. Nevertheless, some went through multiple printings, and some reveal intellectual qualities, or are characterized by other circumstances that command our special attention. One of the most interesting is the anonymous *Peycht Spigel der sünder*, published in Nuremberg in 1510. As self-effacing as the anonymous author tries to be, the text still conveys his personality: an idealistic and yet experienced priest who has struggled with the most fundamental problems of penitents and confessors. At the outset he reveals his reforming inclinations. He tells his readers that he has often wondered why in his age, when "the Holy Ghost has, through printing, opened up the treasures of wisdom and the arts," none of the learned confessors have availed themselves of this opportunity to write a vernacular manual of confession for laymen. In his familiar style he laments the useless works that printers circulate among the laity—silly rhymes and songs—and he attributes this failure primarily to the worldliness of Christians, for whom lawsuits are more important than sacred things. "Thus I, a young confessor," he relates, "have been asked by several penitents to compose . . . a little confessional manual for laymen." He has, he assures us, done it humbly, "nit vil hynein gesezt hab aus eygem kopff," but rather relied on the writings of learned men. What we are given, however, is a long manual (over two hundred pages) whose author's attitudes are revealed in a host of comments and opinions as well as in the selection he makes from the authorities he so honestly respects.[17]

Four other manuals deserve mention here with the *Peycht Spigel* because they all emanate from Germany in the years before and during Luther's spiritual struggle and break from Rome: the *Confessionale* of Engelhardus Kunhofer (Nuremberg, 1502); the *Penitentiarius* of Johannes Romming (Nuremberg, 1522?); the *Short Instructions for Validly Making Sacramental Confession* by Jodocus (Morder) Winshemius (Erfurt, 1515); and the anonymous *Manual for Parish Priests*. This little group also provides an interesting sample of the way in which printed books helped disseminate information on sacramental penance.

---

[17] *Peycht Spigel der sünder* (Nurcmberg, 1510), A2a. Cf. Nikolaus Paulus, "Die Reue in den deutschen Beichtschriften," *ZkTh*, 28 (1904), 15–17.

As its title indicates, the *Manual for Parish Priests* is not only for confessors but covers the basic duties of the parochial clergy. As one might expect, however, it devotes an important part of its contents to problems of conscience and confession. Fifteen editions survive from the fifteenth century, all of them printed in Germany, and at least three editions by the printer Johann Weissenburger appeared between 1512 and 1514 in Nuremberg and Landshut.[18] As a parish manual, moreover, it represents a kind of literature that was probably as influential as any in forming the attitudes and habits of European penitents. The *Peycht Spigel*, for example, is longer, is written in the vernacular, and is designed for laymen. But the *Manual for Parish Priests*, and others like it, undoubtedly touched the lives of far more laymen because it worked through the more literate clergy whose specific calling was to teach such matters. Simple, handy, written in easy Latin without complicated ideas, the *Manual for Parish Priests* was perhaps standard in central Germany in the years before the Reformation, and its popularity is not difficult to explain.

The authors of the other three German manuals can claim some place in the world of humane letters; but it is the *Institutiones succincte* of Jodocus Winshemius that undoubtedly has the best credentials. Its title page is adorned with verses to the reader by Helius Eobanus Hessus and Euricius Cordus, and its introductory epistle to Jodocus Trutvetter is ostentatiously learned and ornate. The manual itself has the distinction of having been praised by Oecolampadius in 1519, who suggested to Johann Froben that he republish it (before, we must hasten to add, Oecolampadius went over to the cause of the Reformation). Nevertheless, Jodocus Winshemius—like Romming and Kunhofer—was concerned with entirely predictable problems which confessional manuals had to take up, no matter what the literary affiliations of their authors were.[19]

---

[18] *Manuale parrochialium sacerdotum* (Nuremberg, 1512): Hain, 10723–10733; Copinger, 3863–3864; Reichling, 979, 616. The three editions by Johann Weissenburger are in the British Museum.

[19] Engelhardus Kunhofer, *Confessionale continens tractatum decem preceptorum* (Nuremberg, 1502); Johannes Romming, *Penitentiarius, in tres parteis, contritionem, confessionem, et satisfactionem discretus* . . . (Nuremberg, 1522?); Jodocus Winshemius, *Institutiones succincte in rite faciendam* . . . *confessionem sacramentalem* (Erfurt, 1516); Nikolaus Paulus, "Ein Beichtbüchlein für Erfurter Studenten aus dem 16. Jahrhundert," *Der*

The manuals just mentioned, however, are only a small sample of the many circulating in the decades before the Reformation. More than ten editions of two different manuals are attributed to Antonius de Butrio.[20] At least a dozen editions survive of the *Confessionale* of Bartholomaeus de Chaimis, and they were published in eight cities, from Milan to Mainz.[21] Jean Columbi wrote a dull general confession;[22] Antoine Faren had his Latin *Confessionale* published in French as *La Pratique de soy bien confesser*;[23] and there were varying degrees of success for short treatises by Jacobus Lupi Rebello, Olivier Maillard, Jean Quentin, Matthew of Cracow, Jacobus de Clusa, and Jacobus Philippus (Bergomensis) Foresti.[24] It is at the same time surprising to see the numbers of anonymous works printed in the fifteenth and

---

Katholik, 19 (1899), 92–96; idem, "Die Beichtbüchlein des Jodocus von Windsheim," ibid., 382–384; idem, "Noch einmal das Erfurter Beichtbüchlein des Jodocus Morder von Windsheim," ibid., 20 (1899), 94–96; idem, "Johann Romming und dessen Beichtbüchlein für die Nürnberger Schuljugend," ibid., 21 (1900), 570–575.

[20] Antonius de Butrio, *Directorium ad confitendum. Modus confitendi* (de Vulteriis: Rome, ca. 1474); idem, *Speculum de confessione* (Johannes de Westphalia: Louvain, n.d.); *GKW*, 5827–5830.

[21] Bartholomaeus de Chaimis, *Interrogatorium siue Confessionale* (Valdarfer: Milan, 1474); Michaud-Quantin, *Sommes de casuistique*, 76; *GKW*, 6540–6551.

[22] Jehan Columbi, *Confession generale auec certaines reigles au commencement tresutile: tant a confesseurs que a penitens* (n.p., 1520?); *GKW*, 7168. See also Marcel Viller et al., eds., *Dictionnaire de spiritualité, ascetique et mystique, doctrine et histoire* (Paris, 1932), II, 1134–1135; J. Balteau et al., eds., *Dictionnaire de biographie française* (Paris, 1933–), IX, 350.

[23] Antoine Faren, *La Pratique de soy bien confesser* (Guillaume LeRoy: Lyon, 1485?); *GKW*, 9718–9721.

[24] Jacobus Lupi Rebello, *Tractatus fructus sacramenti penitentie* (G. Mercatoris: Paris, 14[9]d), *BMC XVth*, 8, 61; Oliver Maillard, *La Confession generale de frere oliuier maillart* (G. LeRoy: Lyon, 1485?), *BMC XVth*, 8, 239; idem, *Oeuvres françaises—Sermones et Poésies*, ed. by Arthur de la Borderie (Nantes, 1877), 164ff; Jean Quentin, *Examen de conscience (pour soy cognoistre et bien se confesser)* (F. Baligault?: Paris, 1500?); for Matthew of Cracow [attributed to Thomas Aquinas], *De modo confitendi et de puritate conscientie*, see Michaud-Quantin, *Sommes de casuistique*, 79–80; *BMC XVth*, 8, 44; and ibid., 9, 183; Jacobus de Clusa, *Confessionale compendiosum et utilissimum* (Nuremberg, 1520); Jacobus Philippus (Bergomensis) Foresti, *Confessionale seu Interrogatorium* (B. Benalium: Venice, ca. 1497); Hain, 2814–2815, Copinger, 950, Reichling, 1463; in the sixteenth century two Latin editions were published in Antwerp (1506 and 1513), and the British Museum has one published in Venice (1510?).

sixteenth centuries, mirrors of sinners, diocesan manuals, and treatises on how to confess. On confession alone, the *Gesamtkatalog* lists thirty-five different editions of anonymous works—including some multiple printings of the same books—and that figure brings us up only to the year 1500.[25]

Such then are the short works that will be cited in the following study. As with the summas, they have been no more than sampled. And while it is true that they are generally unimaginative and ordinary, they provide invaluable evidence for habits and assumptions precisely because they intended to simplify doctrine for practical application.

Finally, no survey of the pastoral literature of the pre-Reformation era can neglect the preeminent authority of Jean Gerson; and among his manuals, the *Opus tripartitum* is certainly the most remarkable and influential. Its three parts—an exposition of the Ten Commandments, a treatise on confession, and a preparation for death—were written separately, but were soon put together to make the little book that became so famous. At least sixteen different printings are counted for the fifteenth century, and the book's success continues in the sixteenth. Originally written in French, it was first printed in Latin and eventually translated into Spanish, Flemish, Swedish, German, and back into French. But its potential for molding opinion surpassed even its wide publication. According to the eighteenth-century editor of the *Opera omnia*, the bishops of France thought so highly of it that they chose it as a special means of instruction for both priests and laity; pastors were to read it to their people and it was inserted into their liturgical books. Indeed, we know that the bilingual edition of the *Opus tripartitum*, the *Instruction des curez*, was explicitly commended by many bishops: in Paris in 1506, Evreux in 1507, Le Mans in 1508, Chartres in 1531, and probably others. The admonition of the Bishop of Le Mans is self-explanatory: "The *Instruction of Curates* for teaching the simple people: curates, chaplains, masters of schools and hospitals, and others throughout the Bishopric of Le Mans are enjoined to keep this book with them and read from it." The Bishop of Le Mans is worried, he continues, about the education of the simple people who seldom hear good preaching. To make up for this failure of

[25] *GKW*, 7341–7375. Michaud-Quantin has correctly noted that *GKW*, 7292–7340, are really taken from the *Lumen confessorum* of Andreas de Escobar, and should not be listed under anonymous works: see above, n. 16.

instruction, he urges the use of this book "by the venerable doctor in theology Master Jean Gerson, most Christian doctor, once chancellor of the church of Paris, great and prudent zealot of souls, and singular consoler of consciences." Such praise is typical of the attitude of ecclesiastical authority in the early sixteenth century to the Chancellor of Paris, the Most Christian, the Consoling Doctor.

Gerson wrote many treatises that were popular and influential: *On the Art of Hearing Confessions*, *On Nocturnal Pollution*, *On the Remedies against Pusillanimity*, and many others that bear on the problems of the cure of souls. In addition, ten printings of his *Opera omnia* appeared before 1521, and among those we know were responsible for these editions are such famous names as Johann Geiler von Kaisersberg and Jakob Wimpfeling. These are only some of the reasons that Gerson dominates this literature, not just through the *Opus tripartitum* or his other great manuals, but simply by the ubiquity of his opinion and the authority accorded it. His is the greatest voice in the cure of souls.[26]

Devotional Literature

The fifteenth and sixteenth centuries are replete with devotional classics, popular then and for the most part unread now, that deal with the great themes of repentance, confession, forgiveness. In addition, there is a huge variety of literature in other forms—sermons, poems, treatises, and manuals—that most properly belong with the books that sought to edify, to encourage contemplation of the life of the spirit and the last things. Some of these books obviously belong in the class of devotional literature: Stephan Lanzkranna's *Heavenly Road*, Jacobus de Gruytroede's *Golden Mirror of the Sinful Soul*, or the anonymous *Garden of the Soul*. But the purpose of other literature is so similar that it is pointless to separate them: the various collections of Lenten Sermons of Robertus Caracciolus, for example, or the *Golden Work of True Contrition*, by Johannes Ludovicus Vivaldus, must have appealed to audiences with the same tastes and needs as those

[26] Jean Charlier de Gerson, *LInstruction des curez pour instruire le simple peuple* . . . . *Opusculum tripartitum* (Paris?, 1510?); Du Pin, I, 425; Michaud-Quantin, *Sommes de casuistique*, 80–82; Jean Gerson, *Oeuvres complètes*, ed. by Palémon Glorieux, 7 vols. (Paris, Tournai, Rome, and New York, 1960—), I, 83–85, hereafter cited as Glorieux.

who read the *Heavenly Road*.[27] This literature has been invoked only occasionally in this study, primarily to show how other literary forms used ideas about repentance and confession. But one set of works, based on the poem "Poeniteas cito," has been more extensively used. The difficulty in classifying this work betrays the artificiality of sharp divisions between pastoral and devotional literature. Its popularity with publishers, moreover, demonstrates the potential of a didactic poem to disseminate simple instruction to a wide audience.

The poem is about one hundred and ten lines, mostly in unrhymed hexameters. Probably written in the late twelfth or thirteenth century, it expounds, without doctrinal peculiarities, a fundamental teaching about sin, confession, confessors, penitents, contrition, satisfaction, and correction. Many of its lines enunciate doctrinal commonplaces, but two sections in particular are among the most widely cited texts in the literature on confession. In the course of the middle ages, the poem acquired glosses, commentaries, and vernacular translations.[28]

In the fifteenth century no fewer than six different forms of the "Poeniteas cito" were printed. One version reproduces only a text of 113 lines of Latin verse.[29] Another version supplies a marginal

[27] Robertus Caracciolus, *Sermones . . . . De quadragesima: de penitentia . . .* (Lyon, 1513); *GKW*, 6061–6108; *Hortulus anime* (Nuremberg, 1511); *BMC XVth*, 1, 114, 160; 2, 366, 533, 536. Jacobus de Gruytroede, *Speculum aureum anime peccatricis* (U. Gering and G. Maynyal: Paris, 1480); sometimes attributed to Denis the Carthusian; see *BMC XVth*, 1, 282; 2, 326, 364, 534, 608; 3, 644; *GKW*, 5, 721. Stephan Lanzkranna, *Himelstrass, im latin genant Scala celi* (Augsburg, 1510); *BMC XVth*, 2, 351. Joannes Ludovicus Vivaldus, *Aureum opus de veritate contritionis* (Saluzzo, 1503); J. Baudrier, *Bibliographie lyonnaise*, 14 vols. (Lyon, 1895–1912, 1950–1963), vol. 11, 198, 200, and 217, notes five early sixteenth-century editions in Lyon.

[28] The text of the poem alone is printed with the works of Peter of Blois in *PL*, 207, 1153–1156. See also Michaud-Quantin, *Sommes de casuistique*, p. 19 and n. 10; *BMC XVth*, 9, 187; Morton W. Bloomfield, "A Preliminary List of Incipits of Latin Works on the Virtues and Vices, Mainly of the 13th, 14th, and 15th Centuries," *Traditio*, 11 (1955), 259–379; Samuel Harrison Thomson, *The Writings of Robert Grosseteste, Bishop of Lincoln, 1235–1253* (Cambridge, 1940), 257–258; Johann F. von Schulte, *Die Geschichte der Quellen und Literatur des Canonischen Rechts*, II, 528; Louis J. Paetow, ed., *Morale scholarium of John of Garland (Johannes de Garlandia)*, Memoirs of the University of California, vol. 4, no. 2 (Berkeley, Calif., 1927), 83–84.

[29] [Poeniteas cito], *Penitentiarius magistri iohannis de galandia* (Caillaut: Paris, n.d.). See *BMC XVth*, 8, 51 (IA. 39503). This edition is probably Pell. 9585. In addition, Pell. 9583, 9584. Hereafter cited as [Poeniteas cito], *Penitentiarius*.

and interlinear gloss, to clear up possible ambiguities in the poem,[30] while still another enhances its didactic mission by alternating the Latin verses (totaling 111 lines) with a German rendition that runs to 170 lines.[31] The other three versions include prose commentaries, but differ greatly. One selects and rearranges only 34 lines of the poem for explication, and then appends a short general confession.[32] A second presents the longest commentary of all on 118 lines of Latin verse and 196 of its own German rendition.[33] But by far the most important version is the 111-line poem with commentary and interlinear gloss that is usually entitled *Libellus de modo poenitendi et confitendi*. Between 1485 and about 1520, at least fifty-one editions appeared, six in Cologne and a dozen or more in each of Antwerp, Deventer, and Paris.[34] This popular version offered solid, unsophisticated doctrine in twenty pages or less. All six versions remind us that late medieval literature on confession often exhorted but rarely polemicized. Thus for printers and pastors alike, this poem could be a perfectly appropriate place to begin instruction on penance. Its concise, memorable verses, with their various glosses, translations, and commentaries, are an important source for this study.

A Practical Literature

Let us restate the most important characteristics of this literature. First, it was popular. Publication records prove this popu-

---

[30] [Poeniteas cito], *Penitentionarius de confessione* [Grüninger: Strasbourg, c. 1497]. See *BMC XVth*, 1, 112 (IA. 1535). Probably in addition, Goff P-849 (probably the same as Reichling 289); and Pell. 9582.

[31] [Poeniteas cito], *Penitencionarius* [Printer of Capotius: Leipzig, 1490?]. See *BMC XVth*, 3, 636 (IA. 11777). Another edition in the British Museum: [Höltzel: Nuremberg, 1505?]. Perhaps in addition, Hain 13164. Hereafter cited as [Poeniteas cito], *Penitencionarius* (Latin and German).

[32] [Poeniteas cito], *Confessionale pro scholasticis et aliis* [Quentell: Cologne, 1490?]. See *BMC XVth*, 1, 273 (IA. 4773); 9, 81 (IA. 49904). In addition, Campbell 488, 492.

[33] [Poeniteas cito], *Summa penitentie* [Wagner: Nuremberg, 1490?]. See *BMC XVth*, 2, 464 (IA. 7994). I can find no other edition of this version—the longest and in many ways the most interesting of the six.

[34] [Poeniteas cito], *Libellus de modo poenitendi et confitendi* (Hopyl and Higman: Paris, 1495). See *BMC XVth*, 8, 136 (IA. 40134). In addition to the twenty-three editions in the British Museum, twenty-eight more can be established: Hain 11492, *11493, 11496, 11502, 11503; Pell. 9587–9589, 9591; Campbell 1131, 1139, 1140, 1143, 1143a, 1145–1147; Kronenberg 1135a; Goff M-771, M-776, M-777, P-847; BNC 65, 150, 249, 546, 773, 1918.

48

larity both for the fifteenth and sixteenth century. Summas and manuals for confessors appeared everywhere in Europe, in Latin and in vernacular languages, and in multiple editions. St. Antoninus's *Confessionale—Defecerunt*, Andreas de Escobar's *Modus confitendi*, and Guido de Monte Rocherii's *Manipulus curatorum* were among the most frequently published books before 1500. And the problem of how to make a good confession appears in devotional books that enjoyed a similar popularity.[35]

Second, this literature was practical. The summas and manuals for confessors were designed for use. A priest could find out what he wanted to know by consulting them because they were organized especially with that in mind. No better example of this practicality can be imagined than the creation of the alphabetical summa, which makes it possible to get information immediately on a specific topic. But we also find in the literature as a whole a host of devices to expedite the retrieval of information. Elaborate tables of contents, exhaustive indices, numerous cross references, careful identification and separation of specific questions, clear and orderly organization—these are some of the means by which authors and printers created a useful genre. It is worth noting that a table of contents or a long index takes up paper and costs money: we must assume that the gains in usefulness were judged worth it.[36]

[35] Thus Franz Falk, *Die Druckkunst im Dienste der Kirche zunächst in Deutschland bis zum Jahre 1520*. Schriften der Görres-Gesellschaft zur Pflege der Wissenschaft im katholischen Deutschland (Cologne, 1879), 38, argues that the central religious concern of medieval Catholicism is confession and communion in a worthy manner: "Deswegen begegnen wir in jenen zahlreichen Lehr-, Gebet-, und Erbauungsbüchern immer wieder der Belehrung über die Beichte und die Ermannung zu würdigen Empfange der h. Sacramente der Busse und des Altars, so in der Himmelstrasse, Seelentrost, Licht der Seele, u.s.w."

[36] Thus the *Astesana* states this purpose directly: "Incipit tabula totius huius operis seu summe. [C]upiens ego frater astesanus compilator huius summe ad honorem dei vtilitati communi seruire tabulam istam super eandem summam secundum ordinem alphabeti studui componere *vt facilius quod quisque* requisierit in ea valeat inuenire" (italics added). In substantial agreement with my characterization of the literature on forgiveness is the description of the summas in Josef Georg Ziegler, *Die Ehelehre der Pönitentialsummen von 1200–1350. Eine Untersuchung zur Geschichte der Moral- und Pastoraltheologie* in Michael Müller, ed., Studien zur Geschichte der katholischen Moraltheologie, vol. 4 (Regensburg, 1956). Ziegler argues for their practical orientation as mediators between the university and the parish church and as conveyors of simplified teaching: "Alle Autoren gemühten sich eben dem Seelsorger eine möglichst klare und unkomplizierte Applizierung

In addition, authors tried to add to the utility of this literature by employing, whenever possible, verse, mnemonic devices, formulas, and definitions. It is clear once again that the intention is to make information readily accessible—and putting it into easily remembered form is one of the most effective ways to insure easy use. Thus there was much, even in the more sophisticated summas, that a simple priest could commit to memory and draw on.

Third, the literature on forgiveness was cautious, respectful of all authority, and yet varied both in its form and its opinions. Its caution leads often to what we call plagiarism; and one can never be certain that a striking phrase or passage has not been borrowed from some more illustrious source without a credit.[37] Yet on almost every question we shall discover a certain range of opinion that derives, paradoxically, from pastoral authorities' habitual respect for the judgments of all the saints, theologians, and canon lawyers. Since those authorities, as Abelard had proved long before, did not agree with one another, there was inherent in their method and style a tendency toward some diversity. It would heighten interest if we could represent pastoral

der Antworten auf der tägliche Leben zu erleichtern" (pp. 15–16). Ziegler also describes two goals very similar to discipline and consolation: "Ihre Verfasser wollten dem Seelsorger vor allem dazu verhelfen, den rechten Zuspruch wie das richtige Bussurteil für das Beichtkind zu finden. Diese doppelte Zielsetzung entspricht der zweifachen inneren Entstehungsursache der PS[Pönitentialsummen]. Einerseits wurden sie gefordert von dem 12. Jahrhundert beginnenden Individualismus des Hochmittelalters, anderseits waren sie eine notwendige Folge des im 13. Jahrhundert sich durchsetzenden rechtlichen Zentralismus der Kirche," ibid., 4–5. Ziegler thinks historians have overemphasized disciplinary aspects at the expense of pastoral counsel and comfort, which distinguish the summas from the early penitentials. Pastoral comfort, according to Ziegler, becomes even more important in the "ethical" period ushered in by the *Astesana*, when summists turn to theologians rather than canon lawyers, who had dominated the previous "canonical" or "dogmatic" period of the summas for confessors (ibid., 3–18).

[37] The *Summa rudium*, "Prologus," A2a, affirms the opinion of the editors of the *Summa* of Raymond of Peñaforte (above, n. 2 and text) that avoiding originality is the best assurance of trustworthiness. After naming the authorities from whom this work is culled, the author assures simple priests that his summa is aptly named and they can read it without fear or scruple: "Quia relator huius opusculi sum non inuentor. Et de mendica scientia mea nihil opposui sed immo diuersas et varias materias in vnum corpus collegi." Note that he also calls the admired John of Freiburg the "compiler" of the *Summa confessorum* (see above, n. 3).

theology embroiled in raging controversies over the issues raised by the forgiveness of sins. But the truth is that an outspoken criticism, like the one Sylvester directed against the *Angelica*, is rare. And even when authors specifically disagree with one another, they are not trying to create a doctrinaire system but merely looking for a safe solution to a particular problem. Even Sylvester uses the *Angelica*; and he agrees with his Franciscan rival far more than he disagrees. When we assemble a large number of books on sin and confession and related subjects, therefore, we inevitably find a range of opinions. To describe the condition of the institution of forgiveness on the eve of the Reformation faithfully, we have to describe this range of opinions. Thus we shall find neither a uniform set of practices and doctrines nor a theological war. Rather we shall examine a range of ideas, beliefs, habits, rules, and attitudes and try to discern the system within this diversity.

In attempting to respect the range of opinion and still make sense of the institution as a whole, the analysis that follows may appear to resort too often to summas and longer works on confession. A more abstract and learned literature may seem at times to be emphasized to the detriment of the teachings of ordinary manuals, which were perhaps more available and intelligible to simple priests. Nevertheless, I think that extensive use of this literature is justifiable. To begin with, it was a popular literature. In addition, it is illuminating precisely because it intentionally explains more. At the same time, it is practical, conservative, and authoritative. And finally, in the attempt to reconstruct a mentality, the summas and longer works help not only to explain the thinking behind the commonplaces of the manuals; they also show us where speculation occasionally strayed beyond the acceptable limits of consensus. In short, there is admittedly a danger in mistaking the opinions of intellectuals for the understanding of ordinary curates and laymen. But that danger has not been ignored in the interpretation that follows. And the popularity, practicality, conservatism, and authority of this literature make even the most academically inclined authors less liable to the intellectuals' vices of irrelevancy, naïveté, and singularity.

Finally, we must speculate on the role that printing played in the transformation of religious life at the end of the Middle Ages. The availability of printed books must have made a difference: certainly for the clergy, religious and secular—but also for the laity. And the practical, popular literature on the forgiveness of sins was magnificently suited to the functions of discipline and consolation through the forum of penance on the eve of the Reformation.

As we have seen, the institutions of forgiveness in Christian antiquity and the early middle ages relied principally on ascetic public acts to ensure obedience and offer consolation. Of course they demanded contrition and belief in divine mercy. Nevertheless, they were systems of shame and, above all, expiation. Private auricular confession, on the other hand, gradually turned the institutional energies of ecclesiastical penance inward. In the penitentials it still focused on expiatory, albeit private, acts of satisfaction for sin. But by the thirteenth century it had become primarily a private act, protected by the seal of the confessional, emphasizing the inner preparation and disposition of the penitent seeking help from a sacrament dispensed by a priest. It would be foolish to suppose that society itself, or even the church, renounced public shame and the mentality of expiation. The church and the secular community had a rich variety of means in law courts, public punishments, social exclusion and disapproval to exact retribution and keep shame alive.[38] Indeed, there is still an element of shame, whose value authorities proclaim, in telling sins to a priest. But sacramental confession, the principal means of forgiveness of sins, goes another route. The law is applied to the inner forum—the conscience of man—and forgiveness is offered only to those who achieve that inner preparation. From a penance of shame and expiation, the church, through centuries of development, had turned to a penance of guilt and remorse.

And surely the task of reaching the Christian community and teaching it to feel guilt and seek its cure in priestly absolution was well served by the advent of printing. Practical manuals and detailed summas were available in ever-increasing numbers. And if there was not an absolutely uniform understanding about what it all meant in detail, there was perfect agreement that forgiveness of sins had to bring a guilty, sorrowful penitent to a priestly confessor. The books served the institution as it disciplined through guilt and consoled through the hope of forgiveness.

[38] On the persistence of public penance, see H. C. Lea, *History of Auricular Confession*, II, 73–93. Cf. Rosalind Hill, "Public Penance: Some Problems of a Thirteenth-Century Bishop," *History*, n.s. 36 (1951), 213–226.

The most traditional picture of the Reformation emphasizes the immorality or inadequacy of the clergy. But the massive attempt to instruct clergy and laity on the proper way to confess indicates—as any biography of Luther must show—that the church may not have been doing too badly, but rather too well. Indeed, both views are not irreconcilable: if there was a campaign to reach out more effectively, and if the clergy did not seem intellectually or morally fitted to lead that campaign, the tensions would naturally have been enormous.

But clerical abuses are not the subject of this study. We shall now turn to the teachings that were so widely disseminated in the years before the Reformation in the literature on the forgiveness of sins. We shall now examine the common practice and theory of sacramental confession, instrument of discipline and hope of consolation.

Part Two

The Teaching on Sacramental Confession
at the End of the Middle Ages

CHAPTER III

THE PRACTICE OF AURICULAR CONFESSION

The Necessity of Sacramental Confession

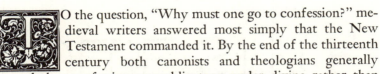O the question, "Why must one go to confession?" medieval writers answered most simply that the New Testament commanded it. By the end of the thirteenth century both canonists and theologians generally agreed that confession was obligatory under divine rather than human law. To prove it, they cited a host of scriptural passages, both plausible and implausible.[1] The most common and potent argument based sacramental confession on the power of the keys, the power to bind and loose from sin, whose principal source in Scripture is Matthew 16:19, in which Christ says to St. Peter: "And I will give thee the keys of the kingdom; and whatever thou shalt bind on earth shall be bound in heaven, and whatever thou shalt loose on earth shall be loosed in heaven." Almost of equal importance is the power Christ grants to His apostles in John 20: 22-23: "Receive the Holy Spirit; whose sins you shall forgive, they are forgiven them; and whose sins you shall retain, they are retained." Other texts were also popular, however. For example, Christ's command to the ten lepers in Luke 17:14—"Go show yourselves to the priests"—was cited as an explicit reference to the obligation to be cleansed by the church. And the admonition of James 5:16—"Confess, therefore, your sins to one another, and pray for one another, that you may be saved"—was proof for some that there is an obligation to admit one's sins to a priest.

[1] For a good review of the traditional texts and the Biblical citations used by Eck, see Heinrich Schauerte, *Die Busslehre des Johannes Eck*, in *Reformationsgeschichtliche Studien und Texte* ed. by J. Greving, vols. 38-39 (Münster, 1919), 144-151. As always in the pastoral literature, the arguments that the authorities use are derived—perhaps without exception—from the "doctors" and "masters." Especially influential are Thomas and Duns. The early church used Matt. 16:19 and 18:18 more than John 20:22-23 to validate the power of forgiveness; see Karl Rahner, *Theological Investigations*, II, 140.

Perhaps the most imaginative departure from the literal text, however, is the interpretation of Christ's words to the disciples after Lazarus appears still bound in cloths and bandages (John 11:44). Farfetched as it may seem to us, the command, "Unbind him and let him go," was occasionally interpreted as a figurative reference to the priestly power of loosing from sins.[2] Thus it was not difficult to find in the New Testament a text prescribing the confession of sins.

But not all arguments were universally and uncritically accepted: medieval exegetes had their own standards and they could apply them. Thus some found it difficult to prove that Christ had Himself instituted sacramental confession to priests, and many were content to see in the New Testament an "implicit" or "tacit" institution by Christ. John of Freiburg, for example, says quite plainly: "Therefore He instituted confession tacitly, but the apostles promulgated it expressly."[3] And Jacobus de Clusa quotes St. Bonaventure: "Thus confession was intimated by the Lord; instituted by the Apostles; and promulgated by James the Bishop of Jerusalem." Astesanus of Asti, in another manifestation of scholarly caution, unequivocally rejects the relevance of "confess, therefore, your sins to one another," with the argument that the text does not specify "to a priest" rather than to a layman. At the same time Astesanus dismisses as also irrelevant the second part of that citation—"and pray for one another"—denying that it has anything to do with forgiveness in the Sacrament of Penance. Nevertheless, Astesanus finds it reasonable to say that the obligation to confess is a positive precept of God, and his argument is typical. If the power of remitting sins granted in John 20:22-23 is arbitrative, he reasons, if it is up

[2] Teetaert, *Confession aux laïques*, 360–365, 452, 460–465. The *Supplementum*, however, argues the necessity of confession under divine law simply by citing theologians and canonists while neglecting the favorite places in Scripture ("Confessio 2," 1).

[3] Teetaert, *Confession aux laïques*, 441–442; Jacobus de Clusa, app. 4 to *Confessionale compendiosum et utilissimum*, D4a; cf. Michel, "Pénitence," *DTC* 12¹, 1025. Theologians, in their summas and commentaries on Peter Lombard, considered all of these issues in greater detail and with more imagination than even the best of the summas for confessors. One example of greater thoroughness is Duns Scotus' consideration of the problem, if confession to priests is necessary, why is it not observed in the Greek Church? (*Quaestiones*, dis. 17, q. 1, 10, *Opera* 18:508–509). The summas for confessors are not interested in this question.

to the priest to decide whether someone's sins are to be retained or forgiven, then the knowledge of sins is necessary. If the priest must know the sins to decide, then confession is necessary. Going beyond this text, Astesanus argues that confession of sins is likewise necessary on other, rational grounds: one is obliged to recover the grace lost by sin, and love of God demands that one do everything in one's power, including confession, to have one's sins forgiven.[4]

The energy spent on these arguments suggests a nagging doubt. Despite the consensus on the divine nature of the obligation to confess that reigned after the thirteenth century, religious authorities could still search for more convincing proof that the obligation was based on more than an ecclesiastical regulation. For in spite of their familiarity with the favorite texts from Matthew and John, they had to face the possibility that confession was, perhaps, not an ancient tradition handed down from the Apostolic Church after all. Important authorities, especially among canon lawyers, had preferred not to affirm that it was such, or that it could be found in the New Testament.[5] Was it, then, an innovation of the thirteenth century, and nothing more? It is as an answer to that particular question that we should understand attempts to find "confession" in the natural law, or prefigured in the Old Testament.[6] Guido de Monte Rocherii, for example, explains a variety of origins for confession that put it safely beyond the objection that it was a recent invention. Interior confession, he says, is a precept of the law of nature in the sense that if a man knows he has offended God ("which he does not see except through some ray of faith"), reason teaches him to acknowledge his guilt before his Creator. Vocal confession to God, he continues, became necessary immediately after the Fall, when man was in a condition requiring a medicine not only for original sin but also for his subsequent actual sins. Guido follows the opinion that God's question to Adam, "Where are you?" is to be understood as urging Adam to confession. Vocal confession to

[4] *Astesana*, V, 10, a. 2, q. 1. The need to know sins in order to retain and forgive was stated by William of Auvergne, who nevertheless objected to a purely judicial understanding of the role of the priest. Michel, "Pénitence," *DTC*, 12¹, 956.

[5] Duns Scotus, *Quaestiones*, dis. 17, q. 1, 10, *Opera*, 18:508–509, argues against the glossators and canonists who cannot find an explicit law making confession obligatory.

[6] Schauerte, *Busslehre*, 141–143.

a man, however, was only instituted under the New Law by the Incarnate Christ. And it was fitting that confession to a man be instituted then and not earlier because of its goals: it was established to make known and delete sins and to effect a reconciliation with God and His Church. But these goals are proper to the New Law, the law of true light in which the Church was founded and in which the Incarnation made possible this act of double reconciliation.[7] What Guido has argued is that confession of sins is rational as well as scriptural, and both arguments can support its necessity.

The attempt to find confession in the law of nature is entirely predictable, given the preoccupations of medieval thought in general and the confessional literature in particular. Rationality, after all, was above, and judged, mere positive law. At the same time, however, everyone was careful to distinguish between the natural and the supernatural form of confession and forgiveness. For natural law, and even Mosaic prefigurations, had a limited value in justifying the actual practice of the late medieval church. The uniqueness of the New Law and its continuity with the present institutions of the church had to be preserved at the same time that the reasonability of confessing was defended. At this point, however, we must call attention to an anomaly characteristic of medieval theological argument.

To establish continuity between the ancient and contemporary church, arguments from history, as well as reason and Scripture, seem to us relevant and essential. Yet, just as the recourse to rational demonstration was predictable, so also is the infrequency of historical proof. The energies of those who wrote on the confessional were directed to showing that it is reasonable in itself to confess, and reasonable to find the obligation to confess to priests in the New Testament. Historical arguments are rare.[8]

Nevertheless, it was universally recognized that there had been important historical changes in the development of confession; everyone understood that *Omnis utriusque sexus* had played a

[7] Guido de Monte Rocherii, *Manipulus curatorum*, II, 3, 1, fol. 72b–73a; cf. I, 1, fol. 3b–4a. The *Eruditorium penitentiale* (A. Caillaut: Paris, 1490?), C1b–C5a, finds the Old Testament calls to repentance a precedent for confession and sees an analogy to confession in the nature of things—the ocean, wine, and parts of the body are examples—which seek to cleanse themselves.

[8] *Astesana*, V, 10, a. 2, q. 1; Cf. Duns Scotus, *Quaestiones*, dis. 16, q. 1, 9, *Opera*, 18:508.

crucial role in the regulation and definition of sacramental penance.[9] Indeed, if the decree of 1215 might raise some doubts about what had been observed in the ancient church, the respect for canon law in this literature leads authors to examine the consequences of that decree. Here the argument for the necessity of confession leaves the realm of positive theology and enters the world of practical administration. We leave exegesis of Scripture and take up exegesis of *Omnis utriusque sexus* and other ecclesiastical legislation. And once again it is important to repeat that medieval authorities were not completely naïve. No one, for example, argued that the obligation to confess once a year, for all practical purposes at Eastertime, could be found anywhere in Scripture. Nor could anyone argue that the directive to confess only to one's own priest was scriptural either. Both clearly derived from *Omnis utriusque sexus*. Yet the decree of 1215 had made both regulations part of positive church law. They were unquestionably binding, and their consequences for the practice of confession, both as a consoler of individual penitents and as a way of controlling their conduct, were immense.

Jurisdiction—defined in answer to the question, "To whom is one obliged to confess?"—is therefore part of the discussion of the necessity of confession. As we have seen, the original intention of *Omnis utriusque sexus* was at least in part, if not primarily, disciplinary. Whenever the literature of the confessional demands the jurisdiction of bishop or parish priest be rigidly adhered to, we recognize this function. For example, Guido de Monte Rocherii explicitly recalls the disciplinary purposes of the law when he explains that the bull requires all adults to confess for three reasons: so that they could express their need before God; so that there would be proper reverence for the Holy Sacrament, which must be received at Eastertime; and so that the pastor could know his sheep and thus not fail to detect heresy.[10]

---

[9] Indeed, as we have just seen, this recognition of the role of *Omnis utriusque sexus* was at the root of the doubts about the divine institution of confession to a priest. Other examples of the authorities cited (especially the decree of 1215) as bases for the obligation to confess: *Eruditorium penitentiale*, B8b–C1a; Lupi Rebello, *Tractatus fructus sacramenti penitentie*, par. 27, 38; *Peycht Spigel*, B7a–B8b; Godescalc Rosemondt, *Confessionale*, 7, 95, fol. 192a–b. None of these citations contains anything original or unusual; but even though they deal in theological clichés, it is always important to know which clichés are circulating.

[10] Guido de Monte Rocherii, *Manipulus curatorum*, II, 3, 2, fol. 73b.

This pastoral control is publicly announced in the "Great Confession of Easter," to be recited in all the churches of the diocese of Lisieux. At the end of this general confession the curate is to tell the congregation that he forbids under pain of excommunication anyone from another parish, no matter what his status, to receive communion "in this church or parish" without producing explicit permission from his pastor or superior. Similarly, he forbids his own parishioners under pain of excommunication to receive communion outside of the parish without permission from him. As might be expected, the curate's jurisdiction in confession is also jealously guarded:

> Likewise I forbid under pain of excommunication any man or woman to receive the Body of Our Lord in this church or parish unless he has confessed to me or to my deputies or to someone else who has good authority to do so.

Reverence for the Sacrament and knowledge of his sheep: the Bishop of Lisieux was making sure that the sacraments of the parish church promoted the obedience as well as the piety of the community.[11]

Other regulations reinforced the authority of the clergy and limited the penitent's choice of a confessor. Some of the rules were highly complex, such as the cases reserved to the bishop, which will be discussed later. The authoritative *Raymundina* and its gloss have lengthy discussions of proper jurisdiction,[12] but the most modern ideas on the subject before the Reformation are summarized in the *Sylvestrina*. The question posed is, "Who, in a broad sense, is the proper priest of laymen?" Sylvester's answer may not describe the reality of how confessors were alloted, but it reveals the church's interest in jurisdiction as a way of maintaining effective discipline: he offers a model that neatly balances the ecclesiastical against the secular hierarchy. The king, he explains, confesses to the bishop of the city that is the seat of his realm. Minor princes present problems if they have more than one episcopal city in their territories, but in general they should confess to the bishop of the principal county or duchy. Officers

---

[11] *Manuale secundum usum lexouiensem* (Rouen, [1523]), fol. 115b.; cf. Dennis E. Rhodes, "A Problem in the Liturgical Bibliography of Normandy," *Gutenberg-Jahrbuch*, 1968, 188–190.

[12] *Raymundina*, 449ff. Cf. *Supplementum*, "Confessio 3," which is also an extremely detailed discussion of jurisdiction.

of the government who do not have a permanent residence must confess to some appropriate bishop or curate according to where they spend most of their time. Townsmen and other laymen who do not have any special offices are under the jurisdiction of the curates in whose jurisdictions they principally live—if they spend an equal amount of time in two jurisdictions, they may take their choice. And by ancient custom the Emperor and the Empress confess to their own chaplains. In addition, there are equally detailed rules for the proper confessors of the regular clergy.[13] Except for the case of the Emperor, who has a personal chaplain, there is an obvious design here: the function of control is served as the great of the church are pitted against the great of the world. How else, in fact, could obedience be maintained and effective sanctions applied? At least that is the ideal.

It would be misleading, however, to represent these rules governing the choice of confessor as rigidly enforced. Undoubtedly the proper lines of authority were most faithfully observed by priests and monks. Thus in the religious orders the frequency of confession as well as the choice of confessor were carefully regulated. Similarly, the *Manual for Parish Priests* is strict on this question when it deals with ordinary priests. In caring for the souls of others, the manual warns, priests must not neglect their own; they should confess at least once a year to the bishop or his penitentiary, or to someone else having the bishop's powers. Ordinary priests, it explains, are not entrusted with the cure of other priests' souls, except in case of necessity. Yet the same manual urges that any parishioner who asks permission to go to another priest should be granted it freely, to avoid any occasion for remaining in sin. In the same spirit, the *Supplementum* advises that a confessor freely grant this permission. The penitent's good motives ought to be believed, "because it is not probable that he is going to penance with deception." Already, on the authority of William of Rennes, priests who demand money for this permission have been called guilty of simony.[14]

---

[13] *Sylvestrina*, "Confessor 1," q. 3, par. 3, I, 153; ibid., q. 2, par. 3, q. 8, par. 8, I, 155. Cf. *Supplementum*, "Confessio 3," 14–17; and Jacques Toussaert, *Le Sentiment religieux en Flandre à la fin du moyen âge* (Paris, 1963), 110–119.

[14] *Manuale parrochialium sacerdotum*, V, A4b, B2b; *Supplementum*, "Confessio 3," 5, "Confessio 1," 15. Cf. *Peycht Spigel*, B8b–C1a; [Poeniteas cito], *Libellus de modo poenitendi*, A6a–b; and [Poeniteas cito], *Confessionale pro*

The most notable, and controversial, exception to the rule that one must confess to one's own parish priest derived, of course, from the various privileges granted to the mendicant orders to hear confessions of laymen who were not officially under their pastoral call. The mendicants exercised and tried to defend and expand these privileges. Their interest in confession thus explains why the summas of confessors were written by Franciscans and Dominicans. Probably it is to his fellow mendicants that Angelus de Clavasio refers when he notes, in an offhand manner, the relaxation of the rules that defined one's "proper" confessor and bolstered parochial discipline: "For today there are many priests whom we may call our own and to whom we may legitimately confess."[15]

---

scholasticis, A6a; the first gives several reasons for confessing to someone other than one's own priest, the other two summarize Hostiensis's ten reasons for this exception (after both note that jurisdiction normally belongs to the pastor). It is usual for summas and manuals to enumerate reasons for one to confess to a priest other than his pastor. See Louis Binz, *Vie religieuse*, 222–231; and Medard Barth, "Beicht und Kommunionen im mittelalterlichen Elsass," *Freiburger Diözesenarchiv*, 74 (1954), 91, and esp. 95ff., whose conclusions for Alsace are probably more typical than the *Manuale parrochialium sacerdotum*'s careful delineation of the area of choice of confessor for priests: "In der Wahl des Beichtvaters hatte der Priester von Stadt und Diözese Strassburg volle Freiheit. Die Bestätigung hierfür liefern die Synodalstatuten, welche die Bischöfe Friedrich von Lichtenberg (1300) und Johann von Dürbheim (1310) erliessen (Barth, "Beicht und Kommunionen," 91).

[15] *Angelica*, "Confessio 3," 15. Barth, "Beicht und Kommunionen," 94–95, describes an enmity so severe between the secular clergy and the mendicants that it led into open armed conflict. For the importance of the role of confessor in the history of the Franciscans, see John Moorman, *A History of the Franciscan Order from Its Origins to the Year 1517* (Oxford, 1968), 94, 121–122, 170, 181–183, 202–203, 363–364. Moorman does not emphasize the importance of Clement V's *Dudum* for defining the privileges of the friars, as Sylvester and others do (see below, n. 18 and text). A famous campaign against the friars, in favor of the sole jurisdiction of parish priests, was conducted in the fourteenth century by Richard FitzRalph, Bishop of Armagh (c. 1300–1360). Six editions of his *Defensorium curatorum contra eos qui privilegiatos se dicunt*—printed in Lyons, Paris, Rouen, and Louvain in the last quarter of the fifteenth century—are in the British Museum. There were at least one edition in the sixteenth and five in the seventeenth century. See Aubrey Gwynn, "The Sermon-Diary of Richard FitzRalph, Archbishop of Armagh," *Proceedings of the Royal Irish Academy*, 44 (1937–1938), 1–57; idem, "Richard FitzRalph, Archbishop of Armagh . . . ," *Studies. An Irish Quarterly Review*, 22 (1933), 389–405, 591–607; 23 (1934), 395–411; 24 (1935), 25–42,

We have seen that confession was thought to be necessary according to the dictates of reason, Scripture, and the church. But the most compelling argument for its necessity was the insistence of the clergy that only by virtue of the Sacrament of Penance could a man's sins be forgiven. In a popular metaphor taken from Jerome, it was called the second plank after the shipwreck by authors from Raymond of Peñaforte and William of Rennes to John Eck and Geiler von Kaisersberg. The clearest explanation of Jerome's metaphor comes from the *Astesana*. Baptism is the first plank, it explains, because metaphorically speaking, like a sailor who saves himself from the perils of the sea by clinging to a plank of the wrecked vessel, so we cling to Baptism after the shipwreck of human nature in the sin of Adam. Penance is the second plank and the only aid by which we can reach the safety of salvation (after, it is clear, the first plank has been lost through actual sin).[16] Why confession was necessary to save a shipwrecked man, how it worked, what its advantages were—all of these were problems with a variety of acceptable solutions in the era before the Reformation. But almost everyone agreed that confession was necessary in some way, and virtually all understood this necessity to be based on the power of the keys, a power entrusted to priests by which they could apply the passion of Christ and the forgiveness He won to the sins of penitent Christians.

This relationship to Christ's sacrifice, moreover, is absolutely essential. A law, an argument, or a metaphor that makes a point

---

558–572; 25 (1936), 81–96; 26 (1937) 50–67; John Trevisa, tr., *Dialogus inter militem et clericum,* [*and*] *Richard FitzRalph's Sermon: "Defensio curatorum"* . . . , ed. by Aaron J. Perry, Early English Text Society, Original Series, 167 (Oxford, 1925); and L. L. Hammerich, *The Beginning of the Strife Between Richard FitzRalph and the Mendicants. With an Edition of His Autobiographical Prayer and His Proposition Unusquisque,* Det. Kgl. Danske Videnskabernes Selskab., Historisk-filologiske Meddelelser, XXVI, 3 (Copenhagen, 1938). Jean Gerson, "Discours sur le fait des mendiants," Glorieux, VII, 978–992, follows FitzRalph (whom he mentions, p. 989) in his defense of the rights and privileges of curates, especially to preach and hear confessions; see esp. pp. 987–991.

[16] Jerome, Epistle 84, *PL,* 22, 748; Schauerte, *Busslehre,* 70 and n.; Johann Geiler von Kaisersberg, *Navicula penitentie* (Augsburg, 1511), fol. 3b, (3 Kal. March); *Astesana,* 5, 2, a. 3; Duns Scotus (*Quaestiones,* dis. 14, q. 4, 6, *Opera,* 18: 157) argues that the Sacrament of Penance must be necessary for forgiveness, for if contrition alone forgave sins, then penance could not be called the second plank after the shipwreck.

about the ecclesiastical institution alone is far from complete. After all, forgiveness was won by Christ, and even the most hardened canonist had to understand that dogmatic truth. Thus the *Angelica* explains that the sacraments mediate the benefits of the passion of Christ and this application in sacramental confession achieves the remission of sins. If someone were to reject confession, therefore, he would show contempt for his own salvation.[17] And the *Sylvestrina* explains quite as dogmatically that the priest's absolution opens up paradise and grants the hope of salvation, which we cannot have without Christ, to Whose passion we submit ourselves in confession by virtue of the power of the keys.[18] Once again, behind the agreement to a metaphor—that the keys place us in contact with the suffering of Christ and make justification possible—there will remain a multiplicity of explanations. We shall see the necessity of confession and absolution defended on the grounds that it is easier, or surer, or safer, or more meritorious, or characteristic of obedience. But we shall always see its necessity defended. Ultimately the power of the keys has to be grounded in the passion of Christ. Yet the reverse is also true—the benefits of Christ become available only through the keys.

This understanding of the sacrament and the keys does not solve all problems, then, but it defines the religious meaning of the institution and illuminates many of the doctrines that regulated it. In the first place it is evident that if the power of the keys is entrusted to priests, then there is little to be gained by confession to a layman. We have already seen that confession to laymen was held acceptable under certain circumstances by theologians before the thirteenth century. Indeed, some argued, and St. Thomas was among them, that in cases where a priest was not available, confession to a layman, if it could be done without harm, was mandatory. But the logic of forgiveness through the keys makes the value of confession to a layman subsidiary at best. What is the point if the real advantages are in the priest's special powers? Of course theologians and religious writers in general who esteemed the practice of confessing sins in itself and for itself, tried to prolong the life of confession to laymen. Nevertheless, none of the writers whose works circulated in the late fif-

---

[17] *Angelica*, "Confessio 2," 1; "Confessio 7"; "Remissio."
[18] *Sylvestrina*, "Confessio 2," q. 7, par. 6.

teenth and early sixteenth century gave a great deal of emphasis to such confession even in case of death in the absence of a priest. Guido de Monte Rocherii says that a dying Christian can and ought to confess to a layman, but he is careful to specify that it is not a sacrament and he also directs the layman to bless but not absolve the dying man.[19]

Andreas de Escobar's *Interrogations* goes furthest in the direction of power to the layman when it says "a layman can absolve a dying penitent when a priest cannot be found—laycus potest absolvere penitentem in articulo mortis: cum non possit haberi sacerdos." He expresses this unusual opinion in a chapter entitled "Tract Concerning Absolutions," and the context makes it clear that he fully intended to call what the layman did in this case absolution, even if it is not certain what he meant by that word.[20] Nevertheless, the authority of one canon lawyer—even a widely read one—should not be overestimated. Furthermore, even Andreas grants the power only in this particular necessity.

It is far more typical to regard confession to a layman as no more than a pious act that can have vague spiritual benefits but is far from an obligation. Thus the opinion of the *Angelica* expresses the common understanding with admirable clarity. The kind of confession that is a work of virtue opposed to hypocrisy can be made to a layman, it explains, but sacramental confession can only be made to priests. In the absence of priests it may be virtuous to incite one's feelings of shame by confession to a layman; but it is in no sense a necessity and it should not be done if it might pervert the layman who listens to the recitation of sins. More important, only in a case of the greatest urgency, that is, the imminence of death, is one excused from the necessity of confession only to his proper priest. In this case the *Angelica* shows what a profound sense had evolved of the sacerdotal power to forgive sins: it is even permissible under those circumstances to confess to a heretical or excommunicated priest (provided there is no danger of contamination with his errors) and receive his

---

[19] Guido de Monte Rocherii, *Manipulus curatorum*, II, 3, 4; the *Raymundina* (III, 34, 15–16, pp. 451–452) also holds it to be obligatory to confess to a layman *in articulo mortis* if there are no priests, but William of Rennes' gloss mitigates this duty by calling it a counsel, not a precept. In the same place Raymond advises against confessing to a heretical or schismatic priest.

[20] Andreas de Escobar, *Interrogationes*, C3a.

absolution, because his power to forgive is part of the indelible character of the priesthood.[21] It should not be surprising to hear a pious author say it is more profitable to confess to a heretical priest than a faithful layman: the *Angelica*'s theology of the keys, as we shall see, makes this conclusion incontrovertible.

From the evidence so far presented, the necessity of confession to a priest in the late medieval church—aside from objections condemned as heretical—seems to have been unassailable. In its most general sense—confession as the inner admission by fallen man of guilt before his omnipotent and good Creator—it seemed to some a part of the natural law, something natural reason could perceive. More specifically, the obligation to confess to a priest of the New Law was found in the New Testament, in some way an institution of Christ Himself, one of His sacraments, that almost everyone thought had been practiced in the Apostolic Church. No one doubted, moreover, that this sacrament was made obligatory once a year for every adult Christian by the ecclesiastical decree of 1215, which also specified to which priest the faithful were bound to confess. Finally, it was necessary for the work of justification. Only the power of the priest could apply the merits of Christ and the forgiveness won by His suffering to the individual sinner. And for that reason the Sacrament of Penance was aptly called the second plank after the shipwreck: for its necessity is inseparable from a sense of danger and urgency. Heretics—Albigensians, Waldensians, John Wyclif, or even Peter of Osma—might free themselves from this sense of urgency and reject this necessity. But could an obedient Catholic even have reservations?

In fact, at least one hesitation remains for our consideration. The men who wrote on confession were familiar with an institution as well as the Bible and the canon law, and their thinking inevitably was influenced by their practical experience. As we shall see, the work of confession was not easy, and these authorities knew it. When Godescalc Rosemondt said that in his opinion it was the most onerous and difficult of the precepts of God and

---

[21] *Angelica*, "Confessio 3," 1–2. Cf. Teetaert, *La Confession aux laïques*, 563–566. Godescalc Rosemondt (*Confessionale*, 7, 74, fol. 128a–b) thinks that even an ignorant priest who has the power validly absolves. See also Rudolf Stanka, *Die Summa des Berthold*, 34; Bartholomaeus de Chaimis, *Interrogatorium*, I, A2a–b; Johannes Nider, *Expositio preceptorum decalogi* (Paris, 1482), 9N, Pla.

the church,[22] he was not flirting with heresy but merely repeating a common observation. Confession to a priest was not only a necessity but a burdensome one, and that burden could constitute an objection to its divine origin.

Ironically, Duns Scotus used the widely recognized difficulty of confession to argue that it was divinely instituted, and both the *Angelica* and the *Sylvestrina* followed him on it. Angelus begins his proof of the divine institution by giving the usual reference to Chapter 20 of the Gospel of St. John; but he goes on to say that there is an even more convincing argument that confession was not a human invention:

> But the truer argument by which it can be proven that [confession] is of divine law is that it is not to be believed that the Church and the Apostles would have imposed that most dangerous yoke on men unless Christ had given that precept explicitly [verbaliter] to the Apostles.

Those who read the *Sylvestrina* in preference to the *Angelica* would have found the argument in virtually the same words: ". . . neither the Apostles nor the Church would have introduced so great and so very dangerous a yoke on the people unless they had received it verbally from Christ."[23] The naïveté of this argument is touching. Caught in the dilemma of accepting the necessity of confession, and at the same time recognizing that while His yoke was supposed to be easy this yoke was definitely not, they tried to find in the contradiction itself a proof of the divine institution of confession. But this argument for the neces-

---

[22] Rosemondt, *Confessionale*, 1, 1–2, fol. 2a–b.

[23] *Angelica*, "Confessio 2," 1; *Sylvestrina*, "Confessio 2," q. 4, par. 4. Cf. H. C. Lea, *History of Auricular Confession*, I, 169—who cites, besides the *Angelica*, John Duns Scotus, Gabriel Biel, and Domingo de Soto in their commentaries in *In quartum librum sententiarum*, dis. 17, q. 1. See Scotus, dis. 17, q. 1, 10, *Opera* 18: 508: "Sic tertium membrum teneatur scilicet quod confessio non cadit nisi sub praecepto Ecclesiae, non potest faciliter improbari, nisi quia vel Ecclesia non attentasset tam arduum praeceptum imponere omnibus Christianis, nisi esset praeceptum divinum, vel quia non invenitur ubi ab Ecclesia imponatur istud praeceptum, quin ante hoc Sancti: reputarent hoc praeceptum de confessione obligare." Johannes Romming, *Penitentiarius*, ch. 14. B1b, echoes this sentiment in his manual: "Certe nec ecclesia nec apostoli hoc iugum hominibus imposuissent nisi Christus verbaliter apostolos iussisset." And Olivier Maillard says that his first motive in writing his manual was that Duns Scotus had called it the most difficult commandment of the New Law (*La Confession*, A2b–A3a).

sity of confession will work only if one already accepts the practice of confession as ancient, even apostolic, and has confidence in the unbroken continuity of divine guidance in the traditional visible church. A generation of reformers was about to appear who agreed that confession was a burden but did not believe in its antiquity or trust in the charity and infallibility of the hierarchy that imposed it.

The Frequency of Confession

Every Christian who had reached the age of discretion[1] was required by the legislation of 1215 to confess at least once a year. Most Christians probably managed to confess no more than that, at Eastertime. Alain de Lille complained in the twelfth century that clergy as well as laity barely confessed once a year, and even that, he lamented, was more out of habit than sorrow for sin. It is unlikely that the frequency of confession dramatically changed after 1215. Some modern historians contend that no more than yearly confession remained the rule through the fifteenth cen-

---

[1] A variety of opinions existed on the age to begin confession, communion, and religious education in general. Some of the criteria were capability of discerning right from wrong; understanding of the mystery of the Eucharist; or, most simply, capacity to commit sin. Estimates varied from seven to fourteen years of age, with a general agreement that the age could vary from person to person. Such individual differences might be discovered by questions put to children by their elders. There was also a common belief that the age differed for boys and girls. The [Poeniteas cito], *Confessionale pro scholasticis*, B1a, explains that the Gloss's criterion, ability to discern between right and wrong, is met when the person is closer to future puberty than to past infancy: it suggests ten or more years for boys and adds that sins of lust can be committed at fourteen years. Robertus Caracciolus, *Sermones . . . De quadragesima: de penitentia*, 28, ch. 1, q. 3, cites the same authorities; notes that some put the age at seven; and concludes with passages objecting to the assumption underlying the use of age of puberty that only sins of lust are important, while, at the same time, lamenting that children are now guilty of lust before actual puberty. The *Supplementum*, "Confessio 2," 3, specifies seven years as the age when a boy or girl is "doli capax" and hence obliged to confess. Cf. Rosemondt, *Confessionale*, 7, 93, fol. 151b–152a; Andreas de Escobar, *Interrogationes*, B4b–C1a; Fantinus Dandolo, *Compendium pro catholicae fidei instructione* (Antwerp, M. van der Goes: 1490?), "De Penitentia." The best summaries of the variety in practice are in Toussaert, *Le Sentiment religieux*, 107–109; H. C. Lea, *History of Auricular Confession*, I, 400–404; Gabriel Le Bras, *Les Institutions ecclésiastiques*, in Fliche and Martin, eds., *Histoire de l'église*, vol. 12[1] (Paris, 1964), 126–127.

tury,[2] and to explain this infrequency they find fundamentally practical motives keeping the faithful away from confession. The most obvious discouragement was plain expense, which came primarily from what Germans called the *Beichtgeld*, the "alms" customarily given to the confessor. By definition a voluntary gift, it was nevertheless a hardened prerogative of the clergy and considered a normal part of a parish priest's revenue. That such a mentality would lead to other corrupt practices was inevitable. Apparently one of the most difficult to root out was the habit of confessors to impose penances consisting in the purchase of masses, with the stipulation that the masses be purchased from the confessor himself. Over twenty synods forbade this practice between 1195 and 1446.[3] Probably even more important than

[2] Peter Browe, "Die Pflichtbeichte," 342–343, 346–347; Louis Binz, *Vie religieuse*, 403. Cf. Toussaert, *Le Sentiment religieux*, 112–113, 117; his summary (p. 121) is taken from a moralist's perspective: "Des indices différents convergent vers une conclusion assez reticente. Raréfaction probable de la confession chez les plus dévotes personnes, alignment du nombre des confessions sur celui des communions pour les braves gens, désaffection du sacrement de Pénitence en general, restriction de la fréquentation de ce sacrement, relégué, chez les masses, aux derniers moments de la vie ou pour de très grandes circonstances. La confession, généralement, compte beaucoup de fidèles et connait des abstentionnistes plus ou moins passagers, assez nombreux cependant: ainsi en témoignent une liste d'excommuniés, une multiplication d'avertissements sévères et la précision de sanctions dans les statuts diocésains, quelques autres indices épars enfin." For the kind of sanctions employed to enforce the law of yearly frequency, ibid., 109–110. See also H. C. Lea, *History of Auricular Confession*, I, 187–217. For precisely the opposite estimate of the importance of confession, see E. Delaruell, E.-R. Labande, and Paul Ourliac, *L'Eglise au temps du grand schisme*, 14[2]:656. "La fin du Moyen Age a été une époque favorable au sacrement de la confession; il y eut même une sorte d'inflation dans certains milieux dévots, puisqu'on voit des religieux se confesser tous les jours. Cette tendance est évidemment liée à l'obsession du péché, à la crainte du Jugement, avec la hantise de l'attaindre inopinément. A ces sentiments se rattache le développement des indulgences: ce fut un des bons effets de leur multiplication que de pousser à des confessions plus fréquentes, afin de les obtenir." Not all moralists would have agreed that the multiplication of confessions was in fact a healthy thing: see, for example, Peter Browe, *Die häufige Kommunion im Mittelalter* (Münster, 1938), 108. Medard Barth ("Beicht und Kommunionen," 96–99) offers more concrete evidence of the importance of confession even in the earlier period (1282–1371). Barth has found many examples of legacies, some of them substantial, left to confessors; and he argues that this was common throughout Germany.

[3] Browe, "Die Pflichtbeichte," 351–362; H. C. Lea, *History of Auricular Confession*, I, 404–411; Toussaert, *Le Sentiment religieux*, 112–113.

financial abuses, however, was the parish clergy's inadequacy in numbers, talent, morality, and power to absolve. The last of these, insufficient jurisdiction, was caused chiefly by the plethora of sins reserved to the bishop, and more will be said of them later. The other defects in the parish clergy, of course, are the chief material of many histories of the Reformation, and they must always be given their place in any explanation of the events of the sixteenth century religious revolution.[4]

Nevertheless, the later middle ages witnessed a sharp attack on the neglect of the Sacrament of Penance. The call to frequent confession by synodal statutes in the fifteenth century[5] was echoed time and time again by those who wrote and preached on the forgiveness of sins. These men thought the motives for delaying confession were purely moral, the errors and vices of sinners.

The analysis of tardy repentance derived from the *Raymundina* is typical of this thinking. Four motives hinder immediate confession: shame at telling one's sins; fear of being unable to fulfill the works of satisfaction imposed; too great a hope of pardon, of finding a time in the future to repent and be forgiven; and finally, desperation at obtaining mercy from God.[6] Olivier Maillard incorporated these motives into his metaphor of overcoming ten barriers to enter the gate of penance and regain the city of grace; the other barriers, which include love of sin, fear of restitution, and shame at doing good, similarly emphasize the willfulness and hence culpability of sinners.[7] As we shall see later, moralists blamed most consistently the hope of a long life, which the *Golden Mirror of Sinners* of Jacobus de Gruytroede traces in typical fashion to the devil, who tempts men by saying "you are young—you will live, do penance, and go to confession."[8] An interesting insight into the attitudes of late medieval preachers of repentance is found also in the treatise of Antoine Faren, who includes among his barriers to confession "incredulity": many, he warns, delay because they do not believe in the immortality of

---

[4] Browe, "Die Pflichtbeichte," 362–368; Toussaert, *Le Sentiment religieux*, 117–122.

[5] Browe, "Die Pflichtbeichte," 346–347.

[6] *Raymundina*, III, 34, 67ff., 498ff.; Antonius de Butrio, *Directorium ad confitendum*, 6; *Supplementum*, "Penitentia 4." Strangely enough, this moralistic emphasis and analysis is essentially what Toussaert offers in *Le Sentiment religieux*, especially 119–122.

[7] Maillard, *La Confession*, A2a.

[8] Jacobus de Gruytroede, *Speculum aureum*, B5b–6a.

the soul, the resurrection of the body, the punishment of sinners, and the reward of virtuous men. "And that barrier," he notes with disarming confidence, "is easily broken by considering what men have lived according to the Christian law."[9]

These themes were so common in late medieval preaching that they may seem too trite to be significant. But their basic assumption deserves explicit notice: to remain impenitent is a failure of reason and piety, for which man is held responsible. Such an attitude gave ample opportunity for expanding on the necessity to confess frequently. Man can and should repent and confess without delay. If he does not, he is morally culpable. Some authorities, as Guido de Monte Rocherii noted, used this moral truism to explain the intention of *Omnis utriusque sexus*. They argued that the decree of 1215 did not mean sinners should be encouraged to delay confession until Lent. On the contrary, it was directed against, not in behalf of, negligent Christians to ensure that they would not delay any longer than Lent.[10] The ideal, which was increasingly demanded from the time of Guido to the end of the middle ages, called for speedy and frequent recourse to the Sacrament of Penance. The question is, How far beyond the minimum requirements of yearly confession could medieval pastoral theology go?

In the course of the middle ages four new occasions were introduced, in addition to the Lenten requirement, when confession of serious sins was said to be necessary. Two were universally accepted: Christians in the state of sin must confess immediately when they are in danger of dying, either through sickness or because they are about to be placed in some other notable peril; and they must confess before receiving the Eucharist, or, according to some, before receiving any other sacrament except Baptism, or before performing any solemn religious act, such as saying the mass. Two others were almost as universally recognized: if a sinner has someone available who can absolve him of his sins and for some reason it is doubtful that within the year he will have a similar opportunity, he must not delay; and if the sinner's conscience dictates to him that he confess immediately, he must obey it.[11]

[9] Antoine Faren, *La Pratique de soy bien confesser*, A7a-A8a.

[10] Guido de Monte Rocherii, *Manipulus curatorum*, II, 3, 3, fol. 74b–75b.

[11] Guido de Monte Rocherii, *Manipulus curatorum*, II, 3, 3, fol. 85a–b; *Angelica*, "Confessio sacramentalis," 31 (Angelus adds special vows to more

These four occasions of immediate confession not only illustrate the late medieval call to more frequent repentance; they also underscore the function of this essential ritual. The first two circumstances are easiest to understand. To participate in a sacrament and to die were the most serious and "dangerous" acts of a Christian. They required sinlessness, guiltlessness, a clear conscience. No one could have thought it safe to approach the altar for communion, consecrate the Eucharist, or die, in the state of sin. Once again, the underlying assumption is that confession is necessary for justification. The other two circumstances are also significant. The requirement to confess without delay if one doubts that a priest with adequate powers will be available within the year is an affirmation of the Easter duty. This obligation was taken so seriously that pastoral theologians were willing to be more stringent than the letter of the text and require penitents to plan ahead. Finally, the special attention paid to the dictates of conscience reemphasizes the personal, psychological meaning of the teaching on confession. To affirm the Easter duty was to affirm ecclesiastical authority and the functions of discipline and control. To affirm the conscience was to recognize that, as always, its promptings constitute moral obligation and also that, as always, the forgiveness of sins is unintelligible apart from the consolation of the sinner and penitent. One must follow his conscience; by obeying it and seeking forgiveness in confession, the urgings and doubts will be removed.

Beyond these four cases it was common for medieval writers and preachers to sing the praises of frequent confession for a variety of reasons. Godescalc Rosemondt admits that there are only a few circumstances that bind one to confess without delay. But he adds that such an instance arises when there is a danger that one will forget one's sins if one goes only once a year. Thus,

---

frequent confession, as among some religious orders); *Sylvestrina*, "Confessio 1," q. 2, par. 3; Gerson, *Opus tripartitum*, I, 17, and II, Du Pin, I, 440c; idem, *De Differentia*, Du Pin, II, 499a–b; [Gerson?], *La Confession de maistre iehan iarson* (Paris, c. 1491), A3b–A4a; Nider, *Expositio decalogi*, III, 9R, P2a–b (Nider also adds one for special vows); Stephen Lanzkranna, *Himelstrass*, c. 8, fol. 24a; [Poeniteas cito], *Libellus de modo poenitendi*, A5a; *Supplementum*, "Confessio 2," 7. To these references many more could be added. For a careful discussion of the dogmatic history of confession before communion, see L. Braeckmans, *Confession et communion au moyen âge et au Concile de Trente* (Gembloux, 1971).

on the basis of the obligation to make a good confession, he advises reception of penance four to seven times a year, or else at the major feasts.[12] Jacobus de Clusa uses a similar argument. He inveighs against infrequent confession and holds neglectful sinners culpable for much of what they forget about their sins. He attributes this forgetfulness to tardy and infrequent recourse to confession: the same people, he complains, are certainly less negligent and forgetful in their temporal affairs. The fundamental principle for a moralist like Jacobus de Clusa, then, was simple: the more frequent the confession, the purer it is. The danger that excessive reliance on sacramental penance will lead to scrupulosity is not apparent here. For Jacobus, frequent confession not only helps the sinner remember his sins; he is consoled by it and his conscience is made serene.[13] But Jacobus' real point is that frequent confession helps a man remember his sins, and with this the weightiest of all pastoral authorities was in agreement: frequent confession, Gerson declares in his *Opus tripartitum*, "is highly profitable for the increase of grace and the more distinct recognition and explanation of sins."[14] The idea was a commonplace.

The best authors who wrote about confession, however, went beyond the stock arguments and well-worn citations and drew on their practical experience as confessors. And experience taught the best of them that there was such a thing as too frequent confession. Wessel Gansfort sounds deeply rebellious when he urges that confession to a priest should be omitted if it does not enlighten a man and lead him to a better life—if it hinders praise, love of the law, and interior peace of heart.[15] But there is no more than a difference in tone, if that, between the Master of Contradictions and the Most Christian Doctor when the latter says that if habit is making confession (or the Sacrament of the Altar) of small devotional use, one should abstain from it. With characteristic balance, it is true, Gerson adds: "But if someone

[12] Rosemondt, *Confessionale*, 7, 96, fol. 142b–144a.

[13] Jacobus de Clusa, *Confessionale*, cap. 1, A2a; cap. 8, A4b–B1a. The *Rosella* also argues for frequency on grounds that will be discussed later under the motive of sorrow: namely, that confession should be frequent because it is the surest and safest way to the forgiveness of sins.

[14] Gerson, *Opus tripartitum*, I, 17, II, Du Pin, I, 440c, 445c. Cf. *Peycht Spigel*, C3b.

[15] Joannes Wessel Gansfort, *Farrago rerum theologicarum uberrima* (Basel, 1522), 48a.

feels himself profiting from it more and more and finding greater peace of conscience, he may confess every day and take communion every day."[16] But the danger to which Gerson addresses himself here—the danger to which he and all the great authorities on the practice of confession were attentive—was that of the scrupulous conscience, which magnifies or invents faults to its own torment.

The problem of scrupulosity is ever present, and it could complicate a great variety of questions. The *Sylvestrina* recognizes this danger, for example, when it decides whether a sinner must, if he is to be forgiven, confess immediately after becoming contrite. The answer is No, and the reasoning is revealing. Only the usual four cases require immediate confession, Sylvester explains; otherwise the simple intention to confess is adequate. And this rule is to be adhered to firmly, he continues, even though it is dangerous to defer confession for any reasons. Because while it is "safer" never to delay, it is definitely not "safer" to hold the opinion that a contrite man may never delay. For to teach that the contrite man must always confess immediately would give "fearful men" innumerable occasions of sinning. By that he means that it would impose an impossible burden, since their consciences would repeatedly demand, on pain of sin, that they confess without delay. As Sylvester puts it, the scrupulous man might remember a sin at dinner or in the street and feel obliged to seek a priest; and to satisfy such a harsh requirement he would have to have a supply of confessors constantly on hand to quiet his conscience.[17]

For the most part, as we shall see later, scrupulosity was treated gently. But at times an author could deal with it for what it was supposed to be—a serious spiritual vice—and take a harder line. When St. Antoninus of Florence talks about the order in which a priest should hear penitents, he advises the confessor to receive first and most willingly those who seem to need

[16] Gerson, *De Differentia*, Du Pin, II, 490d–500a.
[17] *Sylvestrina*, "Confessio," q. 2, par. 3, I, 141–142; Sylvester's counsel was probably pertinent, for real problems could be raised by the contrary advice, which urged immediate confession. One example of this contrary advice is in the *Confessio generalis breuis et vtilis tam confessori quam confitenti* (J. Solidi: Vienne, n.d.), 1b: Lacrimabilis quo ad dolorem de peccato commisso/ Accelerata vt scilicet de die in diem non differat sed/ Statim quam citius potest confiteatur.

or want to confess most; or those who rarely come; or strangers, or men of higher rank; or those whose confession seems likely to confer the greatest utility. "And to those who want to confess too often, assign a certain time outside of which you will not hear them; do not make yourself available to them for other conversations; and always use not soft but harsh and severe words with them."[18] On the whole, however, it was generally acknowledged that the repeated and scrupulous confession had to be treated with delicacy. Authorities on the spiritual life thought of it more as a sickness than a vice, and the greatest practitioner of its cure was Jean Gerson. His counsels in *De Remediis* deserve to be recalled here, therefore, to strike a balance with the unusually, and uncharacteristically, harsh words of St. Antoninus, and to emphasize that this problem was normally conceived of not as a matter for discipline but for consolation.

Gerson begins by speaking of those who keep repeating their prayers or starting them over if their minds have inadvertently wandered. "To them," he continues, "we must add those who are not content when they have been 'properly' but not 'sufficiently' contrite and confessed (indeed as far as we can see it is impossible for them to be sufficiently contrite for their sins). They always have a scruple that they have not yet properly confessed. They exhaust themselves and their confessors with repeated confessions, especially of light and unimportant sins. . . . To all of these alike should be given the counsel to trust not in their own justice but in the pure mercy of God; and as they overestimate their own negligence, so let them also exaggerate the infinite mercy of God." Gerson no more intends to excuse bad confessions than to encourage inattentive prayer. His advice, he urges, is for the weak and not the strong. The rule he then invokes as a remedy for scrupulosity recalls a fundamental principle of pastoral theology: in the work of the cure of souls the confessor must deal with men who are not angels and who are very different from one another. As the Consoling Doctor puts it: "Let them remember that common saying, that 'God does not want to demand anything beyond man's power.' "[19] This principle ideally underlies every counsel and precept laid down by the men who

---

[18] Antoninus of Florence, *Confessionale—Defecerunt*, 8; cf. ibid., 6, for gentler advice.

[19] Gerson, *De Remediis*, Du Pin, III, 585c–586b.

tried to find, in the theory and practice of confession, a meeting between man's effort and God's mercy, between the correction of the sinner and the consolation of the penitent.

In conclusion, church law set the minimum frequency for confession at once a year. Four exceptions emerged representing additional requirements. But these cases remained exceptional by their definitions, and tell us more about attitudes to forgiveness than habits of confessing. Moralists saw, on the other hand, two abuses in the practice of the faithful. First, people confessed too little—and in this conclusion there is evidence to suppose that this complaint was justified and that the narrowest compliance to the yearly requirement was the rule for a large portion of Christians in the late middle ages. Second, people confessed too often. For this contradictory conclusion there is the abundant evidence of the confessors who themselves complained about it. It is essential to remember, however, that for all Christians, the tepid as well as the fervent, the confessional symbolized discipline and reconciliation. It was the place of forgiveness, not just for scrupulous monks who ran to it continually, but also for worldly laymen who stayed away.[20] The call to frequent confes-

[20] Toussaert draws the opposite conclusion (except for the importance of penance to the dying [*Le Sentiment religieux*, 113–117]), and thus his rather dramatic and confident conclusion (p. 122): "Il faut rebattre sur une conclusion partielle, quoique non négligeable: le confessional n'existe pas en tant que moyen de sanctification et de rédemption utilisé fréquemment; il n'existe absolument pas comme moyen de formation individuelle des consciences. C'est à partir de ces considérations qu'on comprend . . . pourquoi la tour est penchée." Some simple observations should save us from accepting so negative a judgment on the importance of the Sacrament of Penance. If it was not profoundly significant in the religious life of the late middle ages, why the immense popularity of the literature? why the universality of the call to frequent and early repentance in the Sacrament? why the apparently sincere concern for scrupulous people who repeatedly seek confessors? and, above all, why the hatred of the reformers of the sixteenth century? For additional evidence on the importance of confession at the end of the middle ages, see E. Jane Dempsey Douglass, *Justification in Late Medieval Preaching. A Study of John Geiler of Keisersberg*, in Studies in Medieval and Reformation Thought, ed. by Heiko A. Oberman, Vol. I (Leiden, 1966), 154–155 and n.; and the article by Barth cited above, n. 2. It may not be impossible, however, to resolve these contradictory judgments on the frequency and importance of confession. Those who emphasize the infrequency of confession, and the tepidity of repentance that infrequency implies, think that the institution is ineffective if Christians confess only once or at best a few times a year. But to demand much more than that would require a degree

sion at the end of the middle ages was loud and insistent. Furthermore, the importance of the minimum requirement should not be ignored: Christians had to make it to confession at least once a year. And then there was always that most urgent necessity: making it at the end.

A final observation should reveal the complexity of this problem and cast doubt on easy solutions. If we make a statistic—the relative frequency of confession—the sole measure of the power of sacramental confession to discipline and console, we impose criteria that are too modern. We cannot deny, of course, that when pastoral authorities complained that sinners neglected penance, they meant that people did not confess often enough. Yet when we ask what should have satisfied these moralists, we cannot supply a statistical answer. They did not campaign for a monastic regime of weekly confession for the laity. They asked only that Christians confess when it was appropriate and necessary. Even religious authorities who worried more about infrequency than excessive repetition did not propose ambitious schedules for frequenting the sacraments. If we accept that fact, we can reorient the investigation of the importance of confession and reevaluate it in the light of other evidence.

Frequency of communion supplies an obvious if imperfect analogy. The long-standing prejudice against frequent communion persisted in the late middle ages: the Eucharist was seldom received for a number of reasons.[21] The anomalous custom of distributing "blessed bread" rather than the consecrated Host tells much about this dominant medieval attitude.[22] There is an interesting parallel to this custom in the development of a non-sacramental general confession, which was publicly recited in

---

of social control the medieval church was unlikely to achieve for the whole population. Those who emphasize confession in medieval religious life, on the other hand, look at its ever-increasing importance among the clergy, secular and religious, and among certain groups of laymen. This emphasis is realistic as a measure of the importance of confession in spite of the objections one might raise against its elitist implications. Finally, as is argued below, frequency is not the only criterion in evaluating sacramental discipline.

[21] Peter Browe, *Die häufige Kommunion*, 133–163.

[22] Browe, *Die häufige Kommunion*, 23; Josef A. Jungmann, *The Mass of the Roman Rite: Its Origins and Development (Missarum Solemnia)*, tr. by F. A. Brunner, 2 vols. (New York, 1951–1955), II, 452–455; A. Molien, "Pain bénit," *DTC*, 11², 1731–1733.

Germany as an adjunct to the sermon.[23] In both cases a ritual appears as a substitute for a sacrament—a ritual that is clearly not a sacrament, yet is strongly reminiscent of the sacrament. To be sure, the fear of sacrilege and the consequent stress on scrupulous preparation is more serious for the Eucharist than for penance. Nevertheless, whatever particular explanations are relevant, medieval spiritual authorities did not think the force of the Real Presence in the Christian community depended on the frequency of its reception.[24] And we might even suggest that receiving absolution was related to individual contrition, as receiving the Eucharist was to spiritual communion or simple adoration.

Thus confession, which was undoubtedly more frequent than communion, was not conceived of as a repetitive individual routine except among monks or unusually pious laymen.[25] Rather, it was normally tied to seasons and crises: to dangerous journeys, marriage and childbirth, serious illness, the possible absence of a priest-confessor, and to the feasts of All Saints, Christmas, Pentecost, and, above all, to Lent and Easter. In the early middle ages, confession before Ash Wednesday prepared the faithful for Lent. *Omnis utriusque sexus*, by effectively demanding confession during Lent, reaffirmed its place in the rich liturgical context of that penitential season.[26] In some places in Germany this seasonal quality was heightened by the requirement of the *confessio bina*—the double confession—both of which were to be made before Easter.[27] Had those who imposed

---

[23] Jungmann, *The Mass*, I, 492–494; Michaud-Quantin, *Sommes de casuistique*, 71–72, 82 n. 12; Peter Browe, "Die Kommunionvorbereitung im Mittelalter," *ZkTh*, 56 (1932), 395.

[24] Browe, *Die häufige Kommunion*, 162.

[25] Browe, *Die häufige Kommunion*, 23, 41, 42, 55, 59–88, 92–97, 108, 118–121, 148, 149, 192, and passim; idem, "Die Kommunionvorbereitung," 397–407, which concludes: "Während man in einigen Orden nur dann beichtete, wenn man kommunizierte, war in den meisten anderen die Anzahl der vorgeschriebenen Beichten viel grösser als der Kommunionen. Die Beichte war das eigentliche Sakrament des Mittelalters, durch das sich fromme Mönche und Nonnen zu bessern und zu vervollkommnen suchten; die Kommunion trat in Vergleich dazu weit zurück."

[26] Browe, "Die Kommunionvorbereitung," 388–393.

[27] Browe, "Die Kommunionvorbereitung," 395–397; Johann B. Götz, *Das Pfarrbuch des Stephan May in Hilpolstein vom Jahre 1511. Ein Beitrag zum Verständnis der kirchlichen Verhältnisse Deutschlands am Vorabend der Reformation*, Reformationsgeschichtliche Studien und Texte, ed. by Joseph Greving, vols. 47–48 (Münster, 1926), pp. 88 and n. 42, and 160; Gebhard

this requirement wished, they could have relied on the disciplinary benefits of diocesan regulations making confession and communion obligatory in other seasons. Their decision to emphasize
the Lenten confession in this fashion makes sense, however, if we
recognize that sacramental confession derives strength from its
place in the calendar, not just its relative frequency. With or
without a double confession, the intense pastoral activity associated with sacramental confession at this time of year makes it
not unreasonable to think of it as a seasonal "celebration." Sermons exhort sinners to repentance. Pastors must inform their
flocks of the yearly obligation, teach them how to discharge it,
and try to see that they do. Most obvious of all, those charged
with confession are consigned to sit long hours in the churches,
and in some cases are even given detailed itineraries for visiting
the various places in their jurisdiction.[28] If there was a time to
venerate your patron saint, pray for your dead relatives, get your
throat blessed, invoke a variety of protectors, or celebrate the
wonderful events in the lives of Christ and Mary, so there was
also a time, most clearly and emphatically defined, to confess
your sins.

This seasonal liturgical characteristic—the public side of private confession—existed alongside a more modern reliance on a
repeated individual observance. If you believe it is easy to commit a sin, and not only necessary but also easier to be forgiven by
a priest, then you will inevitably make confession repetitive. Religious observance will then be measured by the statistical standard of frequency, a tendency that is undoubtedly discernible in
the late middle ages. Nevertheless, the church as a whole had not
yet arrived at that simple solution before the Reformation,
when confession still bore the stamp of Lenten rituals. We must
therefore affirm the importance of sacramental confession in the
face of what looks like a bad attendance record. For the institu-

---

Mehring, ed., *Stift Lorch. Quellen zur Geschichte einer Pfarrkirche*, Württembergische Gesichtsquellen, vol. 12 (Stuttgart, 1911), 147, 163.

[28] Mehring, ed., *Stift Lorch*, 133–134, 147, 163; Götz, *Das Pfarrbuch des
Stephan May*, 87–91, 160; Adolph Tibus, *Die Jakobipfarre in Münster von
1508–1523. Ein Beitrag zur Sittengeschichte Münsters* (Münster, 1885), 23–25,
94–97 (cf. 72–74, 114–115); Franz Falk, ed., *Die pfarramtlichen Aufzeich-
nungen (Liber consuetudinum) des Florentius Diel zu St. Christoph in
Mainz (1491–1518)*, in Erläuterungen und Ergänzungen zu Janssens Geschichte des deutschen Volkes, ed. by Ludwig Pastor, vol. 4, no. 3 (Freiburg
im Breisgau, 1904), 13–29, 41–45:

tions of forgiveness provided an effective system in which deviance was defined, correction proposed, and reconciliation offered. This system of ideas and behavior dominated, whether the faithful confessed often or only one time during the season devoted to the penitential mentality.

The Conduct of Confession

There was an etiquette for confession because it was a difficult business. The formalities were simple and designed to remove any initial hesitation and embarrassment. There were apparently slight variations according to the customs of different lands and ages, but on the whole there was uniformity. The general intention of giving the priest a form to follow and getting him to instruct the laity to use it is striking in every case.

Priests were directed to hear confessions in an open or public place in the sight of all (presumably in the church, even though it is not always explicitly stated). Prelates were especially likely to stress this requirement, and many explained that it was to avoid all occasion or suspicion of evil. The confessional box with a partition between priest and penitent was not used until the second half of the sixteenth century, and the fifteenth and early sixteenth century illustrations generally show the priest seated, the penitent kneeling in front of him.[1] In addition to the precaution of a public place, almost all the authorities warn that when a woman comes to confess, the priest should place her at his side so that he cannot look into her face. Antonius de Butrio adds,

[1] Confession in an open place: Odo of Sully, *Synodicae constitutiones*, PL, 212, 60–61; *Manuale parrochialium sacerdotum*, V, B1a; *Officarium curatorum insignis ecclesiae Eduensis* (Paris, 1503), fol. 12a; Hermannus de Schildis, *Speculum sacerdotum de tribus sacramentis principalibus* (G. de Spira: Speier, ca. 1479) [17a]; Gerson, *Opus tripartitum*, II, Du Pin, I, 445C; idem, "Sermo de officio pastoris," (1408), Glorieux, V, 141; Jacobus de Clusa, *Confessionale*, A3a (ch. 3–4); Amann, "Pénitence," *DTC*, 12¹, 925. For the confessional box, see Lea, *History of Auricular Confession*, I, 395. Although there are occasional references in the secondary literature to fifteenth century confessional boxes, no evidence is cited. Toussaert corroborates Lea's dates: he finds no evidence of confessionals in Flanders before the seventeenth century and none in Belgium before the middle of the sixteenth century (*Le Sentiment religieux*, 104 and n.). Toussaert's evidence for the conduct of confession in Flanders accords with the description I have given here (ibid., 104–122).

"especially if she is young." St. Antoninus of Florence advises confessors not to stare or look frequently at youths and noblemen; but the practice of looking directly at any penitent, no matter what his age or sex, is discouraged because of the tendency to inhibit and confuse the telling of sins. Jacobus de Clusa even suggests that it is prudent for the penitent and confessor to hide their faces so that only their voices can be heard, and we can see in this advice a foreshadowing of the partitioned confessional. Others direct the confessor to fix his eyes on the ground, keeping a humble countenance. As in the illustration, the confessor is to sit. A few authorities, and among them is Guido de Monte Rocherii, direct the penitent to sit also. The *Tractatus de instructionibus confessorum* says that the penitent should kneel at the beginning and then, to tell his sins, sit at the feet or side of the confessor according to the custom of the land. Most, however, direct the penitent to kneel, women with their heads covered and men with their hats off. Angelus de Clavasio in one place says the penitent should kneel and in another argues that it is not absolutely necessary for him to kneel or to take off his hat, since it is internal more than external humility that is wanted here. But Godescalc Rosemondt expands on the more common opinion— that it is proper to have humility of posture as well as of mind— by addressing the penitent: ". . . throw yourself at the feet of the priest, the representative of Christ, no matter how great you are; not standing, or sitting, or lying out on the altar as has become the unworthy custom in many places." In short, there is much evidence to suppose that a variety of postures was permissible for the penitent, but the vast majority stipulated that he kneel before the priest. Some of the authorities also advise that proper greetings be exchanged; for example, to the penitent's "Benedicite" the confessor was to answer, "Dominus sit vobiscum." And some also explicitly direct the penitent to clasp his hands.[2]

[2] Examples of sitting and kneeling are found in *Tractatus de instructionibus confessorum* (Pr. of Aristeas: Erfurt, 1483?), A4–A5; Antonius de Butrio, *Speculum de confessione*, I, A3a; idem, *Directorium ad confitendum*, 1; *Summa rudium*, ch. 31, fol. 30b (which tells the priest to decide). Examples of sitting only are found in Guido de Monte Rocherii, *Manipulus curatorum*, II, 3, 8, fol. 86b–87a; *Astesana*, V, 16. Examples of kneeling only are most common: *Angelica*, "Confessio sacramentalis," 1, and "Interrogationes"; [Poeniteas cito], *Confessionale pro scholasticis*, B2b; Antoninus, *Confessionale—Defecerunt*, 8 (if kneeling is possible); Andreas de Escobar, *Interrogationes*,

It was usual early in the confession, before the actual telling of the sins, for the confessor to ask some preliminary questions or the penitent to volunteer the information. If the priest does not know the penitent, he must find out to what bishopric and parish the latter belongs, in order to make sure that the confessor has jurisdiction. At the same time he is advised to find out the penitent's profession and social or marital status so that he can hear the confession more intelligently and be ready to ask pertinent questions about the sins he is told. Sometimes the confessor is instructed to ask the penitent if he is under any sentence of excommunication, and whether he comes to this confession with adequate preparation and the right intentions. And sometimes he is told to ask about the penitent's last confession: when it was; whether the penance imposed then was finished; whether any sins were concealed. J. P. Foresti wants the confessor to ascertain at the outset if the penitent is a public sinner: whether he frequents prostitutes, keeps a concubine, or practices usury. In addition, these introductory questions often are to include a brief catechetical examination or instruction. Most of the directions for these exercises tell the confessor to find out if the penitent knows the Lord's Prayer, the Hail Mary, and the Creed. Antonius de Butrio thinks the Creed may be a bit too difficult to demand; but Andreas de Escobar adds to the usual three prayers the Ten Commandments and the twelve articles of faith.[3]

Some manuals and summas tell the confessor to encourage the penitent to make a good confession. Often this encouragement is only mentioned briefly; the confessor is to promise pardon or he is simply to urge a full and honest confession. Following the lead of the *Raymundina*, however, many take this opportunity to incorporate their views on the qualities of a good confessor into the actual form of the confession. Thus either immediately before

---

C1a, B3a–b; Rosemondt, *Confessionale*, 1, 1, fol. 6b–7a; *Raymundina*, III, 34, 30, pp. 464–465. Jacobus de Clusa, *Confessionale*, A2b; cap. 3: "Cautum est etiam facies habere tectas vt sola vox possit audiri." Cf. *Manuale parrochialium sacerdotum*, V, A4b.

[3] *Raymundina*, III, 34, 30, pp. 464–465; *Angelica*, "Interrogationes"; Andreas de Escobar, *Interrogationes*, B3b; *Confessionale ad usum Albiensis diocesis* (P. Maréchal and B. Chaussard: Lyon, 1499), A2a–A3b; *Peycht Spigel*, C8b–D1a; Foresti, *Confessionale*, fol. 1a–b; de Butrio, *Speculum de confessione*, I, A3a; idem, *Directorium ad confitendum*, 1; Jacobus de Clusa, *Confessionale*, A3a, cap. 3–4.

or after the introductory questions the confessor is directed to comfort the penitent and increase his confidence. Jacobus de Clusa explains that this encouragement is designed to make the penitent confess openly and completely. The confessor should tell him that God already knows his sins and that the more openly he confesses, the more fully he will be pardoned and the more the confessor will esteem him. The confessor will never reveal his sins, but if any remain hidden they will be exposed to the sight of God, the angels, and the whole world, on the day of judgment. Better now, before one man, than then, before all: the argument is a commonplace, but it is not customary to recall it at this point in the confession as a matter of routine. Several authorities tell the confessor to speak of the mercy offered to the truly repentant. The confessor should receive the penitent kindly and graciously, says Andreas de Escobar, and tell him that he is confessing to a representative of Christ. Then he should be comforted by recalling that Christ died for us sinners, that He is gentle and merciful and will be forgiving to the sorrowful. For Peter denied Him and Paul persecuted Him, David committed murder, Mary Magdalen was a sinner and the Canaanite woman was caught in adultery; "and yet all of these have been sanctified because they repented and confessed." Thus in the general directions for confession some of the authorities instruct the confessor to include, as a matter of form, encouragement based on the benefits of Christ's passion and the mercy that is offered even to great sinners who truly repent.[4]

After these preliminaries—whatever the detail stipulated by the author—the penitent is ready to tell his sins. At some point he is to make the sign of the cross, either at the very beginning after he greets the priest, or else before he starts to tell his sins. Usually he is directed to begin with a general admission of sinfulness in the form of a prayer that begins, "I confess to almighty God," in which the penitent names the Virgin, the saints, and the priest as those to whom he acknowledges that he has sinned; and

[4] Odo of Sully, *Synodicae constitutiones*, PL, 212, 61; *Raymundina*, III, 34, 30, pp. 464–465; Guido de Monte Rocherii, *Manipulus curatorum*, II, 3, 8, fol. 86b–87b (derived from the *Raymundina*); de Butrio, *Speculum de confessione*, I, A3a (also similar to the *Raymundina*); idem, *Directorium ad confitendum*, 1; Andreas de Escobar, *Interrogationes*, B3a–b; *Officiarium curatorum . . . Eduensis*, fol. 12a; *Manuale parrochialium sacerdotum*, C3b–C4a; Antoninus, *Confessionale—Defecerunt*, 7; Jacobus de Clusa, *Confessionale*, A3a, cap. 3–4; *Angelica*, "Interrogationes."

after saying "mea culpa," he interrupts this prayer to begin the recitation of his sins. The confessor is urged at this point to let the penitent follow his own order if he cares to. Only necessary interruptions are proper, and the confessor is to delay his special questions until after the penitent has told all the sins he can remember. Both the anonymous *Peycht Spigel* and the *Manipulus curatorum* of Guido de Monte Rocherii commend to the literate the practice of writing down their sins on a paper and reading them off to the priest, but the search for a full confession seldom is taken to such lengths. If the penitent does not have an order of his own in mind, the confessor may teach him to confess according to the seven deadly sins or the Ten Commandments or some more elaborate combination of categories of sins. According to the *Angelica*, if a penitent has no plan, he should be told to begin with the sins that are most troublesome to his conscience. As we shall see, there are many conditions that the authorities see as desirable in the recitation of sins, but it is enough here to note that in general they look for a succinct and frank recitation that avoids euphemisms and irrelevancy. After the penitent has told all he can remember, he completes the prayer of general confession, if he has begun with it, by beseeching God, Mary, the saints, and the priest for their mercy. He may add some formula indicating sorrow for forgotten as well as confessed sins. The confessor may then ask any questions he feels necessary to the correct understanding of the sins he has just heard. He may also try to ascertain the extent of the penitent's sorrow and intention to amend. Then most of the manuals direct the confessor to impose a penance—prayers, fasting, alms, and so on—and then absolve the penitent; but a few reverse the order and place the absolution before the imposition of the penance.[5] There is disagreement also on whether, in pronouncing absolution, the priest should place his hand on the penitent's head. Andreas de Escobar explicitly directs the confessor to do so, for example, but St. Antoninus, on

[5] Guido de Monte Rocherii, *Manipulus curatorum*, II, 3, 6, fol. 84a; *Angelica*, "Confessio 5," 1, and "Interrogationes"; *Peycht Spigel*, C8b–D1a, C3b–C4a; *Tractatus de instructionibus confessorum*, A4a–A5a, E4a–E6b; *Manuale parrochialium sacerdotum*, V, A4b–B1a; Antoninus, *Confessionale—Defecerunt*, 7–8; Lupi Rebello, *Fructus*, 13–18, fol. A3a–A4b; [Gerson?], *La Confession*, A4a–A7a; *Speculum celebrantis*, in *Statuta synodalia lexouiensia* (J. DuPré: Paris, ca. 1483), C2a; Rosemondt, *Confessionale*, 1, 1, fol. 6b–8a; ibid., 7, 81, fol. 132b; Andreas de Escobar, *Interrogationes*, C1a; cf. Richard Stapper, "Das Lumen Confessorum des Andreas Didaci," 279.

the authority of St. Thomas, rejects the practice as improper (not *decens*), especially with a woman.[6]

With the absolution or the imposition of the penance, the confession is over. The penitent offers his "alms" and, asking the priest to pray for him, leaves. To the modern reader, paying the priest seems perhaps the most inappropriate and repugnant aspect of the conduct of confession. As we have seen, it was probably an important factor in discouraging frequent confessions, and it is safe to assume that even contemporaries, accustomed to such realities, did not find it entirely felicitous. Nevertheless, not all good men of the fifteenth and sixteenth centuries considered the practice of giving alms to the confessor an irredeemable or inexcusable vice. Of course it is true that religious authorities were wary of abuses. The sale of the sacraments had long been forbidden, and all were anxious to avoid the possibility of being accused of simple marketing, which would have been simony. The *Manual for Parish Priests*, for example, forbids the clergy to ask for anything for hearing confessions, lest the poor who do not have it be discouraged from going. Likewise it commands priests not to give as a penance the purchase of masses, for the temptation for the confessor to traffic in his own masses was all too obvious. Nothing, however, is said to forbid a gift. The good author of the *Peycht Spigel* is characteristically ingenuous on the subject. He warns his lay audience against offering bribes: "You must not boast about riches or promise to give the confessor a large gift so that he will be kind to you; nevertheless you may do what you wish—you do not owe him anything." On the other hand, he has no horror at the customary *Beichtpfennig*: "Although you are not obligated by law to give anything to your confessor, nevertheless it is seemly to give something, as much as you want to, according to your status; and say 'here father or sir, take my alms and pray to God for my sins'; and depart from him with thanks." Nor is this attitude unique. Even more at home with the custom is the *Tractatus de instructionibus confessorum*. The *Tractatus* declares that the priest may not require any payment for confession, but at the same time it shows no desire to tamper with accepted customs, which it urges be followed. How little scandalized churchmen were at this practice is then nicely

---

[6] Andreas de Escobar, *Modus confitendi*, B2b; Antoninus, *Confessionale —Defecerunt*, 48.

illustrated by the following bit of etiquette: a confessor should not reject a small offering from a penitent, as some proud prelates do! For even if the penitent is not obligated to give, it is, we are assured, fitting and pious to do so.[7]

The most prominent feature of both manuals and summas bearing on the conduct of confession is usually the part devoted to the questions. The confessor is supposed to use these questions to guide his penitent to a complete confession, especially when there is some doubt about the recitation of sins. The questions have a long history, with obvious roots in the penitentials. As early as the twelfth century there had been a reaction against the unashamed detail encountered in someone like Burchard of Worms, and thus Odo of Sully, Bishop of Paris, included in his synodal constitutions the caution that although there should be detailed questions for common sins, unusual ones should be approached with circumspection.[8] Similar advice in the *Raymundina* became the classic position on the conduct of the confessor's interrogation:

> After he has heard the confession, let him begin to inquire distinctly and methodically . . . . Nevertheless, I advise that in his questions he not descend to special circumstances and special sins; for many fall severely after such an interrogation who otherwise never would have dreamt of it.

Yet Raymond and his descendants flatly reject the contention that questions are improper; human simplicity and shame make it necessary for the confessor to clarify what the penitent has said and what the church teaches.[9]

Some authors emphasize investigation more than discretion, but virtually all include both. The *Confessionale—Defecerunt* of St. Antoninus of Florence, for example, repeats both parts of Raymond's opinion, that it is necessary both to question and to

---

[7] *Manuale parrochialium sacerdotum*, V, A4b; *Peycht Spigel*, C4a, C5a; *Tractatus de instructionibus confessorum*, A4a; cf. Barth, "Beicht und Kommunionen," 91–92.

[8] Amann, "Pénitence," *DTC*, 12^1, 924; Odo of Sully, *Synodicae constitutiones*, PL, 212, 60.

[9] *Raymundina*, III, 34, 30, p. 465; cf. ibid., 28, p. 462; Guido de Monte Rocherii, *Manipulus curatorum*, II, 3, 9, fol. 87b; *Supplementum*, "Confessio 2," 5.

be discreet. He expands on this, however, by noting that St. Thomas teaches that to ask all the many possible questions of each penitent would be useless and at times damnable. Questions must be tailored to the age, condition, status, or country of the penitent. The confessor should begin generally and go only so far as is necessary to identify the sin. The danger with which Antoninus and all of the authorities were concerned arose principally in the investigation of carnal sins. His example gives a good idea of where the line was to be drawn; if, he explains, a man confesses to unnatural intercourse with his wife, no more questions need be asked—it is sodomy no matter how it was done and one has to know nothing more. "But in fact for other sins that are not carnal it is not so dangerous and scandalous to delve into particular circumstances."[10]

Almost identical advice is given by Antonius de Butrio, who cautions that questions about sodomy and masturbation should not get too detailed unless there is good suspicion, for many are taught sins in this way. But, he continues, every priest, in the interests of detection of sin, ought to know and teach the Ten Commandments, the articles of faith, the seven sacraments, the seven carnal and spiritual sins, and the sins committed by the five senses. "And because I realize that many priests do not know these," he continues, "I have pointed out many necessary things in this work for their use."[11] De Butrio's list of areas for interrogation is long, but it cannot compare with the variety that some suggest as appropriate guides to inquiry into the penitent's life. J. P. Foresti, who insists that only relevant questions be asked of each penitent, offers this abundance of possibilities: sins against the seven commandments of the church, seven sacraments, Ten Commandments, seven deadly sins, seven virtues opposed to the seven deadly sins, seven gifts of the Holy Spirit, four cardinal virtues, five bodily senses, five spiritual senses, seven corporal works of mercy, seven spiritual works of mercy, along with particular questions to be asked of temporal lords and princes, secular judges, notaries and procurators, school masters, scholars, phy-

---

[10] Antoninus, *Confessionale—Defecerunt*, 5. On the other hand [Poeniteas cito], *Libellus de modo poenitendi*, B4a, cautions against detailed interrogation into sins of avarice ("et specialiter de turpi lucro non debent fieri subtiles inquisitiones ne posterius committant talia peccata") in addition to those of lust.

[11] de Butrio, *Speculum de confessione*, II, A3b.

sicians, public officers, burghers, merchants, artisans, tavern-keepers, and farmers.[12] Clearly only some of these questions would apply to any single penitent, and one is surely permitted to remain skeptical that, for example, the seven spiritual works of mercy ever entered into the interrogation of either average or extraordinary sinners. Unhappily, the problem that remains most difficult to solve is what kind of balance was struck in practice between discretion and brevity on the one hand and thoroughness and prolixity on the other.

The summas for confessors provide some useful clues. The *Angelica*'s article "Interrogationes" gives the standard advice that the confessor should be cautious and conscientious, but on balance careful questioning wins out. On the one hand, a confessor is not supposed to go into excessive detail, and Angelus seems to excuse him from examining seriously someone who appears to be lying. Nor is the confessor guilty of mortal sin if he unintentionally fails to interrogate—if, for example, he forgets. On the other hand, the confessor who is negligent in his inquiry is guilty of mortal sin. The good confessor must try to discover the sins of confused, forgetful, and diffident penitents. In addition to these explicit directions, and threats, the massive detail of "Interrogationes" is even more persuasive evidence that Angelus wanted confessors to be thorough. The article is well over twenty thousand words, and its contents are an index of the moral questions of the summa itself. Thus in treating the problem of interrogation, the *Angelica* suggests to a confessor that every sin may have special circumstances that require special investigation. And if other summists do not have so elaborate an article on interrogation; and if they also recognize the limits that must be placed on the examination of penitents; they too, by their specific directions and by the very structure of their works, stress thoroughness above caution.[13]

[12] Foresti, *Confessionale*, "Tabula," A2b–A4b, fol. 1a–b.

[13] *Angelica*, "Interrogationes"; *Sylvestrina*, "Confessor 3," q. 14–15, par. 17–18; *Astesana*, V, 16 (a place cited by Angelus); *Supplementum*, "Confessor 2," 5; Tentler, "Summa for Confessors," *Pursuit of Holiness*, 114–117. Cf. Jacobus de Clusa, *Confessionale*, cap. 23, B4b (which contains questions especially for unlearned, timid, and rude penitents), and app. 3, D3a (which quotes Hostiensis, who warns that not everything written in the literature on confession is to be followed to the letter; that the discreet priest will be selective; that these are not precepts, but counsels for simple confessors); *Tractatus de instructionibus confessorum*, A2a, A4b–A5a, C4b–E3b; de

Additional evidence that the questioning of penitents was taken very seriously is contained in the first words, the incipit, of the manual of Antoninus of Florence, which refer directly to the obligation of the confessor to search into sins: *Defecerunt scrutantes scrutinio*—"the inquirers have failed in their inquiry." And Antoninus immediately explains: "those who inquire into the sins of others are confessors, and their inquiry is the questioning done in confession." The good confessor will fulfill this office diligently. Failure is an offense against God. Such is the first lesson of one of the most widely published books in the fifteenth century.[14]

It is also the obvious lesson of the most complete program of interrogation in the literature, the treatise *On the Confession of Masturbation*, attributed to Jean Gerson.[15] It is more explicit than the technique of Gerson's *On the Art of Hearing Confessions* for extracting information from penitents unwilling to disclose sexual sins, and it is remarkable because of its unsurpassable frankness. It begins:

> "Friend, do you remember when you were young, about ten or twelve years old, your rod [*virga*] or virile member [*membrum pudendi*] ever stood erect?"

If he answers No, the author insists, he is immediately convicted of a lie, because it is common knowledge that this often happens to all boys, unless they are physically defective. At this point, therefore, the confessor is to urge the penitent more and more openly to tell the truth. If the penitent is a youth, the confessor is advised to continue in this fashion:

> "Friend, wasn't that thing indecent? (Amice, numquid istud erat indecens?) What did you do, therefore, so that it wouldn't stand erect?" And let this be said with a tranquil visage, so that

---

Chaimis, *Confessionale*, III, 1–2, C8b–D5a; *Confessionale* (Albi), A3bff.; Andreas de Escobar, *Interrogationes, passim*; *Manuale parrochialium sacerdotum*, V, B1a; Rosemondt, *Confessionale*, 1, 1, fol. 6b–7a, and 7, 80, fol. 131a–132a.

[14] Antoninus, *Confessionale—Defecerunt*, the incipit. Cf. *Supplementum*, "Clavis."

[15] Gerson, *De Confessione mollitiei*, Du Pin, II, 453–455. Glorieux (*Oeuvres*, I, 49) raises a doubt about its authenticity: "Explicitement attribué à Gerson, dans la table, malgré sa forme indirecte." In the second half of the treatise there are persistent references to what the "master" has said on the subject.

it will appear that what has been asked about is not dishonorable or something to be kept quiet, but rather as a remedy against the alleged awkwardness of the aforementioned erection.

If the penitent still refuses to answer, the author advises the most direct confrontation:

"Friend, didn't you touch or rub your member (virgam) the way boys usually do?" If he entirely denies that he ever held it or rubbed it in that state it is not possible to proceed further except in expressing amazement and saying that it is not credible: exhorting him to remember his salvation; that he is before God; that it is most serious to lie in confession, and the like.

If, however, the penitent admits that "he held and rubbed it," the author advises this line:

"Friend, I well believe it; but for how long? an hour? a half hour? and for so long that the member was no longer erect?" And let this be uttered as if the confessor did not think this unusual or sinful. If the penitent answers that he did so, then there is the evidence (habetur intentum) that he has truly comitted the sin of masturbation, even if on account of his age pollution did not follow.

The audacity of this interrogation is even more marvelous than its guile. Yet the author is willing to go even further in the discussion of this vice in the confessional. He begins by raising the question of loss of virginity through masturbation, and concludes that it can be restored through penance only if there has been no physical pollution. He then urges confessors to inveigh against this sin. If it is committed with a companion, it descends to another form of sodomy. Many adults commit it, and confessors should find out if they have, through some variation on the questions above. For some adults do not confess it, initially because they are ashamed, and then because they have forgotten it. Others who are ashamed admit that they intended never to confess it. And some say that they have never confessed it because their confessors have never asked about it. The author, however, is decisively in favor of interrogating on this subject. He wants parents and teachers to lecture against it to their children, warning against the loss of virginity and their perpetual damnation.

He wants people to understand that one should seek a confessor after committing this crime just as quickly as if one had lain with a woman. Furthermore, he is much less worried here about the danger of teaching the young how to sin than most of the authorities on interrogation. In the author's view, the corruption of nature makes it certain that youths of thirteen to fifteen will be strongly inclined to this vice: they naturally feel the urge to deal with the "itch" of their erections as they would with an itch anywhere else on their bodies. It is much better to take the chance of teaching vice to a few than to allow this damnable vice to increase and remain unconfessed. The author, a determined foe of unnatural sexual vice, uses the confessional to ask questions about it and suggest remedies against it. Accordingly, he asks penitents to discourage it in friends whom they know to be guilty of it. In private they are to preach against it, reminding their companions that the sin is vile, just as their own confessor has said: that severe punishments are meted out by public law for it; and that fire and brimstone descended on Sodom and Gomorrah to punish it. To the penitents themselves he prescribes a variety of defenses against temptation: sobriety, good company, abstinence, prayer, imitation of the saints, rising from bed, beating the breast, flagellation, sprinkling with cold water, and spitting on the ground while renouncing the devil.

The aggressive tone and clinical detail of this investigation into masturbation are not characteristic of the literature on the forgiveness of sins. Indeed, except for its intense practicality and its vehement condemnation of unnatural vices, this language is not characteristic of Gerson himself. Nevertheless it is a valuable representative of one extreme in the spectrum of artful interrogation. *On the Confession of Masturbation* has advised confessors to be thorough and clever in dealing with the sin most likely to raise demands for caution from the authorities on pastoral care. Yet even the most cautious would have had to admit that if the author was right about the extent to which this sin was being hidden, then there was an obligation to find it out.

Two final points of etiquette are directly relevant to the conduct of confession. First, there is unanimous agreement that it is improper to name anyone else in confession. One should recite one's own sins; there is no place for shifting the blame for one's own failures onto others or damaging their reputations. The confessor is expressly instructed not to ask who the partners in sin were and the penitent is strictly forbidden to volunteer the information. Gerson has a disconcerting exception to this rule in his suggestion that it might be all right if no harm could come to the people named and, on the contrary, their reformation might be abetted. Another exception must be made, says Gerson, for the confession of incest: if, for example, the sin has been committed with one's only sister, one must confess it even though it necessarily reveals her identity. In such a case, however, Gerson tries to preserve the rule by advising the penitent to find a confessor who does not know the party to be named. In brief, the overwhelming consensus condemns naming anyone else as a sinner in confession.[16]

Second, the confessor is warned to conceal any disapproval he might feel at the penitent's sins. Clearly this could be a serious and common problem. The *Peycht Spigel*, therefore, has advice for the penitent faced with a short-tempered priest: if he seems too harsh, or registers amazement, remember it is a matter of his soul also. "Be humble, obedient, and patient with your confessor, for he too is a man." Despite the apparent reasonability of the *Peycht Spigel*'s attempt to make laymen understand the difficulties of the priest, however, other authorities are generally outspoken on this matter. They admonish confessors not to show amazement; exhibit a contorted face; show revulsion (no matter what enormities are confessed); rebuke the penitent; or exclaim "Oh, what vile sins!"[17] In part the motive for this rule was to obtain a complete confession, which would be difficult if the penitent were shamed and harassed while he told his sins. But there was a less narrow, a more compassionate intention at work here as well. Just as it was decreed in the severest language that the

---

[16] Gerson, *Opus tripartitum*, I, 17, Du Pin, I, 440D–441A. This admonition not to reveal companions in sin is universal. A few typical expressions of it: Andreas de Escobar, *Interrogationes*, B3b; Rosemondt, *Confessionale*, 1, 1, fol. 6a–b (which includes Gerson's example of confession of incest with one's only sister); *Peycht Spigel*, C4a; Antoninus, *Confessionale—Defecerunt*, 7; *Manuale parrochialium sacerdotum*, V, B1a.

[17] *Peycht Spigel*, C4a. Like the ban on naming others, the admonition to avoid expressing displeasure or revulsion during the recitation of the penitent's sins is a commonplace; a few examples are: de Chaimis, *Interrogatorium*, III, 1–2, C8b–D5a; Andreas de Escobar, *Interrogationes*, B3b; Guido de Monte Rocherii, *Manipulus curatorum*, II, 3, 8, fol. 87a–b; de Butrio, *Speculum de confessione*, IV, A6b; Olivier Maillard, *La Confession generale*, A2a; Rosemondt, *Confessionale*, 7, 81, fol. 132b.

priest could never violate the sacred seal of confession and divulge anyone's sins; just as the naming of companions in sin was condemned; so the caution against showing displeasure was designed to make the experience of the confessional more secure and less threatening. Indeed, the rules of conduct all functioned in this way. They helped to make a trying obligation less anxious. How successful they were is one of the historical problems at hand. But that such rules were designed to allay apprehension and diminish the pain of confessing seems indisputable. Such a conclusion is reinforced, moreoever, when we examine the way writers on sacramental confession described their ideal of the good confessor.

The Expert Confessor

It was common in medieval literature to answer a question by reciting pithy and easily remembered verses, and topics in the conduct and doctrine of confession often received this poetic treatment. The qualities of the good confessor are summarized in this way, as in the following jingle from a manual for curates in the diocese of Autun:

> Audiatque presbyter in ecclesia in loco eminenti confessiones:
> Vultum mulier non respiciens;
> omnes patienter audiens:
> veniam petentibus promittens:
> penas portabiles infligens.[1]

> Let the priest hear confessions in an open place in the church:
> At the faces of women not staring;
> everyone patiently hearing;
> pardon to supplicants promising;
> bearable penances imposing.

In literary merit the translation is not much inferior to the original, and the teaching contained in it does not go much beyond the commonplaces of etiquette. Andreas de Escobar's rhymes are more explicit, as he tells us the confessor ought to be

> dulcis in corrigendo (soft in correcting)
> prudens in instruendo (prudent in instructing)
> pius in puniendo (conscientious in punishing)

[1] *Officiarium curatorum . . . Eduensis*, fol. 22a.

affabilis interrogando (courteous in questioning)
discretus penitentiam iniungendo (discreet in imposing
a penance)
mitus confitentem audiendo (gentle in hearing the penitent)
benignus in absoluendo (kind in absolving).[2]

But again this is simply a listing of virtues appropriate to a good confessor, similar to that of the "Poeniteas cito," which tells us in meter that the confessor should be "agreeable, friendly, kind, prudent, discreet, gentle, devout, and pleasant."[3] But the poem, offering more than a list of virtues here, has this to add about the good confessor:

Let him keep secret—as if it were his own crimes—the sins of
the guilty
Let him be slow to punishment and quick to compassion,
Lamenting as often as he is forced to be severe;
He should pour out a mixture of oil and vinegar,
At times like a father chastising with the rod,
at times like a mother proffering her breast.[4]

All of this rhymed and versified teaching is common and unoriginal. It would be surprising if it were not, since its purpose was to put into a memorable form the clichés about the virtues needed in a good confessor. Yet it perhaps influenced medieval practice and it certainly contributes to our understanding of medieval practice. For it is popular, simple, and didactic, as it emphatically asserts the desirability of humane qualities. It focuses not just on the rules of etiquette, but tries to get at the proper attitude towards sinful and ashamed penitents. No one forgets that the confessor is a punisher and corrector of vice: authority and discipline are faithfully represented. But the emphasis in these verses is on persuasion, friendly and gentle, with only the most prudent use of sanctions to discourage sin.

Before any personal qualities, of course, the priest must have the "key of power," that is, he must be an ordained priest with

---

[2] Andreas de Escobar, *Interrogationes*, B3a.

[3] [Poeniteas cito], *Penitentiarius*, A3a, lines 54–55; "Confessor dulcis, affabilis, atque benignus, Sit sapiens, iustus, sit mitis, compatiensque." Cf. *Astesana*, V, 16—one of the authorities who use this list.

[4] [Poeniteas cito], *Penitentiarius magistri iohannis*, A3a, lines 56–60. The glosses and commentaries of the various versions of the "Poeniteas cito" supply more explicit descriptions here.

jurisdiction over the penitent and his sins, and thus have the power to absolve. Most writers demand, in addition to power and the personal qualities of gentleness and sympathy, a certain amount of talent, which they generally identify with the "key of knowledge." The first key, of power, requires no talent or intelligence; and at times even those who think talent and learning mandatory admit that power is really the essential, that a priest with jurisdiction can usually absolve even if he is sinful and ignorant. But the confessor was not supposed to be sinful or ignorant, and authorities on confession can expound at great length on the second key as it ought to be in the hands of a good confessor.[5]

In the first place, everyone agreed that it was necessary for the confessor to understand sins. He had to be able to identify the offenses against God that were serious enough to lose the grace of salvation and require confession to a priest to be forgiven. He had to be able, therefore, to tell the difference between a mortal and a venial sin, not always an easy task as we shall see later. Yet the confessor declaring what was and was not a serious sin had to follow opinions that were often complicated and even contradictory. How learned did a priest have to be? How ignorant might he be and still validly absolve?

An author with rigorous standards for the performance of this "highest art of arts" could demand much from a good confessor. Godescalc Rosemondt, for example, wants a priest who has been given the burden of the cure of souls to be well informed. He must know the decalogue, the commandments of the church, and other relevant ecclesiastical statutes. He must be able to tell not only what sins are mortal, but also which ones are likely to arise in a particular confession. He must know the impediments to marriage and the ecclesiastical excommunications and censures. He must understand the Easter duty and the general conditions of a good confession as well as the obligations to make restitution and remove occasions of scandal. Finally, he must know enough in difficult cases to doubt his own judgment and seek more learned counsel. This list is not imposing simply because of its

[5] For an excellent exposition, with many texts, of the development of the theology of the keys and the difficulty of explaining the key of knowledge, see Anciaux, *La Théologie*, 539ff., and especially Stephen Langton on the key of knowledge (p. 569). See also Hödl, *Geschichte der scholastischen Literatur*, 380–382 (and his references).

complexity, however, but even more because of the demanding way in which Godescalc presents it. Indeed, all the summas for confessors deal with this kind of knowledge, and often more extensively than Godescalc's *Confessionale*. But few castigate unlearned priests as severely as he, comparing them to physicians who dispense medicine indiscriminately and ignorantly, not knowing what illness it is for, caring only for their own profit. These ignorant confessors are accused of being motivated by greed, and of rushing through a series of confessions to the peril of souls. One can only conclude that for Godescalc Rosemondt it was serious to fail in knowledge, and he was not alone in this attitude. Jacobus de Clusa is even more rigorous in his demands; he wants most of the same things that Godescalc Rosemondt requires for a learned and conscientious confessor; and he is especially harsh on those whose ignorance leads them to absolve too easily, impose too slight a penance, and fail to seek the advice they need in difficult cases.[6]

The *Sylvestrina* provides a contrast that is worth noting. The confessor must have three things necessarily, it declares: power, knowledge, and prudence. A fourth quality is sanctity of life, and while it is desirable, Sylvester could not insist on it absolutely lest the taint of Donatism be introduced. When Sylvester talks about knowledge, however, he is similarly cautious. As usual, the confessor is held responsible for telling the difference between what is and is not a sin, and between mortal and lesser sins. But usually, he assures us, somebody who is told to hear and teach in confession does so legitimately. And if the confessor knows how to read and has seen the *Confessionale—Defecerunt* of St. Antoninus or some other book of that sort; if he is not too stupid to realize when he does not know enough; if he does not plunge into rash judgments when he should not, then he can safely expound in the confessional.[7] Sylvester has not praised ignorance here,

---

[6] Rosemondt, *Confessionale*, 7, 75–76, fol. 128b–129b; Jacobus de Clusa, *Confessionale*, app. 2–3, D1b–D3a; cf. *Supplementum*, "Confessor 2," 4.

[7] *Sylvestrina*, "Confessor 3," par. 1–4; *Supplementum*, "Confessor 2," 4, and "Clavis." On the virtues of the confessor, see [Gerson?], *Le Confessional aultrement appelle le Directoire des confesseurs . . . de nouuel mis de la langue latine en langue francoyse* (Paris, 1547), A6b–A8a, hereafter cited as *Directoire*; Johannes von Dambach, *Consolatio theologiae* (G. de Spira: Strasbourg, c. 1478), XIV, 8, 2; de Schildis, *Speculum sacerdotum* [16a]; *Angelica*, "Confessio 4"; [Poeniteas cito], *Libellus do modo poenitendi*, A6a, B2b, B3b, B5a–B6a; de Chaimis, *Interrogatorium*, II, B7a.

and he has sent the confessor to a literature that will teach most of the things that Godescalc Rosemondt wants his good confessor to know. Furthermore, both Sylvester and Godescalc agree that priests cannot be expected to know everything, and thus they stress the importance of knowing when one does not know enough, so that one can seek more learned advice. Nevertheless, Sylvester's emphasis is important because it reflects more directly the development of sacramental theology. For he counts on the power of the sacrament, not the talent of the confessor, even though he is dealing with the key of knowledge. Sylvester gives priority to the efficacy of the sacrament, and is content with a conscientious confessor who does his best. Godescalc Rosemondt wants more, and he makes it clear.

These differences are in tone and emphasis, however, not substance. There is a large area of agreement, even among authorities who range from lax to rigid. Thus everyone says a confessor must recognize a mortal sin when he hears one. And many share the opinion that there is a science to which one must refer if difficulties arise, and they tell confessors to go to expert men and books to find solutions. Even Sylvester, who wants confessors to avoid the worried analysis of their own intellectual credentials, holds these opinions and thereby admits that there are intellectual principles, a science, an expertise. Furthermore, without leaning toward Donatism, or Wycliffism, all agree that the confessor should himself be without sin. It was entirely orthodox to hold and teach that the priest in sin who uses the keys does so validly but sinfully. And from these requirements, including freedom from sin, it was easy to move to the enunciation of those highest ideals characteristically used to judge the medieval clergy, characteristically difficult if not impossible to live up to.

One example of more than commonplace standards for the good confessor occurs in Jean Gerson's *On the Art of Hearing Confessions*.[8] This treatise sets down briefly and clearly some general rules that the author says he knows from experience are profitable for confessors. There emerges from these rules an interesting conception of the most desirable qualities in those who practice "the art of arts, the guidance of souls."

Of course the ideal confessor must first of all be spiritually minded—free from the cares and desires of the flesh. He should be patient, and not hurry through confessions. Indeed, Gerson

[8] Gerson, *Tractatus de arte audiendi confessiones*, Du Pin, II, 446B–453A.

thinks it would be better to put some penitents off until after Easter than to rush them, even though one runs the risk that they will not return. The good confessor's only concern must be the salvation of souls: wealth, beauty, and learning will not count with him. In short, he must be pious and conscientious.

Nevertheless, Gerson's model confessor is distinguished primarily by his knowledge, tact, perseverance, and, above all, his skill. He should know, "like the most learned physician of spiritual diseases," all the classes and kinds of sins. He must also know the conditions of men and the sins most likely for each. In the pursuit of this knowlege he should learn from the manuals; but he must also learn what they have left out. Furthermore, his knowledge must extend to people as well as sins so that he can learn to question prudently and effectively. Thus he must be able at the outset to ascertain how much shame a penitent feels and reassure him that confession is completely secret (that the confessor would rather die than reveal anyone's sins). The object is to root out suspicion and discomfort and implant love and tenderness. This task is especially important in the confession of youths, women, and simple people, for they are most likely to be so ashamed that they will hide sins. They are to be encouraged to make a general confession: and the confessor must know how to probe and question in order to get a complete confession from them. His manner must be easy and affable. If he is austere he will only discourage sincerity, especially in the obstinate. He must also evaluate the penitent's desire to confess completely and honestly: someone caught dissimulating two or three times should be sent away and told to come back when he is better prepared. On the other hand, the confessor should applaud those who are honest about their sins, and the worse the sin, the more they are to be congratulated for their honesty. Gerson does not forget the usual cautions: make sure the penitent is discouraged from naming companions in sin; avoid inciting temptation; do not be offensive. The primary goal, however, is completeness, and the good confessor is known by his ability to achieve that goal. In the interest of the conscience of the penitent, Gerson asserts, the confessor should try to get explanations of sins that fully satisfy him. Even when it comes time to reproach penitents for having committed "enormous sins," the confessor must be careful not to lead the penitent to deny what he has already admitted. Not only must the confessor obtain a full explanation of the sins, therefore, but he also must be constantly gentle, kind, compassionate, and consoling.

Once again, Gerson is thinking especially about sexual sins, and it seems that his ideal confessor will apply his talents particularly to their discovery and correction. His complaint is by now familiar: some penitents hide sins of the flesh so tenaciously that it is almost impossible to extract them. It is the task of the good confessor to deal skillfully with such penitents—the kind of people who deny they have ever had an erection or a sinful desire. Thus he must make penitents understand that it is necessary to talk frankly about impurity. He will ask leading questions and move gradually to the most serious sins. And he must constantly put the penitent at ease by appearing unconcerned, averting his eyes and saying; "I see, you have done such and such—tell it all and I will be patient"; and, "If you tell all the evils of the world, you would not for that reason be considered the worse—therefore tell it boldly." Now the ultimate goal of confession for Gerson is correction. He wants the good confessor to condemn sins and urge reform to make ignorant penitents realize they have unknowingly committed serious sins; to require restitution; to insure the intention to reform. But the most striking talent of Gerson's expert confessor is the combined abilities to uncover, reassure, and console. Not only is he clever. He is also sensitive.

The author of the *Peycht Spigel* draws his own picture of the ideal confessor, which is reminiscent in many ways of Gerson's, but which stresses simple moral virtues much more decisively.[9] Both experience in the confessional and the literature about it inform this exalted ideal, which is poignant if only because it is expressed so shortly before the attack of Martin Luther. The ideal is doubly poignant because the *Peycht Spigel* gives little intimation of the troubles that were about to befall Roman Catholic attitudes toward sin and habits of confessing.

The good confessor, the *Peycht Spigel* explains, prepares for his task by searching his own conscience. He prays for help, uses the power of the keys with prudence and fear, knows his jurisdiction, and refers great sins to his superiors. Despite this pious deference, however, he is thoroughly competent. He can question men according to their rank, status, and occupation, and he dismisses them with instructions to return later if a difficult case

[9] The following description is a paraphrase of the *Peycht Spigel*, C1a–C2b.

forces him to consult his books. When great sinners come to confess with sorrow and devotion, he rejoices; nor does he ever express horror over sins, but, on the contrary, he is pleased if the confession is complete and nothing is kept back. Never does he leave a penitent without consolation, yet he incites contrition in sinners and convinces them to leave their sins. Assumed in all this advice is a difficult directive for the good confessor: he must not be rushed. He must take time for these and other tasks. When he searches into the penitent's worthiness—his sorrow and intention to amend—with the penitent's interests foremost in mind, the confessor must let him speak and help him over any difficulties that arise. Thus the good confessor carefully directs the penitent, does not allow him to talk about the sins of others, and is especially diligent with the young who are ashamed. In his inquiry into sins of the flesh he is always careful not to teach evil; similarly he avoids useless discussion and allows no hint of scandal to be aroused. He demands restitution and asks questions appropriate to the status and occupation of the penitent. Thus he is never satisfied with a vague and general confession, but asks about the circumstances of sins. He does not prefer the rich to the poor, and he does not concern himself with his penitent's alms. Above all, he continually watches out for his penitent's well-being: he encourages married people to live together lovingly and truly; he only imposes bearable penances; and he would rather die than break the seal of the confessional. Still, his questioning is thorough, and he asks about many sins in case shame, ignorance, or forgetfulness need to be overcome. He instructs his penitents especially to make sure that they do not lead lives that are bad examples to others, and he makes great sinners aware of their reprehensible lives. Those who do not want to stop sinning he does not absolve, and that refusal extends to those who are involved in trades that cannot be performed without sin. Finally, he admonishes the sick to receive the sacraments; and "he stays by the dying man so that he does not despair, and strengthens him in belief and hope in the mercy of God." The *Peycht Spigel*'s conclusion to this is part optimism and partly an exhortation to obey the authority of the clergy: believe that every confessor is like this ideal, the author admonishes, or else pray to God that He give you such a one; for no one knows how care-filled it is to hear confessions. Indeed, the calling of confessor, according to the *Peycht Spigel*, would not only be an emotional strain; it would be utterly exhausting.

In conclusion, what emerges from all the discussions of the expert confessor and the proper conduct of confession is a set of high and perhaps unrealistic ideals tempered by a more sober sense of what one can reasonably expect from penitent and clergy. The formalization of rules of etiquette belongs to the search for a reasonable minimum and a way to guarantee it in practice. Follow these forms, we seem to be told, and the worst excesses of clerical ignorance and tactlessness will be avoided. Similarly, the forms will assure that the penitent understands the obligation to be honest about his sins and repentance. Finally, the forms try to contribute something, necessarily limited, to the correction and consolation of the sinner.

The greatest danger in the standard form of confession undoubtedly came from the interrogations. Interpreted too literally or unimaginatively, some of these programs of inquisition could surely have led to psychological and spiritual disaster. At the very least they could have led to inordinate tedium. But the literature reveals an awareness of this danger; and even if the striking aspect of the interrogation seems to us their excessive detail, the good confessor is one who avoids temerity.

It would be misleading to suppose that those who wrote about sacramental confession clearly distinguished the merely adequate from the best confessor. Nevertheless we often see authors go beyond what was absolutely necessary, and the ideal confessor some of them wanted would have had to have rare qualities indeed. He had to do far more than observe the etiquette and avoid temerity. He had to be a talented, learned, and understanding physician to sick souls. It is difficult even to guess how many confessors began to approximate these ideals, or how many failed completely to observe them. We know that it was a common practice in the middle ages for pious laymen to express their gratitude toward their confessors by including them in their wills.[10] We are also familiar with the literary convention of the greedy, lecherous confessor—from Boccaccio and Chaucer to Margaret of Navarre. Intimations of both possibilities occur in

[10] Barth, "Beicht und Kommunionen," 95–97. Barth also refers to medieval ideals of the good confessor, especially in Johann Geiler von Kaisersberg (pp. 94ff.).

the literature on forgiveness. Throughout the *Peycht Spigel*, for example, there are constant hints of abuses as the author implicitly condemns the greed, laxity, or ineptness of the clergy he knew. But it is just as important to note that the author had high ideals for the minister of the Sacrament of Penance, and he wrote as if they were still relevant for the German clergy of the early sixteenth century.

The Good, Complete Confession

A good confession is the work of the penitent. And it should be obvious by now that a primary goal of the literature on the Sacrament of Penance is to instruct and exhort penitents to confess well. These works are written primarily for confessors to read, and they want to insure a supply of good priests with proper training. But their ultimate, practical effect is supposedly the forgiveness and reformation of repentant sinners, and these results can only be obtained if the sinner cooperates as he is taught to do.

There are, moreover, three elements in the work the penitent has to do if his confession is to be good. The first is concerned with the performance of the penitent before the priest; the recitation of his sins must conform to certain standards. The second has to do with his inner emotions: his sorrow must be real and of a certain nature. The third deals with his future intentions, and perhaps even his future behavior: his sins should be a part of his past.

That there is a work that the penitent must perform is a basic, ancient, and enduring assumption of the Sacrament of Penance. Indeed, even the most convinced predestinarians, if they retain an ecclesiastical rite of forgiveness or reconciliation, assign for all practical purposes some kind of work for the penitent to do, no matter how committed are their theologies to human impotence and iniquity. Yet that proposition says very little about attitudes, habits, and institutions; for what we want to know is the content and meaning of this work and these standards and requirements.

DEFINITIONS

The concise definition of penance or confession with which authorities customarily begin can itself reveal something about what a penitent must do or feel. Two examples in particular illustrate that there are differences about what is important in confession, and that even simple formulas can say something about these differences.

Some think of forgiveness primarily in terms of sorrow and a change of life. They are inclined to stress the virtue of penance, and for the literature we are concerned with, the most authoritative voice is that of Raymond of Peñaforte, who stands in the contritionist tradition of Peter Lombard. The definition the *Raymundina* selects is as popular as it is simple:

Penance is repenting past evils and not committing them again.[1]

This accent on sorrow and amendment survives even in the late middle ages (and, we might add, flourishes in the religious thought of the Renaissance). For these contritionists the best confession is one that leads to a change of life. The work of the penitent is preeminently one of sorrow and reformation.

Others follow the theological developments of the thirteenth century and emphasize sacramental power. There is a great variety of opinion and definition in this group, but the clearest statement of the logical consequences of this theology comes, predictably, from the followers of Duns Scotus. Thus Jacobus Lupi Rebello proposes a definition that is apt in its wording and necessary in its logic. The essence of penance, he declares in pure Scotist language, does not include confession, contrition, and satisfaction, even though they are traditionally assigned to it:

for the Sacrament of Penance *is* that *absolution* of a priest having jurisdiction.[2]

---

[1] *Raymundina*, III, 34, 1, p. 437. Alain de Lille's definition (*PL*, 210, 302B) has a similar emphasis on reformation: "quia poenitentia est, peccata deflere, et nolle amplius committere." But the word *nolle* rather than *non* might be taken as stressing the desire rather than the fact of reform. Even Godescalc Rosemondt, in the sixteenth century, defines penance or contrition as "praeterita mala plangere et plangenda iterum non committere" (*Confessionale*, 10, 3, fol. 170a). Cf. Guido de Monte Rocherii, *Manipulus curatorum*, II, 3, 1, fol. 52a–b; Jodocus Winshemius, *Institutiones*, A4a–b.

[2] Lupi Rebello, *Fructus*, a. 23. Nicolaus de Ausimo (*Supplementum*, "Penitentia 1," 1) explicitly affirms the importance of this definition. The *Pisanella* had used the older definition of Peter Lombard and Raymond of Peñaforte. Nicolaus sees the flaw in this definition and identifies a different essence of the Sacrament of Penance: "Penitentia est vnum de sacramentis ecclesiae quo bene dispositis semper remittuntur peccata . . . ."

Now Raymond was interested in having penitents confess properly, and he was similarly committed to the participation of priests. And the Scotists had nothing against sorrow, amendment, or the conscientious recitation of sins. Nevertheless these definitions emphasize different things. They tell us something by what they put in and leave out; and they represent the two most different opinions about what really counts in the forgiveness of sins. Those who preach sorrow and reform follow the Master of Sentences. Those who pin their hopes on sacramental absolution follow the subtle Duns. Some, of course, do both. And no matter what their opinions on the essence of penance, all will get around to the discussion of the performance of the penitent.

THE SIXTEEN CONDITIONS

The temptation to quote a pithy verse was apparently irresistible to medieval religious writers, and even respectable theologians doted on the habit. The qualities of the good confession, like those of the good confessor, were therefore summarized in the kind of mnemonic formulas we are already familiar with. The versified conditions of a good confession are tedious and ordinary, it is true; nevertheless they are invaluable because they represent a widely publicized specimen of clerical instruction on this subject.

The most popular verse finds sixteen conditions of a good confession. The version that follows is ascribed by St. Antoninus of Florence, Angelus de Clavasio, Sylvester Prierias, and Godescalc Rosemondt to St. Thomas's commentary on Book IV of the *Sentences*, and Angelus and Godescalc are probably correct when they say that all the doctors take it up when they comment on Book IV, distinction 17, question 14:

Sit simplex, humilis, confessio, pura, fidelis,
Atque frequens, nuda, discreta, libens, verecunda,
Integra, secreta, lachrimabilis, accelerata,
Fortis, et accusans, et sit parere parata.[3]

[3] The most readily available example of these lines is St. Thomas Aquinas, *Summa Theologica*, III, Q. 9, a. 4. If the "Poeniteas cito" is in fact late twelfth or early thirteenth century, then the appearance of similar verses there obviously antedates St. Thomas. There are fourteen conditions in lines 15–17 of "Poeniteas cito," *PL*, 207, 1153, and in all printed versions except [Poeniteas cito], *Confessionale pro ccholasticis*, A4a, which has thirteen. Cf., Antoninus, *Confessionale—Defecerunt*, 8; *Supplementum*, "Confessio 1," 2;

> Let the confession be simple, humble, pure, faithful,
> And frequent, unadorned, discreet, willing, ashamed,
> Whole, secret, tearful, prompt,
> Strong, and reproachful, and showing readiness to obey.

It would not be worthwhile to catalogue the slight variations on these sixteen conditions, or even the ones that depart substantially by selecting as few as five. But a summary of the *Sylvestrina*'s explication will give a good idea of the meaning of these most common thoughts about good confessing.[4]

Sylvester explains that confession must be "simple," concentrating on the sin itself and not lapsing into storytelling. If it is to be "humble," the penitent must have an inner recognition of his lowliness and infirmity, and show humility in his external bearing by kneeling, uncovering his head, wearing somber apparel, and so on. "Pure" requires the penitent to have the right intention. By "faithful" Sylvester means truthful, without falsification; and here he disagrees with others who take this attribute to mean

---

Angelica, "Confessio sacramentalis"; Rosemondt, *Confessionale*, 1, 1–2, fol. 2a–b; *Sylvestrina*, "Confessio 1," q. 1, par. 2; *Astesana*, V, 8; Andreas de Escobar, *Modus confitendi*, B2b; Guido de Monte Rocherii, *Manipulus curatorum*, II, 3, 6, fol. 83a; [Gerson?], *La Confession*, A3a–b; Columbi, *Confession generale* A2b; [Poeniteas cito], *Libellus de modo poenitendi*, A5b–A6a; [Gerson?], *Directoire*, C1b–C5b. For the use of this verse in manuscript manuals, see Michaud-Quantin, *Sommes de casuistique*, 86. The authorities just cited are in almost complete agreement on the sixteen conditions of confession. The following authorities have many of the same conditions as the above, but differ substantially in various ways: *Raymundina*, III, 34, 22, 455ff.; *Tractatus de instructionibus confessorum*, A2a–b; Schauerte, *Busslehre des Eck*, 173–176; Geiler von Kaisersberg, *Navicula*, March 7, fol. 9a–10a; de Butrio, *Directorium*, 2; *Hortulus anime*, fol. 153b–155b; *Eruditorium penitentiale*, C7a–C8b; Franz Falk, ed., *Drei Beichtbüchlein nach den zehn Geboten aus der Frühzeit der Buchdruckerkunst*, Reformationsgeschichtliche Studien und Texte, ed. by J. Greving, vol. 2 (Münster, 1907), 81; Matthew of Cracow, *De modo confitendi*, C6a. Another example of a disagreement in definition that does *not* have doctrinal importance is Nicolaus de Ausimo's addition of "Catholic" and "hopeful of pardon" to the *Pisanella*'s explanation of *fidelis* (which is the same as Sylvester's).

[4] *Sylvestrina*, "Confessio 1," q. 1, par. 2. Sylvester returns to many of these "conditions" in much greater detail further on in this article. Gerson, *Opus tripartitum*, I, 17, Du Pin, I, 440C–D. For other stabs at originality here, see Winshemius, *Institutiones*, A5a; Rosemondt, *Confessionale*, 1, 1, fol. 2b–3b; *Eruditorium penitentiale*, B8b–C1a; and Geiler von Kaisersberg, *Navicula*, March 7, fol. 9a–b.

faithful to Catholic belief and the hope of pardon, because faith and hope belong to the substance and not the quality or condition of confession. By "frequent" he means often, for the purpose of telling both new and previously confessed sins, and by "prompt" he means sought without delay, immediately after sinning. "Unadorned" refers to the desirability of a clear recitation of sins, with the minimum of obscurity, but within the bounds of "discreet," which warns against lascivious language that might be a temptation to the priest. (Once again Sylvester takes note of a difference of opinion: John of Freiburg says that discreet means the penitent should find a fit and discreet priest.) "Voluntary" confession should preclude force not only literally but also in the motives of the penitent: thus confession should not spring from the coercion of human shame or fear of exclusion from the church or the sacraments. Yet if the penitent is not supposed to be driven to confession by shame, nevertheless he is supposed to be "ashamed" when he gets there. He should not boast of his great sinfulness; rather he should feel ashamed of his sins internally because they are offenses against God, and show it externally, as he reveals them to the priest. To compound our difficulties in figuring out the place of shame in these conditions, however, Sylvester declares that while shame before the priest is itself virtuous and a work of satisfaction, the confession should at the same time be "strong" so that nothing is omitted out of fear of getting too harsh a penance, or out of shame. In addition, the confession should be "whole," without holding back any mortal sins; "secret," on the part of both confessor and penitent; "tearful," with at least an internal sorrow for sin; and "accusing," of the penitent and not anyone else. Finally he urges that a good confession show "readiness to be obedient," that is, of course, to the priest. Not all of these conditions are essential, but the *Supplementum* was wrong, Sylvester concludes, in trying to reduce them to eleven since, as he has just shown, they are distinct and do not overlap.

We cannot claim that the sixteen conditions represent a great contribution to religious education or observance. Clearly we have here no more than a form to aid the memory, and the poem's store of learning and potential for teaching are quickly exhausted. Indeed, we cannot even point to unanimity in the number or precise meaning of the conditions. Yet the verse was immensely popular and the text itself has something to say. When an author comments on it, furthermore, he has to explain it in terms of what he knows and thinks is right; and we cannot ignore the evidence that results.

Nevertheless, it is possible to get the essentials of this message across in far briefer form if one disregards the sixteen conditions. Jean Gerson, for example, is more direct and succinct, and, one feels, more memorable. At one place in the *Opus tripartitum* he describes a good confession simply:

> Let the sinner accuse himself humbly, and not derisively; honestly and not deceitfully; purely, directly, and sincerely, avoiding irrelevancies; and above all discreetly, so that he does not reveal those who were his companions in sin.

In another passage he advises the penitent simply to confess voluntarily and fully to the best of his ability, and then amplifies this advice by cautioning him against lying or excusing himself.[5] It is a fresher and more persuasive approach to instruction, but there is nothing original in it; and here, as elsewhere in this literature, one finds a weighty unanimity even when authorities seem to disagree.

THE COMPLETE CONFESSION

Of all assumptions the most universal is that a good confession must be complete. This is the first, necessary condition, and it is a truly ubiquitous criterion by which the work of the penitent is judged. Its importance has already been made clear in the discussion of the confessor's interrogations. It is implicit in much of the etiquette of the confessional, which was designed to make penitents at ease so that they could tell their sins without being tempted to conceal them out of shame. It appears in several ways in the sixteen conditions of a good confession. To exaggerate the importance of completeness seems hardly possible. It was and has remained indispensable to forgiveness in the Roman Catholic Sacrament of Penance; and it constitutes an essential difference between Catholic and Protestant forgiveness of sins.

If the penitent wants to make a complete confession, he must first examine his conscience thoroughly to find out what sins have been committed and need confessing. He must do so, moreover, in the same thorough way and for the same purpose that the confessor conducts his interrogation, that is, according to some

[5] Gerson, *Opus tripartitum*, II, Du Pin, I, 446A.

categorization of sins. It is to be done methodically, deliberately, and extensively. Stephan Lanzkranna's *Himmelstrasse* devotes a chapter to this obligation. He advises the penitent to examine his conscience according to some confessional manual's version of the kinds of sins and their circumstances, and he urges that the worse the sinner, the more diligent the examination ought to be. And if a confessor finds his penitent unprepared, he should not absolve him.[6] Such a threat underlines the prominent place confession—that is, complete confession—occupies in this outline of the heavenly road. Furthermore, it was not uncommon for an author to commend a general examination of one's whole life, and suggest other helps to the recollection of sin such as a review from one's youth to the present of his various companions, occupations, habitations, ages, and so on.[7]

The potential for scrupulosity here is evident, and some authors try to save their discussion from an excessively legalistic tone. Engelhardus Kunhofer, for example, equates examination of conscience with the classical imperative "know thyself." He urges sinners to "read the book of their consciences" to prepare for the day when they will stand before the tribunal of Christ. In similar fashion J. L. Vivaldus indulges his rhetorical proclivities by quoting Seneca to show how useful for self-improvement it is to call oneself to account daily; he cites Augustine, David, Nebuchadnezzar, and Hezekiah as evidence that one can be led to salvation through the recognition of one's own iniquities.[8]

For everyone, however, the examination of conscience was serious, and better authors could state this truism convincingly. Thus in the *Opus tripartitum* Gerson flatly asserts that a careful examination is necessary to revive from the state of sin to the state of grace. For, he argues, in order to confess well, it is essential that the penitent prepare, before he comes to the priest to tell his sins, by a diligent and prolonged search of his conscience, "as if he expected to find some great treasure there." Many simple people, however, are guilty of inexcusable negligence and ignor-

6 Stephan Lanzkranna, *Himelstrass*, ch. 5, 12a–b; c. 38, 52a.

7 This advice is usual, although it is especially characteristic of authors who are concerned about penitents who forget easily or else do not go to confession even yearly; see, for example, Alain de Lille, *Liber poenitentialis*, PL 210, 279–304; [Gerson?], *La Confession*, A3a–b.

8 Kunhofer, *Confessionale*, A1b; Vivaldus, *Aureum opus de veritate contritionis*, 6b–19b.

ance, and consequently Gerson offers a mirror for sinners in which they can examine themselves according to the seven deadly sins. At the close of this exercise, Gerson assures those who cannot find any sins to confess that they will be saved by a general avowal of sorrow for forgotten sins; if they remember sins later, they are required to confess them at the proper time and place. But, Gerson warns, forgetting sins through negligence is a serious fault. And although he has offered the standard teaching that honest forgetting excuses one from the obligation to tell all the sins one has actually committed, the sense of his argument emphatically demands a diligent examination of conscience.[9]

THE GENERAL CONFESSION

The examination of conscience could be aided by what medieval authors called a general confession.[10] This popular genre is usually organized, like the interrogations, according to the five senses, seven deadly sins, Ten Commandments, and so on, but it is more succinct and has the distinctive feature of prefacing the example of the sin by a formula, such as "I have sinned in . . . ," or "I admit my guilt at having . . . ." Some were intended to be said publicly by the whole congregation; others apparently were simply to be used, like the second part of the *Opus tripartitum* and countless other manuals, as a mirror of sinners to prepare the penitent for his confession. The usefulness of the general confession to be recited by the whole congregation is nicely

[9] Gerson, *Opus tripartitum*, I, 17, Du Pin, I, 440C; ibid., II, Du Pin, I, 442A–B, 446–447A. In addition to "completeness" as it has been discussed here, authorities were concerned with divided confessions (especially in the earlier period). It eventually became an undisputed condition that one had to tell all one's sins to one priest—not some to one and the rest to another.

[10] The best discussion of the definition and purpose of the genre is in Michaud-Quantin, *Sommes de casuistique*, 68–72, 82n., 86–90, 95–97. Cf. Charlotte Zimmerman, *Die deutsche Beichte vom 9 Jahrhundert bis zur Reformation*, University of Leipzig Dissertation (Weida i. Thür, 1934), 8–48; *Supplementum*, "Confessio 1," 10–12. In the mid-eleventh century Adelmann von Lüttich opposed the general absolution often joined to the general confession on the grounds that it interfered with discipline: "Adelmann verurteilt dieses Vorgehen als einen Missbrauch und eine Irreführung des ungebildeten Volkes. Es sei dadurch die Meinung aufgekommen, dass auf diese Weise alle schweren Sünden ohne besondere Beichte wergeben würden. *Die leichte Art der Vergebung gefährde die sittliche Ordnung*" (Ludwig Ott, "Das Opusculum des Hl. Thomas . . . *De forma absolutionis*," 109–111 [italics added]).

summarized by the *Libellus de modo poenitendi*, which asserts that it is good for the remission of venial and forgotten mortal sins and teaches the *"rudes"* to identify sins and distinguish among them. Just such a public ritual is *The Great Confession of Easter*, inserted into the Diocese of Lisieux's manual for priests, which the Bishop commanded his parish clergy to own and use. This general confession begins by implying one of the oldest functions of the institutions of forgiveness, the maintenance of the purity of Eucharistic devotion: "Good people, today you ought and are obliged to receive the Holy Sacrament of the holy Church, the precious body of our Lord Jesus Christ . . . ." And it concludes with a general absolution, carefully worded so that it cannot be mistaken for sacramental absolution, but still holding out a limited forgiveness: "And by the authority entrusted to me," the priest declares, "I absolve you from all your sins, whether in thought word or deed, that you have committed unintentionally [*negligenter*]."[11] In-between this statement of purpose and the concluding general absolution there is a very ordinary list of sins designed to stimulate awareness and remorse through public recitation.

More famous, widely published, and influential, however, was the *Modus confitendi* of Andreas de Escobar: it is the best example of the genre. Andreas begins by urging the importance to every penitent of "this general confession," which, according to the Master of the Sentences, has great power for the remission of mortal, venial, and forgotten sins and brings to mind the actual sins one has committed. For this reason, we are told, Andreas— monk, bishop, and Roman penitentiary—offers this general confession, "which contains all sins" (some editions modestly put it "almost all") collected from the fathers. They are listed as succinctly as possible, he tells us, because he has treated sin more extensively in his longer *Lumen confessorum*, a work that for some reason, as we have seen, was never published in its entirety. The goal of brevity brings out all the characteristics of Andreas's legalistic mind. Mnemonic devices of the most banal sort abound. "SALIGIA" will help the penitent remember the names of the seven

---

11 [Poeniteas cito], *Libellus de modo poenitendi*, A5b (cf. [Poeniteas cito], *Confessionale pro scholasticis*, B2a–B6b); *Manuale sacerdotum secundum usum lexouiensem*, 113a; *La Grant confession de pasques* (Caillaut: Paris, c. 1492), A5a–A6a.

deadly sins (Superbia, Avaritia, Luxuria, Ira, Gula, Invidia, Accidia), and "VAGOT" the five senses (Visus, Auditus, Gustus, Odor, Tactus). The Ten Commandments are contained in a popular verse that begins, "Unum crede Deum, nec vane iura per ipsum." But while Andreas mentions many sins, he does nothing more than list them. Under avarice there is a rather puzzling collection, from a casuist's point of view, as the text provides a mixture of less easily defined sins such as love of wealth or stinginess of alms, and more familiar offenses such as simony, theft, and fraud. The collection of sins under lust is as bizzare as the stilted language describing them: "Likewise I have sinned in the sin of fornication and lust: for by enjoyment and rumination on the gluttony and pleasure of the body I have had physical pollutions; with lustful words, touches, embraces, and kisses; and at times I have known and enjoyed women foully with indecent acts; and if not in act nevertheless in thought, and thus I have desired to perform and commit adultery, incest, rape, and sins against nature." Neither sensitive nor profound, this section must nevertheless have caught even the most hardened reader's attention. Andreas ends by making it clear that he intends his *Modus confitendi* as a generally useful preparation for auricular confession. Thus he appends a common formula in which the penitent admits his guilt —*dico meam culpam*—to all his sins, asks pardon for them, and finally petitions God, the saints, the Holy Roman Church, and the authority of the keys for strength to persevere and for a good death. Andreas's general confession is thus designed to aid the conscientious penitent examine his conscience before sacramental confession; and it is evident that this unsurpassably popular manual understands one principal thing about a good confession: it must be complete.[12]

DANGERS

But the unfettered cultivation of self-knowledge and rumination on sins held terrible dangers, and clerical writers, especially theologians, were anxious to prescribe limits and remedies. John Eck, for example, argues that while examination of conscience is necessary, and was practiced in the ancient church, one must

[12] Andreas de Escobar, *Modus confitendi*, A2a–A3a; B1b–B2a. For the history of the mnemonic SALIGIA, see Morton W. Bloomfield, *The Seven Deadly Sins* (Lansing, Mich., 1952), 86–89, 106–107, 117–118.

beware of excesses. A brooding and anxious search for sins leads only to the suffering of consciences, Eck warns; and he notes that this kind of vice is familiar to such writers on the spiritual life as St. Bernard and Gerson. But in calling for the observance of a just mean here he does not fail to stress the importance of a diligent examination, and he places himself squarely in the traditions of confessional literature by suggesting numerous categories of sin for the penitent's consideration, so that he will forget nothing when it comes time to confess.[13]

Even more sensitive than Eck to the problems of the scrupulous conscience is the fourteenth century Dominican author of the *Consolation of Theology*, Johannes von Dambach. To those consciences depressed and perplexed by the burdensome requirement of a complete confession, Johannes offers comfort in a variety of ways. Not all details of sins need be told, he advises, but only circumstances that change a sin's gravity. Furthermore, while the shame of telling one's sins to another is a salutary deterrent and should not be an excuse to conceal pertinent information, there are cases where the troubled conscience may omit something so as not to become embroiled in insoluble tangles. For the strong such an omission might be sinful; but for the weak even the requirement of a full examination of conscience must be less seriously understood. The spiritual authorities, Johannes von Dambach continues, all advise the scrupulous against too severe an assault on their consciences. "Indeed, if a scrupulous man were to confess according to all those things that have been written for confessions, he well might need to keep a confessor in his purse." Thus in the examination of conscience before confession the scrupulous person can omit some difficulty when he fears he will become embroiled in an erring conscience. For it is presumptuous to trust too much in the goodness of one's own confession:

> Indeed, however much some strive to justify themselves before God through the manner of their confessing, none should presume they can satisfy divine justice. For that reason it is sometimes necessary—especially in the case of scrupulosity— to leave something to simple mercy, in the spirit of humility, and hope trustingly in the Lord.[14]

Men like Johannes von Dambach, Gerson, and Eck exemplify medieval spirituality's attempt to broaden and humanize the

[13] Schauerte, *Busslehre des Eck*, 162–166.
[14] von Dambach, *Consolatio theologiae*, XIV, 8, 9; XIV, 18, 10–11.

institutional life of the church. They saw that it was vulnerable to legalism and formalism. They tried to correct it. The paths to a more spiritual understanding of the way to forgiveness are varied, but they all go in the same general direction and it is a direction that the sixteenth century reformers will follow as well. These points of contact with Protestant spirituality are as significant as the differences that are so apparent between the revolutionary solutions of the Reformation and the merely revisionist solutions of the middle ages and the Catholic Reformation. And we cannot understand the practice and theory of sacramental confession in the later middle ages unless we recognize that problems of conscience—its suffering and consolation—were central concerns of orthodox medieval doctors.

Nevertheless it would be seriously misleading to imply that this subtle confrontation with the problems of scrupulosity dominated discussion of the examination of conscience. It is possible that Andreas de Escobar was aware of the torments of perplexed penitents just as his contemporary Jean Gerson was, but there is little evidence of such a sensitivity in Andreas's writings. Furthermore, even the authors who took up the problems of the conscience burdened with the enumeration of sins did not propose a root and branch solution. These men were attentive to the needs of the pusillanimous; but they also had the hardened sinner on their minds. None of them advocated a lax examination of conscience. None of them released the penitent from his obligation to look at himself in that awesomely revealing mirror of sinners, which was to contain, as Andreas de Escobar put it, all, or almost all, sins. The penitent was to examine himself, his own individual sins, his own peculiar vices, in order to expose them to the priest. That burden might be softened, but it could never be totally dispensed with.

Indeed, the mind of the hierarchical, sacramental church was far from a reform that would threaten the cherished goal of completeness. The *Peycht Spigel*, for example, offers a telling criticism of the practice of a "general" confession, not because it engenders scrupulosity but because its misuse can lead to inadequate realization of one's sins. Thus the author complains that there are too many general confessions both in practice and in print. They are almost worthless, he says, because they ignore the circumstances of sins and do not elicit either shame or fear. In brief, they are too obscure:

That is a blind confession, which no one understands. It is as if someone carried around a covered dish and said, "I'm carrying something and nobody sees it or can guess what is inside."

The harm done by a vague manual of general confession is far surpassed, the *Peycht Spigel* continues, by the dangerous habit of making an imprecise or obscure confession to a priest. It is the priest, therefore, who is to be blamed first for accepting such a confession. In contrast to this intolerable laxity, a conscientious confessor asks about the circumstances of the penitent's life and sins. For the author of the *Peycht Spigel* the good confessor, as we have seen, is a special kind of priest who will frankly censure a penitent for his lack of application to the work of confessing. The good confessional manual does the same, and its list of sins for the examination of conscience is necessarily long and elaborate: for men and their sins are too complex and too different to get them all in a few pages. Even at that the author notes that his own manual has no sections on investigation of sins according to different professions and statuses, which would require a whole other book. Thus the penitent is to examine his conscience according to all possible categories, and he is urged to consider especially the much neglected nine sins against one's neighbor and the first two commandments of the Decalogue. For the way is narrow and few find it. Good confession involves childlike submission; and you will be held accountable, the author sternly warns, for every useless word; nor will you find that all ignorance is excusable. These are familiar yet sobering thoughts; but their purpose amply justifies their harsh tone. For it is not enough, we are told, to go to a physician and say, "I'm sick." He must know the details of your illness if he is going to cure you.[15] The premise is as old as the medical metaphor; the short manuals and the long summas agree that if you are to be healed you must, to the best of your ability, tell everything.

AGGRAVATING CIRCUMSTANCES

To be complete, the examination of conscience must discover not only all mortal sins, but also their "aggravating circumstances," which must be confessed. This means that the penitent must tell the priest anything about the sin that makes it more blameworthy and offensive to God's law. It is customary to enu-

[15] *Peycht Spigel*, A2b, C5a–C7a.

merate these circumstances by resorting, once again, to one or both of two didactic jingles. The longer contains around fourteen categories, as, for example, in the following widely used version:

Aggrauat ordo, locus, persona, scientia, tempus,
Etas, conditio, numerus, mora, copia, causa,
Et modus in culpa, status altus, lucta pusilla.

Sin becomes more serious according to order, place,
   person, knowlege, time,
Age, condition, number, duration, wealth, motive,
And manner of sinning, high status, and weak resistance.[16]

The *Astesana* comments sensibly that for brevity's sake this verse is better left unexplicated, especially since, as it notes, all the circumstances can be encompassed in the shorter and even more popular verse, which is found in the venerable *Raymundina*:[17]

Quis, quid, vbi, per quos, quotiens, cur, quomodo, quando,
Quilibet obseruet, animae medicamina dando.

And we are even fortunate enough to have a sixteenth century English rendering (of a slightly different version which omits "how many"):

Who, what, and where, by what helpe and by whose;
Why, how, and when, doe many things disclose.[18]

Originally criteria for verisimilitude—to help the rhetorician make narrative credible by directing his attention to the particu-

---

[16] "Poeniteas cito," *PL*, 207, 1154, lines 42–44 (which, as in all versions, omits *persona*). Cf. Columbi, *Confession generale*, A4b; [Gerson], *Directoire*, Q7b; [Poeniteas cito], *Penitentiarius*, A2b; [Poeniteas cito], *Libellus de modo poenitendi*, B1a; [Poeniteas cito], *Summa penitentie*, C1b–C2b; [Poeniteas cito], *Penitentionarius. de confessione*, A3a; [Poeniteas cito], *Confessionale pro scholasticis*, B1a–b; [Poeniteas cito], *Penitencionarius* (Latin and German), 3a–b, whose German rendering is: "Gelogenheyt offte schuldt gebirt/ Da von dye sunde vil grosser wirt/ Orden kunst czeyt vnde stadt/ Altter weil czal gutter rath/ Dy weysse vnd kleiness wyder streben/ Den sunden beschwerung geben."

[17] *Astesana*, V, 7; *Raymundina*, III, 34, 29, p. 463. A common variant of the list quoted here substitutes *quibus auxiliis* for *per quos, quotiens*, thus giving seven instead of eight.

[18] D. W. Robertson, Jr., "A Note on the Classical Origin of 'Circumstances' in the Medieval Confessional," *Studies in Philology*, 43 (1946), 6–14.

lars of action—these eight circumstances are found in Cicero and transmitted to the medieval world by Boethius. They are described by Victorinus and appear in twelfth century theological works and commentaries on Cicero and Boethius. The *Raymundina* has eight circumstances and St. Thomas only seven; but the popularity and authority of both Thomas and Raymond assured the wide usage of one or the other. The literature on penance interestingly attempts to assign authorship to these verses. The *Astesana* attributes them to Cicero and Boethius; the *Angelica* traces them to the pseudo-Augustine and ultimately to Aristotle; Engelhardus Kunhofer cites the *Raymundina*; J. L. Vivaldus finds them twice in the works of St. Thomas, notes their origins in Cicero's rhetoric, and cites variations on them by Aristotle as well as Raymond; and Godescalc Rosemondt apparently knew no instance of them before the fourteenth century, for he ascribes them to Petrus de Palude.[19] Whatever their origins, real or fancied, their relationship to the Roman rhetorical tradition is singularly apt: the authority of classical antiquity, its facile appropriation for Christian uses, the ethical basis of rhetoric itself, and the peculiar emphasis of the literature of confession on propriety of forms—all of these make the circumstances a modest model of the way medieval intellectuals used the pagan heritage for their practical ends.

The aggravating circumstances are supposed to be generally applicable to any kind of sin, but the habit of explaining "how" as referring to natural or unnatural leads one to suspect that sexual sins were particularly kept in mind. When Gerson decides to illustrate them, however, he specifically mentions sins of violence. Thus he explains that "who" means young or old, cleric or layman, married or single; "what" refers to whether it involves sacred objects; "where" asks whether the sin occurred in a sa-

---

[19] Robertson, "Circumstances," 6–14; Johannes Gründel, *Die Lehre von den Umständen der menschlichen Handlung im Mittelalter*, Beiträge zur Geschichte der Philosophie und Theologie des Mittelalters, vol. 39, no. 5 (Münster, 1963), 38–39, 395–396, 418, 650–651; *Astesana*, V, 7; *Angelica*, "Confessio sacramentalis," 23; Kunhofer, *Confessionale*, C3b–C4a; Vivaldus, *Aureum opus*, 135a; Rosemondt, *Confessionale*, 1, 1–2, fol. 2b. For an early literary usage in Walter of Theouranne's *Vita Karoli*, with Professor Ross's detailed explication, see Galbert of Bruges, *The Murder of Charles the Good, Count of Flanders*, tr. and ed. by James Bruce Ross, Records of Civilization, Sources and Studies, ed. by W.T.H. Jackson, rev. ed. (New York, Evanston, Ill., and London, 1967), 3–75.

cred, public, or private place; "by what means or aids" asks whether it was committed with a sword, fist, or stick; "why" searches for the motive, for example vengeance or theft; "how" seeks to know whether a blow was sharp or gentle; and "when" refers to the possibility that the sin was committed in a holy season, such as a feast day or during Lent. Gerson's choice of sins of violence may be somewhat original, but his explanations are commonplace. The authors who advise the penitent on how to examine his conscience are, in fact, fundamentally agreed on the meaning and necessity of telling the aggravating circumstances. They are deeply concerned with scandal, for example, and generally want the penitent to realize that he must confess it if his sin is notorious. Motives are also important—St. Antoninus says "why" is the most important of the eight circumstances. There is also general agreement that sacred things, times, and places are relevant to confessing, and that the higher one's status or office, the worse the sin. In addition, pastoral authorities feel that the more intentional, the worse the offense, and that those who suffer severe temptation are less culpable than those who do not. And although it is sometimes omitted from the list of aggravating circumstances, "how often" takes a prominent place in the search for a complete confession.[20]

It is rare to find novel opinions or disputes in the discussion of the aggravating circumstances. Common interpretations were routinely repeated or ignored, even though the author of the *Peycht Spigel* thought that inquiry into the circumstances of sins was not all it might have been. Nevertheless, it is obvious that the

---

[20] Gerson, *De Confessione mollitiei* (appendix), Du Pin, II, 456C–D; cf. Glorieux, *Oeuvres*, I, 49, *Pro Poenitentia septem psalmi*; Antoninus, *Confessionale—Defecerunt*, 4; *Compendium theologiae*, Du Pin, I, 413D (cf. Glorieux, *Oeuvres*, I, 41); Andreas de Escobar, *Modus confitendi*, B2a–b; idem, *Interrogationes*, B3b–B4a; de Butrio, *Directorium*, appendix; de Chamis, *Confessionale*, III, 1–2, C8b–D5a; Guido de Monte Rocherii, *Manipulus curatorum*, II, 3, 5, fol. 80b; Dietterle, "Die Summae confessorum," *ZKG*, 24 (1903), 528–529. For vernacular versions and explanations, see [Gerson?], *Directoire*, P8b–Q3b; *Peycht Spigel*, B6b–B7a; Falk, ed., *Beichtbüchlein* (Augsburg, 1504), 84–85; Joseph Fritz, "Zwei unbekannte Bearbeitungen des Modus confitendi von Andreas Hispanus," *Der Katholik*, 4th ser. 10 (1912), 64; Stephan Lanzkranna, *Himelstrass*, ch. 6, fol. 17a; A. Faren, *La Pratique*, A6a–A7a. For other variations, see Alain de Lille, *Liber poenitentialis*, PL, 210, 285C–288C; Jodocus Winshemius, *Institutiones*, D4a; *Hortulus anime*, fol. 155h. For circumstances applied to sexual sins, see *Manuale parrochialium sacerdotum*, V, B1b–B2a.

circumstances, like the interrogations, raise problems; and thus it is not too surprising to find that the *Sylvestrina*, in an interesting passage, provides a measure of dissent as it attempts to protect the penitent from too severe an interpretation of "how many" imposed by its rival Franciscan summas, the *Angelica*, the *Supplementum*, and especially the *Rosella*. Sylvester says he follows his fellow Dominican St. Thomas who, unlike the *Angelica* and *Rosella*, does not put great stock in counting. St. Thomas takes it up only once according to Sylvester, and there he specifies that one is obliged to confess the number of sins only so far as a frail human who adequately prepares is capable. Sylvester certainly knew how often the confessor was told to have his penitent calculate number by estimating how often per day or week a sin had occurred and how long in days, weeks, months, or years that sin had been habitually committed. He opposes this venture into quantification, however, as he concludes that the penitent should give a number if he can, otherwise a simple estimate will do. He also notes that at times the number is implicit in the confession itself and nothing more need be said about it. The real danger is simply willful deceit.[21]

It is, of course, no more than a measure of dissent that Sylvester offers here. He may even have exaggerated his differences with the *Rosella*. But small as it is, there is significance in this additional evidence that pastoral theology was capable of seeing the danger of too burdensome an interpretation of the completeness of the work of confession.

AMENDMENT OF LIFE

If a confession is to be a good one, however, it must be more than just complete. Mechanical recitation of all remembered sins is not enough, for all agree that a good confession must, in the broadest sense, be sincere. The penitent must be contrite and he must *intend* to stop sinning,

Now sorrow and the intention to amend are intimately, perhaps inseparably, related. Nevertheless it is necessary to delay consideration of contrition, which belongs to the more theoretical problem of the cause of forgiveness, with its complicated investigation into the degree and nature of sorrow. For contrition is elusive—difficult to define in words and identify in experience.

---

[21] *Sylvestrina*, "Confessio 1," q. 11, par. 11–12. Cf. Antoninus, *Confessional—Defecerunt*, 4.

The intention to amend, on the other hand, is somewhat more concrete: it is easier to talk about it, easier to apply criteria to detect it. Thus we shall look at "sincerity" for the moment only in terms of the intention to amend, which is more obviously a simple quality of a good confession. It is enough here to remember that a repentant heart was required for a good confession and, indeed, had been thought indispensable to forgiveness since the days of the ancient church.

No one argued that the intention to amend was a promise, as if the penitent entered into a contract in which forgiveness would be void if he did not keep his word. The confessor, in fact, may not extract a promise not to sin; and if a penitent falls into sin again, his lapse is not taken as positive proof of his deceit, even though he had said he intended to avoid all sin. A number of authors vaguely talk about theologians who teach such a rigid doctrine, and no one is exactly pleased by recidivism. But the consensus is that the sincere penitent must only intend to amend his life. How carefully such a distinction must be defined is revealed in the *Sylvestrina*, which notes that it is one thing to want to avoid sinning and quite another even to expect that one actually will. The first, the desire to avoid, belongs to the will; the second, the prediction that one will avoid, belongs to the intellect. Sylvester thinks that there are many who want to amend their lives but do not think they will be able to. They are not culpable of a bad confession. Rather, the guilty ones are those who so lack displeasure for sins and the will to change that they wish, positively, not to amend. Such hardened sinners commit mortal sin by the very act of seeking absolution. Yet even here the tolerance of frailty admits of still another distinction: it is entirely proper for someone who does not have sorrow and displeasure for his sins to go to the Sacrament of Penance so that he can arouse these emotions.[22]

Nor is Sylvester representative of the most laxist thought on this issue. In a more complicated speculation, the rationale of which will become clear in the discussion of the cause of forgiveness, many authorities argue that the intention to amend need not even be a positive one. These theologians believe that honest reception of the Sacrament of Penance requires nothing more than that the penitent *not intend to sin* at the time. Dishonesty or insincerity is thought to occur only if the penitent "places an ob-

[22] *Sylvestrina*, "Confessio 1," q. 21, par. 25.

stacle" in the path of the sacramental grace—that is, if he actually intends to sin at the time he confesses and is absolved. The psychological merit of such a theory is obvious: for it is much easier to be certain while you are confessing that you are not positively intending to commit a sin than to know whether your intention to stop sinning is truly sincere. But it is of the highest importance to the understanding of the institutions of forgiveness at the end of the middle ages to realize that this "mildest" of opinions was not the accepted one. As Gerson puts it, the opinion that the sinner is obliged to have an actual intention to stop sinning is more probable and safer.[23]

Thus in the matter of the penitent's intention the mean was again observed. The confessor might not demand any hard and fast promise from a penitent guaranteeing he would not sin in the future. Nevertheless, the penitent was expected to have a firm purpose of avoiding sin and its occasions. True to this notion of the mean, requiring sincerity while recognizing man is weak, is the prescription for those impenitent souls who admit they are inadequately sorry and unprepared to give up their favorite sins or to make restitution. Such a person cannot, of course, be absolved, even though he confesses his sins completely. On the other hand, neither is he to be sent away in despair. He should be admonished, encouraged, and told to perform some pious act, not as a penance but rather in the hope that its performance will lead him to eventual reform; as Gerson puts it, until "God deigns to enlighten him into the true way." Since the twelfth century

---

[23] For the doctrine of the obex, see below, "Sorrow and the Keys: From Attrition to Contrition" (p. 263ff.). Cf. Lupi Rebello, *Fructus*, 25; Gerson, *Regulae morales*, 101, Du Pin, III 103B. [Gerson?], *Directoire*, A4b–A6b, argues that those who return after Easter to their old sins offend against the prerequisite of a "firm purpose of not relapsing or returning to their sins," and asserts they should not commune at Easter! Such an opinion, however, does not necessarily mean the confession of a relapsed penitent was necessarily invalid: we should rather understand this rigorous stand as the complaint of a moralist against the laxity of the theologians' definition of firm purpose. See also Stephan Lanzkranna, *Himelstrass*, ch. 49, fol. 153b, which speaks of "ain gantzen fürtsatz sich hynfür mit der hilf gotes zehüten vor allñ tod sünden"; Maillard, *La Confession*, A2b–A3a; idem, *La Confession generale*, A2a; Winshemius, *Institutiones*, A4b–A5a; [Poeniteas cito], *Confessionale pro scholasticis*, A1b, B2a–B2b; [Poeniteas cito], *Libellus de modo poenitendi*, A2b.

confessors had been advised to deal with the impenitent in this tolerant fashion.[24]

REITERATION

In this scholastic tradition it was only natural for authorities to establish negative, disqualifying criteria. Thus there is a definition of a bad confession, which gives a more precise notion of the good. In brief, the writers on confession want to know in what specific cases confession is invalid and must therefore be repeated in its entirety. The most important ideas on this subject are summarized by St. Antoninus of Florence, and there is little or no difference between him and the *Raymundina, Astesana, Angelica, Sylvestrina,* Andreas de Escobar, Bartholomaeus de Chaimis, or Antonius de Butrio. Antoninus finds four common cases in which the penitent is required to repeat this confession: the first two cases have to do with failures on the part of the penitent, the third and fourth with failures on the part of the priest. They are called the four cases for reiteration.

First, if a penitent intentionally omits a mortal sin or a sin that he has a probable doubt is mortal, then he must re-confess entirely because his confession was not complete. This does not include, however, the case in which a penitent discovers he has forgotten a sin in his last confession; then he would only need to confess the forgotten sin at the next opportunity, not repeat the whole confession. Second, a penitent must reiterate his whole confession if he has failed to do the penance given him by the priest either through contempt or culpable negligence. But if he forgets a penance and then later remembers it, he may then perform it and save his last confession from being invalid, unless a time limit for completion has been imposed. (Antoninus does not seem to approve of such a practice, however, for he advises a second confessor to assume that the time limit imposed by the first referred to the duration of the penance and not to a specific period outside of which the penance would be worthless.)

The third case involves confession to a priest lacking power to absolve a particular penitent. The most usual problem here arose from the custom of reserving certain serious sins to higher eccle-

---

[24] Gerson, *Opus tripartitum*, II, Du Pin, I, 446B–C; Amann, "Pénitence," *DTC*, 12[1] 896. See also Antoninus *Confessionale—Defecerunt*, 6; Rosemondt, *Confessionale*, 7, 90, fol. 139a–b.

siastical authorities, but any impediment to the exercise of the key of power—excommunication or lack of jurisdiction, for example—could cause invalidity. Interestingly enough, Antoninus advises confessors not to pry too curiously into the penitent's past confessions: unless it is well known that a previous confessor did not have the authority to absolve, he cautions, it is not necessary to conduct an investigation to find invalidating circumstances. Fourth, a confession must be repeated if it has been made to a priest who has inadequate knowledge, and this case Antoninus describes as "difficult and intricate." His judgment was, as we shall see presently, an understatement.

Finally, Antoninus feels compelled to take up two cases that others also add to the usual four. Some doctors, he tells us, think that if someone makes a complete confession but is disposed not to abstain from sin, he must repeat his confession, but this cannot be forced on him since there is disagreement. And well there might be disagreement, for the implication that lapsing into the old sins invalidates their previous forgiveness is not a salutary contribution to consolation or a faithful reflection of opinion on the purpose of amendment. Probably what is meant here is that the intention at the time of confessing was faulty, but even that qualification does not remove all the dangers, for it was only natural to test that intention in the most obvious way—did the sinner stick to his resolve? The last case concerns a penitent whose absolution is complicated by his having been excommunicated. The difference between this and the third case is not clear; Antoninus simply advises the safer choice of confessing again.[25]

JUDGING CONFESSORS

Should we take these authorities seriously when they teach that penitents are supposed to examine the intellectual credentials of their confessors? Like speculation on the key of knowl-

[25] Antoninus, *Confessionale—Defecerunt*, 6; *Angelica*, "Confessio sacramentalis," 20 (which denies reiteration is necessary in the sixth case); cf. ibid., 8–19, and "Confessio 5," 10; *Sylvestrina*, "Confessio 1," par. 4–5; *Astesana*, V, 18, *Raymundina*, III [5]4, p. 484; de Butrio, *Speculum de confessione*, II, 2, C3b–C6a; Faren, *La Pratique*, A2a–b; [Gerson?], *La Confession*, A3b–A4a; [Poeniteas cito], *Libellus de modo poenitendi*, A5b; Alain de Lille, *Liber poenitentialis*, PL, 210, 300B; *Eruditorium penitentiale*, D3a–D4a; Jacobus de Clusa, *Confessionale*, C. 6, A3a–A4b; Foresti, *Confessionale*, fol. 3a–b; Rosemondt, *Confessionale*, 7, 82, fol. 133b; [Gerson?], *Directoire*, S6a–T3a.

edge, the fourth case for reiteration—the ignorance of the priest —invites questions about the sensitive relationship between the power of the priest and his intellectual qualifications. It seems almost inconceivable that these conservative authors really wanted such an inquiry. For in a world in which anticlericalism is endemic, the specter of Donatism—the belief that sinful priests do not have the power to administer valid sacraments—is always fearful. They must have been aware of it. For Donatistic doctrines strike at the heart of both functions of the Sacrament of Penance—consolation and social control. If the penitent must himself certify the knowledge and hence the power of the priest, he is placed at the mercy of insoluble doubts about the validity of his absolution. And to invite constant scrutiny of the clergy seems to make effective authority and discipline well nigh impossible. Why, then, raise the question at all?

Clearly the motive is moralistic and hence disciplinary: the limited willingness to raise the question of the incompetence of the priest is rooted in the desire to make control more effective. In the first place, moralists find bad priests intolerable. And discipline is pretty worthless if it does not extend to those who are primarily responsible for its observance. Furthermore, it should be evident that sanctions in this system of control still depend on the cooperation of the individual conscience and not simply the commands of an authoritarian clergy. The system works on guilt and responsibility; it will not work, for example, if the forum of penance is run by total incompetents who forgive indiscriminately, and one way to guard against this kind of disaster is to make it clear that such a priest is not legitimately performing his office. The penitent must therefore be made to shun such incompetence, put it out of business, and return to the healthy control of a competent priest. At any rate, that is a logical reconstruction of the thinking behind this requirement of the good confession.

If the whole problem has any institutional significance, we might reasonably expect pastoral theology to answer some simple questions. For example, how ignorant can a priest be and still validly administer this sacrament? Or, under what circumstances must it be admitted that a priest's incompetence is so blatant and debilitating that no one may excuse himself from going elsewhere for the forgiveness of sins? The answers, however, remain unsatisfying in a most puzzling way.

Jacobus de Clusa considers the choice of a confessor a moral issue, which he discusses in characteristically grave language. He urges penitents not to go to young and inexperienced confessors. "I do not know of a more difficult and dangerous work than the office of hearing confessions," he warns, "but many do not realize this." For while it is easy to listen to a confession and grant absolution, the correct use of the keys, as Christ intended, is a terrifying responsibility. Some are given this charge to whom one would not entrust the care of donkeys. But whereas the best bodily physician is always selected, any physician of souls will apparently suffice.[26] Jacobus is obviously convinced of the seriousness of this decision, then, but he does not specify the failings in confessors that should cause penitents to avoid them.

Godescalc Rosemondt's clarifications are at least amusing. If one knowingly chooses a confessor who does not hear well or does not understand the language the penitent will confess in, then the whole confession must be repeated. If the priest falls asleep, the confession must also be repeated. But Godescalc is apparently anxious to save the penitent from scrupulous doubts, for he entertains the possibility that one might not realize his confessor did not speak his language, had fallen asleep, or was deaf. In that case, of course, ignorance of these failings excuses the penitent from confessing again. On the other hand, there is one real obligation imposed on the penitent: if he realizes that his confessor is not paying attention—if the questions are irrelevant, for example—then he must find another priest and confess again. And lest we think that we are dealing with Godescalc's unique sense of humor, Jacobus Foresti solemnly brands those who knowingly confess to a sleeping or deaf priest guilty of mortal sin.[27]

The *Angelica*, on the other hand, is both serious and vague. Invalidation of confession for the priest's ignorance is said to occur when a penitent knowingly confesses to a priest who does not know how to bind and loose from sin. It is difficult to imagine what such a rule could mean; it is much like the common advice to seek an expert rather than an inexpert confessor. One suspects that Angelus's vagueness may even have been intentional; and it is not inconceivable that some authors simply felt they had to keep all four of the traditional cases for reiteration, but in effect

[26] Jacobus de Clusa, *Confessionale*, c. 3, A2b–A3a.
[27] Rosemondt, *Confessionale*, 7, 82, fol. 133b; Foresti, *Confessionale*, fol. 3a–b.

eliminated the fourth case by thoroughly obscuring it. Thus the *Supplementum* is no clearer. In his clarification of the *Pisanella*'s terse statement—"if he did not know how to distinguish"—Nicolaus argues that the essential power of the keys exists in jurisdiction and not in knowledge. But he goes on to charge penitents who purposely choose a priest less adequate in "knowledge and conscience" with the obligation to repeat that confession, which was "not pleasing to God and invalid." Indeed, even the *Sylvestrina* is evasive: it merely identifies this impediment as a notable ignorance that renders the priest unable to distinguish between mortal and venial sin.[28]

Godescalc Rosemondt extricated himself from the dangers of judging priests by interpreting the case in the fundamentally absurd terms of confessors who were asleep, deaf, or incapable of understanding the penitent's language. Angelus de Clavasio, Nicolaus de Ausimo, and Sylvester obscured and virtually ignored the problem. The most sensible response of all came from Raymond of Peñaforte and Antonius de Butrio, whose prudent circumspection undoubtedly provides a key to the understanding of this dilemma. Raymond and Antonius stipulate that if one thinks his confessor is "inexpert," the penitent must ask his permission to seek a more "expert" priest.[29] Clerical authority is preserved. The likelihood of the case arising seems greater; it might, for example, be revealed in the course of confession that the technicalities of the situation were too great for the confessor. And there is little apparent encouragement here of uncontrolled judgment of the holders of the keys. Yet the intention of the fourth case is preserved: the penitent must take it upon himself to insure in honesty that his priest is adequately representing the authority of the church in binding and loosing sins.

All things considered, however, even the brief opinion of Raymond and Antonius is not fully satisfying and we have seen ample cause for the judgment of Antoninus that this case was difficult and intricate. Was the problem real? Were confessors dozing off? Were there priests so notoriously ignorant that it was

---

[28] *Angelica*, "Confessio sacramentalis," 9; *Sylvestrina*, "Confessio 1," q. 3, par. 4–5; *Supplementum*, "Confessio 2," 8.

[29] Antoninus, *Confessionale—Defecerunt*, 6; de Butrio, *Speculum de confessione*, C6a; *Raymundina*, III, [5]4, p. 484. "Poeniteas cito, *PL*, 207, 1155, ll. 52–53; B. Kurtscheid, *A History of the Seal of Confession*, tr. by F. A. Marks, ed. by Arthur Preuss (St. Louis and London, 1927), 78–79.

common knowledge that they did not know how to "bind and loose" or tell a mortal from a venial sin? Did any penitents suffer doubts about the intellectual competence of their confessors? Were the flames of anticlericalism fed by those who called on the faithful to make sure they confessed only to experts? Probably no one will ever know.

THE SHAME OF THE CONFESSIONAL

We have seen that there was general agreement on the defining characteristics of a good and a bad confession. Everyone knew it had to be complete and sincere. Everyone knew that in some cases it could be so bad that it had to be repeated in its entirety.

There is less agreement, however, on what kind of emotional experience confessing sins to a priest should be. Differences here may not be explicit or immediately apparent; the interests of harmony and the service of the mean often temper the language of pastoral and moral theologians. But surely a great gulf exists between Andreas de Escobar, so much the canonist, and Jean Gerson, so much the practitioner of the cure of souls. And sometimes close analysis reveals almost as great a gulf between conflicting opinions within the same author. Whenever we find evidence on the experience of confessing, however, its importance to our understanding of the social and psychological functions of the Sacrament of Penance is self-evident. On one hand we have the attack on scrupulosity; here authors stress the dangers of pious excess. They are wary of an intemperate reliance on the complete enumeration of sins. They are suspicious of the worried search for conditions invalidating sacramental forgiveness. On the other hand, we see the affirmation, even the exaltation, of a personal sense of shame. Shame is a tool of discipline and a potential barrier to consolation. It also occupies a prominent position in the history of penance, in the literature of the late middle ages, and in the criticism of Rome in the Protestant Reformation. For all of these reasons, then, the insight it provides into the experience of confessing takes on particular significance.

A venerable tradition, which no one seemed willing to challenge, held that shame before the priest was indeed desirable in the confessional. As we saw in the historical introduction, the considerable and consistent lightening of penitential exercises led many theologians to conclude in the early middle ages that the act of confessing should itself be considered a penance; in that way they apparently felt they could reply to the accusation of laxism. For it was obvious that in instituting private confession, the church had eliminated the grim experience of public shame attached to the expiation demanded in canonical penance. As a substitute, ecclesiastical authorities offered the shame of the penitent before the priest. And these opinions are ancient. They appear at the very inception of the literature of the confessional with the manual of Alain de Lille, who explains that one of the causes for the institution of the confession of sins was that it incites shame. Furthermore, sinners could not avoid shame: for it was popularly taught and believed that if one did not disclose his sins to a priest in private, they would be disclosed to all—saints, angels, and all creation—at the Last Judgment. As the "Poeniteas cito" puts it: "Confession will hide sins at the Last Judgment so that neither God nor the devil nor he who comitted them will see them." This sentiment, which was already current in the eighth century, became a commonplace. Another commonplace, this one taken from Augustine, was designed to shame people out of fleeing from the humiliation of avowal. As the *Speculum aureum* explains it: "There are many who feel no shame at sinning but are ashamed to do penance. Oh, incredible insanity."[30]

Certainly there was no intention, or even a possibility, of reviving the old reliance on public shame and expiation. Nevertheless, even the authors we associate with a more enlightened pastoral concern cannot escape completely from this mentality. Johann Nider may have been a theologian of consolation, but he found no difficulty in affirming that shame had its place as a work of satisfaction, diminishing the suffering of purgatory.[31] For Guido de Monte Rocherii, shame is a great punishment and a salutary one; whoever is ashamed for the sake of Christ is worthy of pardon. Godescalc Rosemondt shares these general sentiments, and, like Guido, is quick to point out that he is not talking about the shame that leads to the hiding of sins. You must have shame—but

[30] Alain de Lille, *Liber poenitentialis*, PL, 210, 299A; Amann, "Pénitence," *DTC*, 12¹, 888; Jacobus de Gruytroede, *Speculum aurem*, B3b. Cf. [Poeniteas cito], *Libellus de modo poenitendi*, B2a, which asserts the poem means "quod nec deus nec demon id est diabolus nec ipse peccator posset videre illa"; and [Poeniteas cito], *Summa penitentie*, C4a, which says, more circumspectly, "quod deus suum peccatum haud videt."

[31] Nider, *Expositio decalogi*, III, 9B, 08a.

not too much. Once again pastoral care tries to strike a mean. Thus it is no accident that Guido's judgment that shame must be for Christ's sake follows his demand that a penitent feel both sorrow and joy in the confession of sins. Like the thief at the right hand of Christ, one must at once feel sorrow for his sins and joy at their forgiveness.[32] Medieval thinkers lived easily with that kind of paradox, and the shame of the confessional enjoyed such a paradoxical position. In one sense it was considered a menace. In another sense it was held in mighty esteem. But it is important to stress that even when shame is esteemed, it never becomes the central element in discipline. Shame before God is more frequently extolled than shame before the priest. And shame before the priest is itself restricted to the secrecy and privacy of the confessional. Shame may reinforce guilt; but shame never displaces guilt. Social control through sacramental confession can only be effective if religious values have been internalized, so that sins will cause pain and repentance will be sincere even if no other human is looking.

CONCLUSION: THE WORK OF THE PENITENT

Once again let us turn to the *Peycht Spigel* to take us beyond commonplace rules and themes—the definitions, mnemonic devices, cases for reiteration, and minimal standards—and try to find in its instruction on the good confession a different kind of understanding of pre-Reformation attitudes. It does not deal in novelities and it does not represent the authority of theology or hierarchy. Indeed, few would have bothered to disagree with it. But it talks in simple language about a good penitent's experience, and for that reason it is invaluable.

To begin his discussion of a good confession, the author of the *Peycht Spigel* asserts the most fundamental philososphical assumption underlying the Roman Catholic practice of the forgiveness of sins: "Thus you must awaken, and find in yourself, a true contrition, with your free will and the help of God." Responsible cooperation with unmerited grace is the greatest and yet the most indispensable of all the paradoxes in the literature. The penitent is then told to examine his conscience, uncover every mortal sin for which he has never been contrite, and note aggra-

[32] Guido de Monte Rocherii, *Manipulus curatorum*, II, 3, 6, fol. 84a–b; Rosemondt, *Confessionale*, 7, 84, fol. 134a–135b; *Supplementum*, "Confessio 1," 14.

vating circumstances. Sorrow for sin and the intention to amend are foremost in the catalogue of necessary virtues. The penitent must feel displeasure with himself for having offended God, hate all his sins, and intend to better his life and avoid the occasions of sin. It should give the penitent pain to think that he has angered God and harmed his neighbor; he should wish he had never sinned against God and the salvation of his soul, and, if he is able, he should sigh and weep bitterly. He must also intend to confess aloud all of his sins, be contrite for all of them, and desire to confess all of them. He must renounce all evil desire, people, occupations, and gain; he must make restoration; and he must want to suffer so that he can do penance and make satisfaction. "You must also have trust in the mercy of God that He will forgive all your sins," the *Peycht Spigel* continues, and then it talks in its staccato fashion about the emotion of sorrow for sin. At mass the penitent must think often with sighs on his sins, scold and reprimand himself for having been ungrateful to God, feel remorse at his carelessness in the work of the salvation of his own soul, and be troubled that he has so often and uselessly squandered opportunities for repentance and merit.[33]

The historian is perhaps too aware in these passages of the burden placed on the sinner who is searching for repentance and justification. We think, perhaps too readily, of the agony of an Augustinian monk—Luther was in his mid-twenties when the *Peyscht Spigel* was published. The danger here, of course, is to make Luther's experience universal and find in this and other ideal pictures of the penitent's sorrow, sincerity, and complete confession the unfailing occasions for the torment of consciences. Such an interpretation surely distorts the historical and institutional realities. Even within these works, as we have been seen, there are correctives to what may appear the imposition of an impossible task. For no religious authority wanted to incite despair, and thus most of them held the consolation of the sinner consistently in mind. Nevertheless, reform of the penitent was just as consistently in mind, and everyone assumed that change had to occur in the will of the sinner, and first of all in his attitude toward sin. Thus laxism and consolation could be blended with rigorism and social control. And when the *Peycht Spigel* dwells on the need for a true sorrow and an effective intention to amend, it moves in the rigorist world of moral persuasion. Its

[33] *Peycht Spigel*, C3a.

concerns here are with inner transformation, and it bases this work of personal reform and revivification in the forum of penance.

The *Peycht Spigel* wants to root out sin, therefore, but it would never demand an unfailing change of life as proof of sincerity. Reformation of morals was on the author's mind, but cautiously. There were, however, stronger voices urging spiritual transformation—voices that found the only convincing test of the intention to amend in the actual reformation of the sinner's life. The notion that the best contrition and sincerity are expressed in a new life free from sin is a humanist commonplace, of course, and no monopoly of the medieval penitential tradition. But it did have an honored place in that tradition, it could take on a rigorist hue, and it could also look very much like the anxiety-producing theology of sinlessness that Luther rebelled against. There is a good example of this tougher attitude in the manual of Jacobus de Clusa.

Jacobus's basic lesson is that there are many confessions but few persevering penitents. As he puts it: "We see, across the breadth of the Christian world, the faithful multiplying their confessions and accepting the penances imposed upon them; but I would that they were always true and pleasing to God and that they might persevere until the end of their lives." If repentance were always sincere, he continues, then we would not see the regrettable return to sin after confession, a return that is especially hasty after Easter. Men are careful to avoid temporal harm, such as infamy, theft, sickness, and beatings, but they are much more lax when it comes to avoiding the far greater harm of sin. Why should this lamentable condition be so, he asks? Because we are unwilling to avoid the occasions of sin and because a perverse society hinders true repentance. There has been a paucity of true penitents from the beginning of the world right up to his own day, and Jacobus finds the best evidence for this fact in the plethora of divine punishments visited on mankind, punishments most clearly recorded in the Old Testament.[34]

---

[34] Jacobus de Clusa, *Confessionale*, app. 2, C2a, C4a. Even the *Supplementum* makes it absolutely clear, however, that a *recidivans* need not confess his sins again unless it is relevant to the fixing of a proper penance ("Confessio 2," 9). Furthermore, to the question "utrum vere penitens possit postea mortaliter peccare," Nicolaus answers that although it might seem that a truly repentant man would never return to his sins, all the authorities

Some of Jacobus's readers might well have responded to these views of repentance with indifference. They might have looked at them simply as the kind of thing preachers and moralists are likely to say and spend a lot of time saying. Others might have found here material to brood on. If one catalogues sins as extensively as medieval theologians did; and if one defines true repentance as amendment of life and perseverance to the end; and if one declares or hints that false repentance invalidates forgiveness; and if one nevertheless sees man as basically and helplessly sinful—then we discover a complex of doctrines that is not cheering. Failure of repentance, after all, is punished by God eternally. And the bad confession is betrayed by a return to sin.

Jacobus may have been more rigorous than most, but in one way his thought is typical. The theory of the good confession inevitably emphasized the work of the penitent and his correction. It encouraged frequent, sorrowful, sincere, and complete confession and went as far as it could in demanding moral regeneration without destroying the psychological assurance to which the Sacrament of Penance was also committed.

(Peter Lombard, Raymond of Peñaforte, Thomas Aquinas, and Petrus de Palude) say that the repentant man turns from sin at the time of his repentance; and they refer to that specific time, not to any time at all (*Supplementum*, "Penitentia 1," 4, 10).

CHAPTER IV

SIN: THE SUBJECT OF CONFESSION

The Sense of Sin

THE examination of conscience, interrogations, general confession, forms of etiquette, and the like, were all designed to get at sin. In different ways they encouraged the penitent to think about his sins, identify them, classify them, and tell them. By these means sacramental confession inculcated an attitude toward sin and the self. To be sure, all recognized that it was possible for a penitent to forget a sin, or not to realize that some act or desire was a sin. But the fundamental assumption is that the average Christian can know and weigh his sins, because the church teaches the essentials of morality and because rational man—free and responsible—can apply this teaching to his life.

Nowhere in the practice of forgiveness is the relationship between consolation and discipline more delicately balanced than in the knowledge and recitation of sin. As we shall see, one of the cornerstones of the sacramental system of consolation was complete enumeration of sins. From this work, sincerely if imperfectly performed, the penitent was to find comfort, because even if it was difficult, he had honestly tried and done his best. Yet this enumeration could hold its terrors for the penitent and work against his consolation because he might well fear that he had not done his best. For that reason the requirement of a complete confession could to some extent be mitigated, to assuage the fears and bolster the confidence of the penitent.

On the other hand, defining and telling sins was as relevant to discipline as to consolation. It represented an inventory of undesirable behavior—physical, verbal, and mental—and the ultimate goal, never to be realized, was the elimination of all items in the inventory from the lives of Christian individuals. Yet at the same time the whole notion of a complete confession could impede the very function we most directly associate with it, that is, social control. For if some vice was to be eliminated through this means, some evil corrected, it had to be a certifiable sin. If some virtue was to be encouraged, its opposite similarly had to be an identifiable sin. For the confessor did not hear a rambling tale or inquire generally about good deeds or the good life. He heard sins, asked about sins, and forgave sins. Sin is the subject of confession, and if one wanted some vice uprooted or some virtue cultivated, one had to have it defined in terms of sin so that it could be judged in the forum of penance. Given the nature of the institution of sacramental confession and the rules that governed it, therefore, it could only control things called sins.

First, to introduce certainty and relieve the anxiety of doubt, and second, to provide content to the norms this institution would enforce, there developed, predictably, a moral science. It classified offenses. It applied normative principles to life and human nature. It searched for completeness, clarity, and universality.

VARIETY

Getting at sin was a complicated task for the penitent, as we have already seen. The modern reader is bound to be struck first of all by the overwhelming detail possible in the confessor's inquiry, or the penitent's introspection into and relation of his sins. Ten or twelve categories of sin are not unusually high, and the potentiality of such a profusion of sins for unsettling even conscientious believers (perhaps especially them) is alarming. An amalgam of the usual ways of sinning, including the gifts, doctrines, faculties, virtues, counsels, and laws one can sin against, would look like this:

Ten Commandments
Seven Deadly Sins
Twelve Articles of Faith
Five Senses
Eight Beatitudes
Six or Seven Corporal Works of Mercy
Six or Seven Spiritual Works of Mercy
Four or Five Sins Crying to Heaven for Vengeance
Six Sins Against the Holy Spirit
Nine Sins Against One's Neighbor
Seven Gifts of the Holy Spirit
Four Cardinal Virtues
Three Theological Virtues
Twelve Fruits of the Holy Spirit

The first dozen categories are entirely ordinary and even the briefest manual of confession is capable of devoting almost all of its attention to the enumeration of sins covered by them.[1] Still other ways of classifying sins are possible, however: sins of thought, word, and deed; sins against the natural law; sins of omission and commission; sins called the "five outward signs," which turn out to be embracing, kissing, gestures, suggestions, and writing; and the innumerable sins associated with particular statuses and professions.[2]

Furthermore, within any one of these categories there are unlimited possibilities for elaboration. Jean Columbi wrote little rhymes to describe the virtues opposed to the seven deadly sins, and through the cooperation of his printer was able to present what must have seemed to them a striking visual effect: the virtue is printed on the left hand side of the page—for example, *Humility*—and its contrary vice written *upside down* across from it on the right—in this case an inverted *Pride*. Columbi also devoted some space to the "types" and "principal branches" of the seven deadly sins, and in this he followed an old habit that would be roundly criticized by the reformers of the sixteenth century. The types and principal branches of pride, we learn, are ingratitude, boasting, flattery, hypocrisy, derision, ambition, presumption, curiosity, and disobedience; of avarice they are simony, theft, usury, sacrilege, fraud, and prodigality. The seven deadly sins are all treated in this fashion, as are the Ten Commandments, the

---

[1] Andreas de Escobar, *Modus confitendi*, A2a–B1b; [Poeniteas cito], *Libellus de modo poenitendi*, C2b–C4a; Maillard, *La Confession generale*, A3a–A8a; *Hortulus anime*, 155b–158a; Falk, ed., *Drei Beichtbüchlein*, 86–95; Johannes Wolff, *Beichtbüchlein des Magisters Johannes Wolff (Lupis), ersten Pfarrers an der St. Peterskirche zu Frankfurt a M. 1453–68. (1478)*, tr. and ed. by F. W. Battenberg (Giessen, 1907), 21–39 (146–165); ibid., "Für die Anfänger, Kinder und andere, zu beichten in der ersten Beichte," 1–5 (122–127); Winshemius, *Institutiones*, A5b ff.; de Butrio, *Directorium ad confitendum*, 3. For the history and meaning of the seven deadly sins, see Morton Bloomfield, *The Seven Deadly Sins* (Lansing, Mich., 1952). See also Siegfried Wenzel, *The Sin of Sloth: Acedia in Medieval Thought and Literature* (Chapel Hill, N.C., 1960), esp. pp. 63–96 and 164–187.

[2] For the five "outward signs," see Falk, ed., *Drei Beichtbüchlein*, no. 12. Identification of sins of omission, thought, word, and action, and of sins by status and profession, is extremely common. Some even speak of sins against the natural law. Thus Jacobus de Clusa (*Confessionale*, B2a–b) holds that both the positive and negative versions of the golden rule are precepts of the natural law "infused into the minds of men from the beginning of the world."

corporal and spiritual works of mercy, and the seven sacraments. If the variety discovered in Columbi's classification of sins did not raise scruples, his explanation of sins against the Sacrament of Penance should have succeeded, for it encouraged the penitent to doubt the sincerity of every one of his past confessions. After such detail the manual ironically finishes with the imprecation, "Estote simplices sicut columbe." A pun on the author's name (*columba* is Latin for "dove"), it advises readers to be simple as doves—like Columbi.[3]

Love of detail invades the devotional literature's examination of sin as well; Jean Mombaer's widely published *Rosetum* gives a vivid illustration. In one edition a huge tree of sin covers two folio pages. The trunk is made up of the seven deadly sins; the roots are various sayings about sin, including such favorites as, "Desire is the root of all evil," and, "By the envy of the Devil death entered into the world." At the top we are not surprised to find the tree crowned with the inscription, "Every tree that does not bear good fruit is cut down and thrown into the fire." Ornamentation at the top, roots, and branches (the branches are made up of the "offshoots" and "kinds" of the seven deadly sins) is overpowering in its detail.[4]

At times a writer will comment on the sheer bulk of this material. We have already seen that pastoral authorities interested in the consolation of the tender-minded cautioned against too scrupulous an examination of conscience. Similarly, Jacobus de Clusa notes that many people think that no transgression should be called a mortal sin unless it is condemned specifically in Holy Scripture, as, for example, the list that St. Paul gives in Galatians 5. Jacobus faithfully adheres to the more usual custom of proliferating the varieties of sin, however, and his discussion is rich in different perspectives. As we might expect, Jean Gerson offers a voice of true moderation. Although his *Opus tripartitum* takes up sins against the Ten Commandments in the first part and the seven deadly sins in the second, he concludes his discussion of the latter with the advice that they are enough for a good examination of conscience. The seven deadly sins, he notes, will provide all the insight necessary into the sins according to the five senses, works on mercy, articles of faith, and the Ten Command-

[3] Columbi, *Confession generale*, B1b ff.
[4] Jean Mombaer, *Rosetum exercitiorum spiritualium* (Basel, 1504), fol. 118b–119a.

ments. One need not add anything to them unless there is some particular circumstance he wants to explain.[5]

Gerson's decision to cut away the morass of categories seems to us prudent and correct, and the Reformation's angry protest against such legalism appears similarly justified. For if ever a Whiggish complaint against the tyranny of clerics over laymen rang true, surely it is here. Medieval love of trivia seems to combine with more repressive motives to produce a regimen that is not only absurd but inhumane. And to some extent that judgment is defensible.

But there is a logic behind this proliferation. For moral reformers found themselves virtual prisoners of a theology and an ecclesiology that dictated such a strategy. If the confessional is a primary institution for control, it must be used according to the rules, which, as we have already noted, demand that discipline be exercised by identifying and condemning sins. Now it is true that there were other ecclesiastical institutions exerting control in medieval society. The sermon, the canon law court, the community of the parish, and many forms of public pressure, all provided the clergy with a variety of institutionalized sanctions. Nevertheless the confessional does have a peculiarly powerful rationale and an especially effective way of reaching people, for it was here, in the forum of penance, that a priest representing the traditional, hierarchical church directly confronted and corrected the fallen, the unreformed. It was here that the church demanded all sins of every adult Christian be acquitted. It was here that vice was judged and sentenced, that virtue was hopefully encouraged. If moralists object that the faithful usually went only once a year, realists may reply that this is not a bad record. And if skeptics doubt how much change sacramental confession produced, those who ran the church would answer that no matter how people behaved after they performed the Easter duty, everyone had to satisfy the ecclesiastical law. And that, of course, is a most important point: no matter how effective in defeating sin this institution actually was, the hierarchical church had a theology and practice that made it seem central and indis-

---

[5] Jacobus de Clusa, *Confessionale*, B1b. Jacobus then goes on to advise confession according to no less than eleven categories (including the natural law, see above, n. 2). Gerson, *Opus tripartitum*, II, Du Pin, I, 445B–C. The use of two different classifications of sin in the *Opus tripartitum* is unquestionably attributable to the separate composition of the three parts.

pensable; and the men who wrote down lists and lists of sins did so on the assumption that here was their best chance for discipline.

The superabundance of sins becomes more intelligible, therefore, and so does the determination to enter into every kind of activity of mind and body. Reformation and sanctification hinged on sanctions against sin. And some moral reformers were faced with the difficult task of subsuming the social virtues they wanted to encourage under the rule of the confessional. Naturally they turned to the works of mercy and tried to classify actions contrary to those works as sins. If they had only wanted to restrain lust, avarice, and pride, they could have been satisfied with the seven deadly sins or the Ten Commandments. But some wanted much more. And some of the more ambitious reformers felt that if charity—giving alms to the needy and feeding the hungry— was to be commanded effectively, lack of charity somehow had to make its way into the lists of sins and become matter for confession. Consequently the branch of avarice on Jean Mombaer's tree of sin includes "tightfistedness and illiberality," and "hardness of heart and inhumanity." His fellow Parisian reformer Olivier Maillard is even more direct. Maillard's general confession begins with self-accusations according to the five senses, which the confessant admits he has not used as he ought but rather turned to "vanities" and "filth." In confessing sins according to the sense of sight, he is to admit that he has looked with pleasure on gold or women, but not with pity and compassion on "the poor of our Lord God who are sick, ill clad, and needy." Similarly, one of the offshoots of Avarice, according to a manual attributed to Jean Gerson, is "hardness of heart toward the poor."[6] The probability of such sins ever having been confessed seems low, as we have noted before. The chances of increasing charity in this ill-defined way seem even slighter. The evidence indicates this failure: no casuistry of charity developed comparable to the casuistry of avarice and lust. The lines between mortal and venial sin here remain blurred, perhaps inevitably, because these tended to be sins of omission. Or perhaps a full casuistry of love might have been constructed. It was not.

[6] Jean Mombaer, *Rosetum*, fol. 118b–119a; [Gerson?], *La Confession*, A2a–b; Maillard, *La Confession generale*, A2b; idem, *La Confession*, A3a–b (where Maillard advises that confession according to the Ten Commandments is best).

As with charity to the poor, so with a whole variety of some-times vague spiritual qualities: there were high ascetic and spiritual ideals that some wanted to translate into the language of sin and absolution. The elaboration of categories of sins should be seen in this light. Jean Mombaer's tree of sin was not de-signed as an instrument of torment. It was intended to describe the totality of sin and virtue and put it all under the jurisdiction of the forum of penance. One may reasonably argue that it was fundamentally imprudent, or even inhumane. But in following this path Mombaer merely continued the journey begun by the Irish monks, the Fourth Lateran Council, and the doctors of the church—Thomas and Duns and their disciples.

GRAVITY

To establish a judicious system for the definition, judgment, and correction of sin, it was thought useful to determine the rela-tive seriousness of different offenses against the laws of God and the church. No one doubted that there were in fact varying degrees of seriousness of sins, and one meets that assumption everywhere: in the theology of Augustine, the poetry of Dante, and the practice of the penitentials, to mention only a few well-known examples. And although most simply assumed this truth, Godescalc Rosemondt took the unusual trouble of asserting it against the Stoics, who, he tells us, erred by teaching that all sins are equal. (One deleterious effect of this teaching, he con-tinues, is the heretical belief that all the pains of hell are equal, an opinion that seems unaccountably offensive to him.)[7] Godes-calc's real interest here, however, is in determining what sins are most serious in themselves.

The lists that we have already seen in various contexts identify vices and sins, but that is only the beginning of the exercise. An intricate dissection of sin was indispensable to the communica-tion of a sense of sin. The branches, roots, and offshoots of the seven deadly sins represent the best efforts of curious ascetics to imagine all possible deviations from the laws of God and the teaching of the church. And what is more, such curiosity nat-urally led to the measurement and comparison of various devia-tions. Like good schoolmasters, the theologians graded sins.

The best illustration of the penchant for grading sins, and one of the favorites in the literature, is the rank ordering of sexual

[7] Rosemondt, *Confessionale*, 10, 2, fol. 164.

transgressions. With the example of St. Thomas as a model, not to mention the penitentials or the earliest manuals of confessors, moralists and pastoral theologians found it almost impossible to refrain from presenting the varieties of lust listed in ascending or descending order of vileness. A rather fine example occurs in the *General and Brief Confession*. Its sixteen grades of sexual sin are in some respects unusual; but they afford a good opportunity to explain what sexual sins were considered worse than others. As was often the custom, the sins are merely named; but their meaning is not difficult to discern.

1. "Unchaste kiss." The first sin is one of action, whereas some would have started with impurity first in thought and then in words. But if one is to begin with actions, then this seems a realistic place to do it.

2. "Unchaste touch." Clearly the manual has a progression in mind; it does not make itself absolutely clear, however.

3. "Fornication." This is where most lists of the gravity of sexual offenses begin. Moral theologians took seriously the distinction between this instance of illicit sexual relations and the graver instances below.

4. "Debauchery." Most explain that this refers to the seduction of a virgin; some therefore refer to it also as *defloratio*.

5. "Simple adultery." One of the partners is married while the other is single.

6. "Double adultery." Both partners are married. The point the manual is trying to make is a common one: it is serious sin to break your own marital vows and it is serious to lead others to break theirs.

7. "Voluntary sacrilege." Sacrilege refers to illicit relations involving anyone who has taken religious vows. "Voluntary" (*placitum*) apparently refers to the cooperation of the religious person to distinguish this sin from abduction below.

8. "Rape" or "Abduction of a virgin." It is clear that the word *raptus* refers both to rape and abduction and perhaps primarily the latter; for the literature often explains that it involves taking a girl from the house of her parents. This and the next two kinds of abduction are, obviously, compounds of the three grades of debauchery, adultery, and sacrilege.

9. "Rape" or "Abduction of a wife." This is adultery aggravated by violence.

10. "Rape" or "Abduction of a nun." This is sacrilege aggravated by violence.

11. "Incest." This sin, so harshly condemned here as elsewhere in the literature, presumably refers to illicit intercourse within the forbidden degrees, not just in the immediate family.

12. "Masturbation." With this sin, the list enters into the "sins against nature." The modern reader may be surprised to find this sin ranked as worse than adultery, rape, and incest. It is the kind of lesson a simple list can teach with precision and decisiveness.

13. "Improper manner." This refers to sexual intercourse, even between married partners, in what some medieval authors considered unnatural positions. As we shall see below, the question was widely discussed. Its explicit inclusion as a sin against nature is by no means universal and certainly does not reflect advanced theological opinion, but it reveals a potential for affecting consciences that is highly relevant to the sense of sin under examination.

14. "Improper organ." No one denied that unnatural intercourse was a sin of the greatest magnitude; and generally it was specifically condemned as more heinous if it occurred between married partners, since it then defiled the Sacrament of Matrimony.

15. "Sodomy." Homosexuality is, like all the sins against nature, invariably condemned as worse than incest.

16. "Bestiality." By common consent the worst of the sins against nature.[8]

There are a host of slight variations in the judgment of the gravity of sexual sins, however, and it is not clear what these variations mean. It might be that when one author makes defloration worse than adultery and another reverses the order, we are witnessing a considered and important difference of opinion. It might be—and one suspects it is more likely—that such a difference indicates the issue was in fact unimportant. But there are clear areas of agreement in the calculation of the gravity of

[8] *Confessio generalis breuis et vtilis*, 6a. For varieties and gravity of adultery: [Poeniteas cito], *Libellus de modo poenitendi*, B4a. For a more detailed explanation of these categories, see Dennis Doherty, *The Sexual Doctrine of Cardinal Cajetan*, Studien zur Geschichte der katholischen Moraltheologie, ed. by M. Müller, vol. 12 (Regensburg, 1966), 121–160.

sins, and it is equally clear that authors deliberately preach against particularly detestable sins simply by branding them as worse than other detestable sins. Thus almost everyone would have agreed with Guido de Monte Rocherii when he summarizes a teaching he attributes to St. Augustine: adultery is worse than fornication; plain incest is worse than adultery; incest with one's mother is worse than plain incest; and sins against nature are worst of all. Most would have agreed with his other grading as well: murder is worse than adultery; and sins against God, such as idolatry, are worse than all the rest. And when Antonius de Butrio wants to revile those who practice unnatural vices, he makes his point by a dramatic example of their comparative gravity: "Likewise, if he has foully touched his own member so that he has polluted himself and poured out his own semen, this sin is greater than if he had lain with his own mother." The language may be shocking, but the comparison is more so: Antonius knew how to make a sin look bad.[9]

Since almost everyone commented on the types and seriousness of sexual sins, it must be considered valuable evidence about the medieval sense of sin. Beyond the didactic purpose of pointing out how bad some sins were, however, the weighing of sexual sins must have been less useful than its popularity might lead us to believe. Before penances had become arbitrary, it would obviously have been practical to determine the precise weight of a sin so that the penance could be meted out accordingly. The

---

[9] Guido de Monte Rocherii, *Manipulus curatorum*, II, 4, 1 (cf. *Raymundina*, III, 34, 34, p. 468); de Butrio, *Directorium*, "Luxuria"; idem, *Speculum de confessione*, III, A5a. Similarly the *Supplementum*, "Luxuria 1," reveals the comparative gravity of unnatural vices with loving detail: "Item inter peccata contra naturam gravissimum est peccatum bestialitatis. scilicet ubi non servatur debita species. Post hoc autem est vitium sodomiticum. ubi non servatur debitus sexus. . . . Magis autem si non sit debitum vas quam non sit debitus modus. Minus autem inter peccata contra naturam est peccatum molliciei quod consistit in sola emisione seminis sine concubitu ad alterum." Other lists of the gravity of sins: Gerson, *Regulae morales*, 99, Du Pin, III, 95A; Nider, *Expositio decalogi*, VI, 2, Z3a–Z5a; [Gerson?], *Directoire*, O3b–O6b; [Gerson]?, *La Confession*, A2a–b, A7a–b; *Eruditorium penitentiale*, H1a–H5a; *Astesana*, I, 2, 46, a. 1; Alain de Lille, *Liber poenitentialis*, PL, 210, 288D–289A; *Sylvestrina*, "Luxuria," q. 1, par. 1; *Angelica*, "Luxuria"; *Raymundina*, III, 34, 31, p. 466; Guido de Monte Rocherii, *Manipulus curatorum*, II, 3, 9, fol. 39a; *Hortulus anime*, fol. 156b–158a; Denis the Carthusian, *Speculum conuersionis peccatorum* ([Johannes de Westfalia and Thierry Martens:] Alost, 1473), X6a.

exact tariffs of the penitential books reveal this practicality in a straightforward way. But penances in late medieval Europe were, in fact, arbitrary. No one could realistically hope to re-establish fixed penalties; and even if some thought the confessor should make the penance fit the crime, there is little evidence that authorities on confessional practice took this seriously enough to advise assigning measurably more severe penances to those who seduced their first cousins than to those who seduced their neighbors' wives. Thus one of the oldest justifications for grading severity exactly had long been obsolete.

On the other hand, John T. Noonan has argued persuasively that the classification of economic sins had important consequences: when theologians defined usury as an offense against justice rather than charity, it made a practical difference. For one thing, justice imposed universal and peremptory observance on Christians; the obligations of charity, on the other hand, were serious but admitted exceptions more easily. Furthermore, injustice required strict adherence to the principle of reparation. If one were to be absolved, one had to make restoration, to pay for the harm one had caused.[10] The distinction between the two classes of sin is, therefore, practically significant, and it shows how the science of morality could have palpable consequences even when appearing to be most theoretical.

Finally, it is not simply that the ranking of sexual sins could teach moral lessons or that the classification of usury as injustice caused penitents more than the ordinary amount of trouble. In a legal tradition, with a law that was supposed to be enforced, there were other ways to wield sanctions against sins judged to be grave and perhaps dangerous. As we shall see later, the custom of reserving certain more serious sins to higher ecclesiastical authorities was an important part of medieval ecclesiastical discipline. In such a system the very habit of grading sins, and the rules that govern it, will inevitably affect the lives of the faithful.

MORTAL AND VENIAL SINS

The great problem in the forum of the conscience, however, is not the weighing of sins or the recognition of aggravating circumstances. Rather it is to determine the degree of culpability of an individual sinner and his particular acts: and the critical

[10] John T. Noonan, *The Scholastic Analysis of Usury* (Cambridge, Mass., 1957), 30.

determination is the line between mortal and venial sin. Those devoted to the life of perfection could worry about lesser faults and try to eliminate them, but the practical problem for everyone is to identify mortal sins. A Christian is held responsible only for mortal sins: they lose him grace and make him liable to eternal damnation. They and only they must be objects of the penitent's act of contrition. They and only they must be confessed. Consequently, identification of mortal sins serves one eminently practical purpose: it gives names to forbidden actions, allowing the penitent to tell them more easily. In addition, of course, it defines unacceptable behavior and at the same time shows the Christian exactly what he is supposed to be sorry for and anxious about.

One is struck by the humility of a usually dogmatic tradition when clerical authorities themselves admit that it is not always easy to tell what sins are serious. The manual of Robert of Flamborough acknowledges this difficulty and reminds us that the twelfth century understood the need for latitude in these matters. In his introductory epistle Robert offers words of caution about the accomplishments of moral science: "Thus you must not expect perfection in this matter. For the heart of man is inscrutable, and who can know it?" And he goes on to quote what became a popular judgment: when people investigate the complexities of human action, he notes, you will find "as many opinions as there are heads."[11]

Quot capitum, tot sententiarum: contentious and yet realistic, medieval theologians saw that their attempt to define the universe with the clarity they longed for would fail when it encountered the inscrutability of the human heart. They had to learn to tolerate ambiguities. Johann Nider's *Consolation of Theology* derives its lessons in this respect directly from Jean Gerson as it warns against precipitate judgment of some act as a mortal sin. Narrow definitions are dangerous here, he tells us:

> It follows that it is the ignorant who look for the distinction or difference between mortal and venial sin in a general rule that makes it evident—particularly and infallibly—whether some action is mortally or venially sinful. And the Chancellor has shown this in his *De vita animi*.

[11] Quoted in Dietterle, "Die Summae confessorum," ZKG, 24 (1903), 366–367.

Indeed, Nider concludes, it would be like asking a physician for general rules that would distinguish in a word between fatal and nonfatal wounds and sicknesses.[12]

Still the distinction was necessary and the task unavoidable. Johann Nider himself developed such rules—more complicated than ones that offered the distinction in a single word, but rules all the same. And the master in this task, for Nider and for many others, was the Chancellor himself. In a work first written in French, *On the Difference between Mortal and Venial Sins*, Gerson outlines the most intelligent opinion of the late middle ages. Through the goodness of God, he tells us, we have been given a number of commandments, which, if we fulfill them, will gain us salvation. And the better they are fulfilled, the greater the reward:

> It is necessary, therefore, to know which commandments are obligatory and which are not; otherwise we shall either violate them through ignorance, or in keeping them we shall doubt too severely that we have violated them, when there is no reason to doubt. In that way we would lose all peace of conscience, by thinking something is a sin that is not, or, on the other hand, by thinking something might not be a sin that actually is.

All cases, he admits, cannot be considered and not all those he considers can be treated at length. There follows, therefore, some brief considerations, and if they are not clear, Gerson says, he is ready to answer inquiries. The principles he then proposes are, above all, definite. A mortal sin must first involve a serious offense against an important commandment. Furthermore, it requires deliberation, certain knowledge, and explicit consent, which are individual aspects of each moral act. In addition to these critical standards, Gerson discusses twenty-three considerations on the seven deadly sins, lying, swearing, fraternal correction, when to form an opinion on the mortal character of a sin, the choice of the lesser of two evils, ignorance, sins of merchants, sound faith, excommunication, the avoidance of a bad priest, venial sin, and a general example for the distinction between mortal and venial sins.

Despite his quest for clarity, however, Gerson, like the rest of

[12] Nider, *Consolatorium timoratae conscientiae* (U. Gering: Paris, 1478), III, 24, M7a–N5b.

146

the authorities on moral theology, is serious in his pessimism about achieving absolute certainty in these determinations. In *De Contractibus*, for example, he lays down a simple, popular rule for confessors: do not lightly brand something a mortal sin. This caution, he continues, is especially necessary when the opinion of only one doctor of the church can be adduced to support the contention that a certain act is seriously sinful. Indeed, it often happens in these cases that a conflicting opinion of another doctor can be found. The argument that follows is reminiscent of Robert of Flamborough, for Gerson then turns to the dire results of such reckless pronouncements. "What a labyrinth of fearful consciences we incur," he warns, if we follow an opinion indiscriminately. "For frequently opinions among doctors are not only different but contrary; at times because of temperaments, at times because of different aspects of the circumstances. . . . Whence arises that comedy, 'as many heads, so many opinions.' "[13]

In dealing with the same question, Antoninus of Florence also advises confessors to be cautious. A penitent who admits to an act that he does not realize is a mortal sin, must be instructed. On the other hand, the misconception of a penitent who thinks his acts have been mortally sinful and have not been—for example, if he thinks he has sinned because he had sexual intercourse with his wife in a penitential season, or on a feast day—must also be rectified. It is true that Antoninus wants the laity to be discouraged from risky choices, however, and he thinks confessors should urge their penitents to take the safer course of action. Nevertheless, he typically warns against defining some action as mortally sinful if there is some doubt among the doctors.[14]

In short, more sophisticated (and more influential) authorities were keenly aware that there was sometimes less than universal agreement in the determination of serious sins. Johann Nider, Jean Gerson, and Antoninus of Florence are not isolated voices either; rather they typify the consensus of moral theologians that it is rash to go around branding actions mortally sinful, that there is a wide range of differences among authoritative and respected doctors. And although everybody knew and agreed on the most

[13] Gerson, *De Differentia*, Du Pin, II, 487–504C; idem, *De Contracibus*, Du Pin, III, 181B–D.
[14] Antoninus, *Confessionale—Defecerunt*, 6.

important sins, it will be obvious that there could be important differences of opinion even in the realm of sexual morality, particularly the morality of the conjugal act.

Yet it is important to recall now that although there was a certain hesitancy and even humility among serious moral and pastoral theologians, the literature that taught about sin before the Reformation often did not come from these exalted sources. Often opinion was informed by simplistic manuals and uncomplicated minds. There was plenty of room in the hierarchical church for clerics who were not well instructed but who willingly and dogmatically pronounced on what was and was not serious sin. The caution of the best is important. But we must never fall into the error of overintellectualizing the common teaching of the church. For there were many books and authors who were not of the best, and they could be filled with conviction.

CONSENT AND MORTAL SIN

After actions that are serious sins have been named and defined, there remain grave problems. For it is then necessary to determine whether this action of this man was a mortal sin. A host of complications can arise here, some of which we have already seen in the aggravating circumstances. For example, how do ignorance of the law, coercion, or just plain weakness affect culpability? What is the difference between a temptation and a sin of desire? Or more specifically, what is said about those inevitable and troublesome concerns of a celibate clergy, lustful dreams and nocturnal pollution? Complications like these were truly vexing to medieval moral thought. Yet they had to be accounted for in a casuistry specifically designed to solve the problem raised by the requirement of a complete, sincere, truthful, and yearly confession.

Perhaps the most difficult problem for the confessional is the determination of the line dividing sin from ignorance, negligence, and temptation. If classification of acts themselves can cause confusion, it is nothing compared to the doubts raised when a penitent, examining his conscience and confessing his sins, has to decide whether he has really fully consented to the thoughts, words, or even actions that trouble him. Pastoral care's solution holds no surprises here. Once again summas, manuals, and spiritual counselors suggest rules to remove perplexity and enable a penitent to assess conscientiously and accurately his own responsibility.

148

Godescalc Rosemondt states the case succinctly: there can be no sin without full consent; children, fools, those who are demented or sleeping, cannot sin mortally. It is a very difficult thing to judge in particular cases, moreover, and certain preachers and confessors act rashly when they declare with ease and certainty that a mortal sin has been committed. Nevertheless, Godescalc, like the rest, offers rules for distinguishing venial from mortal sins on the basis of intention and consent. Thus one of his rules explains for the benefit of the perplexed that venial sins are like detours: unlike mortal sins they do not replace God as the final end but only represent distractions on the way to God. Venial sins may be compared to the choice of a man who goes to Antwerp from Louvain by way of Brussels, always intending to go to Antwerp, but taking a less direct route.[15] The problem here is not only that the figure seems irrelevant; as an explanation of how one is to understand the consent of the will it takes us almost nowhere, even though it is couched in the language of intention. Yet if it is true, as Godescalc says, that consent is necessary for a sin to be mortal, it is important not to obscure the explanation with metaphorical tours of the Lowlands.

In fact, the whole penitential system of the medieval church is founded on the proposition that men are responsible for their own willful acts, thoughts, and words, but *only* if they have actually willed those acts, thoughts, and words. There is a legal sense of responsibility: to be guilty a man must be intentionally involved. To attribute some act to a man, it is necessary that his rational self, not just his material body, participate in it. Vestiges of a more primitive attitude toward guilt persist, it is true, and there are laws and rituals that envisage a spiritual defect for which no culpability can be assigned because no voluntary sin is involved. Some instances of clerical irregularity, and disabilities placed on bastards and pregnant or menstruating women are examples. But these instances are striking simply because, even if they are firmly and widely believed, they contradict this fundamental principle. At all levels the church defines guilt in terms of the assent of the human will.

Gerson states this proposition in striking language in the *Opus tripartitum*:

Although someone may fall into temptation—to lust or anger or some other sin—of great severity or long duration, if that

---

[15] Rosemondt, *Confessionale*, 8, 3, fol. 145b–147b; ibid., 8, 10, fol. 150b.

temptation displeases him, or if he resists it, or if he does not fully and deliberately consent, then he does not sin mortally. On the contrary, often he does not sin at all but rather earns great merit towards God by resisting manfully.[16]

Implicit in the thinking of Gerson, and everyone else, is that something outside of the rational self—something not controlled voluntarily—originates temptation. It could be the devil. It could be the corrupted flesh. But whatever it is, there is no avoiding it while we are in our earthly form.

Consent of the will, then, is a basic test of culpability. The short manuals of confession are just as attentive to this element in the moral act, moreover, as the longer and more theologically sophisticated summas. But the emphasis on consent can make the good life more difficult too, and everyone carefully instructs penitents that it is possible to sin by desire even if one does not act on it. *Manual for Parish Priests* notes: "Be assured that in all sins whose acts are mortal we can sin in volition alone." For, it explains in a theological commonplace, if someone wants to forni- cate, steal, or commit some other mortal sin and does not have the opportunity, there can be no doubt that he sins mortally in that desire. Those who consent to the desire commit mortal sin. But the language is important. The first lesson is that the will alone may be guilty of sin; but it is just as evident that without consent of the will no sin can be charged. In emphatic language Johannes Wolff's *Beichtbüchlein* teaches that a man is not cul- pable for the first temptations that appear in his thoughts; for his desires to be mortally sinful he must give full, free consent in his heart—"das er synen fryhen verharten willen darzu gibt ader hat gegeben in dem hartzen."[17] The *Directoire des confesseurs* is equally direct, as it denies that any sin is mortal that lacks this heartfelt intention: "Et notez bien que iamais peche quon face en quelque maniere que ce soit: nest dist mortel iusques a tant que le cueur de la creature ait premier donne consentement. . . ."[18]

Willful consent not only distinguishes mortal from venial sins, but also affects the general estimation of the gravity of the sinful-

---

[16] Gerson, *Opus tripartitum*, I, 15, Du Pin, I, 439B.

[17] *Manuale parrochialium sacerdotum*, V, B2a; Wolff, *Beichtbüchlein*, 35 (161).

[18] [Gerson?], *Directoire*, G1b. Cf. [Poeniteas cito], *Confessionale pro scho- lasticis*, B4b; François Le Roy, *Le Mirouer de penitence*, 2 vols. (Paris 1507–1511), I, R8b ff.

ness of an action. In simple terms, the more rational and complete the consent, the more culpable the act. Godescalc Rosemondt illustrates this criterion when he takes up the question of whether a man or a woman sins more gravely in committing the same offense. He declares confidently that as a matter of fact men sin more seriously because they are more rational than women; he laments, therefore, the tendency to consider adultery and drunkenness more excusable in men, since moral science proves it should be the other way around. Godescalc's Italian contemporary J. L. Vivaldus is just as attentive to the rational component of the moral act, but he takes an even more masculine view of the case. Absolutely speaking, Vivaldus announces, men are more culpable in adultery and fornication because women are weaker both in mind and body. But *per accidens* the woman's adultery or fornication is graver because of the evil consequences —infanticide, abortion, contraception, replacement of legitimate heirs, or diminution of an inheritance—that flow from the crime of the woman.[19] Medieval prejudices notwithstanding, however, the point in these discussions is the same as in the more significant ones: it is not possible to understand mortal sin apart from willful consent, which determines guilt and the gravity of a sinner's offense.

The common observation that it is difficult to tell when a sin is mortal did not, as we have already said, deter writers from elaborating rules and metaphors for the detection of mortal sin. These rules are especially relevant when problems of measuring consent arise. One particularly ingenious attempt comes from Gerson's *On the Difference between Mortal and Venial Sins*: it describes six stages in the assent of the will to sin by analogy to the betrayal of the king of France by his wife, the queen, for the benefit of his enemy, the king of England. The analogy begins as a messenger from England appears before the queen, but she refuses to hear him. In the second stage she is attracted by the gifts the messenger brings and decides to hear him; but she is displeased by what he has to say and sends him away. In the third stage, however, she hears the message with pleasure, and it is here that mortal sin begins. In the fourth stage she accepts the gifts, and in the fifth she actively seeks to aid the enemy of her husband. In the final degree of surrender she proves herself

[19] Rosemondt, *Confessionale*, 10, 2, fol. 165a–166b; Vivaldus, *Aureum opus*, 56a–b.

obdurate in her infidelity: no threats or punishments from France or ill treatment from England can extract her from service to her husband's enemy.[20] The metaphor seems to strive more for clarity than elegance, and how successful it was in teaching the perplexed penitent to measure his consent to sin is difficult to imagine. Nevertheless, Gerson's intention is not frivolous; he was teaching a simple—perhaps not so simple—lesson of casuistry. It is important, moreover, to understand the attempt in this light rather than in the fanciful language of the *Waning of the Middle Ages*, which sees in this kind of allegory both spiritual vice and the decay of a civilization. Gerson knew what he was doing. His attempt may offend modern Europeans. It may have failed medieval ones. But it was not an idle game. For it responded to the deepest psychological needs of Christians who lived within the framework of the institutions of the forgiveness of sins.

Stephan Lanzkranna's *Himmelstrasse* also offers principles for judging whether sins are mortal, and its seven rules are all grounded primarily in distinctions in the nature of the individual's intentions and consent. Thus it warns that mortal sin inheres in the love of created things above, or exclusive of, the honor of God; but if one loves created things, or himself, without wishing to forgo God's favor or break God's law, "then it may be without a mortal sin." If a man offends God or his neighbor unthinkingly, then it also may be without serious sin. Nevertheless, the *Himmelstrasse* adheres to a popular doctrine that guilt itself can arise solely from an erroneous judgment in cooperation with the will: if one thinks an act is a mortal sin and does it, one commits a mortal sin even if the act is not a mortal sin in itself. Similarly, if a man wants to commit a mortal sin (or wants to commit an act he thinks is a mortal sin), he sins mortally as often as he desires it; and pleasure in the thought of a mortal sin is also a mortal sin. In addition, the *Himmelstrasse* grapples with perplexity in a long discussion urging that whenever one doubts about one's willful consent, one should nevertheless confess the action as a sin because it is "safer." There is a consistency in these counsels; and although they do not represent what we would call laxism, they do attempt to solve doubts by showing how the consent of the will itself is a vital criterion for judging mortal sin. In a similar

---

[20] Gerson, *De Differentia*, 25, Du Pin, II, 502C–504C.

fashion Godescalc Rosemondt has four rules, the *Peycht Spigel* nine, and Johann Nider a multitude; all are designed to make it easier to tell mortal sins; all stress the necessary concomitant of the operation of the will.[21]

From one point of view medieval casuistry can look arid and sterile as it strives for clarity in metaphors and rules. From another, however, it seems to correspond to the best instincts of Western thought, because it emphasizes intention and rationality. All of the humanizing influences of equity and fairness become appropriate to the solution of moral questions. We must nevertheless remember that the standards by which ecclesiastical reformers judged religious practice were not taken from Ulpian and Aristotle—at least not entirely. And while this rationalistic conception of human responsibility may seem to be nothing more than common sense, it could find hostile critics. Even in the middle ages there were doubts. In the Reformation there would be a torrent of criticism directed precisely at these rationalistic principles.

SINFUL THOUGHTS

As we have seen, the doctrine of willful consent and the responsibility for sin meant not only that some actions were not culpable but also that some thoughts were. And a primary goal of all casuistic inquiry into the rules for dividing mortal from venial sins is the distinction between temptations and sinful thoughts. Our whole discussion of consent, moreover, is applicable to this problem; and many of the examples already cited discuss the line between temptation and sin explicitly. This determination is, again, practical, and authors spend time on it because they must teach penitents to know what desires they ought to confess.

The requirement of confessing sins of thought brought forth the wrath of the sixteenth-century reformers from Luther on, and they had good historical grounds for their complaint that it was in some respects an innovaton. For all evidence indicates that in the ancient church this kind of sin, no matter how serious it was judged in the spiritual order, was not a matter for ecclesiastical discipline. But whatever its historical status, looking into sins of

[21] Stephan Lanzkranna, *Himelstrass*, ch. 22, fol. 63a–65b; Rosemondt, *Confessionale*, 8, 4 ff., fol. 147b–148b; Nider, *Consolatorium*, III, 25–28, N5b–07a (much taken, as usual, from Gerson); *Peycht Spigel*, B5a–B6b.

desire was an integral part of the medieval church's control of faithful Christians. Sinners were expected to conform to the words of Christ, which warned that whoever looked on a woman with desire had already committed adultery with her in his heart; and these words were not taken as counsel but as precept. Thus the commandment to control the inner life of desire was as ancient as the Gospels, and the decision to control it in sacramental confession had been taken centuries before the late middle ages, when pastoral and devotional writers were deeply committed to the examination of desire. Their speculation in this area is designed to clarify the teaching about consent, so that penitents could recognize the difference between sin and temptation in their own personal experience.

Gerson explains concisely when evil desires are serious sins and when they are not. If you take pleasure in an evil thought, it is a sin, he says, even though it is something you would not actually do if given the opportunity. But if it is to be sinful, it must entail consent to enjoyment of the pleasure of thinking about it, an inner process that Gerson calls *consensus in delectatione*. Furthermore, Gerson argues that simply to enjoy feminine beauty may be no sin, or no more than the sin of curiosity. Thus the sin comes not from passing thoughts and images, but in prolonged rumination and enjoyment.[22]

Another attempt to describe the difference between sinful thoughts and mere temptations occurs in the *De modo confitendi* of Matthew of Cracow, a treatise that enjoyed the prestige of its false attribution to St. Thomas Aquinas. The description is wordier than Gerson's, and perhaps not so lucid, but its thinking is along the same general lines.

> Indeed, no matter how evil and vicious the thoughts, if they are not purposely sought, or accepted with pleasure, or entertained for a time in the heart; or if you have not occasioned their coming because of intemperance in eating or drinking or some other way; but if they have suddenly come and gone, and you have been displeased with them, or at least have not taken pleasure in them; and immediately upon realizing their presence you tried to reject them as best you could, or tried to drive them out by occupying yourself with reading or holy meditation: such thoughts, I say, are not to be confessed, be-

[22] Gerson, *De Differentia*, 12, Du Pin, II, 497A–C.

cause not only does a man not offend in these, but rather deserves much credit, like the battling and victorious athlete.

There are so many conditions for a conscience to be clear that one must question Matthew's success in consoling a penitent who suffers severe temptations. Yet Matthew himself clearly intends this advice to be an effective check on scrupulosity. In fact, he goes on to condemn the evil practice of confessing these temptations because he thinks it is a vanity too prevalent in his own time; the motivation, he tells us, is the desire to make the confessor think his penitent holy.[23] And although Matthew may seem verbose, his intention was to be as descriptive as possible about what goes on in the thoughts of tempted and sinning Christians.

A final example shows how seriously the problem of sinful thoughts was taken and how subtle the distinctions could become. A popular criterion, taken from St. Thomas, measures consent in terms of a *cogitatio morosa* (a protracted thought) with a *mora perfecta* (the complete entertainment of the thought). Fundamentally the idea is the same as in Gerson or Matthew of Cracow: thoughts are not sinful if they are rejected, or if the individual does not indulge them or take pleasure in them. Yet Godescalc Rosemondt explains that this test does not refer to duration of time. Rather it must be understood as the "completion" of a thought without attempting to reject it.[24]

Is any of this helpful to the perplexed and scrupulous? The authorities on the spiritual life thought so, and they must have known something about it. Certainly one of the difficulties for the modern reader is in appreciating how deeply embedded these assumptions were in the medieval religious mentality. Anyone instructed by a priest who had any contact with this literature— manuals for priests and confessors, summas for confessors, devotional works—must at least have heard the common teaching on the sinfulness of consenting to bad thoughts of any kind. The *Imitation of Christ* talks about these problems naturally and

---

[23] Matthew of Cracow, *De modo confitendi*, 8, A3b.

[24] Rosemondt, *Confessionale*, 5, 1, fol. 37b–39a; cf. ibid., c. 10, fol. 159ff. Rosemondt relies particularly on Thomas Aquinas (*Summa theologica*, IIa IIIae, qq. 153–154, and Ia IIae, q. 74, a. 8), but he also cites Petrus de Palude, Augustine, Gerson, and Adrian "of Florence." Other examples: *Eruditorium penitentiale*, G6b–H1a; [Gerson?], *Directoire*, N6a–P4b; von Dambach, *Consolatio theologiae*, XIV, 8, 3.

casually, as if the reader did not need to be convinced but only reminded. For example, "On Resisting Temptations":

> first there comes into the mind an evil thought: next, a vivd picture: then delight, and urge to evil, and finally consent.[25]

This passage—less specific than Matthew of Cracow and less subtle than Godescalc Rosemondt—introduces, quite incidentally, rules of casuistry into a popular devotional treatise. Other examples could be multiplied indefinitely. With slight differences from author to author, the rules and counsels for telling a penitent when he has sinned seriously and what he must confess are ordinary doctrine. They represent habits of introspection and standards for assigning responsibility that, together with the specific identification of what behavior is seriously sinful, formed the sense of sin of Christians at the end of the middle ages.

SCRUPULOSITY AND THE SACRAMENT OF PENANCE

Is the sense of sin taught in this literature simple scrupulosity? The answer, as usual, is yes and no. It is yes because of the sheer number and variety of sins, the implacable search into the mental life of the penitent, and the relentless demand that he make up his mind about the gravity of an act and the degree of his consent. Know thyself becomes an exhausting activity. A favorite epigram from Gregory the Great even declares that it is characteristic of pious men "to recognize guilt where there is no guilt," and one might justly fear the consequences if such teaching became the guide for average penitents. In fact, it did not. For there is another tendency (already discussed in connection with the dangers implicit in the demand for a complete examination of conscience) which renounces the extremes of scrupulosity. Even the *Supplementum*, which is no haven for laxists, responds to Gregory's maxim with a common sense that is typical of the literature. We are not supposed to say we have done things we have not done, Nicolaus explains in an opinion derived from St. Thomas. Rather we are told to be ever fearful that we might be guilty of such sins as pride and vainglory (and Nicolaus implies in this statement that these are the kind of sins confessors seldom hear about). Then he continues with a warning that not everyone should be exposed to Gregory's hard advice: "In addition, the

---

[25] Thomas à Kempis, *The Imitation of Christ*, tr. by Leo Sherley-Price (Baltimore, 1952), I, 13, p. 41.

previous words are not to be understood as pertaining to a scrupulous doubt, which must be rejected on the counsel of one's pastor."[26]

Indeed, the *Supplementum*'s reasonable advice on this question is only a brief comment on a subject of serious concern in the literature on forgiveness. For, far from intending to create an ethic and a sacrament that would produce scrupulosity, pastoral authorities set out expressly to cure it. Having emphasized the elaboration of norms and the inculcation of guilt, therefore, we must again call attention to the attempt to treat spiritual disease.

The image of the priest as a physician of souls is ancient in Christian culture. It originates in the Gospels and is prominent in the Church Fathers and the early medieval penitentials.[27] To be sure, some of this imagery relates to the function of discipline: the clerical doctor is to cure the disease of sin and prescribe remedies insuring that specific vices do not recur.[28] Nevertheless, even here the healing image implies consolation. Just as the cure of bodily disease makes a patient feel better, so the cure of sin makes the penitent feel better psychologically. Furthermore, the benefits offered go beyond the mere assurance that someone who takes the cure of penance will stop sinning and

[26] *Supplementum*, "Confessio 1," 9.

[27] Adolf Harnack, "Medicinisches aus der ältesten Kirchengeschichte," *Texte und Untersuchungen zur Geschichte der altchristlichen Literatur*, ed. by Oscar von Gebhardt and Adolf Harnack, vol. 8, no. 4 (Leipzig, 1892), 37–147, esp. 125–143; John T. McNeill, *A History of the Cure of Souls* (New York, 1951), 95, 108, 110, 114, 119, 134; idem, "Medicine for Sin as Prescribed in the Penitentials," *Church History*, I (1932), 14–26; McNeill and Gamer, *Medieval Handbooks*, 44; Schmitz, *Bussbücher*, I, 596; J. Laporte, *Le Pénitentiel de saint Colomban*, 51–61; Kurtscheid, *A History of the Seal of Confession*, 10–11; John Calvin, *Institutes of the Christian Religion*, tr. by Ford Lewis Battles, ed. by John T. McNeill, 2 vols., Library of Christian Classics, vols. 20 and 21, 7th printing (Philadelphia, 1975), I, 622, n. 1, and 623, n. 3. *Omnis utriusque sexus* describes the priest's office "ut more periti medici": Hefele and Leclerq, *Histoire des conciles*, 5², 1350.

[28] A few examples in which eliminating sin seems to dominate: Burchard of Worms, *Decretorum libri XX*, PL, 140, Bk. 19, "Corrector et medicus"; Alain de Lille, *Liber poenitentialis*, PL, 210, 285c–286c; [Poeniteas cito], *Libellus de modo poenitendi*, A6a; Nicolaus de Saliceto, *Antidotarius anime* (Paris, 1552), Preface, 2a–3a; Johann Nider, *De lepra morali*, prologue, K1a; idem, *Consolatorium*, III, 6, 8; Jacobus de Clusa, *Confessionale*, ch. 2, A2b; Rosemondt, *Confessionale*, 10, 4, fol. 175b–176a; Kunhofer, *Confessionale*, A1a. See also above, n. 27, and below, "Restrictions," n. 22 and n. 23.

therefore have no more reason to feel anxiety. The greatest promise is that confession is the place of healing.[29] And an important element in that promise of confession is the wise confessor's ability to treat penitents who have taken their sense of sin to excess.

The treatment of scrupulosity was a science of comfort designed for those whose strict consciences led them to exaggerate their sinfulness and to doubt the efficacy of the priest's absolution and their own confession and contrition. Part of this science was devoted to upgrading the power of the sacrament, and those efforts are described below in the discussion of how the sacrament works. But another important part was a direct attack on the excessive sense of sin from which scrupulous consciences suffer. It is a vast and complicated subject—only the dominant themes can be mentioned here. Yet even a brief summary will help to modify somewhat the impression of unyielding discipline that moralists sometimes give.

It is not uncommon in the literature on forgiveness for introductory matter to praise or recommend the work that follows because it comforts troubled, scrupulous consciences.[30] A wide

[29] In addition to the evidence already adduced, one very explicit statement worth quoting is Matthew of Cracow, *Confessionale . . . De modo confitendi*, A2a: "Quoniam fundamentum et ianua virtutum: omnisque gratie: ac spiritualis consolationis principium est conscientie puritas ac cordis mundicia: ad quam principaliter et precipue per puram veram ac integram et perfectam confessionem peccatorum acceditur." Other examples of this kind of assertion: *Eruditorium penitentiale*, C6a–7b; Gerson, *Dialogue spirituel*, Du Pin, III, 813B; Jacobus de Clusa, *Confessionale*, app. 4, D4a; *Peycht Spigel*, C8b; Rosemondt, *Confessionale*, 7, 81, fol. 122b–123a, and 10, 5, fol. 176a; Jacobus de Gruytroede, *Speculum aureum*, B2a–4a; Vivaldus, *Aureum opus*, 152b–153a. Cf. Schauerte, *Busslehre des Eck*, 143. Pettazoni's research in confession of sins in primitive, ancient, and modern religions leads him to conclude that there is one underlying unity: "Mais la confession est et reste toujours délivrance, soit qu'il s'agit de délivrer l'homme de douleurs physiques dont le péché est la cause, ou bien de l'angoisse intérieure et obscure qui lui fait haïr le péché par lui-même" (Raffaele Pettazoni, "La Confession des péchés dans l'histoire des religions," in *Mélanges Franz Cumont*, 2 vols., *Annuaire de l'Institut de philologie et d'histoire orientales et slaves*, IV [Brussels, 1936], II, 893–901).

[30] Thus Johann Nider's prologue to the *Consolatorium*, A2a: "tamen pro presenti vni morbo qui est erronea conscientia principalitar succurrere propono per hunc tractatum qui censeri potest consolatorium timorate conscientie . . . ."; the introductory letter to the *Astesana*, fol. 11a: "In isto

variety of works—from summas to manuals and devotional works —address themselves to that pastoral task. The late medieval masters of that theology of consolation were Johann von Dambach, Johann Nider, and, above all, Jean Gerson. Gerson in particular enunciated the dominant themes with clarity and sensitivity: the attempt to define mortal sin and specify the conditions of culpability; confidence in the reconcilability of conflicting authorities and obligations; the attack on perfectionism and the assertion that obedience to the minimum, God's commandments, is enough; and the fervent invocation of the equity, liberty, and gentleness of the law of Christ. Underlying all strategies in the treatment of scrupulosity is the recognition of human complexity. And while Gerson is not the only one to comment on it, he seems to appreciate it most fully:

> The diversity of human temperament is incomprehensible— not just in several men, but in one and the same man—and not, I say, in different years or months or weeks, but in days, hours, and moments!

If the law—and the insistence that the law could and must be fulfilled—stood on the side of discipline, some doctors of consolation tried to appreciate human weakness, diversity, and perplexity, tried to mitigate the law's harshness, and offered mercy to strict and suffering consciences.[31]

---

sedulus lector habeat quo omnis iniectus mentibus hominum scrupulus: qui animam aut ipsius sinderesim ardentissima conscientie face mordebat: tanti operis beneficio elidatur"; and the introductory letter to the *Sylvestrina*: "Noster autem hic Prierias conscientiis inuectas tanta luce discussit nebulas, laqueosque animarum veluti pedibus praejectos sic dissoluit, vt nunc a falsis, quae vera sunt discernere, atque etiam leui nixu de cunctis dijudicare valeant, ne dum eruditissimi quique, verum et mediocriter docti."

[31] Gerson, *De Perfectione cordis*, Du Pin, III, 446B: "Est incomprehensibilis humanae diversitas complexionis, vel conditionis; nedum in pluribus hominibus, sed in uno eodemque, diversis non dico Annis, non Mensibus, non Hebdomadis; sed diebus, horis, et momentis. . . . Et metrum vulgatum habet: 'Quod natura negat, nemo feliciter audet.' " Cf., ibid., 442–447. See also *Raymundina*, III, 30, 5–6, p. 356, and III, 34, prologue, p. 437; Johann von Dambach, *Consolatio theologiae*, X, 9, 1; XIV, 8; XV, 1; XV, 9–10; Gerson, *De Differentia*, Du Pin, II, 499D–500A; idem, to his brother Nicolas, Glorieux, II, 140; idem, *Regulae morales*, Du Pin, III, 101D–102A; idem, *Doctrina contra nimis strictam . . . conscientiam*. Du Pin, III, 241–243; idem, *De Remediis*, Du Pin, III, 579D–582A, 585A–C, 587D–588B; idem, *De Contractibus*, Du

Finally, in fairness to the complexity of the medieval ethical tradition itself, we should note the extraordinary opinion of Duns Scotus, which is directly opposed to Gregory the Great's encouragement to find sins everywhere. In the Subtle Doctor's discussion of whether those who have not committed serious sins need to confess once a year, he shows the most remarkable optimism about the ability of good people to persevere:

> Nor is it incredible that there are many in the Church who live for a year without mortal sins but rather, through the grace of God, preserve themselves from mortal sin for a much greater length of time; and they perform many works of perfection, from whose merits the treasury of the Church is augmented.

And Duns's optimism found at least one popularizer, as we can see in this judgment of Johann Wolff:

> It is much harder and more difficult to break the commandments than to keep them and not break them. Thus it is still more difficult to serve the evil spirit—for the sake of eternal damnation, torment of fire, and everlasting pain—than almighty God—for the sake of eternal life. For it is much harder to swear, curse, scold, play, throw dice, dance, fight, stab, murder, commit adultery, lie, defraud, not honor your father and

---

Pin, III, 180; Johann Nider, *Consolatorium*, I, 2–3, and III, 1–3; idem, *Expositio decalogi*, III, 9B, 12L; *Supplementum*, "Penitentia 2," 3; "Perplexitas"; Antoninus, *Confessionale—Defecerunt*, 6; *Sylvestrina*, "Dubium," "Scrupulus"; Vivaldus, *Aureum opus*, 151b, 152b–153a; Rosemondt, *Confessionale*, 8, 7; de Butrio, *Speculum de confessione*, 40, C2a; idem, *Directorium ad confitendum*, *De modo confitendi*, 7; Foresti, *Confessionale*, 45a; Joannes Surgant, *Manuale curatorum predicandi* ([Basel], 1503), II, 15, fol. 116a. These highly selective citations illustrate some of the problems and suggested solutions. Cf. Lawrence J. Riley, *The History, Nature and Use of EPIKEIA in Moral Theology*, Catholic University of America Studies in Sacred Theology, 2d ser., no. 17 (Washington, 1948) esp. 53–54; Franz Bürck, "Die Lehre vom Gewissen nach dem hl. Antonin," *Der Katholik*, 39 (1909), 17–37, 81–99; Browe, "Die Kommunionvorbereitung," esp. 407–415; Albert Auer, *Johann von Dambach und die Trostbücher vom 11. bis zum 16. Jahrhundert*, Beiträge zur Geschichte der Philosophie und Theologie des Mittelalters, vol. 27, no. 1/2 (Münster, 1928), 112–157, 166–167, 283, 299–300, 315–316; Helmut Appel, *Anfechtung und Trost im Spätmittelalter und bei Luther*, Schriften des Vereins für Reformationsgeschichte, vol. 165 (Leipzig, 1938), esp. 26–27.

mother, and so on, than to omit these sins. You can more easily love God above all creatures and worship, believe in, hope in, and honor Him than men or creatures.[32]

Speculations on the possibility of avoiding sin are not characteristic of the literature on forgiveness. Nor is the ostensible optimism of Duns and pastor Wolff. And if the treatment of the scrupulous conscience was an important element in this literature, it remained only one element—even among more sophisticated theologians—applicable only in special cases, aimed at what was considered an abnormal spiritual vice. Not until the second half of the sixteenth century would such problems of conscience dominate moral and pastoral theology. Instead the authors of summas, and manuals, and devotional books, were concerned with the more ordinary problems of a vast population of penitents. Authorities in the cure of souls wanted, above all, to instill in the Christian community both a sense of sin and a confidence that sins could be avoided and forgiven. They must have thought that their compromise between rigidity and laxity succeeded. They must have thought they had sufficiently protected penitents from scrupulosity and despair in the discussion of sin. But to us it seems that they managed to emphasize the perilous ease of finding ways to commit sins. They numbered and weighed them. They found them in actions, thoughts, and words. And they carefully placed a tremendous responsibility on the human conscience to determine one's own degree of consent, one's own culpability. This moral science was designed to make

[32] Duns Scotus, *Quaestiones*, dis. 17, q. 1, 32, *Opera*, 18, 579: "Nec est incredibile multos esse in Ecclesia, qui per annum vivant sine mortali, imo per Dei gratiam multi multo majori tempore sine peccato mortali se custodiunt, et multa opera perfectionis exercent, de quorum meritis thesaurus Ecclesiae congregatur. Wolff, *Beichtbüchlein*, 39 (165): "Notwendigkeit der Gesetzesbefolgung und der Busse. Item, es ist viel härter und schwerer, die Gebote zu brechen, als sie nicht zu brechen und zu halten. Darum ist es noch viel mehr härter, dem bösen Geist zu dienen für die ewige Verdammnis, des Feuers Qual und ewige Pein als dem allmächtigen Gott für das ewige Leben. Denn es ist viel härter zu schwören, zu fluchen, schelten, spielen, würfeln, tanzen, hauen, stechen, morden, ehebrechen, lügen, betrügen, Vater and Mutter nicht zu ehren etc., als diese Sünden zu unterlassen. Du kannst leichter Gott lieb haben über all Kreaturen und ihn anbeten, an ihn glauben, hoffen und ihn ehren als die Menschen oder Kreaturen."

people understand concretely and feel acutely their own personal guilt.[33]

Sex and the Married Penitent

THE RIGORISM OF MEDIEVAL MORALITY

We have seen that authorities on pastoral care tried to inculate a strict sense of sin. They identified a rich variety of ways to sin. They tried to measure the seriousness of different sins, and they were especially eager to differentiate between mortal and venial sins. Nor did they hestiate to explore sins of thought and desire with the same thoroughness and precision. In medieval religion the teaching about sin is meticulous and detailed—relentlessly so.

Furthermore, there was always substantial agreement on what the big sins were. One does not need the elaborate classifications of sins to condemn the most important vices—the Ten Commandments or the seven deadly sins can easily be used to proscribe the behavior most authorities want to eliminate.

Yet when we go beyond the universally proscribed acts and vices and get down to particular applications and particular cases, uniformity disappears. On many important moral questions we encounter the difference between a "rigorist" conclusion—which insists on the hard and safe solution to a moral problem—and a "laxist" one—which is satisfied with the milder, merely probable choice. And these classifications, rigorist and laxist, are essential to an understanding of medieval and Reformation thinking about sin and guilt. Now there is a danger in anachronistically imposing these labels to make divisions among moral theologians appear clearer than they were. Sometimes, it is true, an authority tends to be either laxist (the *Angelica* is a good example) or rigorist (like the *Supplementum*). But it would be misleading to represent two clearly delineated and warring groups, laxists and rigorists, whose membership was known and whose opinions were predictable. In the seventeenth century there was in fact open contention between laxist Jesuits and rigorist Jansenists. No such war is waged, however, in the

[33] See John Bossy, "The Social History of Confession in the Age of the Reformation," *Transactions of the Royal Historical Society*, 5 ser., 25 (1975) 21–38, esp. 21 and 33, for a conflicting view.

years before the Reformation. Thus we shall often encounter mild and hard solutions to a problem, perhaps especially in sexual sins, without pretending to define schools of thought. Diverse opinions were possible, uniformity apparently was not. And it would be fanciful to propose that when we encounter laxist judgments, we are finding evidence for a dramatic change toward mildness on sexual questions in the literature as a whole.

By modern standards even the mild opinions of medieval and Reformation moralists are strict. Indeed, we should recall here that sex was not the only area of morality with rigoristic, puritanical rules. If it is fair to accuse Christian churches since the nineteenth century of knowing only one sin, such an accusation against the medieval church would be utterly unfounded. The church remained interested in every aspect of human activity and busily incited guilt in the widest variety of transgressors.

One of the most familiar examples of medieval rigorism is the theological treatment of the morality of economic life. We know a great deal about how scholastics dealt with sins of businessmen and financiers. And although the old view that medieval churchmen were unyielding, reactionary, and omnipotent in their regulation of economic life is obviously exaggerated, they still appear unreasonably restrictive.[1]

Thus it should not surprise us to find that the practical literature is concerned with the widest imaginable range of economic occupations and practices. Imagine the problems that might be stirred up if a confessor followed the *Tractatus de instructionibus confessorum*'s advice for interrogating craftsmen. The *Tractatus* warns that certain professions—law, military, and merchant, for example—can hardly be performed without sin. Thus craftsmen who make swords, knives, and arrows should be told to find out why purchasers want them. The confessor must also discover whether the craftsman is guilty of fraud, and even whether "he has invented some novelty that pertains more to vanity than

---

[1] On medieval economic morality, see Noonan, *Scholastic Analysis of Usury*, esp. 70–81, 171–195; Benjamin Nelson, *The Idea of Usury, From Tribal Brotherhood to Universal Otherhood* (Princeton, N.J., 1949), 3–30; Raymond De Roover, *La Pensée économique des scolastiques, Doctrines et méthodes*, Conférence Albert-le-Grand 1970 (Montreal and Paris, 1971); idem, *San Bernardino of Siena and Sant'Antonino of Florence. The Two Great Economic Thinkers of the Middle Ages*, Kress Library Series of Publications, no. 19 (Boston, 1967).

163

necessity."[2] A manual attributed to Jean Gerson explains that those who intentionally lend anything "for temporal profit"— whether it be money, grain, livestock, or wine—are guilty of usury. The seventh commandment also forbids, according to this manual, any kind of fraud, and lawyers who take spurious cases are condemned here.[3] Gerson himself has a similarly broad conception of sins against "thou shalt not steal." Thus he condemns usury, unjust legal suits, defamation of character, fraud in selling and manufacturing, and simony. He brands others as transgressors of this commandment: spendthrift wives and churchmen; farmers who cheat their neighbors by moving boundary lines; and adulterous women who displace legitimate heirs with the offspring of their illicit unions.[4]

When the *Directoire des confesseurs* talks about economic vices, it condemns public usury, nine hidden kinds of usury, greed, and grinding the poor; then it turns to varieties of "spiritual" avarice. Here it accuses scholars who show contempt for sacred subjects by choosing a more lucrative study: ". . . as those do who prefer to take up civil, canon, or customary law rather than holy theology in order to become lawyers and men of affairs [gens de pratique]."[5] St. Antoninus's *Confessionale—Defecerunt* gets at scholars in an equally thorough examination: confessors are to ask them if they were quarrelsome or disobedient to their masters; if they chose a less apt teacher for a bad reason; if they set improper goals to their knowledge, such as unjust gain or curiosity; if they were negligent in study; or if they succumbed to the temptations of pagan literature. Thus a confessor is to find out whether a student "has studied too ardently in the books of the pagans on account of their beauty, and thus had less time for useful study pertaining to his salvation. . . ."[6] Moral theology, like death, was a great leveler: its absolutes touched the behavior and consciences of student, farmer, bishop, merchant, and anyone else the ecclesiastical authority could think of. Its range of inquiry was, as we have seen throughout this study, as broad as the list of all the virtues, vices, and commandments. And most important of all, its standards, its willingness to set narrow limits

---

[2] *Tractatus de instructionibus confessorum*, E2b–E3a.

[3] [Gerson?], *La Confession*, A7b–A8a.

[4] Gerson, *Opus tripartitum*, I, 10–11, Du Pin, I, 435–436.

[5] [Gerson?], *Directoire*, K3b–L1b.

[6] Antoninus, *Confessionale—Defecerunt*, 35.

to what was allowed the Christian faithful, could be extraordinarily rigid.

Yet sexuality holds a special place in medieval religion. For while it is true that the medieval church could excoriate all kinds of vices and all kinds of sins, it was inordinately concerned with the sexual. From the age of the Fathers, in fact, sex was disparaged and condemned in such excessive language that it is difficult to acquit some of the most prominent Catholic theologians of a heretical dualism. And certainly dualism, transmitted from Gnostics, Stoics, and Platonists, contributed to medieval pessimism about the physical in general and sexuality in particular. As a result, moral theology was plagued by an antithesis, as unrealistic as it was uncompromising, between irrational physical pleasure and rational self-control. The result is evident throughout the intellectual tradition: "The blacker the colors in which sexual pleasure is seen, the brighter shines the ideal of the sexually chaste man."[7] This dark view provides the background for theological speculation. Sexual organs and functions are called *turpia*, shameful things; and authors deprecate indiscriminately the immoral, the ugly, and the unseemly, as if the differences between them were not crucial to a realistic sexual ethic. Popularly, sex became identified not only with sin but with the devil himself, and theologians suggested that God gave Satan a special measure of freedom to intervene in the realm of sexual

[7] Ziegler, *Ehelehre*, 202. Cf. John T. Noonan, *Contraception. A History of Its Treatment by the Catholic Theologians and Canonists* (New York and Toronto, 1967), 90–101, 293, 366–367, 440–448; and ibid. (Cambridge, Mass., 1965), 66–77, 241, 304–305. (Paperback [1967] and hardcover [1965] editions identified below by publication date.) The most forthright critique of medieval rigorism in sexual ethics has come from Roman Catholic scholars (most of them priests). In addition to Josef Ziegler and John T. Noonan, we may add Michael Müller, *Die Lehre des hl. Augustinus von der Paradiesesehe und ihre Auswirkung in die Sexualethik des 12. und 13. Jahrhunderts bis Thomas von Aquin*, Studien zur Geschichte der katholischen Moraltheologie, ed. by M. Müller, vol. 1 (Regensburg, 1954); Leopold Brandl, *Die Sexualethik des heiligen Albertus Magnus. Eine moralgeschichtliche Untersuchung*, Studien zur Geschichte der katholischen Moraltheologie, ed. by M. Müller, vol. 2 (Regensburg, 1955); Peter Browe, *Beiträge zur Sexualethik des Mittelalters*, Breslauer Studien zur historischen Theologie, ed. by F. X. Seppelt et al., vol. 23 (Breslau, 1932); Josef Fuchs, *Die Sexualethik des heiligen Thomas von Aquin* (Cologne, 1949); and Heinrich Klomps, *Ehemoral und Jansenismus. Ein Beitrag zur Überwindung des sexualethischen Rigorismus* (Cologne, 1964).

activity. And fundamental to this complex of ethics, attitudes, and taboos, was a fear of contamination—by semen, or menstrual blood, or the blood of childbirth—which expressed itself in various ways: in numerous discussions of nocturnal emission; in the deeply entrenched ritual of "churching"; or in the isolated, fantastic opinion of the *Summula Raymundi* that intercourse during menstruation can be fatal to the husband, so poisonous is the woman's monthly flow.[8]

It is important to understand the fear of impurity and suspicion of sex and pleasure in medieval religious thought because it is the basis for a mood of pessimism and rigorism that influences the practical literature on sin. This fear and suspicion can be found in the Old Testament, or St. Paul, or the Fathers, or even in ancient pagan sources. But a tradition of unusual severity is established in the early medieval tract *Responsum beati Gregorii ad Augustinum episcopum*, which asserts that one can never enjoy sexual pleasure without sin. A surprising number of theologians promoted this harsh view, but the most influential of them all were the canonist Huguccio and his pupil Innocent III. Indeed, in the thought of Archbishop Huguccio contempt for sex and pleasure probably reached its high point. According to Huguccio, every act of sexual intercourse, even in marriage, involves guilt and sin—*culpa et peccatum*—because every time a man experiences sexual pleasure he is guilty of at least a small

[8] Ziegler, *Ehelehre*, 181–184, 202–207; Browe, *Beiträge zur Sexualethik*, 3–32, 80–113, 121–127; *Summula Raymundi* (Cologne, 1506), "De Baptismo," "De mulieribus menstruosis," fol. 58b: "Secundo est notandum . . . mulieres non debent habere consortia cum viris eorum tempore passionis menstrui. Cuius ratio est ista. quia menstruum est valde immundum et quasi venenum salua reuerentia. et si tunc illo tempore vir coiret cum ea tunc vlterius posset infici cum veneno et cum malis humoribus quo forte morte periret. et hoc esset sibi horibile peccatum. quia mulier hoc patiens si appeteret coitum talem studiose esset homicida." Even if the man escapes unharmed, the *Summula Raymundi* warns that the sperm would be poisoned by the menstrual flow and the offspring would therefore be defective (ibid.); that the dangerous humors of menstrual blood can be emitted through the eyes (fol. 59c); and that women who die in childbirth should be purified before they are buried (fol. 59b–60a). For refusal of burial in consecrated ground to women who die in childbirth (including a twelfth century directive that the unborn and unbaptized child must be cut out and buried outside the churchyard before the mother is buried in consecrated ground), see Browe, *Beiträge zur Sexualethik*, 18–21, 37. In 1420, Martin V *condemned* the following proposition of the Augustinian Nicolaus Serrarius of Tournai: "Non est mulieri opus purificari, quinimo hoc sc. purificari est iudizare" (ibid., 38).

venial sin. To the objection that God could not have commanded men to increase and multiply and at the same time make it sinful, Huguccio confidently replied: "God commands and makes many things that are not and cannot be without sin. Does He not make souls, which cannot exist in this life without sin?" Huguccio's view is so gloomy that even he realized its proximity to heresy, and he exculpated his doctrine by arguing that real heretics called all sexual intercourse *mortal* sin, whereas he was content to define the conjugal act as only a slight venial sin.[9] This is a critical difference between Huguccio and "the heretics," of course. For no matter how extreme the capitulation to dualism appears in medieval theology, it was never complete. When Huguccio insists that marital intercourse is in itself only a venial sin, moreover, he has said you do not have to confess it. And that is the most important distinction for the conscience of the married penitent. Nevertheless, Huguccio had articulated a deep suspicion of sex and pleasure. If it is not pure Manichaeanism, neither is it free of a dualistic conception of the evils of natural physical functions. This dualistic suspicion persists throughout medieval moral theology; and it colors all opinions on sexual morality, even though it was a metaphysical truism that since God had created matter and the world there could be nothing inherently evil in that creation.

The great scholastic theologians of the thirteenth century, however, drew back from this extreme rigorism. Abelard had already asserted that sexual pleasure was natural and that Adam and Eve had experienced it in Paradise. Albert the Great, Thomas Aquinas, and Duns Scotus continued to develop this naturalistic analysis and arrived at a compromise between the ascetic and the naturalistic tendencies in Christian thought. Even though it was no more than a compromise, it made possible a considerable softening of the teaching for confessors on conjugal morality. Thus there was a greater willingness in the high middle ages to admit that sex might be good. Sex did not become completely good. Indeed, it remained for the clerical mind still dangerous. Nevertheless the thirteenth century witnesses the transition to a climate of opinion in which it is possible to talk about sex in less

[9] Müller, *Paradiesesehe*, 282–284; Ziegler, *Ehelehre*, 171-172; Noonan, *Contraception* (1967), 241–243; (1965), 197–198; Brandl, *Die Sexualethik des hl. Albertus Magnus*, 23–24. The *Responsum beati Gregorii* is now attributed to Nothelm of Canterbury: Klomps, *Ehemoral und Jansenismus*, 37.

pejorative, sometimes even complimentary language. By the late fifteenth and early sixteenth century one can find ideas about sex and even pleasure that would shock anyone raised in the gloom of Gregory the Great, Huguccio, or Peter Lombard.[10]

Summas and manuals for confessors strike a compromise, as was their custom, between asceticism and naturalism. Devoted to the "safe," antipathetic to the radical, they generally preserve the feeling that sex is dangerous while they protect the pastoral clergy and their penitents from the extremes of rigorism. The questions they pose, moreover, reflect the issues raised in years of theological debate. What is the natural and legitimate exercise of the conjugal act? How do married partners commit sexual sins? What should motivate the sexual act? What sexual obligations do married partners have toward one another? The questions themselves indicate the hesitancy of medieval religious thinkers to accept sexuality as natural and good. Answers to these questions show the range from prudence to audacity possible in the literature on the forgiveness of sins.

EXCUSING SEX IN MARRIAGE

That marital intercourse had to be "excused" is evidence enough of the magnitude of the difficulty Christian theology had created. But that is how St. Augustine had talked about it, and he remained the guiding authority on marital sexual morality. He formulated the three "goods" of marriage—faith, offspring, and sacrament—and he argued that only the procreation of children and the fidelity of the married partners justified sexual congress. In his view, these goods of marriage balanced the objective evil of the sensual act of intercourse. Thus sex was licit within marriage if the partners went beyond their selfish enjoyment and considered the begetting and raising of children and the performance of a duty to one another to preserve continency. Apparently the goal of Augustine's moral philosophy is to have married partners exclude considerations of pleasure from their conscious motivation and direct their sexual activity toward external, unselfish goods. For Augustine these goods excusing marital intercourse were two, then: begetting children who would be cared for and educated in the faith of Christ; and

---

[10] Ziegler, *Ehelehre*, 165–169, 172–173, 181, 186–189; Noonan, *Contraception* (1967), 309–311, 353–357, 365–381; (1965), 255–257, 292–296, 303–317; Müller, *Paradiesesehe*, 181–279, 299–304.

rendering the marital debt to a partner so that he might avoid incontinency. Strictly speaking, Augustine only freed intercourse for procreation from all sin; every other use of sexuality, even within marriage, entailed some kind of sin, although he considered most such faults among the ordinary daily transgressions, which can be readily remitted through the petition of the Lord's Prayer, "forgive us our trespasses."[11]

The Augustinian conception of the mortality of the conjugal act provides the basic framework within which the practical literature for confessors operates. Perhaps the most important transmitter of these ideas is the summa of Raymond of Peñaforte and the gloss of William of Rennes. Raymond affirms Augustine's three goods of marriage—offspring, fidelity, and sacrament—and he remains faithful to the strictest Augustinian teaching when he says, "These three goods are able to excuse sin if the honor of the marriage bed is served as married partners come together *for the sake of offspring*." Raymond then turns to the most critical moral problem in the literature: the motives of the conjugal act. There are four motives, he tells us, for conjugal intercourse: to conceive offspring; to render the debt; to remedy incontinence or avoid fornication; and to satisfy desire. In an apparent contradiction to his assertion that the goods excuse sin when joined with the intention of procreating, Raymond announces that both the first and second motives are without sin; that the third is a venial sin; and that the fourth is mortal. William's gloss comments on Raymond's classification of the third motive—avoiding fornication—as a venial sin. Some say that this is no sin at all, William tells us, because it uses the act for a good purpose. But Augustine says that there is always some sin when the act is undertaken for any reason but desire for children. William leaves the reader with the impression that he accepts Raymond's classification entirely. Nevetheless William rejects the canonists' discussion of the motives for the conjugal act. There is no sense, he says, in trying to distinguish between remedying incontinence and avoiding fornication. Some find a difference. They think the need to remedy incontinence betrays an inability to control desire, whereas one who wants to avoid fornication merely tries to escape from the temptation of lying with someone other than his wife. The first is motivated by desire for pleasure, the second

[11] Noonan, *Contraception* (1967), 159–166; (1965), 124–131.

by the desire to avoid sin. He sensibly rejects this puzzling distinction, for none of the "masters" use it; and we can hope that he also objected to its obscurity. His prudence is commendable. But the whole hairsplitting discussion reminds us of how unreal this subtle examination of motives could become, and how far from common experience the advice to confessors could stray.[12]

Yet the examination of motives, and the judgment of the conjugal act according to motives, remained typical of the literature on the forgiveness of sins. And when authorities on pastoral care talked about "excusing" the marital act, or the goods of marriage, or the motives for sexual intercourse, they accepted the Augustinian framework and necessarily implied that sex was bad. There were ways, as we shall see, to incorporate the newer ideas of a Duns Scotus or an Albert the Great into the judgment of the marital act. Nevertheless, the whole mentality is a negative one, and even those who try to exalt the physical union of man and wife will, when they accept this framework, begin on the defensive.

THE CONJUGAL DEBT

Some authors use Peter Lombard's labels to describe the moral status of the motives for intercourse in marriage. To pay the debt and to seek offspring is "licit"; to avoid one's own infidelity is "delicate"; and to satisfy one's own desire for pleasure is "intemperate" or just plain "bad." This language too reveals the theologians' suspicion of sex. Yet despite the difficulty that celibate speculators found in justifying a fundamentally sensual act, they still insisted that no matter how ascetically inclined one of the partners in a marriage might be, one could not unilaterally impose abstinence on an unwilling spouse. This meant, of course, that there was still another way for married people to sin.

For medieval casuistry the obligation "to pay the marriage debt" is as serious as the requirement of procreative purpose. Its scriptural basis in St. Paul is clear and specific:

As for the questions raised in your letter; a man does well to abstain from all commerce with women. But, to avoid the danger of fornication, let every man keep his own wife, and every woman her own husband. Let every man give his wife

---

[12] *Raymundina*, IV, 2, 13, pp. 519–520. For a summary of the judgment of motives for the marital act, see Müller, *Paradiesesehe*, 295–318.

what is her due, and every woman do the same by her husband; he, not she, claims the right over her body, as she, not he, claims the right over his [1 Cor 7: 1–5].

This passage was taken as a rule binding each married partner. Refusal of the debt was matter for confession. The moral basis of this obligation is obvious. There is a horror of adultery, both in St. Paul and in the medieval authorities who insist on the payment of the debt, and no antipathy toward pleasure or devotion to virginity could make them forget that horror. Consequently every authority considers the obligation of paying the debt as an essential part of the proper conduct of marriage.

Gerson asserts this duty in the *Opus tripartitum*. Those who refuse the debt without good reason, such as ill health or some other reasonable impediment, he judges guilty of sin. He expands on this in the *Regulae morales*. There he insists that "no spouse is held to pay the debt in notable and certain detriment to her body or to a fetus about to be born." But he also makes it clear that not all excuses are valid: holy time and place do not exempt a partner from the obligation to pay the debt.[13]

Gerson's refusal to accept holy places as justification for denying the debt had been discussed in a work misattributed to him, the *Compendium theologiae*. To the question "Whether one always must pay the conjugal debt when it is sought?" the *Compendium* offers this amusing affirmative reply:

Concerning the payment of the conjugal debt, however, some hold that on every occasion the debt must be rendered to the one seeking it according to the opportunity of place; and they say this because the act has a certain shame attached to it. Consequently *it need not pe paid in public.* But at every hour and every instance when other affairs have ceased [in omni hora omnique dimisso negotio], *if one knows that the other is in a state of dangerous desire, one is obliged to seek out a secret nook and pay the debt* [italics added].[14]

Berthold of Freiburg agrees. You must pay the debt, Berthold teaches, in any private place, even a holy one. You should dissuade your spouse from asking under such circumstances, but

---

[13] Gerson, *Opus tripartitum*, II, Du Pin, I, 444C–445A; idem, *Regulae morales*, Du Pin, III, 106A.

[14] *Compendium theologiae*, Du Pin, I, 292D–293A.

you acquiesce without sin. Should you ask for it yourself in a holy place for the sake of avoiding temptation or for offspring, then it is no more than a venial sin. Berthold's only serious restriction is in his warning that if there is another, unblessed place available, then both sin mortally in not using it. Finally, Berthold probably shows what he really thinks of sex when he notes that a holy place so used needs to be reconsecrated.[15]

The obligation to pay the debt, therefore, was taken seriously enough to make religious writers forget their worries about sacrilege and argue that it took precedence over holy times and seasons. The most authoritative voices of this literature—people like Gerson and St. Antoninus of Florence—leave no doubt about how important paying the debt was in their moral theology. In the early sixteenth century, then, Sylvester is ready to offer a summary of commonplace opinions on the whole range of questions about the marital debt. One is not required to pay the debt to one's own personal danger, Sylvester begins, nor is one required to seek the debt, except to avoid fornication. But it is a mortal sin, "according to everyone," to deny it if there is no rational excuse and the one seeking it cannot be dissuaded. "Nor is one excused by not wishing to multiply one's offspring, or by virtue of anger or hatred or the holy season . . . : but one is required to pay the debt to the other even when the other only asks indirectly, for example by gestures." It is especially common, Sylvester continues, that women are too embarrassed to ask for the debt explicitly, and thus their signs and "conditions" must be considered sufficient communication of their desires.[16]

Sylvester has imposed rigid requirements, which are found in virtually all the authorities on sin and forgiveness. They allow few reasons for a spouse to refuse to pay the marital debt. Could this rigidity lead to scruples and troubled confessions? It is entirely possible, and perhaps even probable. For it created another sin, and good confessors were bound to understand it and deal with it conscientiously.

[15] Berthold von Freiburg, *Summa Joannis, deutsch*, Q. 179, "Ob man die eeliche werck müg tün an heilige stete."

[16] *Sylvestrina*, "Debitum coniugale," q. 8, par. 10; Antoninus, *Confessionale—Defecerunt*, 30. That refusing the debt is a mortal sin is a commonplace opinion. Exceptions to this rule allow refusal when the fetus or the woman is endangered (menstruation, pregnancy, disease). For the obligation to pay the debt to a spouse with leprosy, see Ziegler, *Ehelehre*, 60–61, 111–115, 282–283.

At the same time we must remember that the sin was in *not* having sexual intercourse. Theologians had gone beyond excusing or permitting the marital act. In some instances they found it mandatory. Thus they set limits to their own distrust of sexuality and admitted that there were, indeed, worse things than pleasure. It was not good in all cases to abstain. It could even be mortally sinful.

The suspicion and distrust of sex returns, however, in other cases concerning the marital debt. Moral theologians and those who directly instructed confessors regularly distinguished between paying the debt and seeking it. To seek the debt to overcome one's own desire was, for such authoritative theologians as Albert, Thomas, and Bonaventure, a venial sin. In the minds of these authorities it fell under the heading of what St. Paul had called "a concession" to those too weak to observe a higher degree of self-control. Since seeking the debt was only a venial sin, one would expect that it would not have been a prominent concern for the practical literature on the forgiveness of sins. Nevertheless, the moral status of seeking the debt elicited some inexplicably intricate discussions. The *Angelica* argues that only the sterile are completely sinless in seeking the debt to avoid incontinency—those who are fertile should intend procreation. St. Antoninus calls seeking the debt "indifferent," but only if there is no other way to avoid danger. And Sylvester, discussing the problem in three places, says that seeking the debt to avoid one's own incontinency is venial if there is some other way out of danger; indifferent if there is no other way (the example he uses of this dilemma is of a man who knows he must have a long talk with a woman in private and enlists his wife's aid to prepare for it accordingly); and meritorious if there is no other way and God's grace sanctifies the action.[17]

Now the difference between the complicated judgment of the *Sylvestrina* and the simple classification of the motive of avoiding incontinency as a venial sin is, for the practical purposes of con-

---

[17] Ziegler, *Ehelehre*, 214–218, for the early development and the opinions of Antoninus and Angelus. *Sylvestrina*, "Debitum coniugale," q. 11, par. 13, q. 12, par. 14; "Quarto quando facit ad eandem vitandam in se; et aliter meilus vitare non potest: quia est actus prudentiae vel castimoniae. Supposita vero carentia gratiae praedictus actus dictis quatuor modis [of which *causa vitandi* is one] est indifferens . . . ." Cf. Dennis Doherty, *The Sexual Doctrine of Cardinal Cajetan*, 269-303.

fessing, trivial. Yet it encouraged that habitual examination of the motives for marital intercourse. Thus while finding certain motives venially sinful and excusing slight variations in motive from any taint of sin should not have seriously troubled penitents, it kept alive the illusion that this was a clear and coherent way to talk about the conduct of marriage.

SEX FOR PLEASURE

If the precision of the distinctions between motives for the conjugal act seems curious to a modern reader, the confidence with which theologians separated the motive of satisfying desire from the others is stunning. Raymond of Peñaforte had fixed the habit of discerning four motives for undertaking the conjugal act, and he had pronounced the fourth intention, to satisfy desire, a mortal sin. His immediate authority for this condemnation was an old epigram declaring that everyone who was "too ardent a lover" with his wife was himself an adulterer. The epigram was originally pagan, but was appropriated by a Christian author in the ancient church and thereafter quoted as Christian by Augustine, Jerome, Gratian, and Peter Lombard in their eagerness to impose rational and ascetic limits to the sexual behavior of the married. With such authoritative and influential sources using this epigram, it is not surprising to find a huge variety of medieval literature condeming "too ardent love" as adulterous. "Nothing is more vile," says the *Raymundina*, "than to love your wife in adulterous fashion."[18] Heightening the severity of this con-

---

[18] *Raymundina*, IV, 2, 13, pp. 519–520; Noonan, *Contraception* (1967), 67, 106, 170–171, 241–242; (1965), 47, 80, 135, 197; Ziegler, *Ehelehre*, 210, 218–223; cf. ibid., 255, for a much more optimistic view than I present of the loosening of restrictions on the sexual act after William of Rennes—particularly in the judgment of the sinfulness of sex for pleasure and the marital act enjoyed *ultra modum*. An ancient condemnation of *nimis ardenter* is found in Methodius, *The Symposium. A Treatise on Chastity*, tr. and annotated by Herbert Musurillo, Ancient Christian Writers. The Works of the Fathers in Translation, ed. by Johannes Quasten and J. C. Plumpe, no. 27 (London and Westminster, Md., 1958), "Logos 3," 13, p. 72: "I think that it will be advantageous for you to control your carnal inclinations and not to abuse your vessels for uncleanness just because you are married"; and ibid., "Logos 9," 4, p. 138: "Those, however, who, even though they are not committing fornication, are yet deluded into enjoying their sole and lawful spouses to excess, how will they celebrate the Feast [after the Parousia]?" Editor's notes (pp. 204, 233) admit the obscurity of these passages and speak of an apparent reference to "lack of moderation in the use of marital privileges."

demnation, William of Rennes' gloss on this passage includes lengthy quotations from Huguccio. Thus William reinforces Raymond's strict opinion and introduces into the summas for confessors the sentiments of one of the most dualistic of medieval authorities.

William begins by noting that Peter Lombard calls it a mortal sin to enjoy your wife merely to satisfy desire. Others, William continues, say that if it is done naturally, it is only a venial sin, because then it is done out of the right and "trust" of matrimony. Then William cites Huguccio, who says it is a mortal sin. In avoiding fornication, Huguccio teaches, one chooses a venial instead of a mortal sin; but by satisfying pleasure he understands a situation in which desire has been actively incited—"by hands, or thought, or by using hot drinks . . . , so that he can copulate more frequently with his wife." It is true that Huguccio's opinion has helped make the meaning of "satisfying desire" clearer and more restrictive, and these pastoral advantages may explain why it had a certain currency in the literature on forgiveness. But Huguccio has another, harsher judgment that William cites: "Either coitus is a sin or it is not; but it can never be completely without sin because it always occurs with excitement and pleasure, which cannot be without sin."[19]

With the opinions of Huguccio, therefore, William of Rennes has offered future advisers of confessors and penitents some of the most pessimistic judgments about what was licit within the bounds of matrimony. After the *Raymundina* and its gloss, however, we find a variety in the language of the manuals and summas that uniformly accept the existence of a sin married people could commit by enjoying intercourse intemperately, but do not define or condemn it in even similar ways. Deep-rooted suspicion of sex persists. But more reasonable views are also influential. Perhaps most significant of all, however, is the lack of clarity possible when this case of conscience is discussed. For lack of clarity, as much as rigorism, can lead to perplexity and scrupulous doubts. And vagueness as well as diversity characterize subsequent discussion of this sin. Thus we must listen to the language

[19] *Raymundina*, IV, 2, 13, pp. 519–520; cf. Ziegler, *Ehelehre*, 219–220, 255; Ziegler argues that John of Freiburg is the first of the pastoral authorities clearly to reject the rigorism of Huguccio and reduce the sinfulness of sex for pleasure to venial status if it is performed within the limits of matrimony (that is, you would not do it if she were not your wife).

of these authorities on pastoral care as they try to make sense out of the sin of excessive enjoyment of one's wife.

Some authorities are imprecise in the extreme. Antonius de Butrio condemns even entering marriage for carnal pleasure. "For I have sinned," de Butrio's manual recites, "if I have contracted matrimony *for the sake of pleasure* or beauty or the size of the dowry and not on account of the good of offspring or of avoiding fornication."[20] Denis the Carthusian admits that the conjugal act can be without sin if one intends not pleasure but rather offspring (to educate to the worship of God), or payment of the debt or avoidance of incontinence. But, he warns, many married people commit mortal sins by excessive desire for pleasure because, as the oft-quoted epigram ascribed to St. Jerome has it, "omnis amator feruentior est adulter." And how bad is adultery? Denis has always said, he tells us, that it is ineffably enormous; after homicide it is one of the worst sins one can commit against one's neighbor.[21] For the little manual of J. P. Foresti also, the dangers of marital pleasure are as vague as they are dire. Foresti's confessor is to be guided in his inquiry of married people by these considerations: "If one was too immodest in touches, embraces, kisses, and other dishonorable things (*inhonesta*), it sometimes might be mortally sinful because these things are not consonant with sacred matrimony. . . . If he knew his wife not for offspring or for paying the debt, but only for his own insatiable and uncontrolled pleasure, . . . he has exposed himself on account of this kind of intemperance to the dangers of serious sin."[22]

The language of de Butrio, Denis, and Foresti has untold capacity for harm to consciences. It frustrates the goal of casuistry because it confuses rather than clarifies and disturbs rather than consoles. How could a confessor use such vague guides? How could a penitent decide whether pleasure had exercised too great a role in his decision to marry or whether his act of consummation had been too fervent? What could the penitents of pastor Johannes Wolff make of his formula for the examination of conscience and the confession of sins on this subject?

[20] de Butrio, *Directorium ad confitendum*, "De Peccatis contra sacramentum matrimonii"; for other examples of questioning the motives for marriage, cf. [Gerson?], *La Confession*, A7a–b; Jean Quentin, *Examen de conscience*, "Sur le peche de luxure"; Columbi, *Confession generale*, B7a–b.

[21] Denis the Carthusian *Speculum conuersionis peccatorum*, X6a.

[22] Foresti, *Confessionale*, "De Luxuriis coniugatorum," 17b–18a.

176

I have not had a godly attitude with respect to birth. Or that I have paid the debt but have had too much pleasure etc. Paul: "those who have wives be as if they had none" (1 Cor. 7:29).[23]

Yet even in the sixteenth century this obtuse nagging about motives persists: Godescalc Rosemondt writes a guide for married penitents to examine their consciences in his *Confessionale*: "And I have sought and fulfilled the pleasure of the flesh in illicit manner, and always too ardently; and I have intended minimally the good of offspring, for which matrimony was principally instituted...."[24]

[23] Wolff, *Beichtbüchlein*, 6 (128).

[24] Rosemondt, *Confessionale*, 5, [6], fol. 94b. This definition of "within the limits of matrimony" is susceptible to two interpretations. The more common understanding is, I think, the one based on the question, "Would you have had sexual intercourse with the woman who is your spouse even if she were not legitimately married to you?" A different meaning would be, "Were you so aroused by the desire for pleasure when you had intercourse with your wife that you would have done it with anyone who happened to be there?" The first question is predicated on a specific passion for your wife at the time of consummation. The second is predicated on a general and uncontrolled passion. The first assumes that only one woman is the object of desire but you will have sexual relations with her whether she is your wife or not. Thus Jean Raulin, *Itinerarium paridisi ... complectens sermones de penitentia, ... de matrimonio ac viduitate* (Paris, 1519), *De matrimonio*, sermon 8, fol. 181b–182a, identifies this mortal sinner: "... paratus esset idem facere cum vxore etiam si non esset coniunx." The second assumes that any woman will do; your wife just happens to be there at the time. The *Angelica*, "Debitum coniugale," 21, includes both definitions as it describes the condition of exceeding the limits of matrimony as when "cum quaviscumque alia vel cum ea etiam si non esset sua coiret," and it even adds "vel constituit ibi finem ultimum." Both are also in Antoninus, *Summa theologica*, 4 vols. (Basel, 1485), I, ti. 1, ch. 20, casus 1, where the discussion is based on Petrus de Palude. Klomps, *Ehemoral und Jansenismus*, 35, thinks that the second view is more common and that it derives from Augustine: "Anders wäre es [than the Pauline indulgence for paying the debt], wenn das Lustmotive ehebrecherischer Art wäre, d.h., wenn der Gatte Bereit wäre, mit *jeder anderen* Frau wie mit seiner Gattin zu verhehren" (italics added). Ziegler, *Ehelehre*, 220, also uses this definition. In either case, however, the whole problem with the definition of the sin *extra limites* and *nimis ardenter* is in knowing when it has happened. This difficulty of identifying the sin lead, as it is argued below, to the resolution of the question into two different considerations: the first, the more easily identified condition of self-incitement *ut pluries coire possit*; and the second and even more easily identified condition of explicitly wishing your wife were someone else while you had intercourse with her. Cf. Caracciolus, *Sermones ... De quadragesima: de penitentia*, 29, ch. 1, for a similar treatment in sermon form.

It was possible, however, to define more carefully the sin of too great enjoyment in the conjugal act. The first way was to follow the lead of William of Rennes in quoting Huguccio's opinion that too ardent love meant inciting desire artificially so that one can have intercourse more frequently rather than letting it arise naturally. Bartholomaeus de Chaimis is one of those who accept this definition, and he declares on it with surprising boldness. Marital intercourse for the sake of pleasure, he advises, is mortally sinful if it is intentionally incited and does not simply arise out of natural infirmity. The test is which comes first, desire or an act of the will.[25] Antonius de Butrio, in spite of his vagueness elsewhere, gives this rule for determining when marital intercourse is used for satiating desire: it is mortally sinful "when it is not preceded by but precedes temptation," which one arouses by vilely touching his private parts and inciting lust "so that he might know his wife more times than he has the will."[26] Johann Nider, whose announced concern for the consolation of the penitent did not lead him into milder opinions on the conjugal act, is also explicit. He is discussing the act when it is "intemperate," which, he tells us, "is generally performed with mortal sin":

> The second kind of intemperate intercourse occurs for the sake of satisfying desire and the man provokes himself to this through meretricious caresses, or on purpose uses hot and strongly inciting drinks, or in some other way summons, as it were, this act from himself for the sake of satisfying pleasure.[27]

Some authorities explain, therefore, that when they condemn the intemperate enjoyment of conjugal rights they mean specifically auto-erotic incitement to a desire for intercourse that would

[25] de Chaimis, *Interrogatorium*, III, 3.

[26] de Butrio, *Speculum de confessione*, 60, C7b.

[27] Nider, *Expositio decalogi*, VI, 4, B2b. Berthold von Freiburg, *Summa Johannis, deutsch*, "Von dem eelichen wercken / wenn die sünd seÿen /vnd wenn nit," also defines the marital act "mit überigem wollust" as occurring when one does not need it but rather incites desire so that he can more often enjoy intercourse. Such married people are, as is traditional, condemned as mortally sinful for acting like prostitutes. But interestingly enough, Berthold sees the possibility of excusing such behavior if the motive is to have children: "Wär aber dz sÿ hindernuss häten zů den wercken / als ob ir eins zekalt wår vnd vnfruchtper / vnd gerñ kinder håten / vnd dēn ir eins das ander reÿczt mit greyffen / oder heÿsse kost ÿsst vnd starcke tranck trinckt / auff das dz sÿ kinder mochten machen das war nit sünde."

not ordinarily arise. Certainly this definition is clearer than the vague rumblings against desire and pleasure and immodest behavior we find in Foresti and Denis the Carthusian. Nevertheless it is also true that this is a rigoristic doctrine likely to engender its own troubles; and that the line between normal and natural arousal and forbidden degrees of self-arousal can be, to say the least, baffling.

The second and favorite way to determine the sin of intemperate pleasure in marital intercourse taught penitents or confessors to decide whether the act remained "within the limits of matrimony." You are guilty, according to this criterion, of too fervent and therefore adulterous love of your wife if you would have performed the act even if she were not your wife.

Most of the authorities who use this definition of intemperate intercourse no more than identify and condemn it. The *Tractatus de instructionibus confessorum* brands as mortally sinful an act so lustful that one would do it even if one's partner were not one's legitimate wife, and its brevity and severity are in no way unusual. Foresti warns, for example, that anyone "who has loved his wife so ardently that he would have wanted to lie with her even if she had not been his wife . . . is said to have committed adultery inferentially (*interpretive*)." Jodocus Winshemius cites the *Angelica* as he uses almost identical language: the "ardentior amator" is an adulterer with his wife because he would exceed the limits of matrimony solely out of desire for pleasure. And Stephan Lanzkranna's *Himmelstrasse* brings the worrying about ardent loving to the readers of devotional literature. The conjugal act can be mortally sinful, Stephan warns, when one so passionately desires one's spouse that he would act unchastely—*unkeusch treiben*—with the other even outside the bonds of matrimony.[28]

This second definition of lustful intercourse that exceeds the proper limits of matrimony was popular among ecclesiastical writers. Like the refusal to pay the debt, it found wide currency among the disseminators of moral doctrine and confessional instruction. Yet, like the sin of willfully inciting desire, it is still fundamentally unrealistic and even more difficult to identify. How do you know when you have so desired your wife, or so de-

---

[28] *Tractatus de instructionibus confessorum*, D8b–E1b; Foresti, *Confessionale*, 15a; Winshemius, *Institutiones*, B3b; Stephan Lanzkranna, *Himelstrass*, c.17, fol. 55a–b. See above, n. 24, for the meaning of this definition.

sired sexual pleasure, that you would have done what you did with your wife even if she had not been your wife, or, perhaps, if someone other than your wife had happened to be around? To some authorities both solutions were confusing and dangerous and they tried to clarify or soften the condemnation of going outside the limits of marriage. Antoninus of Florence accepts the traditional formula when he condemns someone who "is carried to the conjugal act with such inordinate affection that even if it were not one's wife or one's husband one would still perform the carnal act with her or with him." Nevertheless he is openly skeptical about the utility of this definition as he adds: "... *yet this is difficult to determine*."[29] It is a brief but salutary caution from a voice of considerable authority. And to the prudence of Antoninus we may add that of Jean Gerson, who articulates a different interpretation of this case of conscience.

Gerson's *Regulae morales* presents a third, milder and clearer teaching on pleasure in marital intercourse. The worst prejudices of Huguccio are removed. Gerson manages to free his moral doctrine from the most excessive suspicion of the carnal as he summarizes his judgment on the four motives for intercourse:

> The enjoyment of a man with his wife is licit for the sake of offspring, of paying the debt, and of preservation from forbidden incontinence. And if nothing but pleasure is sought, but it remains within the limits of the bond of matrimony so that it would not be sought outside of it, and it does not occur with otherwise prohibited circumstances, that is either no sin or only a venial one.[30]

Gerson's tone and emphasis, like St. Antoninus's, direct attention away from scrupulous concern over the degree of pleasure involved in the act. Only one condition is dangerous—not remaining within the limits of matrimony. How do you tell whether you have remained within those limits? In the next paragraph Gerson adds a clarification that was to become a popular way to specify what this formula meant: it is a mortal sin if, while you are having sexual relations with your wife, you think of someone else as the object of the act. Now this circumstance is identifiable and reasonable. It does not ask what might have happened, it asks what did. Taken as a whole, Gerson's concise characterization of

[29] Antoninus, *Confessionale—Defecerunt*, 30 (italics added).
[30] Gerson, *Regulae morales*, Du Pin, III, 95B–C.

the motives for intercourse affirms that something specific has to intervene to make sex for pleasure seriously sinful. And that sin really amounts to a sin of desire, with a definite object. Thus here, as elsewhere, Gerson seems determined to curtail the dangerous and unnecessary multiplication of sins.

Both Antoninus and Gerson were obviously dissatisfied with the customary treatment of sex for pleasure, yet they were too conservative to dispense with it altogether. Although they were reluctant to encourage confessors to investigate the degrees of sexual pleasure, even they felt compelled to include this case of conscience. To an even greater degree, the *Supplementum, Angelica*, and *Sylvestrina* illustrate how intricately the clerical mind continued to investigate the motivation of the conjugal act.

Confessors who read the *Supplementum* on the question of satisfying desire would have found rigid conclusions, hostile to sexual pleasure. Nicolaus of Ausimo's additions to the text of Bartholomaeus of Pisa are an assault on the consciences of married people that is not typical of the summas in general but all too typical of the *Supplementum*. The shadow of Huguccio is cast over this fifteenth century summa.

Bartholomaeus's *Pisanella* had remained faithful to the teaching of Raymond of Peñaforte: the conjugal act is without sin, it argues, for the sake of children and rendering the debt. Bartholomaeus even calls intercourse for procreation "meritorious." Nicolaus, however, adds a commentary of unsurpassable rigor. Yes, the *Pisanella* is correct, he begins, "if the rectitude of the intention is afterwards not somewhat changed (postea aliquatenus non mutetur)." His definition of how the intention can remain righteous is alarmingly rigid: ". . . that is, [if] in the performance of this act there is no enjoyment of pleasure (hoc est in executione ipsius actus nulla voluptatis delectatione teneatur)." Nicolaus then confidently quotes the *Responsum beati Gregorii*'s opinion, which Gratian had put in the *Decretum*, to the effect that it is very difficult to stand in the flame and not feel the heat; such a miracle could only occur as a special gift of God. That is why, Nicolaus assures us, Gregory forbids married partners entrance to holy places after they have had intercourse. The point is obvious. There can be no marital intercourse without some degree of sin because it is inconceivable that the act could be performed without pleasure.[31]

[31] *Supplementum*, "Debitum coniugale," 4.

181

Thus while the *Pisanella* had acquitted intercourse motivated by desire for offspring or by paying the debt from all sin, the *Supplementum* asserts the likelihood of the sinfulness of all marital intercourse because of the inevitable concomitant of pleasure. No doubt the sin is venial and not matter for confession. Still the attitude, which we can easily identify as stemming from Huguccio, is not encouraging.

What of those conjugal relations motivated by desire for pleasure? The *Pisanella* sticks to the familiar teaching, which Bartholomaeus ascribes to St. Thomas, that this is only a venial sin if it remains within the limits of matrimony. It is otherwise if it exceeds those limits, "so that even if she were not his wife he would do the same": in that case it is a mortal sin. For, as we are accustomed to hearing, whoever loves his wife adulterously is an adulterer.

"Indubitably true," Nicolaus asserts in his comment, because the mere intention to commit a mortal sin (what sin? we might ask) is a mortal sin. To prove this point he offers one of his rare citations to the New Testament. The warning in Matthew 5:28 that whoever looks at a woman and wants to commit adultery with her is already guilty in his heart is of doubtful relevance, but Nicolaus invokes it. For although the passage from Matthew might have been used to restrict the definition of "outside the limits," as Gerson had—by calling it the express desire for someone else—Nicolaus does not clarify anything. The *Pisanella* had given the stock explication, asking would you have done it even if she had not been your wife? Instead of working on this question, however, Nicolaus turns to broad threats about the dangers of sensuality. His comments on Ecclesiasticus 19:2 fit the general tone perfectly:

> "Wine and women make even wise men fall." And surely a spouse ought to be utterly discreet and fearful, so that when he is inflamed with desire he does not transgress the limits of matrimony, even in intention.

But it is when Nicolaus turns to the motive of satisfying desire that the influence of Huguccio is most evident. Taking the description of the man who satisfies desire from Huguccio, Nicolaus condemns as mortally sinful anyone who purposely arouses himself. This judgment is more reasonable, he explains, because there are only three cases in which married people are allowed to have intercourse: offspring, paying the debt, and avoiding fornication. "It follows therefore that other cases fall under the prohibition of fornication, which is a mortal sin because it violates the sixth commandment of the Decalogue." Indeed, Nicolaus takes this opportunity, in this practical reference work for confessors, to deliver a sermon. He quotes the severest attacks on lust. He cites the Book of Tobias, and says that those who undertake or use matrimony for pleasure are given over to the devil. It is true, he admits, and one wonders how reluctantly, that marriage was given as a remedy. It was not given, however, "for the fulfillment of pleasure (non autem ad implementum voluptatis)." In the world view of the *Supplementum*, seeking pleasure is devilish and damnable. The confessor who consulted these pages would have learned to conduct a scrupulous inquisition into the motives of married Christians. And the guiding principle behind that inquisition would have been that sexual pleasure is sinful.

Another example of a dispute between text and commentator on sex for pleasure occurs in a sixteenth century edition of the *Angelica*, which is provided with an extensive gloss by Jacobus Ungarelli, and an occasional gloss on that gloss by Ungarelli's superior in the Franciscan order. Under "Conjugal Debt" Angelus de Clavasio answers the question whether marital intercourse "for the sake of satisfying desire" is a mortal sin. Some, he tells us, hold it is always a mortal sin for that motive; and this case is said to occur when desire is aroused by thoughts, touches, and hot drinks "so that one can copulate more frequently (ut possit pluries coire)." But Angelus declares that the more common and more reasonable opinion holds that it is not a mortal sin so long as one would not do it if she were not one's wife; and the emphasis, as with Gerson and Antoninus, is on the normally venial nature of the fault. Ungarelli's gloss disagrees in its usual, rigoristic fashion: "Nevertheless," he protests, "it can be said that the first opinion is the more rational." In fact, he sees only two causes of intercourse free from sin (for children and to pay the debt), and the third, avoidance of fornication, is excused from sin on account of its purpose. The rest are sins against the sixth commandment. Ungarelli's scorn and condemnation for pleasure seekers is unrestrained: those who undertake intercourse for pleasure exclude God from their minds, act as brute beasts, lack reason, and if they begin marriage for this reason, are given over to the power of the devil. The gloss on Ungarelli, however, calmly notes that William of Vaurouillon, a fifteenth century Franciscan and disciple of Duns Scotus, agrees with the *Angelica*'s opinion, "which seems more rational."[32]

We have not examined the dispute between the *Angelica* and Ungarelli's gloss because it might possibly have reached an extensive, literate public. It is not even likely that the comments of an obscure glossator would have influenced many confessors. Nevertheless, it shows how tenaciously a rigoristic teaching on sex for pleasure could hang on. Ungarelli is criticizing the work of a fellow Franciscan, a renowned and respected authority. Obviously his commitment to a rigoristic solution was carefully considered. And while the final word, the gloss on Ungarelli, decides in favor of Angelus's milder and "more rational" opinion, Ungarelli's words remain in print to remind us that even in the sixteenth century those in charge of instructing the pastoral clergy could cling to the most severe moral judgments. Put this evidence along with the vague condemnations of "too ardent lovers" in the manuals, or with the fulminations of the *Supplementum*, and one can imagine the grave distress created for married penitents. To take pleasure in sex is for these rigorists fundamentally evil. There are ways that sexual pleasure in marriage can be so great that it is mortally sinful. Yet who can deny that pleasure in sex is virtually inevitable? And who has found a way to measure it?

Of all the summas for confessors, the *Sylvestrina* defines most sensibly and carefully the sin of lustful intercourse transgressing the limits of matrimony. Intention can make the conjugal act a mortal sin, Sylvester says in summary of his authority, Petrus de Palude. He also notes that all authorities agree it is a mortal sin to perform the act outside the bounds of matrimony so that one would do it with anyone and not just one's spouse. But what does this mean? Sylvester chooses the third way of defining it as he quotes with approval an opinion of Petrus de Palude that we have already seen in Gerson's *Regulae morales*: this violation occurs when the intention of the partner suffers a disorder so that another person actually comes to mind—*si actu cogitetur de tali inordinatione intentionis*. Consequently, if another person is not actually desired, no matter what the degree of appetite for pleasure, there is no mortal sin. Indeed, even if someone were so disposed that, if another person came to mind he would then desire

[32] *Angelica*, "Debitum coniugale," 4.

184

that person, there would still be no mortal sin. For we are praised and blamed for acts, not habits or dispositions.[33]

Sylvester, St. Antoninus, and Jean Gerson have mitigated the confessor's obligation to investigate the motivation of the sexual act. In particular, all three attempt to soften that suspicion of sex that is so prominent when pastoral theology tries to find ways to condemn excessive pleasure. Yet even in their language there is a caution that recalls their purpose: to give a safe and sound opinion on all important questions to the widest of audiences. In this case, their teaching was intended to reach all married people. Hence they were restrained, even when it seems likely that, as in the question of the morality of sex for pleasure, some of them were skeptical about how useful the old language was. At the end of the middle ages we find even bolder theologians, who do not write for the pastoral clergy, but who are worth citing because of their break with traditional puritanical attitudes. The Parisian master Martin Le Maistre was one of those who rejected some of the rigorism of the old school. No devotional work, no manual or summa for confessors, could offer an argument like this one, which cuts through the hesitancy and puritanism of the enemies of pleasure:

> Right reason dictates that it is lawful to use . . . copulation for the sake of pleasure, just as it is lawful for me to use lamb or mutton, and, though I suppose both are healthy, to use lamb when it pleases me more. Nor would Aristotle see any fault in this if the use was moderate.[34]

---

[33] *Sylvestrina*, "Debitum coniugale," q. 2, par. 4. Sylvester says he is merely following Petrus de Palude here in his tight definition of *infra limites*. We can find a similar limitation of this sin in the vernacular manual, [Gerson?], *Directoire*, "Luxure de corps," O3b–O4b. When a man or woman has sexual relations with his spouse but in his heart is enjoying another—"Et en ceste volunte accomplissent le faicte comme si ce avoit este a lautre"—it is a mortal and very dangerous sin; we might add, it is a relatively specific one too. See also: [Gerson?], *La Confession*, 6th commandment, A7a–b. "Aussy se elle a acompli son mariage en facon deshonneste en pensent daultruy"; and Foresti, *Confessionale*, 15a, "Si reddendo debitum vxori de alia cogitauit & econtra; semper mor. p. & totiens quotiens hec deliberate fecit."

[34] Noonan, *Contraception* (1967), 372; (1965), 309. Noonan's description of Le Maistre, Major, and Almain forcefully establishes their originality. On the laxist use of the analogy between food and sex, however, St. Thomas had already anticipated Le Maistre: "Praeterea, qui cibo utitur propter delecta-

Another Parisian master, John Major, was similarly critical of the strict view. Major openly rebuts the opinion he thought came to Huguccio from Gregory the Great—that pleasure had to be sinful—objecting that there is no proof for it. And when he looks at the teaching on the motives for conjugal intercourse he says simply: "I find a great variety among the Doctors here, and in my opinion, men who are too hard."[35]

Le Maistre and Major represent one pole for the judgment of the morality of the conjugal act undertaken for pleasure. The canonist Huguccio represents the other. For Le Maistre the pleasure of sex was no more ominous than the pleasure of a good meal. For Huguccio, all sexual acts, even within marriage, partook of desire and pleasure and therefore, to some degree, of sin. Between these two poles stood the mass of practical advisers to those in charge of the cure of souls. Most of them were nearer to Huguccio, because they accepted the possibility that one might sin seriously by an excessive desire for pleasure in the conjugal act. But even these authorities were careful to note that many of these transgressions were only venial sins. Furthermore, some of these authorities realistically tried to clarify what this sin meant in the experience of married life. There were, finally, other authorities on pastoral instruction who stood closer to Le Maistre, and, for a variety of reasons, tried to minimize the concern over sinful indulgence in the pleasures of marital intercourse. Those confessors who read Antoninus, Gerson, Sylvester, or Angelus de Clavasio would have found authorities for limiting, minimizing, or perhaps even ignoring this question. Those confessors who read other works, however, would have found a persistent encouragement to suspect and decry the sexual pleasure of married people.

UNNATURAL ACTS

Sodomy, onanism, bestiality, and other sins against nature, were, as we have already seen, invariably identified as the worst imaginable sexual transgressions. Thus the universal condemnation of contraception and sexual acts in which genital organs are

---

tionem tantum, non peccat mortaliter. Ergo pari ratione qui utitur uxore tantum causa libidinis satiandae"; *Commentum in quartum librum sententiarum*, dis. 31, q. 2, a. 3, *Opera omnia*, vol. 11 (Paris, 1874), p. 127.

[35] Klomps, *Ehemoral*, 51–52; see pp. 52–57 for other opinions of Major and Jacques Almain.

not properly joined as sins against nature meant that the state of matrimony was susceptible to dangers far greater than disorders in the motivations of the conjugal act. The insistence of theologians that these sins are even worse when practiced by married people is faithfully reflected in the vituperative language used to instill repugnance toward unnatural acts. The profound concern of clerical moralists is evident in the following quotation from *Opus tripartitum*. At the commandment, "Thou shalt not commit adultery," Gerson writes:

> By this commandment every association [societas] and carnal union of man and woman outside of the law of matrimony is forbidden under pain of mortal sin; and to assert the contrary is an error against faith. This precept also forbids—as much for those bound in matrimony as for those who are single—every erotic stimulation of the genitals in which the natural order imparted by nature is not served or the parts intended by nature for generation are not properly joined. And this sin is the more serious the further it departs from the natural order, whether between single persons or, which aggravates the sin, between those who are joined in matrimony; whether such contact shall have been with oneself or another person or with respect to a beast of another species, consummated with illicit and foulest satisfaction.

We notice first that this passage begins with a sweeping condemnation of "every erotic stimulation (omnis luxuriosus attactus)." This prohibition is so general that one immediately looks for some clarification. But a manual expressly designed for popular use cannot be too explicit lest the faithful, in the common warning of the literature, be taught how to sin. Thus sexual activity that might be anything from precoital stimulation to masturbation is branded as the vilest of transgressions and there is no guarantee that actions which Gerson would consider entirely innocent might appear to a reader of this passage to be sins against nature.

We notice also in this passage Gerson's customary obsession with the whole class of sexual sins against nature. By far the greatest part of *Opus tripartitum*'s exposition of this commandment is devoted to the confession, causes, and cure of unnatural acts. Yet despite his skill as casuist and consoler, the principal characteristic of his attack on sins against nature is not its clarity but rather its tough words. He seeks to terrify those who recklessly pursue their perverted inclinations:

> On account of this detested sin the world was once destroyed with a universal flood and the five cities of Sodom and Gomorrah were burned with a celestial fire so that their inhabitants descended live into hell. Likewise on account of this sin—which calls forth divine vengeance—famines, wars, plagues, epidemics, floods, betrayals of kingdoms, and many other disasters come more frequently, as Holy Scripture testifies.

The vivid depiction of God's wrath, coupled with a certain generality in the identification of "erotic stimulation" as a sin against nature, does not make this section a model of pastoral instruction.[36]

If Gerson could be vague, there should be no surprise that others were habitually imprecise when they taught about unnatural conjugal acts. Once again it is in the language of moral doctrine that we encounter the possibility of obscurity and perplexity. The *Directoire des confesseurs* tells married partners to determine whether they have had relations in ways other than according to the laws of nature or the propriety of marriage. Strikingly similar is the warning of Jodocus Winshemius that married penitents sin by knowing each other without, or against, natural usage. Winshemius is being intentionally vague, moreover, because he is taking his ideas directly from the *Angelica*'s detailed discussion "Debitum."[37] To other more explicit sins against nature within marriage the manual of Foresti adds this condemnation of nonprocreative sexual activity: "If he was too unchaste in touches, embraces, and kisses and other shameful things (*inhonesta*) this could sometimes be mortally sinful: for these are not consonant with holy matrimony."[38] Even Jean Columbi's general confession includes this kind of language. In one place the congregation is to say: "Likewise in marriage with my spouse I have committed several evil touches."[39] And Antonius

[36] Gerson, *Opus tripartitum*, I, 11, II, "Luxuria," Du Pin, I, 436A–437B; 444C–445A. It is on the basis of this passage that Noonan, *Contraception* (1967), 290; (1965), 238–239, attributes to Gerson the view that coitus *ultra modum* is a sin against nature; see below, n. 50.

[37] [Gerson?], *Directoire*, "Luxure de corps," O2a–b; Winshemius, *Institutiones*, B3b.

[38] Foresti, *Confessionale*, 17b–18a.

[39] Columbi, *Confession generale*, B7a–b.

de Butrio's *Directorium* adds his disapproval of improper marital love: "And if on account of pleasure and lustful stimulation I have approached my wife and performed meretricious and filthy actions."[40]

These condemnations are disturbingly vague. They fail, as Gerson's teaching in *Opus tripartitum* fails—because it is not clear what kind of erotic stimulation and shameful sex play these authors are forbidding. Yet they are saying or intimating that these are unnatural acts. Now it is possible that we are dealing here simply with euphemisms for unnatural intercourse and other contraceptive practices. If that is so then their failure to get across is almost total. It seems more likely that their intention is to discourage sexual behavior of any sort that is not necessarily and directly related to a procreative act. Once again, the suspicion of pleasure dominates.

Elsewhere in the literature, however, the discussion of unnatural acts in marriage could be starkly frank. Authorities define two principal ways married people can commit sins against nature. First they condemned as unnatural intercourse sexual relations *non in debito vase*—that is, not in the proper orifice. Second, they condemned, with a good deal more difficulty and rationalization, sexual relations in which the proper orifice was used, but in which the act was performed in what they called an improper manner—*indebitus modus*. The first variety was easier to define as damnable sin (although such practices as coitus interruptus and coitus reservatus could complicate the casuistry), because it clearly fell under an ancient ban against deliberate frustration of procreation. Improper manner posed more serious problems, however, because its gravity definitely depended on one's view of what habits are natural to man; how serious it is to depart from these natural habits; and how evil it is to enjoy sexual relations and strive to increase that enjoyment by means of these improper manners. The developed casuistry of improper manner referred to "unusual" positions in sexual intercourse, and the definition of what was and was not unusual was outlined by the thirteenth theologian Albert the Great and accepted almost universally thereafter.

For Albert there were five major choices of position. First was the natural position: the woman lies on her back and the man on

---

[40] de Butrio, *Directorium ad confitendum*, "De Peccatis contra sacramentum matrimonii."

top of her. Second is a position that deviates slightly from the natural in which the partners lie laterally, beside one another. Third, a more serious deviation, the partners sit. Fourth and worse is standing. And the fifth and worst is to copulate like animals with the man entering from behind. It is the last of these that is most popularly discussed as the "improper manner" constituting an offense against nature.[41] Others include a sixth position—the man reclining with the woman on top—and call it worse than all but coitus from behind.

The notion that it was sinful to copulate in the manner of brute beasts is at least as old as the penitentials of the early middle ages. Most of them penalize it more lightly than really serious sins such as adultery, fornication, and the like, and it is in that tradition that Burchard of Worms declares: "Have you had relations with your wife or someone else from behind, in the manner of a dog? If you have done so, do penance for ten days on bread and water." Nevertheless some of these early medieval books took it more seriously, and it could even be taxed with three years of penance.[42]

The era of private confession changes the form of this speculation because the problem then becomes differentiating between mortal sins, which are matter for confession, and venial sins, which are not. The question is raised with exquisite simplicity by William of Rennes in his gloss to the *Raymundina*. After discussing the case of too ardent loving of one's wife, he asks: "Does a man sin mortally if he knows his wife not in the customary manner even though he performs the act in the proper orifice?" This blunt question receives an answer of equal candor: "I respond that I believe, without prejudice, that if he does this merely for the sake of seeking greater pleasure, he sins mortally." William continues with what were to become the classic considerations for judging this case. If the wife is pregnant or sick and the husband does not dare approach her from the front, he does not sin mortally by approaching from some other way

[41] Albertus Magnus, *Commentarii in IV sententiarum*, dis. 31, a. 24, *Opera omnia*, vol. 30 (Paris, 1894), 262–263.

[42] Burchard of Worms, *Decretorum libri XX*, 19, 5, *PL*, 187, 957–960. There is a variety of penances in Schmitz, *Die Bussbücher*: I, 282–283 (40 days); I, 453 (40 days); II, 183 ("sicut de animalibus"!); II, 344 (3 years). Cf. McNeill and Gamer, *Medieval Handbooks*, 197, canon 21 (although the translation is euphemistic, the original is given in the footnote)—(40 days).

just so long as there is no improper use of the female genitals and no semen is intentionally or knowingly spilled. Yet, he declares, "it would nevertheless be much safer if he were to consider her as a sister in such cases than to know her in such a way."[43] Both John of Freiburg and the *Summa Joannis, deutsch* agree substantially with William's conclusion. Berthold notes that sitting, standing, or performing the act like irrational beasts from behind "waer alles ein todsuende," and when he notes that there may be excusing conditions such as sickness and pregnancy that make such deviations from normal practice acceptable (just so long as the organs are properly joined), he cites Thomas, Albert, and Petrus de Palude.[44]

Astesanus focuses on the same issues but varies the argument. He declares that the common opinion brands coitus in an abnormal manner but in the proper orifice a mortal sin if it is done solely to increase pleasure, but not a mortal sin if it is because of some good reason. The other view holds that improper manner is always against nature, always a mortal sin, and never excusable for any reason. Those of the milder opinion argue that only coitus not in the proper orifice is truly against nature. He concludes that the harsher opinion is "safer," but he also advises that "the whole thing be left to more worthy judgment [saniori judicio]." Thus far Astesanus has appeared to favor the rigorists, but he has drawn back from asserting flatly that they are right and all deviations from normal positions are mortal sin. But he finishes this section with a curious twist—a hard opinion based on the likelihood of conception.[45] To the question

---

[43] *Raymundina*, IV, 2, 13, p. 520. The *Supplementum*, "Debitum coniugale," 11, follows William's solution and includes some of Albert's considerations as well.

[44] Johannes von Freiburg, *Summa confessorum*, IV, 2, 37; Berthold, *Summa Johannis, deutsch*, "Von dem eelichen wercken," Q. 177.

[45] *Astesana*, VIII, 9, a. 2. Ziegler, *Ehelehre*, 227–231, summarizes the opinion of Astesanus differently. Ziegler notes that there were theologians in the thirteenth century who concluded that intercourse *ultra modum*—that is, *in debito vase* but *non debitus situs*—was always sinful, and he thinks that Astesanus did not even allow it to avoid adultery (*Ehelehre*, 229), because Astesanus followed a rigorist tradition and classified it as *contra naturam*. (For that opinion in the *Supplementum*, see above, "Sense of Sin," n. 9.) I do not find Astesanus so definite. Although Astesanus calls the harsh opinion "safer," he still says he is going to leave it up to someone with better judgment; and while he brands the woman on top as contraceptive in effect, and therefore *contra naturam*, nevertheless he seems to give full recognition to

"What if a mounted woman abuses the man?" Astesanus answers:

It is a mortal sin, because that manner is against nature, since it is not conducive to the infusion of semen with respect to the man, nor to its reception with respect to the woman; and thus the intention of nature is totally frustrated. Thus Methodius enumerates that sin among the causes of the flood; as it is also in the *Historiis scholasticis*[46] saying: Women gone mad, having gotten on top, abused their men.

A whole host of authors trying to be faithful to the moral teaching of the church and hoping to save Christians from the

---

the rationality of the view that coitus *a tergo* is permissible for a good reason. On the other hand, Ziegler also denies that this kind of rigorism rules the pastoral literature: "Trotzdem von einigen Franziskanertheologen aus medizinischen (Empfängnisverhütung) und ethischen Erwägungen (sündhafte Steigerung des Geschlechtsgenusses) eine strenge Beurteilung des Ehevollzuges ultra modum befürworte wurde, setzte sich in der Pastoralliteratur der PS mit ausnahme der Astasana die rigoristische Haltung nicht durch. Der Dominikaner Wilhelm und der Minorit Monaldus werten ihn, aus einem vernünftigen Grunde vollzoge, als lässliche Sünde. Johannes und Bartholomäus sprechen ihm unter diesen Umständen unter Berufung auf Albert und Thomas jede Sündhaftigkeit ab" (*Ehelehre*, 231). But the qualifications Ziegler has included can constitute, as is argued here, the basis for a rigoristic ethic on the marital act *ultra modum*. This is especially relevant when we consider Ziegler's assertion (pp. 213–214) that there is distrust, if not downright condemnation, of coitus *ultra modum* to increase pleasure (and not to protect wife or fetus), which is true not only for his period, which ends with the fourteenth century *Astesana*, but for the subsequent period as well.

[46] Jean Raulin (*Itinerarium paridisi, de matrimonio*, sermon 8, fol. 182b) makes the same reference to this text, which is in Petrus Comestor, *Historia scholastica*, "Liber Genesis," ch. 31, *PL*, 198, 1081. A fifteenth century edition of the *Historia scholastica* (Augsburg, 1473), tries to clarify the *contra naturam* definition of the sin by adding words (italicized here) implying more than coitus *ultra modum*: "Sexcentesimo anno mulieres in uesaniam verse *sese abutebantur* supragresse viris *postea* abutebantur." The original source of this passage (acknowledged by Petrus Comestor) is the *Revelations* of Pseudo-Methodius; for identification and text, see Ernst Sackur, *Sibyllinisch Texte und Forschungen. Pseudo-Methodius, Adso, und die tiburtinische Sibylle* (Halle, 1898), esp. 3–9, 55–59, 61; and Marjorie Reeves, *The Influence of Prophecy in the Later Middle Ages, A Study in Joachimism* (Oxford, 1969), 300, 352. Both English manuscript versions omit identification of this sin: *The Begynnyng of the World and the Ende of Worldes*, ed. by Aaron J. Perry, Early English Text Society, Original Series, 167 (London, 1925), 95–96.

vilest of sins found it necessary to condemn unnatural positions and practices in the marital act. Godescalc Rosemondt, for example, reminds his readers that it is not proper to talk at great length about the various ways to commit sins of lust—one must be cautious not only in books and sermons, he tells us, but even in the confessional. Nevertheless, he finds lust so prevalent among the clergy as well as the laity that a degree of frankness is apparently justified and he identifies the usual varieties, from fornication to bestiality. Under unnatural acts he notes:

> Unnaturalness occurs when the man in intercourse with his wife does not use the proper orifice or organ; or if he uses the proper organ he nevertheless does not use the proper manner ordained by nature and more apt for conception.

He then continues with a form like that of the general confession, written in the first person and designed to aid the examination of conscience. Thus the avowal of sinfulness for the married begins "I have not lived honestly and purely in the state of matrimony as befits good spouses," and reiterates, among a concise list of possible sexual transgressions, his condemnation of unnatural positions: "Also I have not used the proper, natural manner in carnal union as reason and the matrimonial state require."[47] It is a flat condemnation of "improper positions."

In a section of his explanation of the Decalogue that discusses the varieties of "intemperate" conjugal acts, which generally occur with mortal sin, Johann Nider also specifically includes unnatural positions. He notes at the outset that one meaning of sexual intercourse "against the natural manner" is where the proper orifice is not used, and this is always a sin because offspring cannot follow and the intention of nature is therefore totally frustrated. The question of unnatural position, however, leads to a more detailed discussion of the authorities. The possibility of sin arises here when there is nothing physical to prohibit the "natural way." Nider restates the standard classification—laterally is bad, sitting is worse, standing is still worse, and the worst of all is *a tergo*—and then offers his own analysis of the authorities. Thomas cautions that if only the position is in question, it is not, as some say, always a mortal sin; indeed, it is without sin when

[47] Rosemondt, *Confessionale*, cap. 5, tit. 2–3, fol. 39a–40b.

no other way is possible. But Albert and those who follow him call it contrary to the intention of nature, an impediment to conception, and a sign of mortal concupiscence unless some physical cause makes the normal position impossible.[48] And despite Nider's attempt to represent the authority of the theologians, his summary of them is as inconclusive and imprecise as his own judgment on the question. He has gone beyond the kind of blanket condemnation one finds in Rosemondt; but his argument is principally distinguished by its indecision on the moral judgment one should make about the details he scrupulously raises for consideration.

For some reason Nider was more explicit in his *Tractatus de lepra morali*. There he refers to Albert and Thomas, who are said to agree that no position can be mortally sinful in itself if the genital organs themselves are properly joined. Unnatural positions are objectionable, however, and one should use the proper one, "which nature teaches"; for, "when the woman lies on her back and the man lies on her belly, women easily conceive." As for the opinion that the position that deviates furthest from this one—"from behind in the manner of beasts"—is a mortal sin, Albert explicitly disagrees. Nider prefers to conclude his discussion with a more severe note, however, and turns to Petrus de Palude for an argument that the choice of a deviant position purely for pleasure is far more reprehensible:

> If for the sake of pleasure, however, he unnecessarily alters the natural manner, though not the organ, it is a mortal sin; because she is not his wife except for natural acts.[49]

It is a strong condemnation of a particular position, circumstance, and motive. It is more precise than Nider's other teaching. And it reveals one of the most popular pastoral authorities at the end of the middle ages endorsing an extremely severe opinion.

The *Compendium theologiae*, often misattributed to Gerson, is another important voice for rigorism in the determination of un-

[48] Nider, *Expositio decalogi*, VI, 4, B2b. The *Confessionale* of the diocese of Albi reproduces Nider's analysis of the conjugal act almost verbatim from the *Expositio decalogi* (E5b–E6b); all other references to Nider's *Expositio decalogi*, therefore, represent the teaching of the diocese of Albi's manual as well.

[49] Nider, *Tractatus de lepra morali* (Paris, 1479), V, 1, 5, U6a–U7a.

natural vices. The *Compendium* notes that concerning the conjugal act "in uncustomary manner" or "in animal manner" or "not in the manner that nature determines," there is disagreement. The important circumstances affecting this judgment are, most important of all, the proper joining of the genital organs, and also the existence of physical disabilities. Some teach that under the circumstances of physical disability there is no sin because *contra naturam* only means not using the proper organs. Alexander of Hales is harsher. He says that this is also sinful, although these circumstances diminish the quantity of sin. The most liberal voice is held to be Albert, whose familiar judgment holds that "nothing a man does with his wife is in itself a mortal sin when the proper organ is used," but that having intercourse in the manner of brute beasts can be, if there is no good reason for it, "a sign of mortal concupiscence." According to the *Compendium theologiae*'s summary of the teaching of St. Albert, the choice of unnatural positions could be seriously sinful only if done solely for pleasure. Yet the final comment is perhaps as significant as the doctrine itself, for the *Compendium* warns: ". . . it is not expedient, however, for people to know this." Albert's reasonable teaching, even though it contains the warning against pleasure-seeking novelties, is considered too dangerous for popular dissemination.[50]

Finally, we might conclude this review of rigoristic speculation with one of the hardest directions to confessors for investigating

---

[50] *Compendium*, Du Pin, I, 283C–D. Noonan, *Contraception* (1967), 290; (1965), 238, misattributes this work to Gerson (as did H. C. Lea) and concludes that Gerson here, as well as in the *Opus tripartitum*, teaches the harsh doctrine that *ultra modum* is *contra naturam* (see above, n. 36). But Gerson did not write the *Compendium*, which does not seem to me to teach that rigorous opinion anyway. Furthermore, the *Opus tripartitum* does not seem to teach it either. The only passage in the *Opus tripartitum* that might condemn *ultra modum* is the following: "Prohibetur etiam Praecepto hoc tam in matrimonialiter conjunctis quam in solutis omnis luxuriosus attactus membrorum genitalium, quo non servatur naturalis ordo inditus a natura, vel non rite copulantur partes ad generationem a natura deputatae." It seems to me that "naturalis ordo inditus a natura" is intended to identify practices that frustrate procreation. And I do not think the case in which the *"partes"* intended by nature for generation are not joined *"rite"* refers to *indebitus modus* but rather to *non in debito vase*. In short, I can find no concrete evidence to show that Gerson taught that deviation from the "normal" position was mortally sinful. See, for the contrary, *Regulae morales*, Du Pin, III, 95A–C, in which *ultra modum* is not mentioned.

unnatural marital conduct. J. P. Foresti, who had vague but forbidding things to say about unchaste kisses and caresses between married partners, was more specific in his instructions for the interrogation "concerning the lusts of the married." First he rather explicitly condemns coitus in unnatural positions when done for pleasure: "Whosoever has known [his wife] in the proper organ but in a disreputable way, if he did it for pleasure, sinned mortally; not, however, if it was for some reasonable cause." Then he even more explicitly condemns unnatural positions because of their contraceptive effect: "If in knowing his wife he sought to avoid conception or took a position such that it could not happen, he has sinned mortally and as often as he has done it—*about which one must especially interrogate*" (italics added). For our understanding of the practice of confession, moreover, Foresti's terse advice to the confessor that contraceptive practices and positions should be the subject of intense inquiry is most illuminating. Foresti has rejected here the usual cautionary advice to confessors that they avoid descending into particulars lest they teach sin.[51] Four of the most popular books for confessors also discuss this problem, however, and their attitudes and rhetoric on the subject of pleasure, position, and sin are perhaps the most significant evidence we have about the questions confessors might have asked married penitents.

Guido de Monte Rocherii's *Manipulus curatorum* is rigorist on the sin of improper manner but not fully consistent in its advice about questioning penitents about it. In addition to sodomy in which the proper orifice is not used or in which the female genitals are "abused," Guido labels as unnatural "when he does not know her in the natural manner." In asking questions about lust, the confessor is again cautioned against descending to particulars—it is enough to know "who" she was and "how" it was done. Thus, if the penitent is a simple person, the confessor may ask if the act was done in a natural manner, but "he should not ask whether he knew her from the front or from behind." In general Guido advises such questions be avoided, and he adds that the confessor will learn how to ask through experience.

[51] Foresti, *Confessionale*, "De luxuriis coniugatorum," 17b. "Si cognouit in vase debito, sed modo inhonesto. si hoc ad voluptatem fecit grauiter p. secus si aliqua rationabili causa." "Si cognoscendo vxorem quesiuit euitare generationem vel in tali modo stetit quod fieri non possit mor. p. & totiens quotiens. idem *quam maxime interrogandum est*" (italics added).

When Guido turns then to the ways a man and wife can sin mortally, however, he reiterates his condemnation of intercourse "when the man knows her contrary to the manner instituted by nature," and he warns that this is the gravest of sins in a wife.[52] Consequently one has the impression that Guido wants to urge caution but is unwilling to ignore the sin of improper manner.

Antoninus of Florence declares the following instances, among others, of conjugal intercourse to be mortally sinful: when the proper organ is not used; when the proper organ is used, "but in such a way that the semen is not received, in order to avoid offspring"; or when sex play leads to pollution. Antoninus discusses unusual positions at greater length and with a surprising degree of caution. Of three deviations—laterally, from behind, and with the woman on top—some say they can be sinful, especially the last. Thomas and Albert, however, say these positions are not sinful in themselves but can be a sign of concupiscence. Antoninus advises confessors not to declare on this subject or deny absolution to anyone persisting in it; "but condemn and prohibit it as much as you can." Nevertheless when the first two deviations from the norm are used, it can perhaps be completely without sin, especially if there is fear of abortion. Antoninus then is clearly on the side of caution in the confessional even if one detects in his tone a basic repugnance for improper manner. This caution is preserved, moreover, when he summarizes his lessons in a set of questions for the confessor to consider:

> Concerning the above, however, the questions are to be phrased as follows: has the use of marriage been clearly outside the proper organ; has he done something to avoid conception; has the use been in an improper manner, although in the proper organ, and how. . . . And concerning these one must judge the sin mortal or venial according to what has been said above: and on such things you have a fuller treatment in the summas.[53]

It is not unlikely that a confessor who read this whole section would leave improper manner entirely out of his questions. If the problem came up in confession, the confessor could have gained nothing more from Antoninus than a general disliking for an in-

[52] Guido de Monte Rocherii, *Manipulus curatorum*, IV, 3, 9.
[53] Antoninus, *Confessionale—Defecerunt*, 30.

temperate indulgence, and he could not find a clear condemnation of improper manner. If the confessor were so disposed, he could inveigh against the practice—or go to some rigorist authority who would assure him that it was always a mortal sin. Antoninus therefore does not end the possibility of distress for penitents addicted to such practices and scrupulous about confessing them. But he makes things considerably easier.

Compared with the usual pastoral instruction on sins against nature, the *Angelica* allows married partners considerable freedom in their sexual life. Two discussions, one on *coitus reservatus* and the other on improper positions, illustrate the *Angelica*'s laxity.

The first case considers the morality of a man "who before completion of the act withdraws so that he does not emit semen even outside the organ lest he have more children." Angelus says he cites Petrus de Palude's opinion that it is not a mortal sin unless the woman is incited to "semination." Angelus says that Petrus also argues that the same reasoning applies to a man who wants to limit his offspring through continence: the man is not required to complete an unfinished act unless the wife is seeking the debt. The same reasoning excuses from mortal sin "the woman who, after she has been known by the man, goes immediately to urinate, or who stands up quickly to emit the semen so that she does not conceive." Angelus is not entirely happy with this conclusion: ". . . but concerning this opinion I have strong doubts, on account of the canon *Aliquando*, which seems to condemn it as a mortal sin." Nevertheless, Angelus tries to harmonize the milder teaching with the *Aliquando*, which he says can be interpreted differently:

> But it can be said that it is talking about someone who does this purely for pleasure or else who seeks an abortion after conception. But Petrus means when someone does this for a reasonable cause: for example, when he cannot care for them and the like; and before conception occurs in the mother's womb; and thus it would be held [not seriously sinful], although it is dangerous.

At the word "dangerous" the *Angelica*'s rigid glossator Ungarelli comments in a predictable fashion by recalling the punishment of Onan, who was killed by God for spilling his seed on the ground. Furthermore, Angelus himself returns to the canon *Aliquando* as he ends the discussion by warning that it forbids as mortal sin always "giving or receiving poisons of sterility."[54] Yet the permissiveness of this passage, which cites the laxist reasoning of Petrus de Palude, reveals a strikingly different attitude toward sexuality than one finds in the average manual for confessors. Angelus has admitted that it is possible, even though dangerous, to allow a woman to take positive action after sexual intercourse to avoid pregnancy if hardship will result from the birth of another child. And he has thereby narrowed significantly the definition of sins against nature.

With even greater lucidity Angelus pursues the question of "unnatural" positions. Basically he favors the opinion of Albertus Magnus, that nothing a man does with his wife is mortally sinful in itself if the genital organs are properly used; but that "these positions can be a sign of mortal concupiscence." This proposition is coupled with a warning, however, by which Angelus expresses his displeasure at the thought of such practices and yet admits that reason cannot easily condemn them.

> You should truly condemn all these deviations and declare them to be dangerous; and you must persuade them to resist as much as you can. Nevertheless do not rush into a judgment, because a wife is granted so that a man may take pleasure in her to avoid fornication.

This text is designed to teach confessors who have to expound moral theology without harm to the consciences of their penitents. Angelus's caution is merely an explicit example of the general principle we have already encountered in advice for prudent confessors: do not judge actions mortally sinful precipitously and inconsiderately. What emerges from this principle is a laxer rule on "unnatural" positions. Furthermore, Angelus defines the criteria for judging positions more carefully by using the goal of procreation:

[54] Angelus [Carletus] de Clavasio, *Prima pars summae Angelicae cum commento. Summa Angelica de casibus conscientialibus . . . cum additionibus . . . Iacobi Ungarelli patauini . . . necnon et a venerabile P. F. Augustino patauino. . . .* (Lyon, 1534), "Debitum coniugale," 27, fol. 192b. Cf. Noonan, *Contraception* (1967), 359–360; (1965), 298, 348; for Albert the Great on micturating and standing up after intercourse to avoid conception (1967), 252–253; (1965), 206–207.

> And therefore hold this opinion: that however the act is begun, and however it is done; if the semen is emitted in the proper organ and in such a way that the woman can retain it, it is not a mortal sin in itself.

If, on the other hand, the act is done so that the woman cannot "retain the semen," even if it is done *in vase*, it is mortally sinful. This final judgment seems to contradict the possibility that a woman whose actions after natural intercourse impeded conception might be innocent of mortal sin. Nevertheless it removes many of the scruples raised by those who worried confessors about the coital positions of their penitents.

The comments of Ungarelli's gloss are more than one might have wished as an illustration of how a rigorist would respond to this solution. To Angelus's statement that the wife is permitted to assume such positions so that the man may take pleasure in her to avoid fornication, Ungarelli echoes William of Rennes and advises simply that "in all these cases it would be better if the man considered her as his sister." And to the problem of the female's retention of the seed Ungarelli cites the *Astesana* which, as we have seen, says that when the woman gets on top of the man it is a mortal sin because in that position the man is not apt to inseminate and the woman not apt to receive the seed. Ungarelli even includes the *Astesana*'s dire reference to Methodius here: ". . . this was one of the causes of the flood."[55]

The *Angelica*, of course, was influential and Ungarelli's gloss was not. The most important evidence, therefore, is the laxness of the teaching of the great summa. Now the *Angelica*'s language is not unequivocal. Sexual games are not encouraged; questions about the marital act are. Yet on balance there is a certain hardheadedness about the *Angelica*'s milder approach: faithful application of the principles governing the sexual conduct of marriage lead in the laxist direction, and that is the way Angelus is certainly traveling. His effect must have been quite the opposite of that produced by Astesanus, Guido de Monte Rocherii, Godescalc Rosemondt, or even Johann Nider.

The last of the great summas for confessors, the *Sylvestrina*, offers a useful conclusion to the teaching of moral theologians on unnatural practices. Sylvester was as interested in the fine points

---

[55] *Angelica* (1534), "Debitum coniugale," 25, fol. 191b–192b; *Astesana*, VIII, 9.

of this problem as Angelus de Clavasio and almost as worried about it as Jean Gerson. His opinions are not wholly laxist. Yet his dominant concern is to judge the sexual act by the criterion of procreative purpose, and because he consistently adheres to this criterion he avoids some of the cruder judgments of his predecessors. One highly interesting characteristic of these passages, moreover, is their exhaustive consideration of views with which Sylvester ultimately decides to disagree.

His first exploration of unnatural acts begins by asking whether the conjugal act can be a mortal sin if it follows "manners contrary to nature." Everyone agrees, he carefully explains, that the natural position is when "the woman lies on her back and the man lies on her stomach and observes the proper orifice for insemination." St. Thomas finds two ways to deviate unnaturally from this: first by inseminating outside of the proper orifice, and everyone agrees that this is a mortal sin, even for the woman who only suffers it for fear of her husband's hatred, or beating, or infidelity, or any reason other than "absolute violence"; second, by using the proper orifice but not using a proper position. Then Sylvester enumerates the usual positions in this analysis from light deviations to the greatest: laterally, sitting, standing, or with the woman on top, and finally "bestialiter," like an animal. Sylvester blames Petrus de Palude for originating the opinion that the woman on top is mortally sinful, because it is not conducive to insemination and thus seems to hinder procreation. Sylvester's biology refutes that delusion:

> But I say that is false: because the uterus draws the semen to itself even if the virile member does not penetrate the vagina. Thus women conceive in baths where men have emitted sperm.

Petrus de Palude also argues that all the deviations from the normal positions are mortally sinful if done merely for pleasure and not with reasonable justification on the grounds that it is mortally sinful, as they quaintly describe it, to misuse the "custom" and "use" of any of the sacraments not only in their essentials but even in their accidentals. Sylvester can refute that argument too:

> But I say that pleasure remaining within the limits of matrimony does not pervert the use of this sacrament, which is also obviously a remedy; otherwise someone approaching his wife in the natural way for the sake of pleasure would sin mortally.

In other words, the motive of pleasure only becomes sinful if the desire leads one to exceed the bounds of matrimony. And we know that Sylvester had a narrow view of that circumstance, which he defined as occurring only if one actually and intentionally thinks about another woman. It is this intention that governs Sylvester's judgment of sex for pleasure, and whether the position is natural or unnatural can make no difference. Turning to William of Rennes, Sylvester notes that while he does not seem to distinguish "supragression" from the rest, William calls them all mortally sinful when done for the sake of pleasure. Sylvester makes short work of that opinion: ". . . because he does not prove it, I will say nothing about it." The *Angelica* and the *Rosella*, he continues in his combative way, hold that these positions are not mortal sins—even including "supragression"—if the woman can retain the semen, and if she cannot, they are mortally sinful. Here Sylvester recalls his biology. "That conclusion is not rational," he argues, and it turns out he is objecting to too rigid a teaching, for sometimes the *matrix* retains very little of the semen and rejects the rest and yet conception follows. Then, in an apparent reference to his belief that women have been impregnated in the baths by aquatic sperm, Sylvester reasons that if the *matrix* can attract semen over a distance, it can retain contiguous semen even more effectively.[56] All in all, the drift of Sylvester's arguments runs inexorably to laxism. Apply rational standards, stick to the criterion of procreative purpose, learn the biological facts of life, and you end up with fewer mortal sins to worry your penitents. Unfortunately for the simplicity of this presentation, however, Sylvester did not leave it at that. In a separate paragraph he recalls unnecessarily the more stringent attitudes toward sex for pleasure.

In the summary paragraph Sylvester argues three points. First, he says, in all such cases when married people act for pleasure by choosing unnatural positions, they are to be severely rebuked for using beastly habits. We see here the same prejudice against sexual pleasure as infected even Antoninus of Florence and Angelus de Clavasio. Second, married people are to be sympathized with because in these sexual matters they retain little or no rationality. Third, when the female genitals are used, Sylvester declares that he would not dare to call anything mortally sin-

[56] *Sylvestrina*, "Debitum coniugale," q. 4, par. 6.

ful in itself, but only on account of illicit intention, for example, an intention that does not remain within the bounds of matrimony. Then he capitulates to the traditional, restrictive framework. He reverts to the rationale of Thomas and Albert and looks for reasonable motives to justify deviations from the normal position. Physical difficulty, especially pregnancy, plays the most important role in this thinking, even though Sylvester has already provided arguments that fully justify deviations from the normal position: "Whence, if there is a reasonable cause, all those are permissible." It seems superfluous to prove this point, but Sylvester proceeds with it. If the conjugal act can result in procreation and the object of the sacrament can possibly be served, then it cannot be in itself a mortal sin. All the deviant positions, however, satisfy these criteria, for according to Albert conception may occur and the end of the sacrament—offspring or the remedy for corruption—may be served. Sylvester's caution inexplicably increases here. He says that Albert's opinion means that these positions are not in themselves illicit and may be licitly observed for some rational cause: ". . . for example, sickness, or danger of abortion, or natural disposition, or the like." He doubles the caution by citing St. Thomas's opinions to the very same purpose: deviant positions are not in themselves sinful but, in that favorite phrase, may be signs of mortal concupiscence if there is no rational excuse. His final citation is altogether unexpected and anticlimactic. The Archdeacon—who, says Sylvester, "was quite timorous in coming to conclusions"—says that wives who submit to this kind of practice cannot be judged guilty of mortal sin. Why not? "Because they do not have to judge the intention of those asking for the debt so they may thereby refuse it; nor should a judgment be easily pronounced that such a position is a mortal sin."[57]

It is not easy to summarize Sylvester's teaching on unnatural positions, and that is admittedly a disturbing feature of it. One is tempted to apply Sylvester's own characterization of the Archdeacon and pronounce this section of the *Sylvestrina* "quite timorous." To deny that unnatural positions frustrate conception knocks out one objection to them, and to insist that "too ardent desire" is only the specific desire for adultery knocks out the

[57] *Sylvestrina*, "Debitum coniugale," q. 4, par. 7. Cf. Noonan, *Contraception* (1967), 376; (1965), 312, who does not find Sylvester as laxist or as original as I do.

other. Yet one is left with the impression that Sylvester does not fully believe his own restrictive definition of what we mean when we say that a man has allowed desire to take him, in marital intercourse, outside the limits of matrimony. He does not seem to believe in his own definition because he resurrects all the troublesome language of Albert and Thomas when he talks about "signs of mortal concupiscence." Nevertheless, we are not back where we started with William of Rennes or Astesanus of Asti. We are even further from the opaque condemnations of a less learned literature. Even with his conservative finish, the *Sylvestrina* offers more lucidity—more chance of saving penitents from thoughtless intrusions on their peace of mind—than anyone could derive from those hostile or hurried references to unnatural positions that are all too frequent in the literature on the forgiveness of sins.[58] And taking this analysis in its entirety, we

[58] Condemnations of unnatural postions, in addition to those cited above (n. 37–n. 45) are numerous and range from casual to extensive and explicit. *Tractatus de instructionibus confessorum*, ch. 2, "De luxuria," A6a–A7a, condemns any fornication *modo non debito*, and specifies that sometimes *modi inordinati* apply to married people: they are definitely to be corrected because, as Jerome has said, the embraces of a prostitute are more damnable in a wife. The section "De coniugatis" offers a cross-reference to that passage to explain the case "si habuerit modum aliquem inordinatum." The same section condemns abortion and contraception as homicide: "Item Quere si mulier aliquod impedimentum fecit ne conciperet. Et idem hoc intellige de viro. Vel si abortium procurauit. Quia in utroque casu tamquam homicida iudicatur." Bartholomaeus de Chaimis (*Interrogatorium*, III, 3) concludes that it is mortal sin for a woman to be on top or a man to enter from behind if it is done solely for pleasure. Jean Raulin's *Itinerarium paridisi, de matrimonio*, sermon 8, first condemns unnatural intercourse as totally contrary to the procreative purposes of nature, and then goes on to consider "in vase debito sed contra naturalem modum" when there is no physical reason for it. This is always a sin, he warns, but not always a mortal sin. The only distinction he offers, however, does not solve the problem: for he returns to physical reasons and says that unnatural manner is venial if it is chosen to protect the fetus. Stephan Lanzkranna's *Himelstrass* is vaguely sinister on the subject: "Zum anderen mal [the first example is sodomy] / so geschicht es so ain man mitt ainer frawen zeschaffen hat / er thüt es aber nit in ainer solichen mass vnnd weiss als es geschehen soll gewonlich vnnd natürlich vn̄ als frum̄ vn̄ erber leüt das thon. Sunder er thüt das anders dan̄ es sein sol / oder in anderer weiss die mannigfeltig ist / vnd das soll er auch in der beicht melden" (ch. 17, fol. 52b). Dennis Doherty, *The Sexual Doctrine of Cardinal Cajetan*, 122, 128–129, provides an interesting insight into sixteenth century pastoral attitudes. After quoting Cajetan's assertion that all but one position are "contra naturalem ordinem," Doherty explains why Cajetan

have a decisive rejection of the prejudices of the tradition of Huguccio.

Sylvester's tendency to adhere strictly to procreative purpose led him to more rigorist ways on the subject of *amplexus reservatus*—sexual relations that stop short of insemination—and his reasoning on this difficult problem is as provocative as that on unnatural positions. This subject is introduced as Sylvester discusses whether it is a mortal sin to provoke desire "by thoughts, touches, food, and the like." He must have known that this was how Huguccio and those who followed him defined the sin of too ardent love that took one outside the limits of matrimony, but, as we have seen, he studiously avoids that way of talking about it. Instead Sylvester turns to the opinion of Petrus de Palude on that kind of precoital preparation. Petrus argues that if erotic stimulation is desired for itself alone and results in pollution outside of the proper organ, or if it is prolonged with no intention of performing the conjugal act, then it is a mortal sin. But when such stimulation is in preparation for the act, Petrus declares that it is natural, rational, and at worst a venial sin:

> Nevertheless, if these things occur for the sake of avoiding fornication in oneself or another, or for the sake of paying the debt—just as doves and bears arouse themselves, not remaining in enjoyment of these things but only seeking to be prepared for the act—it does not seem to be a sin; because it is permissible to help the body be obedient to right reason. It will be a venial sin, however, if this is ordained for the pleasure of coitus within the limits of matrimony. . . .

Sylvester likes this teaching of Petrus so far, obviously because it confirms his own predilection for judging sexuality according to the standard of procreation. He is therefore disturbed by Petrus' next dictum, which Sylvester finds repugnant to the preceding. For while Petrus states that it is mortally sinful "to spill the seed" to avoid conception, he nevertheless permits the man

---

condemns the position with the woman on the top more harshly in the *Summula peccatorum* ("videtur mortale aut prope") than in his commentary on St. Thomas's *Summa Theologica*: "This opinion in [the *Summula peccatorum*], written in 1523, is therefore stricter—*no doubt as tutioristic for the sake of hearing confessions*—than that expressed In 2-2, completed in 1517" (italics added). Cf. Müller, *Paradiesesehe*, 125 and n. 73.

to withdraw before *either* "inseminates," on the ground that one is not required to resume an incompleted act unless the wife seeks the debt. Sylvester, like Angelus de Clavasio, notes that Petrus permits the woman to avoid conception by quickly standing up or urinating immediately after coitus; but he flatly condemns it as contrary to the canon *Aliquando*, which prohibits all kinds of contraception. The first opinion, permitting coitus reservatus, Sylvester brands as "highly irrational," because it seems to him that if it is a mortal sin to stimulate genitals with the intention of not consummating the act, it must also be a mortal sin to stimulate genitals and even enter the vagina with the intention of not consummating the act. But it is not a sin, Sylvester concedes, if one begins with the intention of consummating the act and then decides for some reason to stop in the midst of the act and withdraw with the consent of one's wife. There are in Sylvester's view two conditions that legitimize noncoital sexuality (if, of course, ejaculation does not occur):

> First, when they are not shameless touches proceeding from lust, but from love, such as kisses and decent embraces. Second, when they in fact proceed from lust but there is no thought of coition, so that it is neither intended nor excluded, and the place is suitable for intercourse if the will for it ensues. Otherwise, however, they are mortal sins, because every lustful action that is not conjugal coitus or ordained to it actually or potentially is illicit.[59]

Once again Sylvester has offered his confessors a detailed and somewhat complex solution to a difficult case of conscience. For while he is almost unique among pastoral authorities on confession in paying attention to marital love and affection, he is still wary of sexual pleasure—especially when it does not lead to procreation or save from adultery. It is not wholly rigorist, but it is certainly not laxist.

[59] *Sylvestrina*, "Debitum coniugale," q. 7, par. 9; Noonan, *Contraception* (1967), 359–360, 404; (1965), 297–299, 336. Noonan's explication overlooks the subtle distinction between intending from the start to do nothing more than enjoy precoital stimulation and not finish the act, and not intending anything specific from the start and then changing one's mind in the middle of sexual activity and deciding not to continue. It is a subtlety, but it does not allow us to categorize Sylvester as an unqualified opponent of *amplexus reservatus*.

In his teaching on conjugal morality, Sylvester tried to bring order and rationality into the realm of the sexual. Perhaps he tried too hard. His consistent emphasis on procreative purpose allowed him to cut away some of the obfuscations about too ardent loving and unnatural acts. On the other hand, this same emphasis meant that the liberal ideas of Petrus de Palude were often unacceptable. If one is to work within the medieval penitential system, then the kind of consistency and clarity that Sylvester offers is undeniably beneficial. It avoids confusion. Nevertheless, when we judge this attempt, one of the best, to advise confessors how to deal with married penitents, we must recall that there is an open invitation to investigate the private sexual lives of the laity, do so in detail, and reform them according to strict standards.

Taken as a whole, the practical literature on sin and confession gave considerable attention to sins against nature. Medieval churchmen were devoted to the idea of the moral goodness of procreation and mistrustful of doing anything for pleasure. They accordingly conceived a horror of unnatural practices, which they sometimes defined with a startling comprehensiveness.

In the most sophisticated authors a more rational moral theology exposed some contradictory and unrealistic attitudes, and those interested in a more consistent moral theology took a closer look at the definition of unnatural practices. Thus authorities such as Gerson, Angelus, Antoninus, and Sylvester adhered to a narrower definition of the unnatural. Consequently, the choice of unusual positions as well as sexual behavior that does not result in ejaculation became less serious. Even careful moral theologians might still hold that copulating with one's wife's "in the manner of brute beasts" was not compatible with the nature of man the rational animal. But their biology and ethics told them that, strictly speaking, unnatural coition meant those instances in which ejaculation—in their view both masculine and feminine —was completed in such a way that the partners acted to avoid conception. And some were at least willing to entertain the possibility that nonprocreative sexual acts between a man and his wife might be legitimate. Indeed, Angelus de Clavasio comes dangerously close to excusing what he considered contraceptive practices.

The literature as a whole, however, maintained a broad definition of sins against nature. Even those who were most consistently devoted to the logically necessary conclusions of scholastic ethics were quite capable of talking the language of dualistic rationalism—capable of providing confessors with a variety of scruples about the morality of the conjugal act. Thus while we detect strong tendencies toward clarifying and rationalizing the teaching on unnatural acts, even some of the most progressive minds, Sylvester, for example, are not completely free from the old pessimism. Most important of all, not all manuals and summas that were circulating in the late fifteenth and early sixteenth centuries had a clear, consistent, and realistic sexual ethic. These books taught confessors to believe that married people committed unnatural acts often and in a wide variety of ways. And they instructed confessors to ask about them.

OTHER RESTRICTIONS ON THE EXERCISE OF CONJUGAL RIGHTS

Restrictions because of holy season or place, the physical condition of the wife, the infidelity of a spouse, and participation in holy rites all determined, at one time or another, whether one could legitimately enjoy one's marital rights. Few of these restrictions remained as strict prohibitions by the end of the middle ages. But the habit of considering all possible questions in this literature insured that authorities would continue to discuss the possibility that these circumstances might make the conjugal act sinful, even if they ended up saying it did not.

The most tenacious rule remained the prohibition on sexual intercourse during menstruation. This prohibition undoubtedly had deep cultural roots, which were reinforced by the stern proscriptions of the Old Testament. In addition, however, there was a widely held biological opinion that the offspring of such a union were likely to be deformed.[60] Among theologians this belief and interest in the welfare of the child led to a compromise with the seriously enforced prescript of the payment of the marital debt. In general it could be venially or seriously sinful to seek the debt if one knew that one's wife was menstruating.

There is a tendency in some of the summas for confessors to reduce seeking the debt (even knowingly) during the wife's menstruation to a venial sin. But the fear of defective children continues to haunt even the most sophisticated authorities.

[60] Browe, *Beiträge zur Sexualethik*, 3–8.

Antoninus of Florence says that it is more common to hold that it is not a sin to ask for the debt during menstruation and he therefore bids confessors not to deny absolution (presumably to those who will not promise to desist); but he urges confessors to discourage asking for the debt during menstruation as much as possible unless there is a fear of incontinency.[61] The *Angelica* and Ungarelli's gloss are strikingly similar to Antoninus on this question. They object on the usual grounds that monstrosities are likely to be born if conception follows, but fear of adultery leads them to permit it. Nevertheless, Angelus, in a disturbing reversion to primitive tests of guilt, thinks that the decision of whether the sin is mortal or venial depends on the condition of the offspring![62] Sylvester also disapproves of intercourse during menstruation. He cannot accept the judgment of Petrus de Palude that it is completely all right, since he believes in the likelihood of defective offspring. His conclusion is based on the teaching of St. Thomas, who, he thinks, did not find it mortally sinful for a man to demand the debt from a menstruating wife to avoid adultery if there was no other way. For the woman, however, there is no similar laxity: ". . . in a woman, however, asking is always a mortal sin, because at the time of menstruation she is not so moved as to be easily in danger of falling."[63] These theologians were only trying to be prudent, and one can sympathize with their concern for the good of the offspring. Yet they tried at the same time to respect the obligation to pay the debt, and even those who believed that deformed children might be born often reduced this case to a venial sin.

But if there was an increased toleration of sexual intercourse with a menstruating woman among the more prominent authori-

[61] Antoninus, *Confessionale—Defecerunt*, 30; cf. *Supplementum*, "Debitum coniugale," 10, for the same solution. See also Ziegler, *Ehelehre*, 232–234, 273–274.

[62] *Angelica* (1534), "Debitum coniugale," 32. The passage concludes with this startling language, designed to give a sure determination for the moral status of seeking the debt during menstruation and risking the birth of a malformed child: "Si autem solum exigit causa libidinis vel reddit. tunc ex futuro euentum cognoscetur si peccauit mortaliter vel non. quia si proles generabitur leprosa reputabitur mortale. quia dedit operam rei illicite [i.e., he observed the obligation of the debtor illicitly] ar. c. j. de psump. Si vero non generetur leprosa erit veniale. Ideo ante euentum debet confiteri tanquam de mortali. c. iuuenis. de spon."

[63] *Sylvestrina*, "Debitum coniugale," q. 6, par. 8.

ties, we can find in others adherence to older, stricter rules condemning it unequivocally. Even Gerson was capable of harsh, unqualified rejection of intercourse during menstruation. His *Regulae morales* state simply that another way for married people to sin is when they "knowingly" have intercourse when there is serious danger of harm to the offspring, "as in the time of menstruation."[64] If the husband does not know he is seeking the debt during his wife's period, he is evidently excused from serious sin, but that appears to be the only concession. Guido de Monte Rocherii also flatly brands as mortal sin knowingly having intercourse during menstruation.[65] Foresti takes the same view and also warns the woman she is supposed to refuse.[66] Seeking the debt during menstruation is "highly serious sin" in the view of the *Tractatus de instructionibus confessorum*, which condemns it twice.[67] But perhaps the frankest language comes from the *Directoire des confesseurs*, as it describes the various ways married people can sin:

> The fifth is when a man has intercourse with his wife while she was menstruating (ou temps de ses fleurs) because the woman is not decent for performing the works of nature, according to the decency of the Sacrament of Marriage. And also because if a child were hereby conceived it would not come to good perfection, just as the philosophers say. For it would have too many members, or too few, or would be hunchbacked or deformed . . . or some sickness might come from it that would take a long time to tell about.[68]

Now the *Directoire* is not a notably sophisticated manual. And while the tone of this passage is perhaps abnormally naïve, it only puts into concrete form the worries shared by other manuals and even summas. Thus another question of conscience might have been added to the toll imposed on married penitents seeking absolution from informed and inquisitive priests.[69]

---

[64] Gerson, *Regulae morales*, Du Pin, III, 95B–C.

[65] Guido de Monte Rocherii, *Manipulus curatorum*, II, 3, 9.

[66] Foresti, *Confessionale*, "De luxuriis coniugatorum," 17b.

[67] *Tractatus de instructionibus confessorum*, "De luxuriis," A6a–A7a; "De coniugatis," D8b–E1b.

[68] [Gerson?], *Directoire*, "Luxure de corps," O3b.

[69] For other opinions on intercourse during menstruation: Burchard of Worms, *Decretorum libri XX*, 19, 5, PL, 187, 957–960, who penalizes it with ten days of penance with bread and water; Stephan Lanzkranna, *Himel-*

When authorities forbade, on pain of mortal sin, intercourse during menstruation, they generally referred to danger of harm to the offspring. But a final example from Johann Nider shows how profound a mistrust of sexuality and pleasure also lies behind this prohibition. Nider cites the opinion of Duns Scotus, who says that someone seeking the debt under these circumstances sins mortally. The rationale of Duns Scotus, fountainhead of laxist judgments, is novel: he argues that the New Law would not demand less chastity than the Old Law, which enumerates intercourse during menstruation among those crimes punished most severely in Leviticus. That argument is, in fact, not typical of the literature. But the prejudice against sexual functions it reveals certainly is.[70] And Nider shares with the *Directoire* a certain suspicion that there is something unclean about menstruation that makes sexual intercourse at this time indecent.

A closely related question concerns intercourse with a preg-

---

strass, ch. 17, fol. 55a–b; Raulin, *De matrimonio*, sermon 8, in *Itinerarium paridisi*, fol. 180b–181a; [Gerson?], *La Confession*, A7b; de Butrio, *Directorium ad confitendum*, "De peccatis contra sacramentum matrimonii"; Berthold, *Summa Johannis, deutsch*, Q. 184, "Ob man die eelichen werck müg pitten / wenn dye fraw schwanger ist oder in der kindspet oder ir krankheÿt hat," which refers to William of Rennes' gloss to the *Raymundina*, IV, 2, 10, "Abstinendum," p. 516; Olivier Maillard, *La Confession*, B2a; Falk, ed., *Beichtbüchlein* (Augsburg, 1504), 89. None of these authorities completely free intercourse during menstruation from sin; some explicitly call it mortally sinful; some distinguish on the basis of motives; some are vague. Typical of a vague condemnation is the following passage from Godescalc Rosemondt's *Confessionale* (5, [6], fol. 43b), in the form of a general confession: "Tempore menstrui, infirmitatis vel alio tempore non debito debitum exegi: . . . frequenter cum preiudicio prolis et nocumento vxoris. Propter enim talem vel similen abusum uxorum nascuntur aliquotiens proles leprose: monstruose et defectus naturales habentes." Cf. Noonan, *Contraception* (1967), 112, 340; (1965), 85–86, 282; Ziegler, *Ehelehre*, 231–243, 273–274, 281.

[70] Nider, *Expositio decalogi*, VI, 4, B2a–b; Duns Scotus, *Quaestiones*, dis. 32, *Opera*, 19, 345. Duns argues that one is obliged to render the debt during menstruation only if there is no other way to obtain offspring (without the danger of their being born defective). "Unde non sine causa in lege Mosaica accedens ad mulierem menstrutatem, debuit mori, nec more infligebatur ibi, nisi pro peccato mortali et gravi; nec est probabile quod in lege Evangelica, quae est lex castitatis, sit minus prohibitus ad menstruatam accedere." The commentary on this passage (*Opera*, 19, 345) argues that Duns favors but does not assert that intercourse during menstruation is a mortal sin, and it lists a variety of theological opinions ranging from condemnation as a mortal sin to freeing it from all guilt. Cf. Jean Raulin, *Itinerarium paridisi, de matrimonio*, sermon 8, fol. 181a.

THE SUBJECT OF CONFESSION

nant wife. Here again the primary motive behind the restriction is the safety of the offspring, and all the authorities stipulate that the ban is to avoid danger to the fetus. Yet once again there are intimations of a more primitive mentality in the persistence of related taboos against intercourse after childbirth and before purification. Thus Olivier Maillard finds that whoever has intercourse during the wife's confinement and before the ritual purification is in danger of mortal sin, and the *Tractatus de instructionibus confessorum* puts it with intercourse during menstruation as "a highly serious sin." Nevertheless, intercourse with a pregnant wife is generally considered a slight sin. Berthold of Freiburg says that while you should not, it is not serious; Johann Nider says that it is definitely not mortal; St. Antoninus says it is at most a venial sin; and even the *Supplementum* decides that if there is no danger of abortion, paying is no sin and asking only venial. And there are some who ignore it or mention it as a possible question for examination without seeming to care deeply about it.[71]

The possibility of harm to the offspring, of course, evokes a real and consistent concern. What strikes the modern reader as odd, however, is the absence of even a rough rule based on nearness to parturition. While most authorities warn against harming the fetus, they do not try to estimate in months or weeks the duration of abstinence. At the same time they deny for the most part that intercourse during pregnancy is a mortal sin unless there is a danger to the fetus.[72] Indeed, it must have been clear

[71] Olivier Maillard, *La Confession*, B2a; *Tractatus de instructionibus confessorum*, D8b–E1b; Berthold, *Summa Johannis, deutsch*, Q. 177: "Von dem eelichen wercken . . . ," Johann Nider, *Expositio decalogi*, VI, 4, B2b; Antoninus, *Confessionale—Defecerunt*, 30; *Supplementum*, "Debitum coniugale," 9. Cf. Burchard of Worms, *Decretorum libri XX*, 19, 5, PL, 187, 957–960; [Gerson?], *La Confession*, A7b; Falk, ed., *Beichtbüchlein* (Augsburg, 1504), 89; Andreas de Escobar, *Interrogationes*, B4a–b.

[72] Burchard of Worms, *Decretorum libri XX*, 19, 5, PL, 187, 957–960; Antoninus, *Confessionale—Defecerunt*, 30; Nider, *Expositio decalogi*, VI, 4, B2b; Stephan Lanzkranna, *Himelstrass*, ch. 17; [Gerson?], *Directoire*, "Luxure de corps," O3b–O4b; Guido de Monte Rocherii, *Manipulus curatorum*, II, 3, 9; *Angelica* (1534), "Debitum coniugale," 33–34, fol. 193b. For a defense of Christian doctrine against the charge that it is inferior to that of Islam, which allows polygamy and eliminates the necessity of sexual intercourse with a pregnant wife, see Raulin, *Itinerarium paridisi, de matrimonio*, sermon 8, fol. 182a–b: Raulin's argument is based on an analogy to farming, used as early as Clement of Alexandria; see Klomps, *Ehemoral*, 18; and

to everyone that the teaching on sexual morality of the church made intercourse during pregnancy almost inevitable. The obligations to pay the debt and avoid adultery could not be revoked for the duration of a normal pregnancy.

Complementary to the softening of restrictions according to the norms of pregnancy, childbirth, and menstruation is a somewhat better consensus that holy seasons, blessed places, and sacred rites are not necessarily violated if married partners exercise their conjugal rights.

There are a number of instances in the literature we are investigating in which the questions suggested for a penitent's examination—either by himself or the confessor—raise the problem of sexual intercourse during holy times or in holy places. Antonius de Butrio's *Directorium*, for example, has a formula in which the penitent admits he has sinned by performing the marital act "improperly," one example of which is "at times of solemn feasts and sacred fasts." There is nothing conclusive about forms such as these: the most dangerous characteristic is their vagueness. But the danger of vagueness is certainly real for a scrupulous person—priest or penitent—who might see lists of sins of only one summa or manual and not understand that weightier authorities might have had something quite different to say on the subject. Even Olivier Maillard guards against this danger when he notes in his very brief manual that although one should abstain from intercourse on feast days it is not a commandment.[73] On the other hand, Jodocus Winshemius, who says he is representing the opinions of the *Angelica*, is not so careful as Maillard. Winshemius says that seeking the debt in a holy season is a sin, especially if it is in contempt of the season and the precepts of the church, although paying it "with sadness of mind" is no sin at all.[74] The

---

Noonan, *Contraception* (1967), 99–100; (1965), 74–75; see also ibid. (1967), 293ff.; (1965), 241ff., for a discussion of the difficulties in finding models of the natural for humans in animal behavior.

[73] de Butrio, *Directorium ad confitendum*, "De peccatis contra sacramentum matrimonii"; Maillard, *La Confession*, B2a. Similar questions are found in [Gerson?], *La Confession*, A7b; and Stephan Lanzkranna, *Himelstrass*, ch. 17; Columbi, *Confession generale*, B7a–b; and *Tractatus de instructionibus confessorum*, D8b–E1b; which specifically says that while the church urges continence, the contrary is no sin. For the severity of early medieval restrictions on sexual intercourse and communion, see Browe, *Beiträge zur Sexualethik*, 39–63.

[74] Winshemius, *Institutiones*, B3b.

difficulty with this decision is in identifying these "precepts" of seasonal abstinence from intercourse. Furthermore, as we shall see, Angelus did not quite say what Winshemius reported. In the manual of Foresti the relationship between the debt and a holy season finds a novel expression. To refuse the debt on a feast day is not, as it normally is, a mortal sin, but only a venial one: and thus the season is in this case an important circumstance. But Foresti also says it is not a mortal sin to have intercourse on the same day after Holy Communion.[75]

Throughout these examples there is a rough consistency, then, but only a rough one. Authorities hesitate to brand the disregard of holy times and places as mortal sin; but they also are reluctant to free it completely from doubt by entirely omitting their moral inspection. Johann Nider's teaching on the subject is a good example. Thus he first classifies seeking the debt on a feast day among sins that are at least venial but specifies that this sin is, in fact, only venial. Then he classifies as evil and "intemperate"—which means generally committed with mortal sin—intercourse "in a prohibited time," and here he specifies that the one who seeks it sins "*potissime*." Intercourse in a holy place, if no other place is available, is "venial"; but if other places are available it is "doubtful." Finally he asserts that intercourse in an unusual place, holy or public, so as to cause scandal, is an "intemperate" exercise of conjugal rights.[76] While Nider does not revert to simple condemnation of intercourse in holy times and places, therefore, he willingly complicates the casuistry of this circumstance.

Astesanus of Asti believes that it is obligatory to abstain from intercourse before communion, an opinion based on Old Testament ideas of ritual purity,[77] which is echoed in other literature on the forgiveness of sins. The *Directoire des confesseurs*, for example, thinks that it is a sin to have intercourse with one's wife at a holy time, such as a vigil ordained for fasting. It is also sinful when they are about to receive the Holy Sacrament because married people act according to lust rather than marriage if they enjoy their conjugal rights then.[78] But the most puritanical discussion of this case is in Nicolaus de Ausimo's *Supplementum*, which painstakingly prescribes harsher restrictions than its

[75] Foresti, *Confessionale*, 17b–18a.
[76] Nider, *Expositio decalogi*, VI, 4, B2a–b.
[77] Ziegler, *Ehelehre*, 164–165.
[78] [Gerson?], *Directoire*, O2b–O3b.

parent *Pisanella*. Two examples are most striking—the questions of intercourse before communion or during holy season.

Under "Communicare," the *Pisanella* had asked whether coition was an impediment to communion and answered according to Thomas Aquinas that if it was without sin—that is, if it was for offspring or rendering the debt—then it was no impediment, unless there was the same kind of corporal uncleanness or distraction of mind that might make nocturnal pollution an impediment. "But when married partners have intercourse dominated by pleasure they ought to be prohibited from this sacrament," and the authority cited is Peter Lombard. Nicolaus begins his comment by reviewing the opinions of other authorities. John of Freiburg teaches the same thing as the *Pisanella*, but Albert the Great says that someone "led by weakness" to the act ought to be dissuaded from communion but not prohibited. Another authority says that all talk of abstaining is a counsel and not a precept. Nicolaus has a different idea however: "But it is certainly true that all matrimonial coition, even paying the debt, is an impediment to communion," as is clear from the familiar warning of Jerome that you cannot find time to pray and ought not to eat the flesh of the lamb if you return the debt to your wife. As a result, permission to exercise conjugal rights before Holy Communion should be understood to apply only to conjugal acts that are completely clear of pleasure and mental distraction. The impossibility of such freedom from pleasure and distraction is so great, however, that one must presume the contrary, and therefore not only asking for but even rendering the debt "seems normally to be an impediment to communion." Exceptions to this impediment are, first, in all cases of necessity, and one presumes that Nicolaus is talking about danger of death. Another exception is granted to the unhappy woman whose husband demands the debt so often from her that she would be in the position of having to abstain from communion for an excessively long time. Nicolaus's true desires are expressed in the decree of a church council which says: "Every man ought to abstain from his own wife before Holy Communion for three or four or five or six or seven days." The solution of Albert, forbidding communion to the one who has exacted the debt but allowing it to the one who dissuades unsuccessfully and renders it, is the last opinion offered for deciding the case. But Nicolaus's concession is at best half-hearted, and he has treated the reader to an awesome piece of rigorism. Under the same heading, the *Pisanella* also considers the morality of sexual intercourse on the same day after one has taken communion, and follows the opinion of Albert the Great: one should not ask for it, and one should even render it only with reluctance; ". . . nevertheless I do not think the contrary is a mortal sin." Nicolaus comments that he finds the same thing in John of Freiburg, but to show his dissatisfaction with it, he offers some damning words about this kind of self-indulgence:

> And I believe that the soul of someone doing this is in bad condition and remains devoid of grace on account of such great irreverence; on account of devotion and reverence for so great a sacrament he ought to abstain as much as he possibly can *not only from such uncleanness*, but also from eating.

Nicolaus's passionate assertion of the incompatibility of communion and marital intercourse is a good illustration of the rhetorical tendencies of this literature, which often left the realm of moral science simply to preach puritanical opinions.[79]

Equally rigid is the *Supplementum*'s judgment on intercourse during holy seasons. We begin with the usual kind of solution to this problem: the *Pisanella* cites the authority of Raymond and does not seem to find the case especially troublesome. You should pay the debt, this solution runs, unless you can prudently and without danger put it off, and you pay it without sin. The sense of incompatibility between sex and holiness is apparent then, but the *Pisanella* does not take it too seriously, for even demanding the debt is only a venial sin as long as there is no contempt for the season. But the consideration of "contempt" for the season gives Nicolaus his opportunity. From the authorities cited it is clear, he says, that everyone agrees that the use of matrimony is not excused from mortal sin "when it occurs in contempt of the season or of ecclesiastical regulation."

> He seems to be contemptuous, however, if he can abstain without great difficulty and yet asks for or freely renders [the debt]. For contempt seems to be nothing other than not to take the trouble to do what one ought. . . . Nor does one seem to be excused if in those times he asks or willingly renders for the sake of offspring.[80]

[79] *Supplementum*, "Communicare," 10.
[80] *Supplementum*, "Debitum coniugale," 7.

216

Given this strict definition of contempt for holy times, the period for abstaining from marital embraces could become unbearably long. And lengthy too would be the interrogation of the confessor.

But the rigidity of the *Astesana, Directoire*, and *Supplementum* is not common. Much more typical is the advice given in Matthew of Cracow's *The Worthy Reception of the Body of Christ*. In answer to the question "whether conjugal coition is an impediment to communion," Matthew explains that if the act was done for the sake of procreation or paying the debt, there is no sin and therefore no impediment "unless there is some bodily impurity of mental dullness or distraction of the sort associated with nocturnal pollution that occurs without sin." In such a case judgment should be left to the individual. If the act has been done solely for pleasure, however, Matthew agrees with many of the authorities who say he ought to be prohibited from communion. After communion he ought not demand or return the debt on the same day—but the contrary is no sin.

> It is also fitting for someone wishing to take communion to abstain from the conjugal act three or four or five or seven days. . . . But that is a counsel and not a precept, and it is to be understood as to seeking, not paying the debt. For if one spouse seeks it the other is required to pay, even assuming he is to take communion, as Landulf says, because it might expose the former to the danger of fornication.[81]

Guido de Monte Rocherii is even simpler: he declares that he does not believe it sinful to enjoy marital rights in times of fasts, saint's days, or days on which communion is received.[82]

This is the spirit that typifies the most authoritative and widely read literature guiding the consciences of the minister and recipient of the Sacrament of Penance. For Gerson there is an impropriety in enjoying sexual relations in holy times and places, but it is not serious enough to override the requirement of rendering the debt: ". . . holy time and place do not seem to be an excuse [for refusing]; rather one spouse is obliged to pay the debt to the other who is seeking it, having begun, nevertheless, by amicably

[81] Matthew of Cracow, *Incitatio ad digne suscipiendum corpus Christi*, Du Pin, III, 314B-C. Cf. Ziegler, *Ehelehre*, 273–274.
[82] Guido de Monte Rocherii, *Manipulus curatorum*, II, 3, 9.

admonishing him not to demand it."[83] And long before Gerson this principle had been accepted. Thus Berthold of Freiburg could argue in the thirteenth century that you owe the debt no matter what the season or how great the feast. Indeed, you should even leave church at the behest of your spouse if he asks:

> And if the married man is in church at the divine service and the other asks him to leave, he should be obedient and do her will—and he does so without sin.

It is better, Berthold agrees, to abstain at times of fast and feast, and although it is only a venial sin to seek it then (for it is against a counsel, not a precept of the church) it could be a mortal sin if it were done out of contempt or with inordinate lust (von vnordenlicher vnkeüscheet wegen).[84] Thus the *Sylvestrina* merely is continuing an already old habit of de-emphasizing the importance of holy seasons when it notes that those who have objected to intercourse in holy seasons, saying that it is mortally sinful if done for the sake of pleasure, must be understood to be condemning contempt of the season; and they deal, it continues, in some cases with exhortations and not precepts.[85]

Two reservations must be registered, however. In the first place, even those who seem generally free from worry about the seriousness of intercourse at fast and feast time retain a sense of the fittingness of abstinence; and at the same time the nature of their concern indicates that there was some doubt that the matter might be serious. Furthermore, in addition to vague references in general confessions and lists of questions about sins, some people express stricter ideas. The *Angelica*, for example, evoked not only a misreading from Jodocus Winshemius but a hostile response from its glossator Ungarelli. Angelus does not see any law forbidding intercourse in holy seasons, and despite some cautions about contempt for the season, does not seem deeply worried about it. Ungarelli does. He reverts to his warnings against lustful intercourse. He argues that if it is sinful for one merely to seek one's own pleasure, it is much more sinful to do so at solemn times. Angelus himself adheres to the popular doctrine that while one may ask for or pay the debt when one is to

[83] Gerson, *Regulae morales*, Du Pin, III, 106A.
[84] Berthold, *Summa Johannis, deutsch*, Q. 178, "Ob man die eelichen werck müg thūn zü heÿligen zeÿten."
[85] *Sylvestrina*, "Debitum coniugale," q. 8, par. 10.

take communion, it is not allowed simply to satisfy lustful appetites. In dealing with the question of asking for or returning the marital obligation in a holy place, Angelus first calls it sinful, but he also argues that it is permissible if the necessity arises: if, for example, one is forced to remain in a church for a long time. Angelus rejects the arguments of Petrus de Palude that even in those circumstances it is not permissible, just as he rejects the notion that intercourse will pollute a holy place. At the words "consecrated place" Ungarelli comments: "Now who would dare such things in the palace of a king? How much more therefore in the palace of the celestial king." The only activities that should go on there, he adds, are those compatible with the divine praises and for Ungarelli that definitely does not include the conjugal act.[86] Once again, the influential opinion is Angelus's, which is not likely to cause much trouble for consciences beyond its concern for contempt for holy seasons. But his fellow Franciscan's gloss reminds us that not all were persuaded by such gentler solutions.

Thus, while intercourse during menstruation is commonly condemned in the literature on forgiveness, the exercise of marital rights during holy times and in holy places, or during the wife's pregnancy, is generally considered at worst a venial sin. Even in

---

[86] *Angelica* (1534), "Debitum coniugale," 29, 30, 35, fol. 192b–193b. Ungarelli's insistence that one would not dare do such a thing in the palace of a king had been used in the same context by Nicolaus de Ausimo (*Supplementum*, "Debitum coniugale," 8), who attributes it to St. Thomas and Petrus de Palude. The use of churches as sanctuaries makes this question a practical one: see Müller, *Paradiesesehe*, 117–118. Another important norm governing the use of marital rights stipulated the loss of those rights for adultery and, accordingly, upheld the right of the injured spouse to deny the debt to his guilty partner, and in some cases actually forbade the innocent party to pay or ask for the debt. For example, if the sin was notorious, or if the admonished sinner persisted indefinitely in his sin, then no matter what the innocent partner wanted, it was considered sinful to pay or ask for the debt for both parties—at least until there was some evidence of amendment. At one time there was an obligation to denounce one's guilty spouse, but at least by the thirteenth century this kind of rigorous prescription is challenged. *Angelica*, "Debitum coniugale," 7–8; *Confessionale—Defecerunt*, 30; Ziegler, *Ehelehre*, 117–121, 254, 274. The *Supplementum* discusses the problem at length and ends by quoting (as had John of Freiburg) William of Rennes on whether the innocent party may ask for the debt from a spouse remaining in adultery: "alii dicunt quod impotentia continendi a copula carnali excusat exigentem in hoc casu, quorum sententia benignior est, licet forte non verior"; *Supplementum*, "Debitum coniugale," 12–15; *Raymundina*, IV, 2, 11, p. 517.

the case of menstruation, there are plenty of authorities who allow it. But if we look at the discussion of these restrictions as a whole, it is evident that even when confessors were told that such practices were not mortal sins, they were told in language that re-emphasized the dangers of sexual pleasure, even for the married.

Our discussion so far has employed value judgments frequently. Some views have been labeled unrealistic, others have been called reasonable. The danger here is obvious: are we simply imposing our own values and our own rationality on a culture that deserves to be judged by its own values and its own definition of rationality? That question demands a careful answer. And so, before we turn to a final evaluation of sacramental confession's sexual ethics for married penitents, it will be helpful to explain some of the assumptions and criteria underlying our analysis.

To begin with, our concern with the function of social control provides important insights into the historical setting of rigoristic sexual ethics. The system of sexual morality developed in the middle ages and incorporated into sacramental confession has many disciplinary functions, some obvious and some not. Most obviously, it can be related to the stability of marriage, the legitimization of offspring, and the regular transference of property. These goals are so expressly in the language of authorities on confession that one is justified in calling them explicit functions of the institution.

An implicit function of sexual ethics in sacramental confession —one that may not be obvious—is the reinforcement of clerical supremacy, to which we have alluded from time to time. The subordination of married laity to celibate clergy is reinforced in many ways by sacramental confession's sexual ethic, one of which is in the extreme ease of committing sins of lust. The casuistry of sins of desire, when applied to sexual impulses, provides opportunities for the imputation of guilt that none of the other deadly vices can match. That guilt must be cured by the absolution of priestly confessors.

To describe the social implications of sacramental confession's sexual ethics, however, does not mean that we have described anything wrong. Property relations were not invented by priests, or even bishops; and it would certainly be surprising to find that sacramental confession was challenging the property structure of late medieval society by endorsing novel marital and sexual arrangements. Furthermore, even if we can show that rigoristic sexual ethics buttress clerical dominance, we cannot reaffirm too often that the clergy were also supposed to observe strict rules. The price they are to pay for power is higher than that of the laity, and it is paid in the same coin of sexual repression. Consequently, observations on the relationship between sexual ethics and property, or sexual ethics and clerical supremacy, need not have pejorative connotations. They are primarily commentaries on how ethics and institutions are integrated.

In a similar fashion, the relationship between sexual ethics, social control, and demography can help us place rigorism in a more neutral light. The recent discovery that most Europeans in this period married late, and that many never married at all, has become a key to our understanding of many problems of social history, and sexual ethics is not the least of them. For if the property necessary to marry and raise a family is in short supply, so that many must wait for years before it is available to them, and many never acquire it at all, then sexual repression will be inevitable. Thus at one level of analysis we might argue that an ascetic sexual morality was functional in the demographic conditions of late medieval Europe. Or, to express it literally, this analysis finds prelates, theologians, and confessors doing the work of the social system by maintaining a sexual ethic compatible with economic conditions.

To be sure, that analysis can be taken only so far because ecclesiastical authorities would have done the work of the social system even more effectively had they simply permitted sexual deviations to relieve the tensions created by scarce resources. To be blunt, masturbation, contraception, and sodomy might well have come to the aid of this population whom we suppose to be suffering from sexual repression. Single people waiting to be married; single people destined never to be married; and married people living on the economic margin and fearful of the burden of additional offspring—all of these people might have been helped by a transformation of sexual ethics that would have sanctioned some obvious forms of relief. Such a simplistic and mechanistic solution, however, was not conceivable. Its premise is that values are totally malleable and almost totally the expression of material forces. In reality, ecclesiastical authorities could not change values as they pleased, even if it was to serve material needs. Authorities on sin and forgiveness were bound by principles. They had a method of solving moral problems that entailed definite scholarly and logical operations. Their opinions, therefore, were not just expedient inventions but rather the product of a particular kind of reasoning about a body of received moral principles. A "rational" solution that offered deviant sexuality to the faithful would not have been plausible. It would have appeared utterly irrational.

Thus examination of the relationship between demography and sexual ethics makes medieval rigorism intelligible on two additional grounds. First, it was functional in economic terms. Second, its peculiar form was to an important degree determined by theological tradition and moral principles.

But to admit these complexities does not make it impossible or undesirable to evaluate the teaching on marital sex. In the first place, we are not looking for a modern, secularized ethic that disregards traditional values and economic realities. Our value judgments are hopefully derived from the intellectual and institutional bases of sacramental confession. We are led to judgments because we have accepted the seriousness of purpose of this literature: to advise confessors; to deal correctly and humanely with married penitents; to solve problems of conscience consistent with theological ideas of divine and natural truth; to offer counsel, forgiveness, and consolation. In trying to maintain a historical perspective, we have been guided by medieval theology's rejection of dualism and its affirmation of a rational as well as a revealed ethic, especially as it was developed in the thirteenth century. That means that the marital act should be treated as a natural consequence of the Sacrament of Matrimony. Thus we ask whether sacramental confession's rules and expectations were compatible with its own goals, including the instruction and consolation of married penitents. This, we must repeat, is only to take pastoral authorities' task and reasoning seriously. They thought of themselves as doctors of souls. It makes sense to ask if they were good doctors. And if we cannot claim a psychological science as sophisticated as scientific medicine; and if we cannot judge their cures as confidently as historians of science can judge those of medieval physicians; we can, nevertheless, claim an understanding of human psychology and human sexuality that surpasses that of the canonists, theologians, and authors of summas and manuals for confessors. With those thoughts in mind, we can turn to a final evaluation of the teaching on the sexual sins of married Christians.

THE NEGATIVE BALANCE

To arrive at a balanced evaluation, we should begin by restating some cautionary notes. Sexual sins, as we admitted at the outset, were not the only concerns of clerical literature on the forgiveness of sins. The vices of scholars and merchants and lawyers and just about everyone were defined and attacked. Standards for judging greed or violence could be as strict as for lust. And so it would be a grave error to see authors of devotional literature or manuals for confessors as uniquely obsessed with sexual problems of the penitent. When St. Antoninus explores "Thou shalt not steal" in his manual for confessors, he writes seven times as much as he does for "Thou shalt not commit adultery." Even within their discussion of marriage, the summas devote an inordinate amount of space to the purely legal questions of vows and impediments. This interest is predominant in the *Raymundina*, which, like its descendants, is far more concerned with legal technicalities than with the sexual conduct of marriage. One example of this legal interest is evident throughout the literature for confessors in the elaborate rules and diagrams laid down for the determination of forbidden and permissible degrees for marriage between relatives. The popularity of Johannes Andrea's *Teaching on the Trees of Consanguinity, Affinity, and Spiritual Relationship* is additional evidence of this interest.[87]

A second word of mitigation needs to be repeated as well: not only were confessors worried about other things, but they were also worried about attacking too directly the sensibilities of penitents—married or single—on delicate matters of sexual behavior. At least they were told to be cautious by most of their manuals, summas, and other literature designed to help hear confessions. Thus we should not imagine that every penitent was asked to review in detail his sexual conduct with his wife since his last confession, recounting the conditions, motives, and positions for the marital act. The penitent is not in fact expected to determine why he wants his wife every time he initiates the conjugal act, and he certainly could not be expected to recall them

[87] There are forty-six editions of Johannes Andrea, *Lectura super arboribus consanguinitatis affinitatis et cognationis spiritualis* before 1500: *GKW*, 1676–1721.

all in the confessional. Interrogation properly conducted was to be diligent, but also prudent.[88]

In addition to these two cautions we must add a positive note to our estimate of late medieval treatment of sexuality. Not only did the pastoral literature find other sins to worry about; not only did it urge confessors to be careful when they explored these delicate problems; it also affirmed in striking ways the goodness of the conjugal act. Here we can even go beyond that instance of requiring payment of the debt and show that it became a commonplace of moral theology to call sinless uses of sexuality not merely "licit," as Raymond of Peñaforte had done, but even *meritorious*. For the history of theology the critical era for this development is, once again, the thirteenth century, when Aristotelians like Albert the Great and Peter of Tarantasia find the exercise of conjugal rights with the proper motives and informed by the love of God not merely excusable but honorable. This attitude often prevailed in later summas for confessors. John of Freiburg includes this classification and Berthold von Freiburg follows him. In the fourteenth century, Astesanus of Asti is even more emphatic as he goes beyond Albert the Great and includes intercourse for the sake of avoiding one's own infidelity among the meritorious acts.[89] Even less academic sources such as the

[88] Ziegler, *Ehelehre*, 226. See, for example, Antoninus, *Confessionale— Defecerunt*. The confessor was not routinely required to investigate the motives for intercourse of all of his penitents. Indeed, as Ziegler (*Ehelehre*) notes, the confessor need not even instruct a penitent to examine his motives every time he has intercourse with his spouse. But Ziegler's characterization of these motives as unimportant for practice cannot hold for the "causa exsaturandae libidinis," because this motive is suspect itself, and is relevant when intercourse during menstruation and in "unnatural" positions are judged. The literature in general kept the question of sex for pleasure alive, as Ziegler admits when he identifies persistent restrictions on marital intercourse, which include forbidding communion after coitus motivated solely by desire for pleasure, and choosing an unnatural position merely to heighten pleasure (ibid., 273–274).

[89] Ziegler, *Ehelehre*, 212–217; Berthold, *Summa Johannis, deutsch,* Q. 177, "Von dem eelichen wercken. . . ." Berthold also says that to have intercourse "durch kinder willen" is not only sinless but "lonper" and "mit lon verdienten von got." The *Angelica* ("Debitum coniugale," 22) has a typical grading: "Nam ex triplici causa sine peccato exigitur et redditur etiam cum merito ex primis duabis." *Causa prolis* and *causa reddendi* are sinless and meritorius —*causa vitandi*, according to Angelus, is generally considered a venial sin. Albert the Great had also considered certain instances of the sexual act

sermons of Jean Raulin, the anonymous *Peycht Spigel*, or the manual of the diocese of Albi refer to the meritorious nature of the act under certain circumstances.[90]

In the *Sylvestrina* the meritorious status of the conjugal act receives a fairly precise theological treatment. After he discusses the cases when intercourse between married partners is a venial sin, Sylvester proceeds to the next question, "In what cases is the conjugal act exercised without sin or with merit?" There are four such meritorious uses of conjugal rights, all of which naturally presuppose the gift of grace. The first is when one pays the debt to one's spouse, for this is an act of justice. The second is the act done for the sake of having offspring and educating them to God—that is an act of worship! Next is to save one's spouse from adultery—an act of charity. The last case is particularly noteworthy because it could normally be classified as venially sinful rather than laudable!

> Fourth, when one acts to avoid the same in oneself, and one cannot avoid it better another way: because it is an act of prudence or chastity.[91]

When we try to understand the sometimes strange thinking of churchmen on the subject of sexuality, we must not ignore this positive side. The attitude toward sex of a Rabelais, or a Montaigne, or even a Le Maistre can be made to appear thoroughly revolutionary. But we see that even conservative clerics like Sylvester could affirm the goodness of natural functions; and thus there is a connection between these conservatives and the more original voices of the age. Moreover, there is evidence that while a certain antipathy to the physical aspects of sex persisted in Western culture, there were also deep counter-currents. Why else would it have become a commonplace in the literature to decide the morality of initiating the conjugal act to gain or preserve good health? Obviously moral theologians were contending

---

meritorius: *Comentarii in IV sententiarum*, dis. 31, F, a. 19, and a. 21, *Opera*, 30, 253–258. Cf. Klomps, *Ehemoral*, 11–16; Müller, *Paradiesesehe*, 282–299.

[90] Raulin, *Itinerarium paridisi, de matrimonio*, sermon 8, fol. 180a ("actus virtutis" and "actus iusticie"); *Peycht Spigel*, K4a–L1b; *Confessionale* (Albi), E5b–E6a.

[91] *Sylvestrina*, "Debitum coniugale," q. 12, par. 14.

with a belief held by some people that sex was not debilitating but rather medicinal.[92]

But if there is this brighter side to the evaluation of sexual functions, the darker predominates. Moral theologians might have been hard on other kinds of sins; they might have worried about too direct an assault on the sensibilities of married people; they could think of the conjugal act as either mandatory or meritorious; and they even found it necessary to discuss the use of sexual intercourse to obtain or remain in good health. Still, the weight of their pessimism and deprecation of sexuality is preponderant over that brighter side.

Indeed, the prejudice that most clearly betrays the culture's true estimate of sexuality is the bizarre belief that it was not helpful but actually harmful to health. For a fine example of this prejudice we may turn to one of Jean Raulin's arguments against polygamy. When coitus is too frequent, he declares, it is very dangerous:

> First, because of the danger of infecundity, as is evident in prostitutes; because from the heat of concupiscence the semen is consumed and sometimes vanishes. Second, because life is thereby shortened, as is evident in the case of Solomon, who, although he was fifty-one years of age, is nevertheless said to have died an old man; and similarly according to Aristotle, sparrows are short-lived on account of frequent coitus.[93]

[92] For example, *Angelica*, "Debitum coniugale," 24: "Utrum cognoscere vxorem causa sanitatis sit licitum. Respondeo. Ri. in iiij. di xxxj. ar. iii. q. ij. quod secundum quosdam sic. vel forte potest dici quod sit veniale peccatum et hoc verius, et sequitur Tho. iii. iiij. di. xxxij." In substantial agreement with this judgment are Berthold, *Summa Johannis, deutsch*, Q. 177, "Von dem eelichen wercken" ("not a great sin according to St. Thomas"); Raulin, *Itinerarium paridisi, de matrimonio*, sermon 8, fol. 181a–b (venial—Raulin calls it an "ineptum medium"); *Sylvestrina*, "Debitum coniugale," q. 12, par. 14 (venial); Antoninus, *Confessionale—Defecerunt*, 30 (venial). Somewhat harder are Nider, *Expositio decalogi*, VI, 4, B2a (at least venial); and Foresti, *Confessionale*, 17b–18a ("not without sin"). The crusaders learned of the healing properties of sexual intercourse immediately after snake bites from the Saracens: see Albert d'Aix, *Alberti Aquensis Historia Hierosolymitana*, V, 40, in *Recueil des historiens des croisades, Historiens occidentaux*, vol. 4 (Paris, 1879), pp. 458–459; but the son of Frederick Barbarossa rejected the remedy: see Hefele and Leclerq, *Histoire des conciles*, 5[2], 1151, n. 2.

[93] Raulin, *Itinerarium paridisi, de matrimonio*, sermon 8, fol. 182b. Raulin does not explain how he knows Solomon was fifty-one when he died.

Although Raulin was defending intercourse with pregnant women as preferable to polygamy with arguments from nature, the source of his metaphors does not hinder him from drawing his own ascetic conclusion. Husbandry, ornithology, and the sorry end of Solomon dictate the rationality of restraint.

Theories about the unhealthy effects of lust were not invented by the medieval doctors, of course, and one author, J. L. Vivaldus, proudly cites the authority of Galen to substantiate his claim that it is harmful to the body, exposes it to illness, and shortens life. The causality is presented in that peculiar language of the learned:

> The complexion of the semen is warm and moist; for it is generated from clear and pure blood, by which the principal and particular members are fed and sustained. Whence if in its emission someone through shameful acts is excessive [modum transgreditur] there will not be enough blood to feed the members. And therefore the man's strength is diminished, the body is dried out, and many weaknesses and various illnesses follow: sciatica, gout, colic, stomach pains and upsets. Among all the parts of the human body, however, coitus is especially harmful to the stomach, eyes, and brain. . . . For, as Galen says, not only does the humor proceed from the members, but also the vital spirit goes out through the arteries with the semen. And thus it is no wonder if he who is devoted to venereal pleasures is debilitated, for as the body is evacuated the vital force is likewise diminished.

Indeed, Vivaldus clearly believes that excessive lust can be fatal, both to the ailing and the healthy. And his attitude here is more than the application of dispassionately accepted medical views. It is founded on his hostility to pleasure, as he makes it clear by continuing with a litany of the evil effects of this vice. Lust clouds the intellect. It infatuates men (the reader is reminded of Adam, David, and Samson). It causes scandal and disgrace. It debilitates all human powers, kills the rational soul, and dissipates one's fortunes.[94]

In addition to the idea that sex is unhealthy, we should recall here the fear of moral contamination from natural physiological functions. The persistence of such questions as whether one may

[94] Vivaldus, *Aureum opus*, 82a.

receive communion after having sexual intercourse, or whether one may have sexual intercourse on the same day after one has taken communion, or whether one may lawfully demand or pay the debt in a holy season, are all examples of how deeply it was feared that the physical corruption of sex might have a spiritual effect. Inexorably the logic of moral science encroached upon these fears. The early medieval notion that some kind of bodily purification was necessary after sexual intercourse was never included in the manuals and summas for confessors; and although Albert the Great had thought the passage of the sun across the heavens could purify a body contaminated by sexual intercourse and prepare it for reception of the sacrament, no idea quite so impractical enters pastoral theology. Yet the old sense of contamination by the physical remained—the sense of uncleanness and the shamefulness of sexuality was very much a part of the summas and handbooks.

A good example of this fear of contamination is in the constant worrying about nocturnal pollution. For a celibate clergy this problem was perhaps especially troublesome, even though, according to the most fundamental principles of ethics, a sleeping man cannot commit a mortal sin. Yet in a treatise whose popularity in print proves the sensitivity of the issue, Jean Gerson discussed at great length whether one may consecrate the Host after a nocturnal pollution. Sexuality—even unintentional and unavoidable—always threatened to be incompatible with the holy. If restrictions against sexual intercourse during holy seasons had been reduced from the absurdly exaggerated periods of abstinence of the early middle ages, it was still, according to a common opinion, possible to commit a mortal sin by enjoying conjugal rights in contempt of the season. Foresti can feed these feelings of contamination by noting that while it is not a mortal sin, nevertheless it is not proper to have intercourse with your wife on the same day you receive communion, just as it is not proper for a menstruating woman to approach the communion rail! To call genitals "the shameful members" betrays suspicion of the body, as do some of the denunciations of revealing clothes. Olivier Maillard rails against women who provoke desire by exposing their breasts, for, he continues, "breasts are a shameful part, as St. Augustine said in *De trinitate dei*, and never ought to be uncovered." Sylvester feels that sex is basically shameful, but he wants to exclude that feeling from the moral evaluation of the act. After discussing those cases when the act is meritorious, "grace being assumed," he takes up the same four cases, "the absence of grace being truly assumed," and judges them *indifferent* because while they lack grace they also lack guilt, "notwithstanding that a man feels ashamed because of it." Three things, he tells us, cause shame: natural weaknesses, such as defecation; guilt; and things sharing the same species as guilt, "such as this act, which is of the same species as fornication."[95]

There were limits to the suspicion of sexuality, and it is rare to find authors who consider lust the worst of all sins. Nevertheless, there are instances of aberrant views on the relative gravity of sexual sins, and those extremes are worth remembering. The *Astesana*, for example, argues—on the authority of Aristotle and Gregory the Great—that gluttony and lust are the worst vices because they reduce men to the level of beasts.[96] Even more shocking is the opinion of the *Eruditorium penitentiale*, which sets out to incite hatred of fornication "because this sin is more detestable than homicide or plunder, which are not substantially evil." It then explains that in cases of necessity it is possible to kill or steal justifiably, "but no one may fornicate knowingly without committing a mortal sin."[97] And it is in essentially the same spirit that some authorities remind us that the penalty for adultery and unnatural acts was once death.[98] This kind of thinking is an exaggeration even of medieval puritanism. Yet it is also true that the climate of religious opinion allowed and perhaps even encouraged such exaggerations.

Still, nothing could reveal more clearly the basic mistrust of sexuality than the common assertion that there are so many temptations within matrimony that it is easier to avoid sins against chastity in the celibate life. This attitude—this judgment on marriage—can be traced to St. Augustine; and it remained in the religious tradition because it was perfectly consistent with

[95] Ziegler, *Ehelehre*, 179–181, 243–250, 253; Maillard, *La Confession*, B1a; *Sylvestrina*, "Debitum coniugale," q. 12, par. 14: "Quia de tribus erubescimus: scilicet primo de culpa, et secundo de habente speciem culpae: vt iste actus, qui est eiusdem speciei cum fornicatione: et tertio de naturalibus defectibus, vt est egestio et huiusmodi."

[96] Ziegler, *Ehelehre*, 160–161.

[97] *Eruditorium penitentiale*, H6b–I1a.

[98] Ziegler, *Ehelehre*, 164–165; Stanka, *Die Summa des Berthold von Freiburg*, 116–118; Foresti, *Confessionale*, 15a–b; de Butrio, *Speculum de confessione*, 61–66, C8a–D1b.

the rigorist teaching on the conjugal act. At the same time, however, it was obviously paradoxical to say that marriage, given as a remedy for concupiscence, is a serious source of sexual temptation. Thus some of the more astute moral theologians were prompted to comment on that paradox. Martin Le Maistre, for example, criticizes the view that marital intercourse solely for pleasure might be a mortal sin as "dangerous for human morals," and he castigates those who find only two valid motives for sexual intercourse, offspring and avoiding infidelity: "I ask how many dangers do they expose the consciences of scrupulous spouses to, for there is many a one whose wife is immediately made pregnant, and after that has happened, they expose to the danger of mortal sin whoever seeks the debt unless it is certain that he does this to avoid fornication."[99]

But if Le Maistre objects to a moral doctrine that needlessly multiplies occasions of sin for married partners, others do not. To some rigorists St. Augustine's dictum that chastity is easier for virgins than for married people is all too true. Even Sylvester succumbs to this mentality when he notes, in his solution to the morality of unnatural positions, that one must sympathize with married people because in the conduct of their sexual lives there is little or no rationality.[100] Nicolaus de Ausimo agrees with this harsh judgment but is far from sympathetic. When he comments on the sin of exceeding the limits of matrimony with one's wife, he emphatically asserts that it is easier to preserve oneself from mortal sin in the religious life, observing strict celibacy, than in married life, enjoying conjugal rights. The blessings of the religious life include absence of incentives to lust and the presence of many, continual remedies. St. Paul may have thought of marrying as an alternative to burning with passion; but Nicolaus manages to evade that teaching. His *Supplementum* depicts married people as constantly exposed to the flame of desire, which consumes their minds.[101]

The most poignant commentary on this paradox, however, comes from Jean Gerson. After enumerating in a brief sentence

[99] Noonan, *Contraception* (1967), 164–165, 372; (1965), 130, 309.

[100] *Sylvestrina*, "Debitum coniugale," q. 4, par. 7.

[101] *Supplementum*, "Debitum coniugale," 4. Nicolaus does not, it is true, entirely ignore the Pauline doctrine that marriage is a remedy; but he is eager here to stress that it is nothing more than a remedy. As he puts it: "non autem ad implementum voluptatis" (ibid.).

the ways the conjugal act can be mortally sinful—during menstruation, outside the proper organ, desiring someone else, from evil motives—he concludes pessimistically:

> Complete abstinence from carnal acts—as in virgins and widows—is often easier than exercising conjugal rights, just as a fever by drinking, a fire by blowing, and an itch by scratching, ultimately become more inflamed.[102]

Gerson's lesson found its way into the *Himmelstrasse*. After explaining that the conjugal act can be sinful if it is done contrary to nature—including improper positions—Stephan Lanzkranna comments: "For that reason a remarkable teacher says that it is easier to preserve chastity and avoid impurity than conduct oneself properly in married life."[103] To Stephan Lanzkranna, the uses of marriage contrary to nature—under which he includes improper positions—are the dangers that render marriage so difficult and celibacy so much safer. But for authorities on sin and forgiveness, these are not the only dangers married people face. Refusing the debt, inciting desire, showing contempt for holy times and places, having sexual relations with a pregnant or menstruating wife, and even seeking pleasure, all provide material for rumination, interrogation, and guilt. And while there are important authorities on pastoral care who decry a senseless rigorism and its anxiety-producing conclusions, for the practical literature on forgiveness as a whole the opportunities for sin in marriage are as plentiful as Augustine, Le Maistre, or Gerson feared. The morality of the conjugal act was only one subject for inquiry in the confessional, and we cannot even be sure how detailed it was. Yet, one can hardly imagine a more sensitive subject or one more likely to arouse scruples. Only a very selective and scholarly reading of the literature on the forgiveness of sins could give a confessor a consoling view of conjugal morality. The best pastoral authorities offer help to troubled consciences, but even the best are only moderately helpful, only intermittently consoling. While they might cure the worst cases of anxiety over sexual behavior, they might also create them. A consistent laxist doctrine did not emerge in the years before the Reformation. On the contrary, pastors now had at their disposal a printed litera-

---

[102] Gerson, *Regulae morales*, 99, "De Luxuria," Du Pin, III, 95C. Cf. Noonan, *Contraception* (1967), 334–335; (1965), 277.

[103] Stephan Lanzkranna, *Himelstrass*, ch. 17, 55b.

ture that emphasized the evils of all but the most restrained exercise of marital rights. It was a literature that could not free itself from the fear of sexual pleasure. The fundamental mood of these celibates ironically comes from St. Augustine (who, after all, had had some experience): they were searching for ways to *excuse* the exercise and pleasure of conjugal intercourse. And if they were willing to find excuses, if we can even find in the *Angelica* and the *Sylvestrina* evidence that pastoral authority was becoming milder and more sensitive to the consciences of married people, it is still true that they found the marital bed a dangerous place for people who would remain faithful to the law.

CHAPTER V

THE WORKING OF THE SACRAMENT
OF PENANCE

Sorrow and the Keys

HE practical literature on forgiveness defined sins carefully and enumerated them copiously. Even for married people it was easy to sin sexually, and this is but one of the areas of life that moralists examined. But if it was easy to sin—in thought, word, and deed—was it also easy to be forgiven? What kind of work did the penitent have to do? What help could he expect from Christ's church and His representative, the priest?

To answer these questions truthfully, pastoral care had to enter a more abstruse theology and consider the process called justification. Religious writers had to explain the role of the penitent's confession and contrition and the priest's absolution in that process by which the sinner was transformed from an enemy to a friend of God. On a simple level we have already solved these problems by describing the "good" confession. But the prescriptions for a good confession do not adequately answer a number of difficult questions. If this teaching is to be successful, penitents and confessors must understand how human effort and sacramentally mediated grace combine to work a miraculous forgiveness. The range of discussion on such questions is naturally immense. In some of the manuals, as a matter of fact, there is no explicit discussion of the theology of justification on any level. In some of the summas, the treatment is skimpy. But most often authors reveal at least an implicit interest in these theological problems, and at times we encounter discussions of surprising technicality.

Because of their practical task, however, the focus of their inquiry (and our analysis) must be on the penitent. The cure of souls was concerned less with theological schools and formulas than with making doctrine clear and useful. To be sure, even the most abstruse elements of the theology of justification as taught by the doctors was relevant to this instruction. But theological formulas and arguments enter for pragmatic purposes. The goal is to make intelligible to the penitent what he must say, do, think, and feel if he is to rid himself of guilt. The academic tradition that fed this pastoral literature, therefore, had to be interpreted judiciously. Theological technicalities, scholastic disputes, and well-intentioned subtleties could be helpful, or irrelevant, or even harmful. And good pastoral care would choose what was helpful and avoid the rest.

It is also evident that there is no greater chance of originality here than in the discussion of moral problems, or the conduct of confession, or any other issue. Differences of opinion exist, but in the theory of how the sacrament works all important opinions are derived from older and respected authorities. We must repeat, this literature discourages novelty. And if some authors offer an interesting or even bizarre opinion, it is nevertheless borrowed. Even Gerson does not innovate when he addresses himself to this kind of practical problem; and acute, perceptive, or experienced as one of his arguments may be, he studiously operates within the constraints of orthodox moral and sacramental theology. Gerson could not—any more than anyone else who wanted to be orthodox—feel free to break out of the constraints his own conscience placed on theological speculation.

Finally, we must recall again the two functions of the institutions of forgiveness that occupy our attention: consolation and discipline. Both are indispensable to successful pastoral care. To assure the penitent that if he fulfills certain requirements and gets certain aids he will be forgiven is patently a work of consolation. But at the same time, to set up requirements a penitent must fulfill serves discipline or social control. Indeed, to define requirements for forgiveness establishes the most general kind of sanctions. For a theory of how the sacrament works can generate rules that will help a penitent know when he is and is not to feel guilty. It is this theory that determines the conditions under which a sinner who has violated prohibitions can acquit himself, and be restored to the company of those who are supposed not to be violating these prohibitions. If a theory does not make it too easy to be forgiven, then a sanction exists for disciplining the faithful and directing their behavior into ecclesiastically approved channels. At the same time, if the theory does not make it too difficult to be forgiven, a mechanism exists for curing anxiety and restoring the deviant to the community of the living faithful.

It should not be surprising that the attempt both to discipline and to console made simple, clear instruction on the working of the Sacrament of Penance difficult to achieve. Add to this the equally significant component of a sacramental theology that had evolved over centuries of change in ecclesiastical institutions and one finds little hope for a unanimous, lucid, and practical theory. In fact, there was a diversity of language and even of conclusions about what a sinner must feel and do and how the Sacrament of Penance helps him if he is to be forgiven and believe he is forgiven. While it is true, then, that there was a broad consensus on the nature of a good confession, and an even more general desire to be orthodox, differences and obscurities bedevil the attempt to offer a simple explanation of how the sacrament worked. Two areas constitute the major concern of this practical inquiry: the nature and role of the penitent's sorrow—contrition; and the power of the priestly keys—absolution.

DEFINITIONS OF SORROW

The most common definition of contrition tries to summarize its moral qualities, not its emotional content:

Contrition is sorrow for sins voluntarily assumed with the intention of confessing and doing satisfaction.[1]

We immediately recognize familiar elements in this formula. Sorrow must be voluntary because the consent of a free will is essential at every point of the moral and sacramental theology of the church. Just as a man cannot commit a sin, neither can he be acquitted of guilt, without the consent of his will. Part of that act of will, moreover, must be directed toward fulfilling the ecclesiastical obligations of confession and satisfaction. This requirement is also crucial. There remained a few in the late middle ages who were so faithful to "contritionism"—forgiveness

[1] Some of the authorities who use this definition: *Raymundina*, III, 34, 8, p. 443; Guido de Monte Rocherii, *Manipulus curatorum*, II, 2, 1; Nider, *Expositio decalogi*, III, 8A, O2a–b; de Butrio, *Speculum de confessione*, 49, C4b; *Supplementum*, "Contritio"; Raulin, *Itinerarium paridisi*, sermon 2, fol. 66; Winshemius, *Institutiones*, A3a; Rosemondt, *Confessionale*, 11, 1, fol. 167a; Jacobus de Gruytroede, *Speculum aureum*, 3, B1a–B3a; *Sylvestrina*, "Contritio," 1; *Angelica*, "Contritio"; [Poeniteas cito], *Libellus de modo poenitendi*, A3a.

235

caused immediately by perfect sorrow—that the necessity for confessing could be something of a puzzle. But even for them an efficacious sorrow had to entail the intention of telling sins to the priest and at least admitting the need to pay a debt of temporal punishment, which could be satisfied through penitential exercises imposed by the priest. This simple definition of sorrow, therefore, forcefully represents the authority of the clergy and the discipline of the church. It tells us that a forgiving sorrow must flow from a will freely embracing it, and must include the explicit desire for the sacramental benefits of the visible church. Vague intentions will not do. Contrition by its very definition binds the penitent to sacramental confession and the ecclesiastical authority that dispenses it.

Some authors resort to an etymological definition of the word contrition in order to say something about the emotion of feeling sorry. Thus the *Sylvestrina* asserts the common belief that *contritio* comes from *con*, an intensifying prefix, and *tero*, the verb "to crush," or "to grind":

> Contrition, from *con* and *tero*, according to its name, means a breaking up, or a smashing of something breakable into its smallest parts, as if all at once it were completely pulverized. And metaphorically it signifies the perfect destruction of the evil will desiring sins. One is said to be contrite for sins when he fully and totally recoils from them through displeasure.[2]

Not everyone interprets the metaphor so concretely as Sylvester, but there is nothing unusual in his going from the notion of a heartrending emotion to the effect of a turning away from sin. The practical question that arises, however, is how do you know that you have the kind of emotion, the smashing of an evil will, that the etymological definition talks about? How do you know when you are "torn apart" by sorrow for sin? We confront here that searching of the human heart that St. Thomas and a variety of authors warn against, but which seems inevitable if you are to have a theory of the sacrament that explains its effectiveness in terms of emotions. Some will indulge in a rhetorical description of emotions in order to awaken a higher purpose, a more profound remorse. But the most important thinking on the sub-

[2] *Sylvestrina*, "Contritio," 1; cf. *Supplementum*, "Contritio," and Guido de Monte Rocherii, *Manipulus curatorum*, II, 2, 1.

ject is more hardheaded. It tells sinners what the absolutely minimum sorrow entails.

St. Antoninus teaches about the necessary emotion in sorrow according to St. Thomas, and his advice is the most common of commonplaces: to be forgiven you need intellectual, not sensible sorrow. By that St. Antoninus and all the others who repeat this dictum mean that you do not have to weep in fact or even feel on the verge of tears. Such a sensible sorrow, Antoninus tells us, belongs to the perfection of contrition and, unlike intellectual sorrow, it can be excessive. The true and necessary contrition must be a habit or a disposition (one might well recall here the phrase "voluntarily assumed" in the most frequently cited definition). Thus contrition must persist as an intellectual or voluntary manifestation not in the sense that one feels continually guilty and miserable as one would expect from a sensible sorrow, but rather as a habit properly understood: a readiness to elicit an intellectual displeasure at sin whenever one remembers one's sins.[3] Jodocus Winshemius is quite as explicit. The sadness one experiences is not a sensible emotion but resides in the mind or will, so that the sinner no longer desires sin, either at that time or in the future. Real tears may follow, but, as Seneca and Ovid suggest, they may be deceiving and they are in any case less important than the movement of the will.[4] Even those who are more enthusiastic for real tears and tangible grief do not think it necessary. Guido de Monte Rocherii, for example, notes that sensible grief is rare: few are capable of it for an hour, and although he thinks it is a mark of great contrition—as in the case of Peter who could not recall his denial without tears—he thinks it evident that such an emotion is not always necessary.[5] Nicolaus de Ausimo also likes real tears, but he is content to urge those incapable of a sensible sorrow simply to be sorry they cannot incite one.[6] The function of discipline is again prominent, therefore, but with moderation.

Some, however, make discipline even more pronounced by tying contrition, by definition, to the intention to amend. The au-

[3] Antoninus, *Confessionale—Defecerunt*, 7. Cf. *Sylvestrina*, "Confessio 1," q. 21, par. 24.
[4] Winshemius, *Institutiones*, A3a.
[5] Guido de Monte Rocherii, *Manipulus curatorum*, II, 2, 4.
[6] *Supplementum*, "Contritio," 6.

thoritative voice of Jean Gerson is only one of many making this identification, but his definition is the most certain: in one place he calls contrition "the intention and the desire of abstaining from sins."[7] We have also seen that those who do not include the intention to amend in their definition of contrition make almost as direct a connection when they call both contrition and the intention to amend necessary prerequisites to forgiveness.[8] It is clear, then, that the definition itself tended to bolster the function of control. The more closely sorrow was identified with amendment, the more it implied obedience to the church. Still we have already seen that the intention to amend was not a contract, and failure to amend did not prove insincerity. And when we consider what religious authorities might have defined as appropriate and essential to sorrow for sin—what excesses of emotionality they might have endorsed—it is also clear that their moderation was fundamentally realistic. It fits best with the ambitious attempt of the medieval clergy to reach and change the whole community of Christians.

SIGNS AND EMOTIONS

Even if the definition of contrition excluded a "sensible sorrow," there was a genuine interest in communicating what it felt like to experience true sorrow. And while the literature defines contrition principally in terms of moral and theological qualities, it also deals with the experience of sorrow, at least to the extent that it is willing to talk about the kinds of emotions that were acceptable and the kinds of signs by which a penitent could discern good sorrow.

When the *Raymundina* discusses sorrow, it talks about six "causes inducing contrition," and in so doing it describes the emotion itself more than its etiology. The six causes are reflection on sins; shame for them; revulsion at their vileness; fear of judgment and the pains of hell; sorrow at the loss of our heavenly Fatherland; and the triple hope of grace, glory, and pardon. That

---

[7] Gerson, *De Differentia*, Du Pin, II, 499C.

[8] This truism is so fundamental that it even appears in the German epitomes of the *Modus confitendi* of Andreas de Escobar: Fritz, "Zwei Bearbeitungen," 62. Cf. Stephan Lanzkranna, *Himelstrass*, 4, 7a; Winshemius, *Institutiones*, A3a; Nider, *Expositio decalogi*, III, 8A, O2b; Raulin, *Itinerarium paridisi*, sermon 2–3, fol. 6b–9a; Jacobus de Gruytroede, *Speculum aureum*, 3, B2a–B3a.

the *Pisanella*, among others, should have repeated these causes is no surprise, for its canonist author shows everywhere the utmost devotion to the opinions of both Raymond and William of Rennes. But it is noteworthy that the *Manipulus curatorum* of Guido de Monte Rocherii should have differed, since Guido in many places did nothing but copy out the words of the *Raymundina*. In talking about these causes, however, Guido implicitly calls attention to a notable gap in Raymond's analysis. For the first and most important cause of contrition, Guido says, is love of God. And although he follows with a list that is almost identical to the *Raymundina*'s, his purposeful inclusion of love as the first and most important motive accentuates the problem of fear versus love in the motivation of sorrow. If Guido adds love, however, he does not omit fear, and we must not think that fear and love are mutually exclusive, for him or for the literature in general.[9]

Fear, in fact, is commonly accepted as a respectable emotion, although it is principally thought of as no more than a beginning to true sorrow. The authorities who accept fear as an adequate beginning to contrition are varied and numerous. The *Astesana* teaches that fear is a part of the process of repentance. And although Astesanus talks about hope in the mercy of God, Who is a kind Father, he makes it absolutely clear that repentance begins not in hope, but in a servile fear that looks at the threat of a just God's punishment.[10] Yet fear is not the goal, for Astesanus or for others. Stephan Lanzkranna is also willing to admit that fear of punishment is a proper beginning to penance. But the *Himmelstrasse* warns that if one goes no further—if he does not love God and righteousness—then his repentance is not enough to take away sins. To dramatize his argument, Stephan tells his version of a popular story of a cardinal who repents only at the end of his life and returns after death to relate that his sorrow, motivated only by fear, did not win him forgiveness.[11]

Even brief manuals make this point. Engelhardus Kunhofer is

[9] *Raymundina*, III, 34, 9, p. 443; *Supplementum*, "Contritio," 5; Guido de Monte Rocherii, *Manipulus curatorum*, II, 2, 6, fol. 70a; [Poeniteas cito], *Confessionale pro scholasticis*, A3b–A4a (which both condemns a "fear" sorrow, "qualem habent fures et latrones qui ad supplicium ducuntur," and accepts fear as one of Hostiensis's seven causes of contrition).

[10] *Astesana*, V, 2.

[11] Stephan Lanzkranna, *Himelstrass*, 4, fol. 7a, 49, fol. 154a.

not so dramatic as Stephan Lanzkranna, but his manual, written not long before the beginning of the Reformation, agrees completely. Many renounce sin and do penance out of a servile fear; but, Kunhofer teaches, this should not be the principal cause of repentance. Furthermore, fear itself should arise out of filial love and the realization that sin offends the goodness of the Father. Similarly, Johann Nider's exposition of the Ten Commandments outlines Bonaventure's stages in the awakening of contrition, which begin in fear but proceed to higher levels of faith, hope, and amendment.[12] The language and the general treatment of these four authors is entirely typical. The idea that fear is an acceptable but insufficient motive for repentance corresponds to the spirit as well as the letter of medieval religion's analysis of sorrow.

There are a number of spiritual guides, however, who seem to depart from this consensus. They go beyond the simple assertion

[12] Kunhofer, *Confessionale*, A2a; Nider, *Expositio decalogi*, III, 8A, O2a–b; Maillard, *La Confession*, A2b. The ubiquity of this solution is *conclusively* established by N. Paulus, "Die Reue in den deutschen Beichtschriften des ausgehenden Mittelalters," *ZkTh*, 28 (1904), 1–36; idem, "Die Reue in den deutschen Erbauungsschriften des ausgehenden Mittelalters," ibid., 449–485; idem, "Die Reue in den deutschen Sterbebüchlein des ausgehenden Mittelalters," ibid., 682–698. Paulus writes expressly to refute the contention of Protestant historians that late medieval religious thought accepted sorrow based on fear alone as adequate for the remission of sins. He concludes ("Beichtschriften," pp. 34–35) that of thirty-four vernacular *Beichtbücher*— in print and manuscript—not a single one finds sorrow out of pure fear as adequate. Three distinguish between a perfect sorrow, adequate outside of confession, and an imperfect contrition, sufficient for the remission of sins in combination with priestly absolution. Even these three, however, do not accept sorrow purely out of fear as sufficient for imperfect contrition. Most do not distinguish between imperfect and perfect contrition. Seven commend contrition without defining it. Eight mention contrition out of love of God without mentioning sorrow out of fear alone. Seventeen, however, require love and specifically reject a sorrow motivated purely by fear as inadequate. Similarly Paulus concludes ("Erbauungsschriften," pp. 484–485) that only one of the forty-one devotional writings—Johann von Paltz's *Dye hymelisch Funtgrub*—teaches that sorrow out of fear of punishment in combination with priestly absolution is sufficient for the remission of sins; and even von Paltz requires a turning from sin and a striving for love. Paulus does not, however, analyze the role of fear that these writings consider acceptable; and his argument underestimates the important issue, discussed below, of the power of the keys, or of priestly absolution, to raise inadequate sorrow (however it is defined) to adequate sorrow. For the most popular literature commonly approves of this view of the power of the sacrament (see below, "From Attrition to Contrition").

that fear is good but not enough, and delineate a narrow and rough path to true, perfect, and necessary contrition. They want sincerity of emotions, and they do not shrink from defining sincerity.

A good example of this contritionist rigor appears in the lengthy analysis of true sorrow by J. L. Vivaldus. The five prerequisites he summarizes in the beginning of his essay are plainly difficult. There the truly contrite man is said to be one who conscientiously recalls all his mortal sins; evokes a true and particular sorrow or detestation for each mortal sin;[13] a general detestation for all forgotten or unknown sins; a genuine intention to abstain, confess, and make satisfaction; and a motion of the free will by which God is loved above all else! But even more demanding is his explanation of the proper motives for contrition, which appears later in the book. First Vivaldus finds a number of motives for sorrow unacceptable: fear of punishment in this world; fear of losing heaven or going to hell; aversion to sin because it is opposed to virtue, honor, glory, and fame; revulsion because sin has bad physical effects, offends vanity, or makes a man "indignum et vituparabilem"—unworthy and contemptible. Vivaldus flatly condemns all of these motives and insists that true sorrow places love of God above all things and proves itself in the turning away from sin:

> But the true, holy, certain, sound, and catholic conclusion is this, which every man who wants to be saved ought to know: that it is expedient to love God the creator of all above all, not merely in word or speech but in work and truth. Therefore it is necessary to abandon sins not for vain considerations, as we have said, but because sins are offenses against God, or are contrary to God, Whom one must love above all things.[14]

[13] A common question asks whether contrition must be a separate act of the will for every remembered and confessed sin, or whether a general contrition for all sins is sufficient. Raymond of Peñaforte (*Raymundina*, III, 34, 10, p. 445) says that contrition ought to be "vniuersalis," and William's gloss comments: "Vniuersalis] debet esse, i. de omnibus peccatis, quae occurrunt memoriae in speciali; de illis autem quae non occurrunt, habenda est in generali." Most have a similar position: see *Astesana*, V, 3, q. 5; Guido de Monte Rocherii, *Manipulus curatorum*, II, 2, 3; Nider, *Expositio decalogi*, III, 8B–D, O2b–O3a; Vivaldus, *Aureum opus*, fol. 155a–b. In opposition to this conclusion are Sylvester (see below, n. 38 and text) and Rosemondt (below, n. 47 and text).

[14] Vivaldus, *Aureum opus*, fol. 155a–b.

Judged by average standards of pastoral theology, these ideals are abnormally high, and we might be tempted to say that such rigor is only possible in the devotional literature, and only from an effusive writer like Vivaldus. Yet even the practical literature is capable of speculating on the heroic requirements of true sorrow. In his exposition of the Ten Commandments, Johann Nider, consoler of consciences and avowed disciple of Jean Gerson, wrote some passages on contrition that may well have been the direct inspiration of Vivaldus's immoderate language. For Nider finds the same prerequisites for contrition (he numbers them in seven instead of five items), which he attributes to Peter Lombard, Thomas, and Duns Scotus. And although he cautions against assaulting the consciences of the pusillanimous, and although we have already seen that elsewhere he accepts fear as a proper beginning for repentance, he goes on to reject the same unworthy motives for sorrow that Vivaldus would find unacceptable. Such unworthy motives, Nider argues, will not take away sin. They are not contrition or even that imperfect sorrow called "attrition." They are only sin. Nider's language is harsh, and although he does not stipulate that future sinlessness proves the sincerity of sorrow, he places excessive demands on the penitent's emotions, just like Vivaldus. True to his pastoral instincts, however, he reasserts the need for caution. These requirements for true contrition, he warns, are the "probable judgments" of the sacred doctors; but whoever wants to preach about them, especially the requirement of a special act of contrition for each sin recalled, or the detestation of all mortal sin because it offends God, "should beware lest he scandalize the people, or cause them to despair." Like the prudent physician, and in the spirit of the pastoral theology of Gregory the Great, "Let him speak with caution so that he may thus frighten and soften the hardhearted, but so that he may not cause the weak to despair of forgiveness."[15]

When he discusses the quantity of contrition, Guido de Monte Rocherii also expresses some uncharacteristically rigorous opinions. To be valid, Guido says, contrition must include a will so displeased by sin that it does not for any reason want to consent, or to have consented, to sin. His argument rests on this principle: "True contrition cannot exist without charity." It is necessary for

[15] Nider, *Expositio decalogi*, III, 8N, O5a–b.

one to love God above all things and not want to sin or to have sinned, for any reason at all. This contrition is the greatest possible sadness, he continues, even though he repeats the common opinion that it is appropriate but not necessary for it to be a sensible sorrow of the sort people in mourning feel.[16] And in a similar fashion, Jodocus Winshemius offers an improvised list of seven requirements for contrition. His discussion is long, Winshemius gravely declares, because the salvation of man turns on true contrition:

> For really very few have true sorrow of contrition according to the prescribed conditions. Therefore blessed Ambrose declares (it is terrifying to say it) that it is easier to find an innocent than someone who is truly repentant.[17]

Winshemius probably did not know, of course, that what Ambrose considered necessary for a good penitent entailed a lot more effort than anyone in the early sixteenth century thought of demanding. But the warning is both sobering and appropriate. For Winshemius, like Vivaldus and Nider, is playing the preacher here. His lesson about the difficulty of achieving sincere contrition is designed intentionally to frighten and hence to transform the irresolute. Like definitions of contrition that bind it to confession or amendment of life, these passages emphasize discipline. And often there is little sensitivity to the dangers such threatening language holds for fearful Christians.

This kind of rhetoric seems especially disturbing in the vernacular manual of Johannes Wolff. Love of God is necessary for salvation, he tells us, and if we lose it through sin, it can be restored through proper contrition, sorrow, pain, and confession ("durch recht rue leyt und smerczen ond bycht"). But there are many kinds of sorrow for sin, and Wolff willingly follows the convention of identifying the unworthy varieties. Merely to recognize that sin is contrary to virtue and carries with it its own pun-

---

[16] Guido de Monte Rocherii, *Manipulus curatorum*, II, 2, 2–3, fol. 66b–68a.

[17] Winshemius, *Institutiones*, A3a–A4b. Although Winshemius is an avowed disciple of Gabriel Biel (he calls him "Gabriel noster"), and although his contritionism (see below) is consistent with that discipleship, this rigorous judgment clashes directly with what Heiko Oberman describes as Biel's pastoral interest in providing a way of justification within the reach of the average Christian (see *The Harvest of Medieval Theology. Gabriel Biel and Late Medieval Nominalism* [Cambridge, Mass., 1963], pp. 157, 160, 177–178).

ishment is to know a sorrow that heathens, Jews, and Turks understand. Also unworthy are the realizations that sin causes loss of reputation, earns eternal damnation, or deprives man of eternal happiness and the vision of almighty God. As long as a man remains in this kind of sorrow and remorse he desires only to seek his own good and escape from what harms him. True sorrow must be founded on more exalted motives: the penitent must realize that his sin is evil because it offends the highest, perfect, eternal, almighty God, his Creator, heavenly Father and Redeemer. The true penitent must realize that sin runs contrary to God's love, honor, and majesty. When a man is contrite out of these motives, when he conceives a "firm and strong intention never again to act against His godly honor and glory," when he intends to confess and do penance and hopes in the bottomless mercy of God and the suffering of his savior Jesus Christ, then he will be forgiven. Everyone should prepare himself for confession by arousing this kind of sorrow.[18] There is another side to Wolff's explanation of how the sacrament works, and we shall consider it when we look at the power of the keys. But his remarks on the ideal kind of contrition, a contrition he keeps calling all men to arouse, represent a common and popular habit of religious writers. They like pure motives, altruistic motives, spiritual and selfless motives. And they do not mind saying so.

The exhortations of J. L. Vivaldus, Guido de Monte Rocherii, Jodocus Winshemius, Johannes Wolff, and Johann Nider can be, if taken seriously and scrupulously, nothing other than threats. Get rid of bad motives or else, they say, and the alternative is of course remaining in sin and ending up in hell. In fact, every one of these men except J. L. Vivaldus will offer a way out of this rigor through various benefits assigned to the power of priests to dispense the forgiveness of Christ. Yet exhortations cannot be

---

[18] Wolff, *Beichtbüchlein*, 36–38 (162–163). Three vernacular works take a similarly hard line on the motives for repentance. Berthold von Freiburg (Stanka, *Die Summa des Berthold von Freiburg*, 34) demands a "willing" confession for inner reasons only and not because of sickness, fear of death, or even obedience to the commandments of the church. [Gerson?], *Directoire*, A3b–A6b, argues under the preparatory conditions that one should confess as often as possible and not merely at Eastertime, out of constraint, because "la confession ainsi faicte nest point meritoire quand a lame." And Stephan Lanzkranna, *Himelstrass*, ch. 49, fol. 153b, demands confession with a sincere contrition for all sins, "die auss der liebe gottes gangen sey / vnd nit allaine ause der vorcht der verdamnuss."

ignored. They talk about the kind of sorrow that is ideally expected in the process of a sinner's justification. And to varying degrees and with varying intensity, they measure true sorrow according to exacting, introspective standards. Yes it is true that Johann Nider cautioned against frightening the pusillanimous, even as his words were probably frightening them. Yes it is true that the discussion of motives was complicated: that almost everyone could find some place for fear of punishment; that Guido de Monte Rocherii could soften his demands on the penitent and urge him to rejoice in the midst of his fear and remorse because he has been freed from sin, has escaped from a shipwreck.[19] But the exhortations to higher levels of selfless contrition stand. Willingness to establish standards—at times rigorous ones —for the sincerity of sorrow is an important part of some of the literature. And it is thus available to encourage obedience to the commandments of God and moral theology, and perhaps to stimulate scrupulosity as well.

TESTING

All the talk about how it feels to be truly contrite was designed not only to make people spiritually better; it also served the practical purpose of giving penitents some way of telling whether they had the emotions they were supposed to have to be forgiven. In its academic form the question asks, "What is the right kind of sorrow?" In a more practical form the question asks, "How can a penitent know whether he has the right kind of sorrow?"

To help answer the practical question, therefore, some good schoolmen thought up tests. Now in a sense the description of the emotion and its worthy and unworthy motives were themselves tests that a penitent could apply by introspection. Religious literature knew a more positive kind of test, however, and its propriety and usefulness were a matter of some concern. As a matter of fact, there is a fascinating example of such a test from a secular author. Jean de Joinville, in his biography of St. Louis IX of France, related an incident revealing that in the thirteenth century this kind of thinking was known outside of the cloister and the university.

"Which would you prefer," the king asks Joinville one day in the presence of some monks, "to be a leper or to have committed

---

[19] Guido de Monte Rocherii, *Manipulus curatorum*, II, 2, 1, fol. 66a–b. See below for Guido's views on attrition and the power of the keys.

some mortal sin?" Joinville is refreshingly candid: "And I, who had never lied to him, replied that I would rather have committed thirty mortal sins than become a leper." Despite the honesty of this answer, St. Louis wanted more; and as Joinville continues the story we find the king offering a moral of extreme severity:

> The next day, when the monks were no longer there, he called me to him, and making me sit at his feet said to me: "Why did you say that to me yesterday?" I told him I would still say it. "You spoke without thinking, and like a fool," he said. "You ought to know there is no leprosy so foul as being in a state of mortal sin. . . . When a man dies his body is healed of its leprosy; but if he dies after committing a mortal sin, he can never be sure that, during his lifetime, he has repented of it sufficiently for God to forgive him."

Without delving too deeply into the theological implications of this opinion, we might note that these hard words offer little succor even from the sacraments of the visible church. Furthermore, St. Louis makes it clear that he is talking about that habitual attitude toward sin that was associated with the definition of, and test for, true contrition:

> "So I beg you," he added, "as earnestly as I can, for the love of God, and for love of me, to train your heart to prefer any evil that can happen to the body, whether it be leprosy or any other disease, rather than let mortal sin take possession of your soul."[20]

Joinville does not comment on whether he changed his mind and heart. And one suspects that few would have been able to improve greatly on his performance on this test. That, of course, is good reason for concern.

The thirteenth century *Compendium theologiae* considers a similar question as if it were well known. The *Compendium* asserts that the confessor who wants to find out whether a penitent has the necessary sorrow should determine whether he would renounce the whole world and undergo death rather than sin again. It is a test that the honest Joinville would not likely have passed, but the *Compendium* advises that if the penitent is cer-

[20] Jean de Joinville, *The Life of St. Louis* in Joinville and Villehardouin, *Chronicles of the Crusades*, tr. by M. R. B. Shaw (Baltimore, 1963), 169.

tain *or even doubtful* not to sin for the whole world or to save his life, then he may be absolved. Only if he is *certain to sin* should he be refused absolution. To reinforce this somewhat milder conclusion, the *Compendium* flatly forbids the confessor to ask such a question directly. He must instead discover this information from other signs of sadness.[21] The *Compendium's* warning against administering these tests is as typical as it is reasonable and necessary. The abuses that could have come from this kind of emotional inquisition are too horrendous to imagine, and one can hardly congratulate a writer for forbidding so obnoxious a practice as actually asking them. The confessor must infer the nature of sorrow, therefore, and not depend on the more precise and heartless questions some had contemplated. But the testing questions keep appearing in the literature.

Indeed, religious writers were familiar with an even more difficult one: does a contrite man prefer hell to mortal sin? St. Thomas considered it inappropriate to ask anyone such a question, and his prudent rejection of it is decisive. The case certainly predates St. Thomas—some say that St. Anselm was the first to pose it—and it finds a later echo in the question of the Presbyterian ordination examination, "Would you willingly be damned for the glory of God?" But it is well known to the practical literature on the forgiveness of sins and several mention it.

The *Sylvestrina* takes up the "hell or sin" alternative, for example, in connection with the problem of determining how sorry one must be to be contrite. Sylvester begins by stating the familiar position that only intellectual, not sensible, sorrow is essential because we are only required to do what we are capable of doing. Still there is no denying that the sorrow we must have should be great and sincere. Indeed, it should be so great that one is ready, in general, to bear any pain rather than sin. One need not, however, test himself or anyone else by asking whether he prefers any particular pain, mortal danger, or hell to sin. To do so would be stupid. The confessor need only ask the penitent if he is repentant. And if the penitent is not sorry enough, the confessor should find out if he wishes he were sorry enough. Unfortunately, Sylvester does not leave the discussion at this reasonable conclusion. Instead he offers a disturbingly scrupulous thought:

[21] *Compendium theologiae*, Du Pin, I, 280D–281B.

To all this I add that since death, according to the Philosopher, is the ultimate of terrors, whoever would rather die than offend God mortally is contrite.[22]

This little appendage appears to be nothing more than a clever aside, showing off a relevant classical allusion and defining in a favorite way conditions under which one can be certain he is truly contrite. Nevertheless, it is at best odd to encourage this kind of self-questioning and possibly tormenting speculation after one has rejected the practice of testing for true sorrow. Sylvester's departing comment is odd because it is undeniable that he would have found almost universal support for his main argument. For authorities on forgiveness reject with finality any suggestion that it is proper for a confessor to ask such a testing question, or even for a penitent to ask it of himself. St. Louis, in other words, had gone too far. The closest one gets to acceptance of this kind of proposition is in the *Supplementum*, in which Nicolaus de Ausimo argues that a contrite man should try for real tears, but if he cannot weep, he should try to incite a high degree of remorse:

> And if he cannot [achieve a sensible sorrow], he ought to be sorry about that, and wish he had suffered death and all evils rather than have committed one sin; and be disposed to suffer death and all evils in the future rather than consent to sin any more.

Nicolaus is guilty of a serious lapse here, because he has presented a criterion that is too difficult and too unbending. Nevertheless it is not a test, but an exhortation. It is undoubtedly a potential menace; but it is not something a confessor is being urged to try out on his penitent. Furthermore the section from the *Pisanella* had, in more characteristic advice, considered the question whether a contrite man should prefer the pains of hell to sin and had quoted the usual answer of St. Thomas: a contrite man loves God above all things and therefore should choose any pain before incurring the guilt of mortal sin. But Bartholomaeus teaches that one need not descend to the consideration of this or that pain, and warns in the usual way that it would be stupid to do so. Most would agree.[23]

[22] *Sylvestrina*, "Contritio," q. 1, par. 2–3.
[23] *Supplementum*, "Contritio," 6, 10.

A final example may perhaps be illuminating. Jacobus de Clusa cites the sophistry of some unnamed authority to dispose of this dilemma. Of course it is preferable to be in hell than commit sin, this argument runs: for to be in hell without sin would mean that one would not feel the punishment of the damned: and to be with sin in heaven would mean that one would not see the glory of God.[24] This mediocre rationalization is unsatisfactory for a number of reasons; perhaps its most glaring flaw is its failure to meet the fundamental needs of confessors and penitents to find a sensible way, and a harmless way, to measure sincerity. Yet it has the merit of rejecting this curious and vexing speculation.[25]

It is not surprising that medieval theologians should have invented these tricky questions to test the sincerity of repentance. They liked clarity and they tried to make profound issues simple for those who had to determine the worthiness of their own inner experience. Nor is it surprising that such questions should have entered into the practical literature, which had an even greater commitment to clarifying these issues for laity and clergy alike. Least of all should it surprise us, if the balance between discipline and consolation was to be maintained, to discover that testing contrition with too hard a question was rejected as more dangerous than beneficial.

Nevertheless, we must find in this penchant for talking about tests the same characteristic we detected in the discussions of worthy and unworthy kinds of sorrow. It is potentially threatening and dangerous. It forced people to a kind of introspective examination that could produce anxiety and doubt. To say that motives are impossible to weigh precisely, and then to talk about what motives are proper and worthy, does not eliminate the search into motives. It encourages it. To offer a test such as "would you rather be in hell than sin?" and then to say that such a test should never be administered, does not eliminate the possibility that people will think or talk in these terms. Thus in the interest of a more sincere and perfect sorrow, and a more virtu-

[24] Jacobus de Clusa, *Confessionale*, 8, B1a.

[25] For others who concur that it is harmful or foolish to contemplate particular tests of sorrow, see Vivaldus, *Aureum opus*, fol. 147a; Johannes von Freiburg, *Summa confessorum*, III, 34, 26, fol. 186b; *Astesana*, V, 9, a. 3, q. 4; Guido de Monte Rocherii, *Manipulus curatorum*, II, 2, 2, fol. 67a–b; Nider, *Expositio decalogi*, III, 8K–M, O4b; Raulin, *Itinerarium paridisi*, sermon 2–3, fol. 3a–5b.

ous life, the literature on the forgiveness of sins purposefully discussed worthiness of motives and tests of sincere contrition: hesitantly and discriminately, it is true, but nevertheless purposefully.

ATTRITION AND CONTRITION

The analysis of sorrow we have examined was not precise, even though the principal task of this literature was to explain what a penitent had to do to be forgiven. Since the most ancient understanding of penance required a contrite heart, one might reasonably expect a simple, clear definition of the sorrow required for valid reception of the sacrament. We have already seen that the discussion of signs and motives, and the attempts at definition, are not easy to apply to one's own experience. They do not eliminate the dilemma of a penitent who wants to know whether he has enough sorrow, or the right kind of sorrow. On the other hand, the brutal tests of contrition the theologians had invented were all too clear and so unsatisfactory that confessors were forbidden to use them. Thus, while testing was the kind of operation this literature tended to favor—practicality and applicability are well served in this fashion—confessors and penitents would have to find some other measure of sorrow than to ask whether death or hell were preferable to a return to sin.

One way might have been the distinction between attrition and contrition. Certainly it would be simpler for us if it were true to depict, as historians often do, an accepted definition of perfect and imperfect sorrow and a central controversy between "lax attritionists" and "rigorous contritionists." In this uncomplicated picture medieval theologians are supposed to have taught that there are two kinds of sorrow a sinner may achieve: one based on love of God, a perfect sorrow called contrition; another based on fear of punishment, an imperfect sorrow called attrition. According to this historical analysis, the contritionists rigidly required perfect sorrow, devoid of selfishness, and rooted in the love of God; the attritionists laxly permitted an imperfect sorrow, devoid of love, and motivated merely by fear. Unfortunately, this neat summary misrepresents the meaning theologians gave these terms. Bernhard Poschmann describes the opinions that actually dominated pre-Tridentine theology:

At the beginning of the thirteenth century the term attrition emerged as a designation of the sorrow which is insufficient for

250

salvation. However, the criterion distinguishing *contritio* and *attritio* was by no means, as in the later view, the motive of sorrow. Originally it was rather a distinction based on the degree of affliction of soul, according as this included a resolution strong enough to confess and make satisfaction. Later, as the doctrine of informing grace—*gratia informans*—became established, it was based on the relation of the sorrow to justifying grace. *Contritio* for the high scholastic period and for pre-Tridentine theology is penance "formed" by grace; *attritio* is "unformed" penance (paenitentia per gratiam formata, paenitentia informis).[26]

In other words, in our period theologians say that the difference between attrition and contrition is not defined psychologically but theologically, according to its formation by grace.

On the other hand, the distinction between attrition and contrition on the basis of motivation was not unknown. This passage from Durandus of St. Pourçain's commentary on the *Sentences* shows that it was possible, as early as the mid-fourteenth century, for a theologian to identify attrition as a sorrow based on fear.

When the will of a man clinging to sin is overcome by fear and by consideration of the punishment owed for sin, and on account of this recoils from sin, he is said to be "attrite"; but when not only from fear of punishment, but also from love of eternal life he totally recoils from sin by fully detesting it, he is called "contrite."[27]

Even this passage is not completely in accord with the later understanding that attrition comes from fear and contrition from love, because it speaks of contrition's love of eternal life rather

[26] Poschmann, *Penance and the Anointing of the Sick*, 164. Cf. Anciaux, *La Théologie*, 473–480. An example of this misconception is Oberman, *Harvest*, 147, 157, and 460, where attrition is defined simply as "Repentance for sins out of fear [. . . *timor servilis*] of punishment by God." The evidence that ordinary pastoral instruction did not propose the adequacy of servile fear is overwhelming: in addition to the references to N. Paulus (above, n. 12) see Joseph Mausbach, "Historisches und Apologetisches sur scholastischen Reuelehre," *Der Katholik*, 15 (1897), 48–65, 97–115, and "Katholische Katechismen von 1400–1700 über die zum Bussakramente erforderliche Reue," ibid., 16 (1897), 37–49, 109–122.

[27] J. Périnelle, *L'Attrition d'après le Concile de Trente et d'après Saint Thomas d'Aquin*, Bibliothèque Thomiste, vol. 10 (Le Saulchoir, 1927), 11–12.

than of God. And although, as we have already seen, St. Thomas himself had thought that desire for salvation was akin to love of God, Durandus's contrition is open to the objection that it too, like attrition, has a fundamentally selfish motivation. Nevertheless, Durandus does talk about these two kinds of sorrow solely in the language of human motives, and he identifies attrition purely and simply with fear of punishment.

But St. Thomas, perhaps the principal authority for those who demand contrition, does not. Nor does the principal authority for those who allow attrition, Duns Scotus. As Poschmann notes:

> It is . . . wrong to regard the attrition of Scotus simply as a "fear sorrow." In reality as compared with his predecessors he assigns a decidedly subordinate position to fear in his teaching on sorrow. It is not enough to fear God: he must also be loved.[28]

Now it is inevitable that attrition and fear will in some sense be associated, if only because attrition is a lesser kind of sorrow and fear a lesser kind of motive. But the evidence for theologians in the period before the Council of Trent is overwhelming: there is no consensus holding that attrition is motivated solely by fear and contrition by love. Rather, theologians distinguish between them on the basis of differences in formation by grace, degree of perfection, and intensity of sorrow.

It should not be surprising to learn, therefore, that it is rare to find someone writing about the practice of confession who departs from the habits of theology and presents, in the manner of Durandus, a stark contrast between attrition based on fear and contrition based on love. One of the commentaries on the "Poeniteas cito" does so, however, in a revealing argument. "What is the difference between contrition and attrition?" it asks, echoing the summas for confessors. The first answer is most usual: attrition is an imperfect, contrition a perfect displeasure for sins. This means, the author continues, that attrition is sorrow for great sins, but not all sins. Then he asserts bluntly that attrition is selfish and worthless. For he defines attrition as a sorrow principally with respect to the punishment the sinner realizes he deserves. This sorrow is without the help of God's grace and begins with love of self rather than love of God. Indeed, it is worse than in-

[28] Poschmann, *Penance and the Anointing of the Sick*, 185–186; cf. 163–196, and esp. 165, 173, 189.

adequate: "Therefore although such people are sorry, they are damned." For they hate sin the way thieves do, because they fear punishment. True contrition, on the other hand, is an entirely different sort of emotion:

> Contrition, however, is a sorrow for all sins, great and small, principally because of the offense against God that a man incurs through sin. This sorrow cannot exist without the grace of God moving the free will to such a sorrow.[29]

Once again this explanation is not perfect for our purposes: it speaks about detestation of sin because it is offensive to God, and we are left to identify this motive, as the author surely intends us to do, with love rather than fear of Him. Still it is clear enough: the difference is principally one of motivation, and attrition is identified simply as sorrow arising out of fear of punishment.

Jodocus Winshemius is another rare example of a writer of practical literature on forgiveness who emphasizes the psychological distinction between attrition and contrition. Winshemius insists that true sorrow must be for all mortal sins, not just one, and that it must be rooted not merely in fear but also in love. Sorrow based on fear is mere attrition, Winshemius contends, and he refers the reader to the *Angelica* to substantiate this contention.[30]

With two such explicit characterizations of attrition as an imperfect sorrow based on fear and not love, we might suspect that this kind of language enjoyed a certain currency at the end of the middle ages—that, in contradiction to what Poschmann claims for the theologians, our more practical writers distinguish attrition by its motivation in fear. Often, however, this distinction is

---

[29] [Poeniteas cito], *Confessionale pro scholasticis*, A3b. This passage is similar to the position of Gabriel Biel: see Gordon J. Spykman, *Attrition and Contrition at the Council of Trent* (Kampen, 1955), 83ff., esp. 85; and Oberman, *Harvest*, 146–160. A passage in the most popular version of the "Poeniteas cito" might also be interpreted as rejecting the motive of fear (and associating it with *attritio*) when it rejects a lesser sorrow because it is *involuntary*: "Unde duplex est dolor pro peccatis: quidam est naturalis; et ille non est meritorius quia non procedit ex dictamine recte rationis; alius est voluntarius et actualis qui procedit ex voluntate libere assumente dolorem cum proposito confitendi et satisfaciendi." [Poeniteas cito], *Libellus de modo poenitendi*, A3a. But this passage is not conclusive, and the heavy influence of Thomas Aquinas (ibid., A4b–A5a) would argue against it.

[30] Winshemius, *Institutiones*, A3b–A4b; N. Paulus, "Ein Beichtbüchlein für Erfurter Studenten aus dem 16. Jahrhundert." *Der Katholik*, 19 (1899), 93–95.

only apparent and derives from the natural association of a lesser motivation with a lesser sorrow. A good example of one who seems to share the view of Winshemius and the commentary on the "Poeniteas cito" is Guido de Monte Rocherii, in his explanation of the stages of repentance. The sinner about to repent, he tells us, thinks first of God's goodness and justice: for all evil displeases Him, He leaves no evil unpunished, and the sinner has committed many evils worthy of severe punishment. Thus fear is born in the heart of the sinner. "And when he thinks further of the piety *and mercy of God*, who is ready to spare every sorrowing penitent and forgive his guilt no matter how great, he hopes for pardon and is thus moved to the detestation of sin." And it is precisely at this point that Guido tells us, "This movement is called attrition, that is, a certain imperfect sorrow." The process continues: God enlightens the sinner who grows in love and detestation of sin. Here we find the crucial change: "Thus servile fear precedes and prepares the heart of the sinner for contrition, but love and the fervor of charity perfect it." Love thus casts out the fear of punishment. But a careful reading of the process discloses that if fear is not absent in attrition, if fear begins the process of sorrow, there are other elements in what Guido calls attrition besides fear. Thus he explicitly describes the attrite sinner as one who thinks of God's goodness, His piety and mercy, and His readiness to forgive any guilt. Clearly Guido means something more by "attrition" than simple fear of punishment.[31]

As a matter of fact, there are similar difficulties in the *Angelica*, to which Winshemius refers his reader to substantiate his assertion that attrition is sorrow based on fear. For when we look where Winshemius directs us, we do not find that simple distinction at all. Angelus poses the problem in the usual way: "How does contrition differ from attrition?" His answer is direct and succinct:

> I respond according to Francis and other theologians, in two ways. First, attrition is an imperfect sorrow; contrition is truly a perfect sorrow. Second, attrition is a sorrow without the grace making one pleasing to God, but not contrition. And therefore contrition and attrition are materially the same—as a dark and illuminated house. Attrition is indeed the light of the dawn, which by increasing becomes noonday, that is, con-

[31] Guido de Monte Rocherii, *Manipulus curatorum*, II, 2, 6, fol. 70a.

254

trition. And observe that according to St. Bonaventure one can be contrite [conteritur] in two ways: one elevating higher, which is the hope of pardon from consideration of divine mercy; the other depressing downwards, which is the fear of punishment from consideration of divine justice.[32]

Now according to Winshemius, the *Angelica* teaches that attrition is based on fear and contrition on love. But a careful look at the text shows this is not the case. Two differences, according to Angelus, and only two, distinguish between the two sorrows: one is perfect, the other is not; and one is formed by grace, the other not. These distinctions are not, it should be obvious, clear descriptions of psychological states or motives. The popular metaphors from light that Angelus invokes do not get us much closer to psychological states. For to say that attrition and contrition are materially the same, and to invoke the figure of brightening, merely emphasizes that these emotions are subtle, exist on a continuum, and cannot be easily catalogued or measured. But what about the opinion of Bonaventure, that one sorrow elevates through hope and the other depresses through fear? Certainly this is what Winshemius was thinking of when he referred his readers to the *Angelica*. The trouble is that there is no certainty that the two directions of sorrow correspond to attrition and contrition. Indeed, the linguistic evidence suggests they do not, despite the question under discussion. For when he says there are two ways to be sorry, he uses the word "be contrite"—*conteritur*—not "be sorrowful"—*dolet*. Now this evidence is not conclusive, for it was certainly possible to call attrition an imperfect way of "being contrite." But even if Angelus, in borrowing this metaphor from Bonaventure, does mean that attrition is the sorrow that depresses through fear of justice and contrition the one that elevates through hope of mercy, it is obvious that he treats this distinction as of secondary value. The most important attributes of contrition and attrition, according to this passage, are theological, not psychological. For the *Angelica* says explicitly that they differ in "two ways," and neither refers to motives. In short, the *Angelica* does not provide confessors with a simple distinction between an attrition of fear and a contrition of love.

As for our two authorities who do distinguish the two sorrows by motivation, Jodocus Winshemius and the commentary and the

[32] *Angelica*, "Contritio" [1].

"Poeniteas cito," we must remember that both define attrition as motivated by servile fear *in order to reject it* as inadequate or even impious. This condemnation, therefore, is identical in spirit and intention to those more rigorous descriptions of perfect sorrow by Johann Nider or J. L. Vivaldus, who reject fear and other selfish motives without identifying them as attrition. Indeed, one suspects that the identification of fear and attrition, the unusual and striking feature of Winshemius, and the commentary on the "Poeniteas cito," was a way to slander the easier theory that attrition in confession is sufficient for forgiveness. By confining attrition to a sorrow motivated solely by fear, one quickly turns it into something that virtually all would have found defective. When we examine the practical literature in greater detail, moreover, we discover that ideas about attrition and contrition conform in a rough and simple way to the theories of theologians.

Some authors argue that only attrition is necessary, and it is obvious that this doctrine is designed to offer an easier way to forgiveness in the Sacrament of Penance. In other words, these authors follow the lead of Duns Scotus. J. Lupi Rebello, for example, describes an attrition so intense that it can achieve forgiveness of guilt outside of the Sacrament of Penance and remission of temporal punishment within it. But he is quite definite that it is only attrition. Similarly Antoninus of Florence, Johann Wolff, and Jean Gerson approve of the opinion that attrition is sufficient. But none of them discuss the distinction between attrition and contrition extensively, and they certainly do not talk about their differences in terms of motives. John Eck shares the essentials of this position, but he normally does not even use the word attrition and specifically notes that there is no accepted definition of it.[33] Thus one group of authorities assert that attrition or some kind of lesser sorrow is sufficient for forgiveness, without exploring its meaning in terms of human emotions.

Other authors leave out attrition entirely and talk only about contrition, which they require for forgiveness. Hermannus de Schildis, for example, tells us that the penitent must have "true contrition of heart" and intend to confess and abstain from all his sins. To confess without this contrition invalidates the sacrament.

[33] Lupi Rebello, *Fructus*, 5–12, 19, A2a–A4b; Wolff, *Beichtbüchlein*, 38–39 (163); Gerson, "De Statuto ordinis Carthusiensis," Du Pin, II, 461A–B; Antoninus, *Confessionale—Defecerunt*, 7; Schauerte, *Busslehre des Eck*, 87–91.

The *Raymundina* and the *Compendium theologiae* also speak only of contrition, and the list of these could probably be lengthened substantially. Contritionists are not rare, and they tend to demand more self-examination and selflessness for sinners to be justified. But few go to the lengths of J. L. Vivaldus, who nicely illustrates an extreme version of this mentality that will not allow an imperfect contrition. We have already seen how demanding his requirements for the motivation and intensity of sorrow could be. Vivaldus is one of those who urges that one turn away from sin purely because it is offensive to God, Whom one should and must love above all things. Yet he is not interested in offering a distinction between attrition and contrition or a perfect and imperfect sorrow. He does not, in fact, effectively clarify the experience of worthwhile sorrow. Thus while his praise of contrition is effusive, he does not hesitate to admit that it is impossible to know whether one has achieved it. And he can indulge in excesses of rhetoric apparently without considering his effect on the cure of souls. Here is one of his more colorful passages:

> Heartfelt contrition is that most efficacious, heavenly medicine that alone causes the vomiting out of the bilious humors from the stomach of the ailing soul. It is the sweetest bath by which the physician of our souls beneficially cures the unwholesome diseases of the human heart.

He continues with a doctrine more pertinent to the discussion of the role of the penitent's sorrow in the process of justification. No sin is too great, he argues, no sins are too numerous, but they can be forgiven "by contrition alone." Furthermore, any amount of true contrition is sufficient to forgive sin. But Vivaldus's exaltation of contrition ends with a familiar catch; no human, only God knows, whether one can attain it.[34]

If we were to contrast the attritionism of Rebello and the contritionism of Vivaldus in terms of pastoral instruction, we would be hard put to discover any definite lessons. Certainly Vivaldus could incite scruples. But even Vivaldus does not say to a penitent: "Here is a lesser kind of emotion, attrition, which you can recognize by the following signs, and you will have to do better than that; and here is that perfect emotion, which you can iden-

[34] *Compendium theologiae*, Du Pin, I, 280D–281B; *Raymundina*, III, 34, 11, p. 446; de Schildis, *Speculum sacerdotum* [14b–15a]; Vivaldus, *Aureum opus*, "Prologue," fol. 3a.

257

tify in yourself by these signs, and only that is enough." On the other hand, neither does Rebello offer that kind of simplicity. This lack of clarity does not mean that Vivaldus, Rebello, and other authors who do nothing more than say one or the other sorrow is sufficient, are not concerned with pastoral instruction. It does not mean that the distinction between attrition and contrition is not important both for the theology of justification and the cure of souls. It merely emphasizes how far we are from a simple doctrine, such as one that would tell penitents that fear was enough, or that love was essential, and that they were to tell whether they were forgiven by examining their motivation.

The most likely place for a full, clear treatment of the sorrow of the penitent and its role in justification is in those practical works that discuss theological questions extensively and technically. An analysis of five of these major works—by John of Freiburg, Astesanus of Asti, Nicolaus de Ausimo, Sylvester Prierias, and Godescalc Rosemondt—shows that they specifically differentiate (like the *Angelica*) between attrition and contrition. They try, to varying degrees to make this difference mean something to a penitent who is examining the worthiness of his own sorrow. But after reading them, one must conclude that even the most ambitious of these attempts to incorporate attrition and contrition into the theology of justification does not provide a sure guide to someone who wants to know whether he is attrite or contrite.

John of Freiburg does not, as the author himself admits, have a conclusive theory of the way the sacrament works. He is, however, an avowed disciple of St. Thomas, and like his master, he does not dwell on the motivation behind true sorrow. What is the difference between attrition and contrition? John of Freiburg answers that attrition, the entrance into contrition, differs materially by being less of a tearing apart; and spiritually by being imperfect. He does not even distinguish them here on the basis of formation by grace.[35]

The *Astesana* has a much more thorough explanation of adequate sorrow. A series of steps culminates in a justifying attrition, which Astesanus carefully distinguishes from true repent-

[35] Johannes von Freiburg, *Summa confessorum*, III, 34, 18; cf. Joseph Göttler, *Der heilige Thomas von Aquin und die vortridentinischen Thomisten über die Wirkungen des Bussakramentes* (Freiburg i.B. 1904), 122–123, who agrees that there is no clear distinction in John of Freiburg.

ance. The doctrine is Scotist, and it outlines a complex interplay between grace and human effort. There is some attention to the analysis of motives and emotions, including the familiar distinction between the degrees of severity by which the remorse of attrition or contrition tears one up. But the critical elements in the process of the perfection of sorrow are "infusion of grace" and "formation by charity." Thus while Astesanus is more complete than John of Freiburg, attrition and contrition still emerge primarily as theological, not psychological concepts.[36]

In the *Supplementum*, Bartholomaeus of Pisa's opinion, like those of John of Freiburg and Astesanus, holds that attrition and contrition differ in perfection and in the extent to which one is broken up. Nicolaus de Ausimo comments on this definition, but not to say anything about servile fear. Instead he urges the penitent on to more profound anguish, sorrow, wrath, and indignation for his sins as he expands on the metaphor of tearing apart. In another passage in which Bartholomaeus upholds the acceptability of attrition, Nicolaus's comment ignores the word attrition and repeats the popular saying that God does not demand the impossible of us. Obviously he is endorsing Bartholomaeus's acceptance of the easier way. And thus the *Supplementum* is willing to accept a less than perfect sorrow and is eager to avoid the impression that the requirements for sorrow are overwhelming. But this concern for the penitent still does not lead to a psychological definition of imperfect sorrow.[37]

Of all the summas for confessors, however, the *Sylvestrina* discusses the process of justification and the role of sorrow in the most complete and detailed theological language. Sylvester's ideas are not novel, it is true, but they are by comparison elaborately spelled out. The differences between attrition and contrition are familiar: intensity of sorrow, perfection of sorrow, formation by grace. These terms do not refer clearly to human experience, but Sylvester uses them to describe the role of perfect and imperfect sorrow in forgiveness. In the beginnings of the process, it is necessary only to be *attrite*, but it must be for each sin not yet forgiven that comes to mind. After the forgiveness of sins, when imperfect sorrow has been formed by grace and thus perfected, it is enough that one feel this newly found contrition in *general* for all past sins. Sylvester then offers two com-

[36] *Astesana*, V, 2, a. 2; 3, q. 5; 9. a. 5; i, 3.
[37] *Supplementum*, "Contritio," 2–4.

ments to help the penitent understand what this means to him.

The first comforts those who think a separate movement of the will for each sin, even if that movement is only attrition, is too difficult:

> But add for the scrupulous, that they are mistaken if they do not believe they have actually felt sorry for individual sins occurring in their memory unless they have consciously said [nisi actu reflexo], "I am sorry."

Sylvester proves this nicely by arguing that it is similar to the case of a habitual fornicator who sees many women in succession: he does not have to say, "I like that," when he sees each one for him to be guilty of having taken pleasure in seeing them. Thus when someone attains a habitual sorrow and intends to be sorry in a general way for offenses against God, he extends this act of sorrow to any appropriate object—that is, to any offense against God and any object of repentance—without actually saying, "I am sorry."

Sylvester's second comment, however, calls for the perfection of sorrow in contrition: For the beginning of attrition is sufficient, and one does not sin by confessing and being absolved if he is only attrite. But he must be contrite as often as he actually recalls his sins if he is to avoid sin in the future.[38]

In other words, Sylvester does not want penitents to feel overburdened by the requirement of sorrow for all remembered sins, but he expects them eventually to become fully contrite. He does not, however, describe the perfection of sorrow in terms of motives or signs or tests. And so Sylvester, like the rest, relies on theology rather than psychology to define his pastoral instruction on the sorrow of the penitent. He shows clearly that even detailed theological treatment could not transform speculation on attrition and contrition into an adequate, practical answer to the question, "How do I know I am forgiven?"

Godescalc Rosemondt was not so enamored of theological terms as his contemporary Sylvester, and the *Confessionale* gives a somewhat different perspective on the work of the penitent. Godescalc teaches that attrition, like contrition, is displeasure and sorrow for sins because they offend God. But attrition is in-

---

[38] *Sylvestrina*, "Confessio 1," par. 1; ibid., "Contritio," par. 1, q. 3, par. 5; q. 4, par. 6.

sufficient to take away sins or produce a state of grace. Thus it differs from contrition in two ways, which Godescalc defines simply, if not clearly. The first difference resides in the work of the penitent; the free will of an attrite man does not include enough effort to be sorry for the offense, so that sorrow is imperfect and not deep enough. The second difference resides in God's grace, which, if it forms sorrow, always produces contrition no matter what its intensity. When he explains forgiveness, then, Rosemondt blends together man's effort and God's grace. Lest there be any doubt which component is more important, the human or divine, Godescalc reasserts first of all that the accompaniment of grace is necessary for sorrow to be contrition, otherwise it is only attrition. And second, he directs attention away from the effort of the penitent by pointing out what must by now be supremely evident: "And it is difficult to know whether sorrow for sins is attrition or contrition."

Even though one cannot tell attrition from contrition with certainty, Godescalc is certain that true contrition is difficult to evoke. And he is anxious to preach this rigorous lesson to his readers. He recalls, therefore, the teaching of his preceptor, Adrian of Utrecht, that it is rash to think that sinners are easily forgiven and say it, as some do, in sermons and confessions. Those who expound so lax a doctrine do not adequately castigate the vices of sinners. Thus he warns against trusting too readily in those words of promise, "in whatever hour a sinner repents." For while we know that all contrite sinners are forgiven, we do not know, he stresses again, whether a sinner is truly contrite. One could fill books with examples of those who could not sincerely repent (how one would know they were *not* truly contrite he does not tell us), and he offers as evidence the cases of Esau and Judas.

All of this talk about the need for a difficult and uncertain contrition could produce gloom and anxiety, however, and Godescalc ends up by urging the usual—that the mean be served here. He calls for moderation in the pulpit and confessional, "so that priests do not impose too rigidly and severely the halter of despair on the people—who want to be led rather than coerced— nor permit the reins to be too lax by offering easy penance to men." To be contrite we must have a heart ground between the two wheels of hope and fear, and Godescalc is far from thinking these sentiments are mutually exclusive: "We hope for mercy in vain if we do not fear justice; we fear in vain if we do not trust."[39]

He may not use as scholastic a terminology as the summas for confessors, but Godescalc Rosemondt's conclusions are entirely traditional. Sorrow is a human emotion and he naturally discusses it in terms of its motivation and intensity. But when he turns to attrition and contrition, he takes up the habits of the theologians and emphasizes the difference in formation by grace and the difficulty of telling which kind of sorrow one has achieved. Thus the language may be fresher, but the doctrine is not. In urging observance of a mean between laxity and rigor, and in offering a bit more discipline than consolation in doing so, he says nothing unusual. Like so many others, he could happily tolerate the ambiguity of encouraging dread and hope at the same time. His teaching on attrition and contrition, therefore, is not so much precise as flexible: ready to bend to the task of comforting the fearful and correcting the recalcitrant, and steadfastly remaining true to theological definitions.

In summary, the theory of attrition and contrition might have supplied confessors with practical distinctions, based on the psychological motives of fear and love, to explain what kind of sorrow a penitent had to have. It did not. There might have developed rather simple explanations, in terms of emotional experience, of the place of sorrow in the process of justification. Thus some might have argued that fear, not attrition, was enough for forgiveness within the Sacrament of Penance, though not outside of it. Others might have rejected fear and demanded love instead of contrition as the necessary culmination even within the sacrament. But when the practical literature examines the motives of love and fear, even when it intends to tell people what are useless and worthwhile emotions, it reverts to the theological analysis of attrition and contrition to explain the role of sorrow in the justification of the penitent. And at the risk of belaboring a point let us repeat: no one confidently offers ways of telling whether an individual's sorrow at a particular time is attrition or contrition by classifying his motivation. When people argued for the necessity of perfect contrition, they certainly meant that love of God had to be present, but they did not necessarily exclude the motive of fear and they did not provide easy test questions

[39] Rosemondt, *Confessionale*, 10, 2–3, fol. 186b–170a.

to determine if or how much love was there. All that we can say is that medieval religious writers had developed a notion of two kinds of sorrow—attrition and contrition—that differed in efficacy, acceptability, perfection, intensity, or formation by grace. And because they tended both to accept fear as a good beginning to sorrow, and to want love as a proper culmination, they naturally associated attrition with fear, the beginning and lower form of sorrow, and contrition with love, the higher and culminating form. They wanted penitents to examine and perfect their motives for repentance: everyone preferred love to fear, some much more than others. But if there was an attritionist school versus a contritionist school, it was not a fear school versus a love school. Confessors were stuck with theological abstractions for their pastoral instruction.

But even this scholastic theology was not without its practical applications. For we see that it was common to define two kinds of sorrow, one of them less perfect and more accessible to human effort. Attrition offered an undefinable and yet available term for those who wanted to exalt the benefits of the sacramental encounter with a priest and his absolution. The analysis of sorrow (especially if it led to the requirement of perfect contrition) could emphasize the work of the penitent and the function of discipline. Making attrition and contrition uncertain gave even more to that function. But the belief in a lesser kind of sorrow, enough for the average Christian who confessed and was absolved, opened up a possibility in theology for consoling the anxious. Thus confessors could assure sinners that the true Church offered special advantages: penitents who might doubt the quality and sincerity of their contrition could throw themselves on that manifest expression of God's mercy, the power of the keys.

FROM ATTRITION TO CONTRITION, THE DOCTRINE OF THE OBSTACLE, AND THE POWER OF THE KEYS

To soften the often harsh demands placed on the penitent's sorrow, theologians and the advisers of confessors asserted a variety of benefits flowing from the Sacrament of Penance itself. We have already traced the general tendency in theology toward a definition of sacramental efficacy deriving from "the work worked"—*ex opere operato*—rather than "the work of the worker"—*ex opere operantis*. We have noted, in addition, that this theological trend effectively proclaimed that any special benefits had to come from the power of the keys expressed, in sensible phenomena, as the absolution of the priest. The great numbers of religious writers who seize upon this as a practical means for explaining the advantages of the sacrament for the penitent make it clear that this kind of thinking was central to the function of consolation.

According to one view of how the Sacrament of Penance works, or might work, the attrition of a penitent may be transformed into contrition. Given the ill-defined nature of the experience of attrition as opposed to contrition, this process is not likely to be readily discernible in the subjective emotional status of the penitent. Thus it is not surprising that a number of authors simply assert that this transformation is true or possible, without trying to go into the dynamics of it. No less an authority than Antoninus of Florence, therefore, can pronounce favorably on this opinion without satisfactorily explaining it. Antoninus refers to St. Thomas's commentary on the *Sentences* to explain the difference between the imperfect displeasure of attrition and the perfect displeasure of contrition. In using this distinction, however, Antoninus reveals a tentative willingness to turn theology into practical advice:

> And because no one knows whether he has grace, which is required for contrition, likewise no one can be certain of his contrition, or, consequently, of his forgiveness. And Richard . . . says in IV, di. 17, that if a penitent in mortal sin is attrite for his sin—as he probably can assume himself to be [so] disposed— then he does not sin in receiving absolution. On the contrary, frequently by virtue of the keys, through the reception of absolution, his attrition is formed [by grace] and becomes contrition [immo frequenter uirtute clauium per susceptionem absolutionis formatur sua attritio et fit contritio].[40]

In one of the most influential of all the writings on the theory and practice of confession, therefore, the doctrine that attrition may become contrition is proposed favorably and yet not clearly explained. What is clear in this context—indisputably clear—is that Antoninus conceives of this doctrine as a consolation to those who are uncertain of their contrition and want some help beyond the sorrow they can muster on their own. The power of the keys is

[40] Antoninus, *Confessionale—Defecerunt*, 7.

to supply this reassurance; but how it is to make up for human deficiencies Antoninus does not explain.

The doctrine is directly associated in the minds of those who use it with Duns Scotus and its popularity is bound up with the affirmation of the power of the sacraments of the church. Some authors invoke it almost in passing, just as Antoninus of Florence does: Johann Nider, Jean Gerson, and John of Freiburg, are examples,[41] as are such theologians as Wessel Gansfort and Gabriel Biel. Some invoke it without even using the word attrition. Thus the *Eruditorium penitentiale* describes one of the advantages of confession:

> For sometimes the sinful man is not contrite before confession, but in that same confession the grace of contrition is given to him and consequently remission of guilt.[42]

Johann Wolff similarly avoids the word attrition while describing the doctrine of the transformation of an attrite into a contrite man:

> If, however, the displeasure, sorrow, and pain are *not enough* for the man to be forgiven his sins *before* he comes to the priest, then *afterwards* [while he is] in the presence of the priest, *out of the strength and power of the holy sacrament* of the confession and forgiveness of sins he will be allotted (as a result of the previous displeasure, which he had before confession and which was not enough for the forgiveness of sins) that *true contrition* and sorrow through which men's sins are forgiven with absolution . . . ; and he becomes restored as a living member of the Holy Church.[43]

In his habitually repetitive and garrulous way, the good pastor Johann Wolff has put into the vernacular the doctrine of Duns Scotus. And without scholastic terminology or subtlety he has conveyed the essential message: contrition is uncertain for fallen man, but the church offers in sacramental confession and absolution a way to make up for human weakness so that penitents may feel more certain of their forgiveness.

The same doctrine can appear in more carefully phrased theo-

[41] Johannes von Freiburg, *Summa confessorum*, III, 34, 26; Nider, *Expositio decalogi*, III, 9A–B, O6b–O7a; Gerson, *De Differentia*, Du Pin, II, 499C.
[42] *Eruditorium penitentiale*, C1a–b.
[43] Wolff, *Beichtbüchlein*, 38 (163), italics added.

logical language. Thus Astesanus of Asti, disciple of Duns Scotus in so many ways, goes into greater detail. He begins by asking whether confession ought to be formed by charity. He replies by noting first that some sacraments acquire grace—Baptism and Penance—and some augment it—Confirmation and the Eucharist. Even to receive the Eucharist, however, one need not have charity certainly (*secundum veritatem*), but only probably (*secundum probabilitatem*). Similarly, one who goes to confession need only have a probable belief that he has charity or the disposition to charity:

> This disposition, however, is attrition, because often in confession and the absolution of the priest it is formed by grace, so that it becomes contrition or contrition follows after it. Whence it is sufficient that a man dispose himself probably for grace through the detestation of all sins.

That disposition is a minimum. To be completely deficient in sorrow—to come to the confessional with a will to sin—means that one approaches the sacrament sinfully. Even the forgiveness of the contrite man, Astesanus continues, is bound up with the desire to confess, to subject himself to the priest, to be absolved, and to perform satisfaction. After he is contrite he confesses; and in the act of confession and absolution either his grace is increased, or, if his sorrow has not been enough to be called contrition, his sins are forgiven him, just so long as he does not place an obstacle to grace.[44]

The idea of the "obstacle" develops out of Scotism's strong emphasis on the intrinsic power of the sacrament, and we shall deal with the exploitation of this idea in greater detail. But here it is enough to see that Astesanus has presented a more theological rationale for this mysterious transformation from imperfect to perfect sorrow. And note that while there is most emphatically a human component—a minimum effort required of the penitent if his sins are to be forgiven—the emphasis is on a process that happens through the work worked.

Another possible explanation of this advantage of confession is possible, however, which tries to give the raising of the penitent's sorrow a simple, psychological meaning. Bartholomaeus de Chaimis, for example, describes a process that takes place purely on a human level between priest and penitent. It does not rely on

[44] *Astesana*, V, 18-19.

the idea of the keys and the efficacy of the sacrament from the work worked. On the contrary, it describes the interaction of confessor and penitent as the latter is led to better and more acceptable sorrow:

> The confessor hearing the sins of the penitent ought to strive as much as possible in the beginning to remove the penitent's shame by not expressing immediately the magnitude or gravity of his sins, but, dissimulating, let him continue to the end of the confession and then expose to him their magnitude and gravity beginning by striking with terror for the lesser ones and provoking him to contrition.[45]

What Bartholomaeus describes is a strategic maneuver on the part of the confessor. Contrition in this context is defined not in its mystical relationship to charity and formation by grace. Rather it is a simple, human requirement that the encounter with a wise confessor may help to evoke and perfect. That meaning of the benefits of confession is, as we have already seen in our discussion of the conduct of confession, common and orthodox. But it is not what we are dealing with here. The doctrines promising special help to doubtful and guilty penitents are principally dependent upon sacramental, not human, aid.

For a striking contrast to the thinking of Bartholomaeus de Chaimis, we may turn to Guido de Monte Rocherii, who articulates the advantages of the sacrament in much the same way as Astesanus. He begins by referring to his discussion of the cause of forgiveness taken from the contritionist *Raymundina*. "Because it has been said above that sins are forgiven in contrition, there remains a doubt about what the priest forgives in absolution by the power of the keys." According to some contritionists, perfect sorrow forgives the guilt (*culpa*), and the performance of penance removes the punishment owed (*poena*). Guido remains faithful to his original position, moreover, by asserting that those who are perfectly contrite go to confession already forgiven. Without suggesting that to achieve adequate contrition outside of confession is extraordinary, Guido concludes: "If, however, he is not perfectly contrite, then by virtue of confession this imperfect contrition becomes perfect, in such a way that from attrite he becomes contrite by virtue of confession; and thus by virtue

[45] de Chaimis, *Interrogatorium*, III, 1, C2a–b.

of confession his sins are remitted with respect to the *culpa*."[46] For Guido, then, it was possible to live with the contritionism of Peter Lombard's followers and the attritionism of the Scotists. Indeed, it was beneficial to do so, for with such a dualism a confessor or preacher could readily spur the faithful on to the heights of a sincere contrition and a meaningful amendment of life while at the same time hold out the comfort of an easier way to those whose experience and temperament might lead them to doubt the quality of their sorrow and intention to reform.

This kind of worried and insecure penitent leads Godescalc Rosemondt to invoke the doctrine of attrition becoming contrition at least twice. Indeed, it must have been very much on his mind, for in the opening section of his *Confessionale* he uses the condition that a good confession must be "tearful" to note that detestation of sins and intention to abstain is enough to gain forgiveness: ". . . for thus by virtue of the sacrament of absolution he passes from attrite to contrite." And he continues with an argument we are already familiar with—that amendment need only be a sincere intention; because men are human and liable to fall, there can be no question of a guarantee. The command is "be unwilling to sin" (noli peccare) and not "sin no more" (non amplius pecces). The context makes it clear, therefore, that any attempt to impugn the sincerity of sorrow on the basis of a return to sin will not affect the validity of the "sacrament of absolution," for in the sacrament the imperfect contrition (whose imperfection or inadequacy, one might argue, is betrayed by the return to sin) is transformed into something adequate for remission.

Elsewhere, Rosemondt uses this doctrine in an entirely different context, for the same consoling purpose. Must one have a special act of contrition for each mortal sin recalled, or is it enough to have a general contrition for all sins? Rosemondt quotes Petrus de Palude, who insists that it is more important to be sorry for each sin than to confess each sin. But Rosemondt thinks this opinion, while safe, is too harsh, for it would find very many not in the state of salvation. He prefers the contrary opinion, that one need only have a general sorrow for all sins, as the more probable one. To be forgiven, he continues, you must examine your conscience, detest your sins, intend to amend, and become generally contrite before confession or during absolution. That is

[46] Guido de Monte Rocherii, *Manipulus curatorum*, II, 3, 10, fol. 95b–96a.

enough. You do not need to elicit a movement of sorrow for each sin:

> For either that movement of detestation and sorrow for all sins recalled before confession and expressed in confession was sufficient so that it may deserve to be called, *de congruo* at all events, contrition; or at least by virtue of sacramental absolution (according to the common and more likely opinion), if previously it was only attrition, then it becomes contrition.

Both of these ways, Rosemondt declares, obtain the remission of sins and the state of grace. And it is this flat offer of forgiveness, through the additional power of the priest's absolution, that constitutes a major theme in the attempt of Rosemondt to console the guilty conscience. Even though he advises that for security one try to be sorry for each remembered mortal sin, he has opposed effectively the safer opinion of Petrus de Palude and confirmed the milder and more probable one, which exalts the power of the keys.[47]

The *Angelica* offers an even more exaggerated version of the offer of sacramental benefits. The assertion that the sacrament can transform an inadequate sorrow into an acceptable one is the foundation of the *Angelica*'s sacramental theory. Thus in asserting that confession truly frees man from the guilt of sin, Angelus stresses in several ways the significance and benefits of subjecting oneself to the authority of the church and enjoying the fruits of absolution, which are just as efficacious as the Sacrament of Baptism. He does not deny the role of contrition: ". . . if someone approaches confession contrite, his grace is augmented in the act of absolution." But the second case seems more critical for sacramental theory: ". . . and sins are also remitted if the preceding sorrow was not sufficient to be contrition, and the penitent does not present an obstacle to grace." It is in defining this obstacle and therefore the minimum requirements for forgiveness that Angelus offers to the world of the confessional a most consoling message.

His clearest statement of the significance for consolation of this doctrine occurs, strangely enough, in his discussion of the necessity of confession, to which we alluded in an earlier chapter. Confession is necessary because it provides the *easiest* and *surest* way

---

[47] Rosemondt, *Confessionale*, 1, 1, fol. 3b–5a; 10, 1, fol. 167a–168a.

to forgiveness, according to Angelus, and therefore anyone who ignores it shows contempt for his own salvation. Its superiority rests first of all on familiar grounds; only in this way can attrition, by the power of God and not the merit of men, be transformed into forgiveness and sacramental grace. Angelus then goes to the heart of confession's consolation, as he defines the magnitude of these benefits:

> From this it is obvious that there is *no other easier way* for finding grace; because here in confession nothing else is required except that a man *not place an obstacle* in the way of grace—which is *much less than having attrition*, which through the means of an appropriate merit (meritum de congruo) is sufficient for justification. *Nor is there a more certain way*; because a man can be far more certain that he does not place an obstacle [to grace], that is, by actually sinning, than that he has attrition. Therefore everyone is bound to recuperate grace through this path of confession, since it is *easier and more certain.*[48]

According to this version of the process of justification in the sacrament, therefore, the power of the keys is so great that only if one actually has an intention to sin—that is, not simply lack a firm purpose of amendment but actually have the intention not to amend—is there an impediment of sufficient seriousness to frustrate forgiveness and invalidate the sacrament. This teaching goes beyond formulas such as those of Astesanus of Asti, Johannes Wolff, and Antoninus of Florence, as it offers something decidedly better than the assurance that confession and absolution can turn imperfect into perfect contrition. We must observe also that it is because attrition was *not* well defined, because it was *not* simply the sorrow of a servile fear, that Angelus finds the doctrine of the obstacle "more certain." Searching into one's sorrow must be uncertain because adequate sorrow, whether one thinks it is attrition or contrition, is not reducible to a simple, identifiable experience. But if the doctrine of the obstacle is more certain, it is undeniably more lax; and we should not be surprised

---

[48] *Angelica*, "Confessio sacramentalis," 8–13, 30; "Confessio 2," and "Confessio 7," (italics added). The gloss of 1534 does not even comment on Angelus's use of the Scotist doctrine of the *obex*. Cf. Oberman, *Harvest*, 149 and n.

that some cannot go along with such mildness. One who can join Angelus, however, is his frequent critic, Sylvester Prierias Mazzolini.

We already know that Sylvester required that the sorrow of the penitent become perfect; even if it begins as mere attrition, it must terminate in contrition if he is to be justified and not sin again. But what does this mean? How does it happen? There are intimations in the discussion of attrition and contrition that this perfection happens almost automatically, or at least that it happens normally within the Sacrament of Penance. In his discussion of confession, Sylvester makes these intimations explicit. Thus he asserts the sufficiency of attrition for forgotten mortal sins: for, according to the Archdeacon, St. Thomas, and other theologians, "in confession one passes from attrite to contrite by virtue of the keys." But this assertion is only a beginning; for in his full discussion of the condition of confession requiring it to be "tearful," Sylvester examines exhaustively the requirements of the sorrow of the penitent and he confirms the theory that finds the highest efficacy in the power of the keys.

Not only does Sylvester deny that a sinner must have actual tears to make a good confession, he goes to some lengths to mitigate the harshness that some versions of worthy sorrow impose on the penitent. Of course some kind of internal sorrow is necessary. But one really only needs to want to be displeased with sin and to want to gain the grace of God. Such an imperfect disposition is attrition, and it is enough:

> Whence in absolution, by virtue of the keys, he is justified, unless he places an obstacle in the way; because [the keys] turn him from an attrite into a contrite man, according to the saints and especially Thomas and Richard.

Indeed, Sylvester tells us, there is even a milder teaching on this subject from Duns Scotus:

> It is argued even more strongly, according to Scotus, that it is enough to have such a displeasure not only formally, but even virtually, by desiring it in its cause, that is, in the justifying Sacrament of Penance. . . . For he holds that for obtaining grace through this sacrament attrition is not required; rather it suffices to have a will to receive this sacrament without ac-

tually [interposing] the obstacle of mortal sin to the action itself in the last instant of absolution, in which the power of this
sacrament resides. . . .

That is a powerful sacrament. All it requires is a penitent who
honestly intends to receive it so that his sins may be forgiven and
who is not, while the priest is absolving him, planning a new sin,
delighting in the thought of an old one, and the like. It is, according to Scotus and Sylvester, just like Baptism: it requires only the
intention of receiving the benefits that the church confers without
actually sinning while one receives it.
Naturally Sylvester is aware that not everyone has embraced
this doctrine. To some, he tells us, it seems that an internal act is
essential to this sacrament, and thus if you are not repentant it is
not worth anything. These critics would compare it to matrimony, which is not binding if someone wants to contract it but
does not want to consent (by which he means, consent to the in-
dissoluble sacramental union). But Sylvester counters this argument with the authority of St. Thomas, and adds that this is not
rational anyway because sometimes sacramental forgiveness can
derive from a future contrition. At that point he uses an argument we have already cited in our discussion of amendment of
life in an earlier chapter. For he stresses that the doctrine of the
obstacle means that someone renders the sacrament invalid by
interposing an actual sin at the time, as for example, if he actually
desires not to give up a certain sin. The desire to sin must be positive, Sylvester explains, and the desire to amend need not be
anything more than that—a positive desire to amend. Even if he
thinks he will continue to sin it does not invalidate the sacrament.
For if one wishes to amend, even if one does not think one will,
then one must be said to have a certain displeasure for sin. At
least one is not taking pleasure in sin, actually sinning, and therefore invalidating the sacrament. According to Scotus, Sylvester
concludes, one does not invalidate the sacrament if one is at least
attrite, or if one intends to receive the sacrament so that one can
feel sorrow.[49]
Sylvester's analysis of the minimal requirements for a sorrow
that will work within the Sacrament of Penance expounds a Scotist position that could only emphasize the consoling help of the

[49] *Sylvestrina,* "Confessio 1," q. 1; ibid., q. 21, par. 24; "Contritio," q. 3–4,
par. 5–6.

keys. Indeed, we shall see in the next section an even more exaggerated version of those benefits. Nevertheless, the ideas of Sylvester are nothing more than an amplification of convictions that are widely held among those who give practical lessons in the forgiveness of sins. It was an extremely common teaching—we have found it in one form or another in Antoninus of Florence, Johannes von Freiburg, Jean Gerson, Johann Nider, Johann Wolff, a commentary on the "Poeniteas cito," Astesanus of Asti, Godescalc Rosemondt, Guido de Monte Rocherii, Angelus de Clavasio, and Sylvester Prierias, and this list could easily be expanded—that it is permissible to go to confession with less than a perfect sorrow. And these authorities find ways to invest that confession, along with absolution, with a power to make up for the defects penitents may fear will invalidate the forgiveness they are seeking. Attrition becomes contrition. The sacrament works on its own power for all those who do not hinder its effectiveness. These ideas are widely diffused and offer consolation to the perplexed.

THE ADORNMENT OF THE SOUL: GUIDO DE MONTE ROCHERII AND SYLVESTER PRIERIAS

The flexibility of pastoral literature finds no better exemplification than the *Manipulus curatorum* of Guido de Monte Rocherii. Guido is a devoted eclectic, and in his views of the working of the Sacrament of Penance he proves true to his penchant for gathering together various opinions as they suit his purposes. We have already discussed some of the positions he endorses. To begin with, his addition of the motive of love to the *Raymundina*'s causes of contrition would seem to place him even more than Raymond in the contritionist tradition. He confirms this impression by his rather high demands for contrition, which is characterized by a will motivated by the love of God above all things and a detestation of sin so great that one would not for any reason consent to sin. Even his discussion of attrition follows the common view that the motivation of servile fear is not enough, and here too he avoids the mildest doctrine. Finally, although he departs easily from his more rigorous tendencies when he argues that through the power of the keys attrition can become contrition, he still recalls his previous conclusion that contrition causes the forgiveness of sins. Yet it is in that discussion of the power of the keys that Guido reveals the extent of his flexibility as he takes a totally different and for him more characteristic stance. As we have seen, he becomes a Scotist, antirigorist and anticontritionist, proposing a theory of the working of the Sacrament of Penance that includes the hard way of forgiveness through contrition outside of the confessional, but emphatically affirms an easier, surer, and more certain way through the power of the keys. Thus one is not surprised to find that Guido examines fully the curious and generally neglected theory of the "adornment of the soul," which concedes much to the enduring effects of the sacrament and allows much to unworthy penitents who come to confess.

In discussing the cases for reiteration of confession, Guido notes that a Parisian master named Godefroid de Fontaines added another to the usual ones: "When someone confesses some sin and does not feel sorry for it or does not propose to abstain in the future, such a man is required to confess again." Revealing a noteworthy sophistication, Guido points out that this judgment implies a certain order in contrition and confession: for Godefroid clearly assumed that contrition must either precede or be simultaneous with confession. In Godefroid's hypothetical case, moreover, not only was contrition absent before and during confession, but its opposite was present. Therefore, he concluded that the confession was worth nothing, and had to be repeated. But Guido knows the clever rebuttal, and he does not keep it from his inquisitive reader:

> Truly, brother Bernard of Gannat, Bachelor of Theology and once abbot elect of Clermont, says, in his *correctorium*, against the said master Godefroid, that such a man is not necessarily held to confess again; but he is held to be contrite again concerning sins previously confessed fictitiously, and for the fiction itself; and by virtue of the confession already made, and of the present contrition, his sins are forgiven him.

The logic of this position is both subtle and compelling. For Bernard simply holds that contrition is just as efficacious in connection with a confession already made as with one being made or going to be made. "For a confession already made had a real existence; and therefore its power can work better than that confession's [power] that is not yet." After all of that, however, Guido confesses he is not sure. He thinks one should at least confess the general fact of the bad confession, and he admits that it would probably be a good idea to confess the particular sins again, as Raymond seems to advise in his summa.[50]

One is disappointed in Guido, perhaps. Since he was bold enough to discuss this theological curiosity, one might wish he had abandoned caution completely and pronounced in favor of the ingenious Bernard. Nevertheless, Guido raised the possibility of forgiveness eventually coming to someone who dissimulated in confession and sincerely repented afterwards, without making him confess again. We can now turn to an authority of even greater stature in the years before the Reformation who granted much more truth to this teaching: Sylvester Prierias.

For Sylvester this case represents a continuation and extension of the powers he attributed to the keys in his section on attrition, contrition, and the obstacle. It occurs in the second part of his long discussion of the condition stipulating that a good confession be tearful. In it he uses the term that is the basis for his and Guido's investigations: the *ornatus anime*, the adornment of the soul. And the specific question asks "whether a confession made *a ficto* without contrition and charity, is valid."

The question really asks, Sylvester begins, "whether a confession that is completed and terminated without contrition and charity is valid." Some cases, however, are not relevant to the problem of the impediment of a fiction. Thus for the penitent who does not intend to receive the sacrament, but goes to confession to mock the church, or for the penitent who intends to receive the sacrament but actually considers that he does not want to avoid sin, the sacrament is completely invalid then and in the future. In the opposite case, it may happen that a penitent goes to confession with some fiction that ceases to exist when the priest is absolving him. For example, a penitent may have an inadequate sorrow, but not so inadequate to make it impossible for it "to be perfected by the sacrament and the use of the keys, and be changed into true contrition." In that case, whether the fiction is confessed or not, the sacrament is valid when it is received.

The real case occurs in two different ways. First, when a penitent unknowingly conceals a fiction, does not have enough sorrow for it to be raised to sufficient sorrow by the keys, does not confess that deficiency because it does not occur to him to do so, and is absolved. Second, when a penitent has some fiction, confesses it, and yet is absolved. In both cases there is the possibility that

[50] Guido de Monte Rocherii, *Manipulus curatorum*, II, 3, 7, fol. 85a–86b.

through the imprinting of an adornment on the soul the sacrament will become valid through this adornment when the fiction recedes.

To make it clear how this action must be understood, however, Sylvester injects a brief explanation of the causality of grace in the sacraments. The doctrine is from St. Thomas by way of Petrus de Palude, both of whom teach that the sacraments confer grace not as efficient causes but as dispositive causes. They do not imprint charity but a disposition to charity. That disposition is called the adornment, and if its opposite—sin—is not present, it is indelible. In other words, whether the sacrament works at the time of its reception or at a later time, it works in the same way. The sacrament works in conjunction with the penitent no matter when it becomes valid, and it does so by disposing him to grace. But it is possible, as we shall see, to dispose for grace without bringing grace about. And this disposition, this adornment, will endure just so long as "its opposite," sin, does not destroy it.

Now Sylvester knows of many theologians who reject the notion that a fictitious confession can become valid when the fiction recedes. They think that such a confession will not take away the guilt or the temporal punishment of sin, and they require repetition of that confession. On this side are Godefroid of Fontaines, Raymond of Peñaforte, Hostiensis, Bonaventure, Durandus, Holcot, and Vincent of Beauvais. To this rather strange list he adds all the canonists, "who, nevertheless, in this wield a scythe in the wheat fields of the theologians." In contrast, however, are St. Thomas, Petrus de Palude, Richard, John of Freiburg, Bernard of Gannat, and apparently Gratian as well. They say that such a confession is valid for the remission of sins when the fiction recedes, just as it is in Baptism, and that one need not repeat such a confession.

Sylvester pronounces simply for the second list: "And this opinion is true." For to every "form" that disposes sufficiently to a certain effect, that effect will follow when the impediment is taken away. He thinks there is a good analogy in physical nature: when a column sustaining a stone is removed, a motion downward follows. The disposition, it is clear, is for heavy bodies such as stones to fall; the impediment is the column sustaining the stone. In the sacrament, this analogy holds. For if the adornment were insufficient as a cause of grace, then penance would not sufficiently cause grace. But it does. And it causes grace only by disposing the recipient to its reception. Therefore, when the impediment to grace is removed, the penitent still remains adequately disposed; grace follows, and the confession is made truly valid.

There are three ways of showing how this opinion can be true. First, it occurs when the fiction represents only some defect in the penitent's sorrow or preparation for confession, and the penitent does not knowingly conceal it but rather thinks he is adequately prepared. That he is mistaken does not remove the fiction with respect to the ultimate end of the sacrament, because adequate preparation is commanded by divine law. But such a fiction does not exclude the essence of the sacrament by the very fact that it is an error and the penitent is not intentionally deceitful. Sylvester leaves us to conclude that in such a case the person is forgiven when his sorrow or his self-examination improves; and we must further assume that the process by which he is forgiven is the operation of the disposition of the adornment in conjunction with his change of heart or reflection. In the second case, a man apparently knows of his inadequacy but does not think it is something that has to be confessed. Here we have a situation exactly like the forgetting of a sin through negligence. Say that such a man did not feel sorrow for his past sins or intend to avoid them in the future, but that it just does not occur to him to tell it. That is still a fiction, but it is also a sacrament if he is absolved. In the third instance, Sylvester cites the case of a man who goes to the same priest to whom he had made his confession with a fiction before. He is not required to tell the sins from his last confession again. He is only required to tell and do penance for the fiction.

To bring more force to this solution, Sylvester adds one more question: "Whether a priest ought to absolve a penitent expressing his own fiction by saying that he does not propose to abstain [from sin]." His answer shows that Sylvester takes the independent power of the keys very seriously:

Everyone says no; because [the priest] ought not to absolve someone who he knows is bound by God. If, however, he absolves him *de facto*, intending to confer a true sacrament, the absolution holds, and it will take effect when [the penitent] becomes contrite, either out of divine agreement, or from the imprinted adornment.[51]

[51] *Sylvestrina*, "Confessio 1," q. 23, par. 2f.

Sylvester has tried to accept the doctrine of the adornment of the soul and make it acceptable to pious ears. In the stark form Guido outlines it, there is something dangerous and innovative about it. But Sylvester tries to assimilate it, in his wordy, theological way, to familiar ideas about the proper preparation for confession. In particular he comes back again and again to the ignorance of the penitent who does not think of confessing his fiction. Sylvester, like St. Thomas, wants to keep contrition as the proper terminus for justification, however, so that any inadequacy is serious or, as he calls it, a fiction. But it is a fiction through negligence, and the adornment of the soul can, in his view, come to the rescue. It can even come to the rescue of someone who admits to the priest that he isn't sorry enough, if the priest in fact absolves him.

What is the significance of this excursion into the theology of the sacraments? Probably not many confessors would have read or could have applied these passages. Nevertheless they reveal important aspects of medieval ideas of justification and the way sorrow and absolution combine to forgive sins. Three observations are pertinent.

First of all, Guido's example points to a major difficulty for all who retain the contritionist position of Peter Lombard, and that would include St. Thomas. Quite simply, if contrition forgives, what does the priest do? We have already noted that St. Thomas includes in his definition of contrition the intention to confess, and this device is a popular one in the literature of forgiveness as a whole. Even those who take a more rigorous "contritionist" position, one more faithful to Peter Lombard, refuse to do without sacramental confession to a priest who holds the key of power. Forgiveness is caused by contrition by virtue of a confession and absolution that is about to be but not yet. But all Bernard of Gannat wanted to do was reverse the order. And there seems little reason to exclude this solution. For if contrition can forgive in conjunction with a confession that is about to be, why indeed can it not forgive in conjunction with a confession that has already taken place? Few took up Bernard's clever alternative, it is true. But many took up an alternative that does away with the temptation to look for such subtleties. For the popular explanation of Duns Scotus—with its two ways to justification and its assertion that the sacramental absolution can raise imperfect to perfect sorrow—makes it far more reasonable to assume that there is a logical order in justification: sorrow first, and then, if the sorrow is not good enough, absolution, which will do any work for the penitent he could not do for himself.

Second, Bernard of Gannat's position, and the whole notion of the adornment of the soul, tell us something important about the limits to mildness. According to this theory, it is possible to have a valid but fruitless confession if some fictitious internal disposition makes the sacrament unable to work forgiveness. Those who believe this to be possible emphasize the distinction between the internal disposition—that is, the contrition of the penitent—and the objective effect of the absolution. They hold that this objective effect, the "adornment of the soul," is produced even if the penitent feigns contrition. Thus, when the fiction disappears— *recedente fictione*, in the language of these scholastics—sacramental grace is regained. In this view confession of sins to a priest is a divine and ecclesiastical precept, but there are apparently no conditions placed upon it other than that it be complete and truthful. Once satisfied, once all sins are told in the forum of penance, the obligation is fulfilled. Priestly absolution does not work on a penitent who is not at least attrite, at least not immediately. But it does imprint that objective adornment by virtue of which he will be forgiven of the sins he has already confessed.[52]

Now despite Sylvester's attempt to rehabilitate this view, the practical literature does not take it up enthusiastically, and the reasons are not difficult to discover. Logical as the theory is, it could not have encouraged the internal discipline so essential in the thinking of all churchmen who teach about confession. On the contrary, it might encourage penitents to seek out the priest and his words of absolution mechanically, without adequate preparation. And, as we have seen time and time again, voluntary cooperation of the free person is the heart of the whole penitential doctrine of the church. It is unlikely that any greater concession

[52] For the *ornatus animae* and its subsequent history, see Michel, "Pénitence," *DTC*, 12[1], 1000–1003; Poschmann, *Penance and Anointing*, 177ff.; Göttler, *Der heilige Thomas*, 21ff., 123, 130ff., 158ff., 180, 226–234; Johannes Capreolus, *Defensiones theologiae divi Thome Aquinatis* . . . , 7 vols., (Turin, 1900–1908), vol. VI, *Defensiones . . . in Quarto Sententiarum*, IV, 17, q. 2, a. 2, pp. 379a–386a; Jean Morin (Joannes Morinus), *De Contritione et attritione. Exercitatio historico-theologica*, in *Thesaurus theologicus*, vol. 11, *Tractatus II de Sacramentis* (Venice, 1762) *Controversia secunda. De Penitentia* . . . . Opusculum VI, 313–431, and esp. 358.

to human weakness would be made than the distinction between perfect and imperfect contrition and the assurance that sacramental absolution can make up for the defective sorrow of someone who is not fully contrite. Even this doctrine is not purely and simply a concession to human weakness, since almost all who conceded the acceptability of attrition thought the penitent should continue his effort to bring his contrition to perfection. Closest in its mildness to the doctrine of the adornment of the soul is certainly the doctrine of the obstacle which holds that one may benefit from the sacrament if one intends only to receive the sacrament and does not impede its efficacy by actually wishing to sin at the time of confession and absolution. But even this view permits the penitent no more than uncertainty about his sorrow. It does not allow a positive deception or dissimulation of his sorrow. And it still honors that central commandment of those concerned with the practical goals of the Sacrament of Penance: a penitent was supposed to do what he was capable of doing— *facere quod in se est*. The theory of the adornment of the soul, however, tends to reduce the effort of the confessing penitent so radically that *facere quod in se est* is emptied of content. Turning away from sin as part of preparation for the sacrament is ignored. And not the will, but only the memory of the penitent is subjected to the obligation to confess his sins. The doctrine of the obstacle had already gone too far for most religious writers. The adornment of the soul could only lose more of them as it threatened to strip the encounter with the priest of any inner spiritual meaning.

Third, the reluctance of the practical literature to take up the adornment of the soul may have been predictable. But this doctrine is only an extreme and unacceptable version of a pronounced tendency in the pastoral theology of the late middle ages: to offer consolation in the form of ecclesiastically blessed and dispensed sacramental help. In the Sacrament of Penance, the center of this help is the absolution of the priest. In the more extreme views, absolution transformed in some way attrition into contrition; or forgave sins almost irresistibly just so long as an obstacle was not placed in its path; or imprinted willy-nilly an objective character on the soul (the comparison with Holy Orders and Confirmation is apt). In everyone's view, however, the absolution of the priest had become a mysterious offering of grace that could counterbalance weakness and doubt.

THE ABSOLUTION OF THE PRIEST AND THE
FORGIVENESS OF CHRIST

No evidence for the increased emphasis on sacramental grace independent of individual effort is more convincing than the development of the *words* of absolution themselves. As with most other elements in this theology, the great change occurred in the thirteenth century. And we can describe that change quite simply: theologians began to argue that absolution in the indicative mood—"I absolve you"—was more appropriate than the deprecatory form—"May God forgive you."

William of Auvergne offers a good example of the kind of language one expects from those adhering to the older view that the priest does very little in causing forgiveness. William objects to the indicative form because of its judicial overtones:

> The confessor should not say, in the manner of the secular courts of justice (more judiciorum forensicorum), "we absolve you, we do not condemn you"; but rather utter a prayer over him that God may offer (tribuat) him absolution, and remission, and the grace of satisfaction. And no one doubts that the confessor may and ought to pray the Father of mercies that He also remit the sinner's sins, which the sinner does not recognize in himself and reveal to this same confessor. Whence in the absolution of penitents priests should not customarily say, "May God remit the sins that you have confessed to me," but "all" [your sins].

In this deprecatory form, the language of absolution itself makes it clear that the priest does little more than pray for the penitent and, perhaps, offer assurance that God has already forgiven him even for his forgotten sins. But in the thirteenth century sacramental theology outgrew this restrictive view of ecclesiastical power and comfort. Consciously and gradually the shift to an indicative form of absolution witnessed this change in thinking. When St. Thomas declared for it, the battle was won, and in the theology of Duns Scotus, indicative absolution plays a crucial role. The practical literature naturally follows this lead.[53] And

[53] Amann, "Pénitence," *DTC*, 12¹, 938; Michel, "Pénitence," ibid., 952; Anciaux, *La Théologie*, 46–49; Ludwig Ott, "Das Opusculum des hl. Thomas," esp. 101–115, 117–135; Hödl, *Geschichte der scholsatischen Literatur*, 382–383 and references. John of Freiburg's formula combines deprecatory and indicative elements: "Dominus te absoluat et ego autoritate qua fungor

sometimes we find the formula of absolution the focal point for a discussion of how the sacrament works. Such is the case with Guido de Monte Rocherii, who considers a variety of ideas on the formula and in doing so may even reveal the lingering hold of older ideas, which he is intent on putting to rest once and for all.

One must realize, Guido insists after discussing sorrow for sins, that God, not contrition or confession, actually forgives sins. Since it is the work of God, the indivisible Trinity, it is logical to ask what the priest does by virtue of the keys. Some say that God cleanses from the stain of mortal sin and the priest absolves from eternal punishment, to which Guido comments, "I confess I do not understand these people." Guido reasons that there certainly can be no eternal punishment for someone whose sins have been forgiven. Others say that a sinner who is contrite is still obliged to confess and make satisfaction, and that the priest releases him from the first obligation and imposes the second. But since the priest says, "I absolve you from your sins," and not, "I absolve you from confession," this second explanation of what the priest does also fails to make sense out of the formula of absolution. Others say that contrition reconciles with God and confession with the Church; and although this is true it is inadequate to explain the power of the keys, which is said to extend to heaven. And some others say that "the priest causes nothing by the power of the keys except demonstratively, whence they say that he absolves in the sense that he shows someone to be absolved." According to this view, when the priest says, "I absolve you" (ego te absolvo), he is really saying, "I show you absolved" (te absolutum ostendo). But this opinion, Guido maintains, seems to give the keys too little. Others say that the priest absolves by virtue of the keys from any guilt he finds, just so long as the penitent does not place an obstacle in the way, and also from temporal or corporal punishment if the penitent will complete the penance the priest imposes. "And that opinion seems reasonable enough to me," Guido says simply. Others say, in addition, that since every mortal sin is an offense against the infinite goodness of God and out of all proportion to our own powers to set right, the power of the keys makes up for this by applying the infinite merits of

---

absoluo te a peccatis tuis"; *Summa confessorum*, III, 34, 89. But the *Astesana* (V, 2, a. 2) has a simple, indicative formula: "Absoluo te ab omnibus peccatis tuis."

Christ's passion to our satisfaction for sin. "Thus I believe that a single Our Father imposed in penance by a priest is more effica- cious than one hundred thousand said on one's own, because it has the merit of the passion of Christ." And, he adds, "This opin- ion is most rational."[54] Whether Guido was summarizing his re- search or plagiarizing someone else's, this analysis of the power of the priest focuses neatly on the words of absolution. It could hardly have been otherwise. One of the profoundest transforma- tions in thinking about the church and the sacraments, then, was signaled by a simple formula's expression in the indicative mood. And writers like Guido, intent on making this mystery intelligible and orthodox, predictably attended to the language they used when they taught priests what to say when they were applying through the keys the benefits of the sacrifice of Christ.

But if Guido represented a school of thought consciously try- ing to divest itself of the contritionism of Peter Lombard, we must admit that the older view still could influence the practical literature in a variety of ways. In the first place, although the *Raymundina* never was printed in the pre-Reformation era, it nevertheless remained an important influence on the thinking of those who wrote about the cure of souls. Raymond's views, more- over, state the contritionist position, with its minimal recognition of the role of the priest, in unmistakable terms. Of all the expla- nations for the forgiveness of sins, Raymond likes the one holding that sins are forgiven any adult who is truly contrite, proposes to abstain, confess, and make satisfaction according to the judgment of the church. According to God's goodness and promise, such a man's sins are forgiven him before a word is spoken. And the only demurral is not in the interest of the sacramental power of the keys: rather, it is Raymond's insistence that contrition does not remit the sins properly speaking, but only God does, through contrition. Raymond then raises the question of temporal priority explicitly in a proposition that would become the occasion for the speculations of Bernard of Gannat:

In this process you will also notice the things that are simul- taneous in time, that is, justification, contrition, and the remis- sion of sins. Some of these, however, naturally take prece- dence: for I must necessarily understand that someone has grace before he is contrite. Grace therefore precedes; love

[54] Guido de Monte Rocherii, *Manipulus curatorum*, II, 3, 10, fol. 95b–96a.

follows, for whoever has grace will love; contrition follows; for whoever loves is contrite; and remission follows.[55]

In other words, there is not much for the priest to do, and the characterization of the formula of absolution as the priest's "showing" forgiveness to the penitent is certainly apt. It is of course still essential to intend to seek the benefits of the keys—and actually to confess "if one has the chance"—for that is essential to Raymond's and everyone else's notions of repentance. But the *Raymundina*'s keys are not impressive, and there are hints of the persistence of this thinking in later writers.

The influence of the *Raymundina*—and its decline—is exemplified by the discussion of the keys in the *Pisanella* and *Supplementum*. Bartholomaeus of Pisa was not completely untouched by theological development, and he looks to his fellow Dominicans Albert and Thomas for the correct formula of absolution, "I absolve you." But the deprecatory prayer *Misereatur tui*—may God have mercy on you—along with the sign of the cross is permitted "so that it may be expressed that the priest does not absolve by his own authority but as a minister." This addition, which Bartholomaeus leaves to the decision of the priest, is explicitly included to emphasize the instrumental nature of the priestly absolution. Indeed, he restates this predilection for the sign of the cross, which he admits is not necessary, but is nevertheless the symbol of the true forgiver of sins, Christ. As for the use of the keys, he describes a modest role succinctly:

What does the use of the keys accomplish? I answer that according to Thomas and Petrus it works instrumentally by disposing to grace and justification, but not principally and directly by causing that grace and justification (efficiendo), because this belongs solely to God.

And then, as if to perplex completely, Bartholomaeus immediately adds: "But just as the absolution is originally effective in cleansing in Baptism, so the absolution is effective now for purification (sed sicut ad mundationem originaliter in baptismo ualet ablutio, ita ad emundationem actualiter ualet absolutio)." One would have thought that this comparison with Baptism is exactly what Bartholomaeus is trying to avoid. But to reassert the contritionism of the early scholastics, he invokes in the very next para-

[55] *Raymundina*, III, 34, 11, p. 446.

graph the explanation of binding and loosing that defines the priest's role as one of "showing" the penitent's absolution. The Lord cleanses the lepers and then tells them to go to the priests, already healed.

Nicolaus's comments on these passages show that he wants to protect the newer versions of priestly power. Thus he invokes the authority of John of Freiburg in order to clarify the first assertion that God, not the priest, forgives. John of Freiburg, Nicolaus says, agrees with the characterization of the priest's action as instrumental only; but John adds, according to the teaching of St. Thomas, a special function for those not perfectly sorry: "If someone was not perfectly disposed for the reception of grace before the absolution of the priest, grace will follow in confession and sacramental absolution if he does not place an obstacle in the way." And to the *Pisanella*'s suggestion that the priest's function is to show the absolved status of the penitent who has already been forgiven, Nicolaus simply points out the contradiction between this explanation and Bartholomaeus's own assertion that absolution is an instrumental cause of grace: "On the contrary," Nicolaus says of the keys, "it seems that they not only show someone absolved, but also absolve, albeit instrumentally, as was said above."

But contrition, as well as God, is a rival of the keys in the tradition of Peter Lombard and Raymond of Peñaforte, and both Bartholomaeus of Pisa and Nicolaus de Ausimo take up this problem. The *Pisanella* characteristically emphasizes the causal role of sorrow: in the Sacrament of Penance its causality is described as material because it is said to be the material disposition for the forgiveness of sins. Yet even the *Pisanella* notes, without making sense out of it, that at least the intention of confessing is required, and that if the intention is not fulfilled there is no remission—in fact there is an additional sin. For Nicolaus there is something wrong here, but he does not seem to know what it is. He recalls the distinction outlined in the *Raymundina* and John of Freiburg between those who say that in cases of necessity, contrition without confession and satisfaction suffices to obtain remission of sins, and those who call the remission wrought by contrition conditional upon confession and satisfaction. As Nicolaus tells it, Raymond pronounces the first opinion "more celebrated," and uses the incident of Lazarus to clinch his argument that remission occurs first. Nicolaus wants to rescue both opinions, however, perhaps in an effort to tie the process of justification more closely to the intervention of the priest than the contritionism of Raymond seems to do. Thus he returns to the raising of Lazarus to point out that although Lazarus was revived by the Lord, he was still bound; it was the Apostles who loosed him. Nicolaus concludes that "full remission" comes only with confession unless confession is truly impossible.[56]

Where does the *Supplementum* stand then on the meaning of absolution? First of all, it is essential to realize that neither Bartholomaeus of Pisa nor Nicolaus de Ausimo apparently cared enough about these problems to solve them. Compared with their concern for legalistic details—excommunications, for example— the working of the sacrament and the role of the keys gets little space and, what is more important, little clarification. Second, both betray the lingering influence of the early contritionism of Peter Lombard and Raymond of Peñaforte. This is especially true of the *Pisanella*, which is one of the rare works on confession that still describes the absolution of the priest as "showing" the forgiveness of Christ and contrition. But Nicolaus too is fond of the parables of the lepers and Lazarus and their implication that Christ cleanses from the worst effects of sin before anyone sees the priest. Third, Nicolaus registers a significant disagreement with the *Pisanella*. His language is mild, but his rejection of the idea of "showing" absolution indicates some awareness of the trend of theological thinking. To be sure, his invocation of Lazarus and the lepers brings an older conception of the function of the priest right back. But Nicolaus at least knew that there was some inconsistency in calling absolution an instrumental cause and then denying any causal significance to that absolution. His own solution, based principally on John of Freiburg's Thomism, is not so self-contradictory as Bartholomaeus's, and it avoids the extreme version of Raymond and Peter Lombard.

At least two authors, Hermannus de Schildis and J. P. Foresti, adopt a view of absolution that deprecates even more than the *Pisanella* the power of the priest. Hermannus de Schildis appears at first to affirm the efficacy of the sacrament "from the work worked" when he endorses the normal indicative form: "I absolve you of your sins." He even explains that it is not necessary

[56] *Supplementum*, "Absolutio," 6; "Clavis," 6–7; "Contritio," 11.

to add, "by the authority I enjoy," a formula that could conceivably be construed as some sort of condition applied to the absolution. But he is not sensitive to the need for enhancing the independent power of the keys, for he also notes: "It is nevertheless a fitting addition when one says, 'I absolve you from your sins which you have confessed and for which you are contrite.'" He justifies additions because there is no fixed form; because, unlike Baptism and the Eucharist, Christ did not institute this sacrament with definite words. Hermannus recognizes that if additions were to interfere with the substance of the sacrament, then forgiveness would not derive its power from the sacrament. But he shows his true inclinations by dismissing that objection: the better theologians and canonists, he tells us, agree that if a sinner is truly contrite, then God absolves him, whereas the priest absolves the penitent from ecclesiastical obligations. Thus the whole force of his analysis of absolution affirms an extreme form of the contritionism. And, when Hermannus takes up contrition itself, his treatment is entirely consistent with this discussion of the formula of absolution. One is obliged, he argues, to confess "with true contrition of heart" and the firm purpose of abstaining from sins in the future. To confess without contrition, or with a dissimulated sorrow, is fraudulent, and he advises such ill-prepared penitents to repeat their confession and include confession of that fiction.[57]

Foresti is clearly in the same camp. He does not want a conditional absolution, it is true, and the formula he settles on is in the indicative mood. But it is essentially identical to that of Hermannus de Schildis and it definitely fails to honor the claims of theology for the benefits of the keys:

> The form of absolution that is commonly observed by all ought to be as follows: . . . May the Lord Jesus Christ absolve you through His most holy passion; and I, by the authority I enjoy, absolve you from all your sins that you have truly confessed to me, and for which you are contrite, and which you have forgotten. . . .[58]

To protect the sanctity of the church from those who would seek forgiveness with a dissimulated sorrow is utmost in Foresti's

[57] de Schildis, *Speculum sacerdotum*, [fol. 13b–15a].
[58] Foresti, *Confessionale*, "Forma absolutionis—alia forma . . . ," fol. 67a–b.

mind. Thus the priest says he absolves. But it really appears that, like the apostles with Lazarus and the priests with the lepers, he is doing something much less dramatic.

Thus the view that forgiveness normally occurred outside of the confessional in an act of God-given contrition persisted. Perhaps it was kept alive by a whole variety of deprecatory prayers reminding people that only God forgives and that His mercy must be granted if sinners are no longer to be held liable. But the overwhelming tendency is to accept divine causality and at the same time assert the causal role of the priest, God's representative, as he applies the keys. And if the deprecatory prayers effectively reminded people of the contritionist doctrine, there was a more direct and powerful assertion of the exalted role of the priest in that simple, almost universally accepted formula, "I absolve you." It is this influence and this tendency that dominates the thinking of those who use the power of the keys to console the penitent.

No one saw the links between the words of absolution, the theory of the working of the sacrament, and the consolation of the penitent more clearly than Jean Gerson. Even in the *Opus tripartitum*, succinct and nontheological though it is, Gerson calls attention to the heart of his concern. He notes that the correct form of absolution is, "Ego absolvo te a peccatis tuis in nomine etc."; and he warns, "Any other additions, conditional or involuted, are more safely omitted." Why does Gerson talk about the simpler form as "safer"? He explains his thoughts in at least three different places, and all of them refer to the confidence of the penitent and validity of sacramental forgiveness.

Gerson wants absolution to be short and simple. It is enough to say that absolution is "for your sins," without adding irrelevancies such as "and their circumstances." Sometimes additions are harmful. To stipulate that absolution is of those sins for which the penitent is "contrite" is dangerous and possibly ruinous. For absolution can remit not only those sins for which one is contrite, but also those for which one is only attrite, by means of grace after one comes to confess. If you specify "contrite," however, you exclude completely those who have only an imperfect contrition, as black excludes white. Finally, this addition injects "a scruple of desperation." "For no one can be certain if he is truly contrite for his sins; when he hears himself absolved from the sins for which he is contrite, therefore, he may begin to doubt and to waver on his absolution." This is especially true for the dying, whom the devil tries to rob of hope and trust so they will feel no devotion or contrition. Yet it is also true of those in health. "Often without any guilt of his own, a man can be deprived of the grace of devotion for a variety of reasons. In this way trust is taken, or diminished, and occasion given for collapse or desperation." For Gerson there is no excuse for taking this kind of chance with wordy additions to the formula:

> For even if it were in fact the case that without contrition sins may not be wiped away; nevertheless a man is often truly contrite, or by virtue of the sacrament contrition is infused in that very absolution, and this condition, as I have said before, remains hidden from him. And when he hears "from those for which you are contrite," he seizes on this opportunity for brooding (mussitandi) and doubting, and, consequently, is in peril.[59]

Two special dangers emerge, then. Superfluous additions may actually affect the extent to which the words of absolution remit sins; and they may cause a perilous scrupulosity in those who fear that their piety is not up to the demands announced in the priest's words of forgiveness. Gerson bases justification and consolation on the power of the priest and the sacrament he dispenses.

The instances of this argument are numerous. Johann Nider's *Manual for Confessors* invokes Gerson explicitly and declares the proper formula to be, "I absolve you from your sins." Nider then immediately notes Gerson's warning: "It is safer to mix in nothing with these formulas."[60] The *Confessionale* of Albi recognizes this

---

[59] Gerson, *Opus tripartitum*, II, Du Pin, I, 447A–B; "Notabile de forma absolvendi a peccatis monitum," Du Pin, II, 482B–D; cf. Gerson to his brother Nicolas on sacramental absolution, Glorieux, II, 133–142 (in Du Pin, II, 406–412), in which Gerson asserts that absolution can forgive sins for which one is only attrite: "immo potest nocere si ponitur hoc adjectivum 'contritis' cum virtus sacramentalis absolutionis valeat super peccata solum attrita licet nondum contrita; et ista est additio quodammodo distrahens quae praesupponit contritionem praecessisse, quae non semper praerequiritur ut dictum est" (Glorieux, II, 134). See also Gerson, *De Statuto ordinis Carthusiensis*, Du Pin, II, 461A–B.

[60] Nider, *Manuale confessorum. De lepra morali* (U. Gering, Paris, 1479), II, 6.

issue as important enough to explain in even greater detail. After declaring for the same formula, it also warns:

> Whence it must be observed that one should not add (ponere) or say "for which you are contrite" in absolution, because this might be dangerous; for one can be absolved not only from those sins for which one is contrite, but also for which one is attrite; and those sins for which one is attrite can, through grace by virtue of absolution . . . , be remitted and effaced. For there are many who are not contrite for their sins when they confess, but only attrite; and nevertheless they are absolved of all of them, except when the sins for which one is attrite are expressly excluded.[61]

This obsession with the correct words is understandable, of course, given the concern of all that the sacrament conform to those rules that will ensure its validity. A number of authorities, however, simply prescribe an indicative form of absolution without coupling an explanation of the formula and the working of the sacrament. Thus Antoninus of Florence, Sylvester, Godescalc Rosemondt, Astesanus of Asti, simply state a succinct, indicative form. Sylvester explicitly prefers "I absolve you" to "I absolve you from your sins," but he does not seem especially concerned at the dangers of the formula he rejects.[62] Some other statements of the proper formula elicit broader explanations. Jodocus Winshemius, despite some contritionist leanings, shows his preference for *ex opere operato* explanation. After asserting that a simple "I absolve you" is sufficient, he explains that these words "signify and cause (efficiunt) from divine institution an internal absolution."[63]

Even the manual of Bartholomaeus de Chaimis, which does not incline towards theological commentary, defines the role of priestly absolution. Bartholomaeus agrees with those who think there is one proper form for this sacrament, and that is, "I absolve you." Furthermore, this formula means, "I give to or confer

---

[61] *Confessionale* (Albi), G5b.

[62] *Astesana*, V, 2, a. 2; Antoninus, *Confessionale—Defecerunt*, 48; *Sylvestrina*, "Absolutio 6"; Rosemondt, *Confessionale*, 7, 99, fol. 14[5]a–b. Cf. *Statuta synodalia Lexouiensia*, "Speculum celebrantis," C2a; *Officiarium curatorum . . . Eduensis*, fol. 12b–14a.

[63] Winshemius, *Institutiones*, A2a. For Winshemius's contritionism and its relation to Gabriel Biel, see above, n. 17 and text.

on you the sacrament or ministry of absolution." Bartholomaeus uses this wordy restatement to deny the contritionist version of the meaning of absolution:

It does not mean, however, as some say, and incorrectly, "I absolve you, that is I show you to be absolved," because it would follow from this that in the sacraments of the New Law there is nothing more than a demonstration or signification, which is false, in that the sacraments of the New Law not only figure and signify like the sacraments of the Old Law, but also cause what they signify. Whence the priest, by virtue of the keys, absolves from mortal guilt, not principally, but as an instrument disposing to the infusion of grace through which there may be remission of guilt.[64]

This version of the efficacy of the Sacrament of Penance is evidently Thomistic. But its exact provenance, or even its exact theological meaning, is not important. What is striking about this and other statements about the proper words of absolution is the heightened consciousness of the intrinsic power of the sacrament. Even when the words of the priest are only "instrumental" causes, it is clear that they have a *causal* role, in some way independent of the work of the penitent. The priest does more than validate the forgiveness of God granted to the contrite man. The priest actually helps. For those who argue that absolution can raise attrition to contrition, or that absolution will work so long as the penitent does not hinder its action by actually intending to sin at the time, the priest does something very helpful indeed. But even for those who want to preserve the notion of an "instrumental" causality, the priest is said to play a role more meaningful than simply to certify that contrition has already wrought forgiveness.

This assertion of the power of the sacrament through a simple, declaratory formula—"I absolve you"—is the dominant trend. It should not allow us to forget, however, that the dominant trend, as evidenced in the majority of the practical manuals and summas for confessors, was not unanimous. Peter Lombard's brand of contritionism was not dead, as we have seen in the views of Raymond of Peñaforte, Bartholomaeus of Pisa, J. P. Foresti, and Hermannus de Schildis. To be sure, these authors were not pro-

[64] de Chaimis, *Interrogatorium*, IV, R2a.

posing their contritionism in the spirit of theological contention, and we could misinterpret them if we were to see here a reasoned rejection of Thomism or Scotism in the manner of a true theologian such as Gabriel Biel. Nevertheless, these authorities offer something different from those espousing the more pronounced versions of efficacy, and they serve to remind us that there was nothing like unanimity on the theory of the way the sacrament works.

In addition, differences in the all-important words of absolution further illustrate the range of variation possible in this literature and this thinking about justification. The extremely popular *Modus confitendi* of Andreas de Escobar is a good example. For in a series of appended sections, Bishop Andreas says he wants to offer ignorant confessors some helpful information. Thus he presents this formula:

> May our Lord Jesus Christ Himself, Who has full power of absolving you, absolve you . . . and by the authority committed to me . . . I absolve you from all your mortal, deadly, and venial sins that you have confessed to me. I also absolve you from all your forgotten sins of commission, omission, and neglect, as far as I can and ought; in virtue of the passion of our Lord Jesus Christ and in the name of the Father, the Son, and the Holy Spirit.[65]

This is exactly the kind of verbosity that Gerson was trying to root out, with one significant exception. For Andreas does not specify "sins for which you are contrite," and thus he avoids, in this maze of qualifications, the most serious and theologically pregnant qualification of all. Furthermore, the mood is indicative. Nevertheless, the formula is involuted. It lacks the confidence and simplicity of "I absolve you." And its conditional phrasing, "as far as I can and ought," might easily become one of those occasions for brooding that concerned the Consoling Doctor.

The *Angelica* is not even consistent in its formulas. Under

---

[65] Andreas de Escobar, *Modus confitendi*, B2b. Compare the formula of the *Alphabetum sacerdotum* (C. Iaumaur: [Paris, 1500?]), A2a, which is not so wordy but which is not Gerson's ideal: "Et dominus noster iesus christus per suam sanctam piisimam misericordiam te absoluat. Et ego te absoluo a sententia excommunicationis minoris si quam incurristi et ab omnibus peccatis tuis." Variations like this are common.

"Confession" Angelus subscribes to the simple "I absolve you from all your sins." Yet when he describes at the end of "Interrogations" the proper form for absolving the penitent, he repeats a formula almost as wordy as Andreas de Escobar's. Both, however, are in the indicative mood, and both are entirely consistent with his pronounced tendency to exalt the keys and the efficacy of the sacrament from the work worked. And while Angelus does not consider minor or even major deviations in the formula crucial, absolution has a real, causal role. Thus if Angelus's priestly reader could learn to absolve from "all your mortal, and venial, confessed, forgotten, and unknown sins, and their circumstances," he would also understand that these words did something real.

For this doctrine permeates the *Angelica*. We have already seen that Angelus endorses the doctrine that the Sacrament of Penance forgives sins just so long as the penitent does not place the obstacle of sin in the path of the grace the priest dispenses. Already, then, it is obvious that Angelus stands squarely with the mainstream of late medieval theology in exalting the power of the keys. And we shall now see that this power must be understood in its relationship to the institutional church founded by Christ.

To the question "whether confession frees from the guilt of sin," Angelus answers "yes." He begins by identifying the source of the sacrament's power: "Since therefore the sacraments are the immediate application of the passion of Christ to us, for this reason every guilt is blotted out through the mediation of the sacraments, exercised in fact or in wish (de facto exhibitis: vel in voto)." Now "penance" is a sacrament, and it is "received" in confession, because in confession "a man subjects himself to the ministers of the church, who are the dispensers of the sacraments." Angelus makes it abundantly clear, therefore, that it is submission to the visible church that insures forgiveness because this is the way Christ has chosen to dispense the grace of His forgiveness. It is thus a simple thing to assert that the combination of confession and the power of absolution remits guilt "unless a man places the obstacle of mortal sin in fact." Even when forgiveness is won through contrition, the power of the keys is evident, "because contrition has the desire of confession attached to it."[66] For remission of sin comes from Christ; and yet it comes only by way of these powerful, visible aids. Because these sacraments are

[66] *Angelica*, "Confessio sacramentalis," 8–13, 30; "Confessio 2," "Confessio 5," "Confessio 7," "Interrogationes."

powerful, they can console. They make up for human deficiencies by applying the merits of the passion of Jesus Christ to the unworthy repentance of sinners. To understand that conviction is to understand the basic premise of the thinking of the late medieval church on the forgiveness of sins, even in its contritionist form. For it is in the willing submission to ecclesiastical authority, entrusted with the power to dispense the grace of Christ, that the work of the penitent—fallen, flawed, and sinful though he is—becomes meritorious. It is this conviction, moreover, that allows us to evaluate the judgments so often made about medieval theology's doctrine of justification, that it was magical and that it displaced the saving grace of Christ.

CHRIST, FREEDOM, AND MAGIC

To the modern mind there is something suspiciously supernatural about the belief that words pronounced by a priest can work an inner change in people whose own inner resources have proven too weak to accomplish that change on their own. Yet we have seen that it was common teaching of medieval theology that if a penitent was only "attrite," the sacrament itself could in some way make him fully "contrite." We have seen that according to some it was even possible to be forgiven merely by not hindering the powerful action of absolution through the intention to sin. And although few subscribed to it, a logical extension of this mentality could hold that absolution produced, in an objective way, an "adornment of the soul" whose forgiving power might be hampered at the time by some dissimulation but which could take effect *after* confession and absolution once that dissimulation had "receded." Finally, in the very attention to the choice of words to absolve a penitent—the belief that complexities might make absolution less powerful—we seem to see the development of some kind of incantation in which the priest's words themselves govern what kind of magical effect will take place in the soul of the recipient.

At the same time, however, historians of the Reformation have often asserted that the Sacrament of Penance was a part of a doctrine of works, a new Pelagianism that emphasized human effort and merit and ignored the necessity of God's grace first, last, and always. Contrition, confession, and satisfaction, according to this criticism, emphasize the work of man and leave out the unique and necessary sacrifice by which Christ alone won forgiveness for sins.

Now both accusations cannot be true. If the emphasis is on magical aids dispensed indiscriminately by the priest, then there cannot be much meaning in the charge that the Sacrament of Penance overburdened the penitent by demanding too much of his free effort. On the other hand, if the penitent was in fact overtaxed and his own will made the center of the process of forgiveness, then there does not seem to be much room for magic. Indeed, if we look at the theory of the working of the sacrament in the context of the evolution of confession, we shall see that neither accusation is helpful for understanding the forgiveness of sins. There is evidence for both accusations. But historical understanding can come only from a total appreciation of the assumptions and attitudes that underlie an institution, a practice. To call it Pelagianism or magic misses the social functions of that institution—to discipline and console the faithful. The sacramentalism of the late middle ages focuses on the obligation to subject oneself to the ministers of the church, who are the proper dispensers of the saving grace of Christ.

By the early middle ages, private penance had confirmed the practice of deathbed reconciliation, in which a Christian "received" penance rather than performed it. But even in the system of the penitentials, *doing* penance was still a fundamental source of discipline and consolation. By the time of Abelard and Peter Lombard, however, inner sorrow was held up as the essential and primary part of forgiveness. The next obvious question, however (which was still being posed at the end of the fifteenth century), asked: If contrition forgives guilt, what do confession and absolution do? And while the contritionist answer might be, "Not very much," the weight of tradition and ecclesiastical authority determined that even for contritionists, confession to priests was indispensable. The papal commandment of 1215 to confess yearly simply confirmed this tradition of confessing to priests and led theologians, and therefore the writers on the practice of confession, to ask why it was necessary and how it made sense. The answers were varied, but all emphasized the unique role of the church in the offer of forgiveness. Even those who wanted to have contrition do virtually all the work still retained the necessity of confession to a priest: even if you never saw a priest, you had to *intend* to confess your sins to be contrite; even if the priest you saw only *declared* that your sins were already forgiven, his role was considered for some reason indispensable; even if forgiveness was wrought *before* sacramental confession, still that forgiveness was defined as sacramental. Indeed, it is precisely in the theory of the contritionists that we see, if not a magical action, at least a most mysterious role for the Sacrament of Penance. The followers of a strict interpretation of Peter Lombard (and Raymond of Peñaforte) are few, however. The dominant theme is the one that emphasizes the causality of absolution, the working of the Sacrament of Penance from the work itself—*ex opere operato*. And those who explain forgiveness and the Sacrament of Penance arrive at a solution that also tries to make sense out of all of these elements. Like the contritionists they try to arrive at some kind of balance between ecclesiastical intervention and internal preparation.

In this discussion, however, we must not forget that the explanation of what priest, penitent, and God do in forgiveness always had to operate within the bounds of the Augustinian theology of grace and freedom. The religious mind wants both free will and providence, Augustine had argued in the *City of God*, and this paradoxical desire still prevailed at the end of the middle ages. To them it was clear. To give up freedom meant giving up human responsibility, and no preacher, confessor, or moralist was willing to do that. To give up grace and providence meant giving up God, and that was even more clearly out of the question. To say that a man is guilty of sin and obligated to repent affirms human responsibility and saves us from fatalism. To say that fallen man cannot become contrite and forgiven on his own, but only through the sacrifice of Christ, saves us from pride. These are the assumptions that underlie medieval ecclesiology, sacramental theology, and even pastoral instruction.

The practical literature on sacramental confession brought these paradoxical ideas as close to earth as they were likely to come. And the institutions of forgiveness must be understood in the context of this Augustinian theology and its basic attitudes toward grace and effort. It would not be difficult to show, on the basis of what we have already described in these pages, that the practical literature on the forgiveness of sins demanded a great deal of human effort. Indeed, it would not be a distortion to say they wanted a worthy, and even *meritorious* preparation, repentance, confession, and amendment.[67] Yet even those who emphasized effort most—the contritionists—were always forced to admit that God alone forgives and that contrition itself is by definition a gift of God's grace. And it is in making it plainer where this grace comes from that we come down to earth, down to the traditional institutions of the visible, hierarchical, sacramental church. For the formulas that exalt the power of the keys and emphasize the automatic efficacy of a sacrament—"from the work worked"—are nothing more than ways to make grace sensible and comfort accessible. Medieval theology did not forget the corruption of man. Pastoral instruction did not exhort without holding out hope of mercy. And the real function of those elements misconceived as "magical" in sacramental theory is precisely to offer hope, mercy, grace, comfort, and, in short, a way to justification that weak and sinful men might believe possible. And what is the power of these sacraments? Nothing other than the grace of Christ.

The ritual of absolution itself is witness to this dependency on the grace of Christ. For while the only necessary words are, "I absolve you," or, "I absolve you from your sins," the normal usage is replete with references to the forgiveness of Christ and the role of His atonement. Deprecatory prayers invoking the mercy of God persist, as we have noted before, as constant reminders of the true cause of forgiveness. Johann Nider explains that the goods conferred on the contrite man are not given because of his sorrow but because of the merit of the passion of Christ. And J. L. Vivaldus reminds the reader of his *Golden Work of True Contrition* that God is, purely and simply, the cause of the forgiveness of sins. Those who adhere to a more strictly sacramental view of forgiveness also revert faithfully to the role of Christ. Only through the atonement can works of satisfaction be worthwhile; and only the power of the keys can apply the atonement to the works of men. It is a commonplace to urge penitents to go beyond their contrition and trust in the mercy of God, or hope in His willingness to pardon. It is a fundamental assumption of this whole literature that confession to priests was founded by Christ

[67] Thus [Poeniteas cito], *Confessionale pro scholasticis*, A1a–b, states that hope of beatitude must originate both in grace and merits: "Dicitur ex gratia et meritis propriis veniens. quod est contra illos qui ex sola gratia dei presumunt venire ad beatitudinem sine suis meritis. Nam dicit Augustinus. Qui creauit te sine te non iustificabit te sine te."

to mediate the grace and forgiveness of Christ. Indeed, we have already seen that the *Angelica* explicitly invokes it as a given when it says: "Since therefore the sacraments are the immediate application of the passion of Christ to us." And it is because this is such an accepted and usual assumption that John Eck's explanation of the form of absolution is so uncontroversial. For Eck the proper way to absolve is as follows:

> May Our Lord Jesus Christ mercifully deign to absolve you, and I, by His authority, which in His place I now enjoy, absolve you from the sentence of minor excommunication, and from all your sins, in the name of the Father, and of the Son, and of the Holy Spirit, Amen.

Eck does not think the imprecation to Christ or even the sign of the cross is necessary. But they clearly fit in with his notion of how the sacrament forgives. For he states simply: "In this form of the Sacrament of Penance sacramental grace is conferred, which the most bitter passion and death of Christ works efficaciously in the soul of the person absolved."[68]

The point of this explanation is not to defend late medieval pastoral instruction from the indictments of superstition or Pelagianism. It is not their Pauline or Augustinian purity that concerns us here. Rather we are trying to make sense out of attitudes, and assumptions, and patterns of behavior. We are trying

[68] Mausbach, "Katholische Katechismen," 122: "Die sittliche Vorbereitung des Sünders wird an keiner Stelle als 'Verdienst' bezeichnet; sie ist überhaupt weniger sein Werk, als ein Geschenk der Gnade, für welches er Gott danken muss. Um so weniger darf er das Ziel derselben, die Aussöhnung mit Gott, von der Anspannung seiner Kräfte erwarten; die Verzeihung und heiligmachende Gnade erhofft er allein von den Verdiensten Christi, die durch das Wort des Priesters ihm zugewendet werden." Similarly, N. Paulus's polemical articles on contrition assert that seventeen of the *Beichtschriften* explicitly direct believers to trust in God's forgiveness—"den Gläubigen dies Vertrauen zur Pflicht gemacht" ("Reue in den Beichtschriften," 35)—and seventeen of the devotional writings do the same—"das Vertrauen auf Gottes Barmherzigkeit anempfohlen wird" ("Reue in den Erbauungsschriften," 485). See also Schauerte, *Busslehre des Eck*, 191–192; Göttler, *Der Heilige Thomas*, 126–128; Nider, *Expositio decalogi*, III, 8D; *Angelica*, "Confessio 7"; Vivaldus, *Aureum opus*, fol. 5b, 9b; *Raymundina*, III, 34, 11, p. 446; Guido de Monte Rocherii, *Manipulus curatorum*, II, 2, 6; *Supplementum*, "Absolutio 6," "Contritio," 2; Andreas de Escobar, *Modus confitendi*, B2b; *Statuta synodalia Lexouiensia*, "Speculum celebrantis," C2a; Antoninus, *Confessionale—Defecerunt*, 48; Rosemondt, *Confessionale*, 7, 99, fol. 14[5]a–b.

to reconstruct a mentality that underlay a whole ecclesiastical regime. And it does no service to historical understanding to focus on one or another theological issue and forget the whole institutional setting in which forgiveness must be understood.

If we recall at this point the language of Luther's theology of the cross, we might be tempted to declare the allusions to Christ in ritual formulas, and the brief references to Him in explanations of sacramental forgiveness, superficial by comparison. Such a comparison would not, of course, be fair. It would expect medieval writers to anticipate and respond to challenges they never imagined possible. And it would look for literary qualities from books whose practical nature makes them unlikely rivals to those of a Luther. One final example from Gerson, however, may help make the reality of Christ's role in medieval sacramental thought more convincing. For in his attack on the flagellants, Gerson conveys succinctly and yet powerfully the belief that we find Christ and His gracious mercy in the sacraments of the visible church.

"The law of Christ is called the law of love," Gerson declares. It is wrong to encumber it with servile burdens. Indeed, the more a law is iniquitous and subservient to demonic powers, the more it will be harsh and cruel. In simple, dramatic language he protests: "But Christ wanted to save us mercifully, through His blood, shed but once." And he identifies Christ's law of love with the sacraments, and especially the Sacrament of Penance, whose consolations are guaranteed in scholastic definitions:

> The law of Christ derives its greatest strength from His mercy and grace—and the vessels of that grace are the sacraments of the New Law, from the power of the work worked. Thus whoever shuns the sacraments, especially the Sacrament of Confession, should be firmly rejected. Experience abundantly proves, however, that the flagellants do not bother with the Sacrament of Confession, or Penance, saying that their flagellation is more powerful for blotting out sins than any confession.[69]

[69] Gerson, *Tractatus contra sectam flagellantium*, Du Pin, II, 660–664. "Lex Christi dicitur Lex amoris. . . . Et inde culpat eos qui servilibus eam premunt oneribus" (660A). "Lex aliqua quanto est iniquior, et daemoniis obsequentior, tanto semper invenitur crudelior et amarior . . . Christus autem ex gratia sua voluit nos misericorditer salvare per sanguinem suum semel effusum" (660C). "Lex Christi maximam sortitur virtutem ex misericordia, et gratia sua, *cujus gratiae vasa sunt Sacramenta Novae Legis ex virtute operis operati*, et ideo

Thus the very harshness of the flagellants' teaching is a sign of its error. Christ's law is not cruel. It is characterized by love, grace, mercy, and forgiveness, which flow to men through the sacraments. And Gerson, the most articulate theologian in this literature, can find no better way to express the power of sacramental confession to mediate Christ's sacrifice than to assert its efficacy *ex opere operato*!

Thus we find that common sense and a sense of mystery came together in the theories about how the Sacrament of Penance works. Authorities on forgiveness addressed themselves to practical questions. They tried to give simple answers that would serve penitents. Definitions of sorrow and speculation on the power of the keys could be put in straightforward, uncomplicated language and applied to ordinary experience. Even scholastic terminology could provide a framework in which practical problems were solved. At the same time, however, there were enough theological differences and conceptual obscurities to ensure that the process of justification would remain mysterious. Theories of forgiveness could not proclaim certain solutions to all problems because they had to work with intangible substances—the sorrow of the penitent, the power of the keys, and the grace of Christ. To admit this does not deny the practical value of theories of forgiveness, which provided the necessary intellectual systems for pastoral activity to be effective—for discipline and consolation to be effective. Nor do we deny the practical value of theories when we assert that the most important result of all theorizing was to translate these intangible substances into the same human experience: a penitent prepared himself, went to a priest and told his sins, heard himself absolved, and undertook some penitential exercises. The unity between these theories and this practice is the basis of institutionalized forgiveness: it allows us to claim that there is a shared mentality that transcends differences in sacramental theory.

In other words, after we examine explanations of how the Sacrament of Penance works, we must return to where we began —the necessity of a sincere and complete confession to a priest.

---

quicquid avertit a Sacramentis suscipiendis, praesertim a *Sacramento Confessionis*, debet rejici fideliter. Constat autem per experientiam in multis, quod taliter se flagellantes non curant de Sacramento Confessionis, vel Poenitentiae Sacramentalis, dicentes, quod haec flagellatio potior est ad delendum peccata, quam quaecunque Confessio" (66oD, italics added).

Theological explanations are relevant, especially because of their pronounced tendency to make the confessional surer and safer; *but all the theories send people to priests to get forgiveness*, even when the power of the keys is not made clear. The best illustration of this truism is literally an illustration—to one of the editions of Stephan Lanzkranna's *Himmelstrasse*, or *Heavenly Road*. A somber foreword, explaining the purpose of the book, begins with this admonition:

> The Heavenly Road (which all men must travel who want to go to heaven) is so hidden that there are few who find it. There are also few who get to heaven. . . .

On the page facing these words is a woodcut depicting a road winding from the earth up through the clouds, with angels helping travelers along the way.[70] At the end of the road is a little doorway-like hole through the clouds. It is the entrance to heaven. At the beginning of the road, on earth, is a priest hearing confession. Some theories of how the Sacrament of Penance works could explain cogently what he was doing there. But virtually everyone would have agreed that he belonged there.

Restrictions on the Working of the Sacrament of Penance

The theory of how the Sacrament of Penance forgives guilt talks in universalistic terms about God's grace, the penitent's contrition and confession, and the priest's absolution. It is abstract language, appropriate to the task. For even this practical literature must resort to theological concepts if it is to explain how divine and human activity are united in a rite that, if done correctly, is necessarily efficacious. Thus theological abstractions become psychologically useful. Confidence in forgiveness, no matter what version of the theology of justification lies at the root of it, comes from the all-inclusive dogmatic claims for contrition, confession, and absolution. Every theological system that explains how men are forgiven inevitably insists that what is done properly here on earth, in the visible church, is also done in heaven. Ecclesiastical forgiveness is valid in God's eyes, and that belief is a principle source of consolation.

Such grand claims would seem to place the Sacrament of Penance and the forgiveness of the repentant sinner above legalistic

[70] Stephan Lanzkranna, *Himelstrass* (Augsburg, 1510).

impediments; but this was not the case. For the teaching on forgiveness at the end of the middle ages betrays its origins. It was the product of a complex historical development, and hence it remained embedded in the institutional structure of the medieval church that created it. Consequently, the working of the sacrament, so absolutely and universally defined in theology, remained subject to significant and in some ways incapacitating restrictions in practice. Some people—the excommunicated—and some sins —those that were "reserved" to a higher ecclesiastical authority —could not be absolved by an ordinary priest. There might also be conditions—in the form of penances or in the requirement of payment of damages to injured parties—that could hinder this earthly quest for forgiveness from becoming divinely valid.

EXCOMMUNICATION

Raymond of Peñaforte, patron saint of canon lawyers and originator of the summa for confessors, provided the literature of the forgiveness of sins with a learned, orderly, and authoritative discussion of excommunication. After telling his reader that the subject is "highly useful and necessary" and promising to reveal all the essentials about it, he offers this simple definition: "excommunication is separation from any communion or legitimate activity." The first excommunication, he thinks, occurred after the Fall, when God forbade Adam to eat from the tree of life. In the thirteenth century, however, cases for excommunication were less poetic and more precise, and Raymond hastens to bring us up to date. Varieties of excommunication are infinite, he states, because there are or could be as many kinds of excommunication as there are kinds of communion. Nevertheless he simplifies them according to the standard distinction between minor excommunication, which only separates from the sacraments, and major excommunication or anathema, which separates from the sacraments, entrance into the church, and all commerce with the faithful. Another key to the understanding of the use of this ecclesiastical punishment is the distinction between excommunications incurred simply by the fact of committing some specifically forbidden transgression (excommunicatio latae sententiae), and excommunications that emanate from some competent ecclesiastical judge and are directed at specific persons or groups of people (excommunicatio ferendae sententiae). Raymond enumerates seventeen cases of major excommunication emanating from a judge, and many cases of minor excommunication (both *latae* and *ferendae sententiae*). Ecclesiastical censures occupy a whole chapter of Book III of the *Raymundina*, which discusses, in fifty-nine articles and over fifty pages, the intricate rules and exceptions by which ecclesiastical authority bound and loosed men judicially: before society, the Catholic Church, and God Himself.[1]

Excommunication is the most awesome weapon in the arsenal of hierarchical discipline. The history of its development and use lies outside the scope of this study, although we should note that evidence from local history shows that the incidence of excommunication was astonishingly high.[2] In practice and theory it was an essential sanction, and thus it had to be of the greatest concern for confessors and their advisers, who tried to ensure its effectiveness by incorporating the teachings of canonists like Raymond of Peñaforte into their manuals and summas. To the modern mind excommunication may look like a social or quasi-political instrument—a primarily public censure that operates in the external forum alone. But to those who submit to the authority of the Roman Catholic Church, its most profound effects are felt in the forum of conscience. The hierarchy binds the faithful in heaven as well as on earth, a claim that is solemnly publicized by the ringing of bells and the extinction of candles, and poignantly symbolized by the refusal to bury those who die excommunicate in holy ground. And thus excommunication produces guilt—judicial, theological, and psychological—and its religious attendant, fear of eternal damnation. For the working of the Sacrament of Penance it takes on special significance because it hedges the forgiveness dispensed by priests with complicated exceptions. The multiplication of censures and excommunications remained a troublesome problem for ecclesiastical reformers from the time of the Great Schism to the Council of Trent. From the fourteenth century on a simple priest could not absolve from an excommunication *latae sententiae*. Furthermore, it had always been a general rule that only the authority who issued an excommunication *ferendae sententiae* could lift it. In other words, ordinary

[1] *Raymundina*, III, 33, pp. 381–436, and especially a. 9–10, p. 386, and a. 18–26, pp. 396–406, for the definitions and rules concerning absolution.
[2] Toussaert, *Le Sentiment religieux*, 110–113, 435–446; cf. Falk, *Florentius Diel*, 42, 44–46, 50; Tibus, *Die Jakobipfarre*, 16, 18, 21, 26–27, 30, 72–73, 78–79, 88 (although Tibus tries to de-emphasize it).

confessors could not validly absolve some excommunicated members of their flock. Thus canon law, and therefore the literature on forgiveness, defines a whole range of disciplinary powers, enjoyed in particular by bishops and popes, that restrict the effectiveness of the keys held by a simple priest. Nowhere is that kind of restriction more painstakingly spelled out, moreover, than in those passages of the manuals and summas for confessors that enumerate the sins that priests without special powers may not absolve: cases "reserved" to bishops and cases "reserved" to the pope.[3]

RESERVED CASES

If a sin is reserved to a bishop or the pope, then an ordinary priest who hears it confessed to him may not absolve it. Instead he must find a way for the penitent to be forgiven through the office of someone with papal or episcopal powers. Part of the problem posed by reserved cases, therefore, stemmed from the annoyance of managing an extra confession to someone with proper authority. This problem was further complicated by the familiar principle that a valid confession could not be divided: that is, one was supposed to tell *all* one's sins to the same priest. How to preserve the rights of prelates, the principle of confessing to one's own priest, and the "integrity" of confession is the subject of some discussion.[4]

The typicial solutions to the problem betray an unwillingness to protest on serious theological grounds. In the *Opus tripartitum*, Gerson tells the confessor to send a penitent who has committed a reserved sin to a higher authority. He allows that authority to hear only the reserved sins—the rest may be confessed to the ordinary pastor—even though his advice ignores the objections he raises elsewhere to such a threat to the integrity of confes-

---

[3] Willibald Plöchl, *Geschichte des Kirchenrechts. Band II. Das Kirchenrecht der abendländischen Christenheit 1055 bis 1517* (Vienna and Munich, 1955), 329–354, esp. 336, 339–341, and 346–349; Gabriel Le Bras, *Institutions ecclésiastiques*, part 1, 246–248; T. Ortolan, "Censures ecclésiastiques," *DTC*, 2², 2113–2136; E. Valton, "Excommunication," *DTC*, 5², 1734–1744; A. Bride, "Réserve, Cas réservés," *DTC*, 13², 2441–2461; Edward V. Dargin, *Reserved Cases According to the Code of Canon Law*, Catholic University of America, Dissertation in Canon Law (Washington, D.C., 1924), 7–9; H. C. Lea, *History of Auricular Confession*, I, 312–346.

[4] H. C. Lea, *History of Auricular Confession*, I, 329–332; Stanka, *Die Summa des Berthold*, 34–35.

sion.[5] In a more detailed discussion Antoninus of Florence considers whether it is better for the confessor to send the penitent to the bishop or take a more active role himself. If the penitent is a simple person and does not know how to confess his sin, then the confessor should give the penitent a written explanation that he can take with him to the higher authority. In such a case the higher authority may absolve or else send the penitent back to the curate. But Antoninus thinks it is best for the confessor (if he can and wants to) to go to the bishop or his vicar personally to get the power to absolve the penitent.[6] That is also the opinion of Bartholomaeus de Chaimis, who differs only in the greater attention he gives to a defense against the charge that this practice divides confession.[7] And the voluminous *Sylvestrina* is even more insistent that no serious problem exists. Sylvester seems to believe that the role of the superior authority is juridical rather than sacramental.[8]

If sacramental confession had been as legalistic as some of its critics have charged, then the problem of reservations and a divided confession would have been examined more methodically. In fact, solutions tend to be mechanical. Even those who worry about integrity routinely accept the customary expedients as correct and legitimate. But reservations caused pastoral problems considerably more serious than the theoretical danger of a divided confession; and it was their threat to the consolation of the sacrament that stirred debate.

Andreas de Escobar and Jean Gerson had much in common. They were learned, influential, and fundamentally conservative churchmen. Both lived at the time of the Great Schism; but their influence endured through their books, including works on confession, into the sixteenth century. Yet as authorities on pastoral care they are often at odds; and on the question of reserved cases they took diametrically opposed positions. Andreas, the dutiful canonist, apparently collected all the cases he could find

[5] Gerson, *Opus tripartitum*, I, 17, and II, Du Pin, I, 441A, 446B.

[6] Antoninus, *Confessionale—Defecerunt*, I, 48.

[7] Bartholomaeus de Chaimis, *Confessionale*, IV, X8a. The *Angelica* ("Confessio 5," 9) agrees with Bartholomaeus that the higher authority only perfects the whole confession of the lower priest, and therefore it is proper for the ordinary priest to hear everything, absolve what he can, and send the penitent off to get absolved for the rest.

[8] *Sylvestrina*, "Confessio 1," q. 19, par. 20.

and put them in his *Lumen confessorum*. This list of reservations was one of the parts of that manual which were printed separately in the fifteenth century—this section under the title *Confessio generalis et casus penitentiales*. In it Andreas does not even hint that there might be something wrong with the practice he is describing. Gerson, on the other hand, severely criticizes the custom of reserving absolution of certain sins to higher authorities. The contrast between them typifies the two tendencies in penitential theory and practice—Andreas upholding the disciplinary function, Gerson laboring for the consolation of penitents.

Andreas finds twenty cases reserved to the papacy and their nature and variety suggest a great deal about how such prerogatives were accumulated.[9] Crimes against the person of clergy and the property and authority of the church are the oldest and most understandable cases in which the papacy required transgressors to go to Rome or a papal penitentiary. This kind of crime receives a prominent place in Andreas's list: striking clerics; burning down churches; associating with those under papal excommunication; falsifying papal letters; violating religious vows and obligations; and failing to protect those who carry letters of excommunication. There are other papal cases whose peculiar nature seems to indicate their origins in specific historical incidents. Thus among the sinners who need papal forgiveness are those who burn or boil a corpse to transfer the bones; inquisitors who, defying justice and their consciences, fail to persecute heretics; people who aid the Saracens in the Holy Land; pirates especially excommunicated by the pope; and any great secular power— from Emperor to count—who gets himself or a close relative into the government of the city of Rome without the pope's permission. The array is broad and the difficulty of finding someone with papal powers of absolution must have been worse than in-

---

[9] [Andreas de Escobar], *Modus confitendi. . . . Casus papales et episcopales*, "Casus papales," E2a–E3b. A mnemonic verse summarizes (with considerably greater brevity) the cases reserved to the Holy See: "Per papam clerum feriens: falsarius; vrens / Soluitur & quisquis audet cantare ligatus / Symon que fuerit; nec fallit regula talis." Special exemptions from the obligation to confess to someone with papal powers are also in a little verse: "Percutiens clerum Romam petat. Excipiuntur / Ut puer: atque senex; egrotus: femina: pauper. / Et claustralis habens inimicos et hostia seruans." The *Sylvestrina*, "Casus," q. 1, par. 1–2, enumerates no less than fifty papal cases, but most have to do with matters of legal jurisdiction over the clergy and other legal prerogatives.

convenient for such sinners. But when we turn to the episcopal cases, we realize that strict observance of Andreas's list would have created a tangle of complications for the Sacrament of Penance far worse than the papal reservations.

There are forty items in Andreas's list of episcopal cases, and we can put them into a few broad categories. Most numerous are crimes involving ecclesiastical authority or holy objects, obligations, and persons: theft or misuse of sacred things; baptizing or standing for one's own children; simony; various sins committed by clerics; clerical irregularity; violations of the liberties and immunities of the church; improper celebration of the mass (neglecting to have correct vestments or a consecrated altar, or not fasting); and various acts related to episcopal excommunication, including the burying of an excommunicate in sacred ground. Sexual sins are the next most numerous category reserved to the bishop, and these include carnal relations with a religious; deflowering a virgin; sexual intercourse with Jewish or Saracen women; sins against nature—sodomy, bestiality, and unnatural intercourse; incest; and sexual relations by a priest with someone he has baptized or confessed. Offenses involving marriage vows are also prominent: leaving a valid, consummated marriage to enter the religious life without the consent of the spouse; installing the offspring of an adulterous union in the place of the legitimate heir; marrying someone after betrothal to another; contracting a clandestine marriage; and marrying after taking a vow of celibacy. Many crimes of violence are also reserved to bishops: accidental assault on one's parents (if it is intentional, Andreas wants to send it to the pope); plotting the death of one's spouse; homicide of any sort; and infanticide—whether intentionally or through negligence. Finally, bishops reserve public usury and failure to make restitution, notorious slander and blasphemy, perjury, and sorcery.[10]

Given Andreas's enormous list of cases reserved to higher authorities, it is little wonder that Jean Gerson protested. The Con-

---

[10] [Andreas de Escobar], *Casus papales et episcopales*, E3b–E4b. Andreas does not include in this extensive list adultery and masturbation—conceivably because he was thinking of the customs of Spain and Italy rather than France. This omission should not lead us to suspect the reliability of Gerson (see below, n. 12 and text), who must have known what he was talking about when he complained about the custom of reserving those sins to the bishop. Cf. Lea, *History of Auricular Confession*, I, 315 n.

soling Doctor was devoted to pastoral care, and he saw clearly the potential harm to conscience this legalistic thicket contained. Thus in at least five different places he called for reform.

Gerson's "On the Power of Absolving and How It Might Be Expedient for the Reservations of Sins to Be Changed" sets out expressly to eliminate inappropriate uses of the reservation of sins. Many sins presently under episcopal jurisdiction could be granted to simple curates, he argues. Among these are all purely secret sins that give no chance of scandal—especially when there is little hope for correction—because in these the sinner usually proves reluctant to seek a prelate and expose himself to that kind of notoriety. When someone is excommunicated by name, absolution can reasonably be reserved to a superior; but excommunication incurred automatically by committing some sin, where an individual is not publicly identified, could be left to ordinary priests. Sexual sins, especially in adolescents, need not be reserved, although Gerson thinks bestiality can profitably be so. Cases involving the breaking of slight vows or making small restitution should not be sent to prelates, although Gerson is willing to see notorious cheaters and usurers forced to seek absolution from a higher authority. Finally, a whole host of minor instances of serious transgressions could be given to curates: hidden heresy; lightly taken blasphemy; daily, not judicial, perjury; harmless sorcery; trivial sacrilege; offenses against parents that do not involve actual attack; and accidental abortion, especially if it remains secret. Scandalous cases that offend the church and the community might easily be known and justifiably reserved to prelates. But the reform he calls for would represent a great improvement on present practice, if only because it would allow penitents to confess all their sins to one man, thus preserving the unity of confession.[11]

Gerson takes up an even more systematic attack in a letter to a bishop written some time before 1408. He begins almost threateningly: "With respect to the forum of conscience, authority in reserved cases (or any other power) has been given to prelates for building not destroying the church, and for the sake of Christian people and their salvation." It has become absolutely clear to some experienced confessors, however, that the strict observance of these reservations, "especially in the more serious

[11] Gerson, "Super Absolvendi potestate, et qualiter expediat fieri reservationem peccatorum," Du Pin, II, 413–414.

hidden kinds of sins of the flesh," actually prevents the confession of such sins by girls, boys, bashful women, and rural simpletons, "from whom the confession of such sins can barely be dragged out, no matter how painstaking, humble, patient, and discreet the confessor may be." Experience shows that all of these people stand in horror of being sent to a prelate or penitentiary, and that no number of penitentiaries in any diocese would solve the problem such cases present. What good does it do, then, to increase the shame and burdens of penitents because of these sins? The difficulties that arise are "so great it can scarcely be believed." The original purpose of reservations, deterrence from certain kinds of sins, is in no way served here, for the sinner can hide this kind of sin from the bishop or anyone else as long as he wants to. And although the ultimate punishment is damnation, reserving the sin does not stop people from committing it, but only deters them from going to confession. Women suffer in particular because they dislike the notoriety of seeking a special confessor. Another old excuse for reservations was that they allowed the use of more severe penances, which only a higher ecclesiastical authority could impose. But now that justification will not hold either, since the penitent need not accept a penance against his will. Thus Gerson implores the bishop to intercede and warns, in language reminiscent of Christ's condemnation of the Pharisees, against closing the kingdom of heaven to the flock of Christ and imposing heavy burdens on weak shoulders. Gerson cannot sustain this adamant tone, however, and he ends not with a threat but a plea: if all hidden sins cannot be turned over to the curates, at least those of the young, especially under fourteen, could be. But, he concludes, the need for reform is urgent.[12]

[12] Gerson, Letter to a Bishop, Glorieux, II, 90–93 (Du Pin, II, 415A–C). Karl Rahner, "Forgotten Truths Concerning the Sacrament of Penance," *Theological Investigations*, II, 140–153, discusses the persistence of *public* elements in modern private penance. He argues that the unforgiven sinner remains publicly "bound," and even must declare that condition by openly seeking a priest-confessor to "loose" him. These public elements of penance would have been even more pronounced in the late middle ages, because people confessed in an open place in the church. But in neither the medieval nor the modern practice is it thought desirable to publicize the exact nature of a penitent's sins. And for Gerson one practical consequence of reservations was precisely that—leading people to suspect those who sought priests with higher powers of having committed enormous sins (and perhaps giving them a hint as to exactly what the sins were).

And that is also the lesson of the "Sermon on the Office of Pastor." The call is plain—"Let the reservation of cases or sins be made more moderate"—and there is a sense of urgency in his conclusion—"it is expedient to relinquish power over hidden sins quickly and easily to curates and ordinaries." The grounds are familiar. Youths under fourteen have bad judgment and little capacity to resist temptation; but they are unlikely to confess their weaknesses to strangers. Special consideration must also be given to the shame and reputation of women who fear that their husbands or parents will suspect them if they are sent so secretly, so far away, and so often to confessors with higher powers.[13]

We can see in this critique of reservations how far the best thinking on pastoral care wanted to preserve the privacy of the penitent. Sending an adulterous wife on a journey to find a priest with adequate power to forgive her is, in an oblique way, a revelation of her sin, a public confession. And the journey itself might be said to constitute a public penance. Now it is not inconsistent with late medieval discipline to impose public penalties: excommunication is a good example. The principle "public penance for public sins" similarly confirms the practice of holding up certain notorious sinners to the disapproval of church and community. Gerson himself asserts in the "Sermon on the Office of Pastor": "We are not talking about public sins." But Gerson, while he may have approved of the public exercise of ecclesiastical discipline where he thought it would do some good, was a consistent defender of the privacy of the confessional. And one of his objections to reserved cases was that sending a penitent to a distant confessor violated that privacy.

Twenty years later Gerson was still writing against reservations, this time in criticism of a Carthusian statute, the wording of which aptly illustrates the uncertainty about priestly absolution that could arise from reserved cases. The statute in question reads:

> Let those charged with hearing confessions not absolve from mortal sin certainly, but rather let them send the penitent to his superior.

The Carthusians may have retained this rule to keep the order as free from the need to reform as their reputation boasted. Good Carthusians are not supposed to commit mortal sins (how

---

[13] Gerson, "Sermo de officio pastoris," Glorieux, V, 141.

broadly the authors of this statute had defined mortal sin is not evident), and when it happens the superiors are supposed to know. Do we not have here a memory of an older discipline, taking us back to the purity of the ancient church? Gerson's extraordinary pastoral insight leads him to precisely the opposite conclusion: "It does not appear that such a reservation is appropriate or consistent with *evangelical liberty*"! Gerson wants reservations only for the most serious sins, even for the ascetic Carthusians. He is especially insistent that such sins be specified, as they are not in the statute under discussion. If these reforms were introduced, he concludes, then the statute and along with it the honor of the fathers of the rules would be salvaged. But once again he echoes Christ's admonition to the Pharisees as he hopes that sinners will be spared "an insupportable yoke on their necks."[14]

Given Gerson's consistent opposition to the abusive reservation of sins, it is somewhat difficult to understand why the *Opus tripartitum*, his most influential guide for the cure of souls, merely implies his criticisms in only one sentence. At the end of the first part, the discussion of the Ten Commandments, Gerson gives this counsel to confessors: "In cases reserved for absolution to the bishop or a superior, however, let the lower priest send the penitent to a prelate or superior able to absolve him; unless perchance there might be imminent danger of death to the penitent, or some great scandal might arise from it, or one might fear, with a probable conjecture, that it would lead to revelation of the sin." He does not then specifically instruct priests to give absolution in such cases; but the description of these cases of necessity more than suggests that priests should take charge of the situation and give absolution. Nevertheless the encouragement for this course of action is not unmistakable. The impression of a more conservative stance on this issue is reinforced, moreover, by the standard treatment of reserved cases in Part Two of the *Opus tripartitum*, "On Confession." There Gerson emphasizes, not the abuse or the exceptions, but the list itself. He begins by asserting the regulation that a simple priest cannot absolve many serious sins unless he has received special powers. The list of such sins is extensive: sorcery committed with holy objects; sacrilegious theft, of holy things or in a holy place; assault on a

[14] Gerson, "De Statuto ordinis Carthusiensis de reservatione peccatorum," Du Pin, II, 460–462; see Glorieux, I, 49; II, 310–311, 321–322.

cleric; simony; heresy; transgressions incurring automatic excommunication; homicide; striking one's parents; perjury in a public trial; notorious adultery; rape; deflowering; seducing a nun; incest within the fourth degree; breaking of vows; infanticide; and, most predictably, sins against nature. The latter are excoriated in particular as "abominable" and "the filthiest" sins, so serious that they are "worse than eating meat on Good Friday." The treatment of sins against nature is especially significant, because we know that Gerson had already raised objections to reservation of masturbation, particularly for adolescents. Nevertheless, he leaves no doubt about what he means, for he specifically condemns the whole gamut of unnatural vice, "whether it be perpetrated on oneself, by masturbation; or whether it is committed with another person of the same sex; or with another person of the opposite sex but in members other than those that nature designates for generation; or finally if it is perpetrated on another species." Gerson's treatment is frank and he concludes his condemnation of unnatural vice by warning that "a sinner is required to confess them explicitly under pain of eternal damnation." Thus Part Two of the *Opus tripartitum* gives pastors a conservative teaching on reservations. Even the exceptions of Part One are gone. Only specification of "notorious" adultery and "judicial" perjury imply his objections to reservation of hidden sins. And he has not raised his usual complaint that the power to absolve secret sins, especially the case of adolescent masturbation, should be given to every curate. On the contrary, he has loudly condemned all sins against nature, admitted episcopal jurisdiction over them, and threatened those who do not confess them—to, we must assume, someone with episcopal powers—with eternal damnation.[15]

Yet Gerson's hesitancy is perhaps explicable. The *Opus tripartitum* follows the safe path because it was designed for wide dissemination, and this would not have been the place to stir up doubts about ecclesiastical authority. Thus even Jean Gerson could not in conscience assault the hierarchy's prerogatives in so popular a work. Indeed, given the intensely cautious nature of this literature, one might easily conclude that those three exceptions to the observance of reserved cases in Part One—danger of death, scandal, and revelation of sin—are in fact a rather bold interpolation. Still, they are not a cry for reform. And we learn

---

[15] Gerson, *Opus tripartitum*, I, 17, and II, Du Pin, I, 441A, 445D–446A.

from the *Opus tripartitum* that the function of discipline could hang on with tenacity in the matter of reserved cases, no matter what the sentiments of a consoling pastor might have favored.

If Gerson's teaching betrays some ambivalence, the instruction that confessors generally received on reserved cases tended, naturally, to be even more conservative. The evidence is overwhelming that the hierarchy, despite the complaints of some reform-minded authorities, tried to preserve and publicize cases reserved to themselves. Bishops and pastoral theologians alike found reinforcement for the reservation of sins in a bull of Benedict XI defining nine cases universally retained by bishops. Five are said to be reserved according to "custom": voluntary homicide or mutilation; forgery and perjury; violation of ecclesiastical liberty; sacrilegious violations of ecclesiastical immunities; and sorcery and divination. Four are reserved according to "law": sins leading to clerical irregularity; arson; sins incurring solemn penance; and major excommunications. And although another set of bulls gave special powers to the mendicants, the reality of reserved cases is everywhere in medieval history. They were so familiar that Chaucer, in the prologue to *Canterbury Tales*, could refer to the Friar's special powers of absolution as if the existence of reservations was common knowledge.[16] They are almost always discussed in the manuals and summas for confessors; indeed, all of those dioceses that used the *Opus tripartitum* as a standard priest's manual would obviously have a simple means of disseminating this information. Furthermore, church councils of

---

[16] *Sylvestrina*, "Casus," q. 2–5, par. 3–5: "Quarto, queritur, quot sunt casus episcopales de consuetudine. Et dico quod innumerabiles, loquendo de consuetudine speciali diuersarum diocesum . . . : sed loquendo de consuetudine generali, secundus Sum Ang. consuetudo nulla est: cum episcopi aloquando plus, aliquando minus sibi reseruent: sed loquitur contra alias Summistas sui ordinis: vt Ros. et Sup. et contra veritatem: quia idem Benedictus in eadem extrauaganti declaruit quod sunt quinque qui scilicet vbique vel quasi episcopis semper reseruantur: licet iis aliquando addant plures, aliquando pauciores." Chaucer's friar is not a model of the good shepherd, and this fact makes his special powers especially inappropriate: "Ful wel biloved and famulier was he / With frankeleyns over al in his contree, / And eek with worthy wommen of the toun; / For he hadde power of confessioun / As seyde hymself, moore than a curat, / For of his ordre he was licenciat. /" *The Complete Works of Geoffrey Chaucer*, ed. by Fred N. Robinson (Boston, 1933), *Canterbury Tales*, "General Prologue—Frere," p. 21, lines 215–220. His popularity with "worthy wommen of the toun" may be a reference to the power to absolve adultery.

every description supported the determination of prelates to maintain this kind of control over the community of the faithful.

The Statutes of the Synod of Lisieux of 1448 are a typical example of the attempt to require pastors to use the pulpit to supplement the confessional as a means of binding conscience and behavior to a stricter adherence to the law. The tone of this synodal directive is entirely consistent with that objective:

> We command and enjoin all priests holding the cure of souls that every Sunday and feast day in the sermons of their churches they themselves declare excommunicated—openly, publicly, and loudly—all usurers, superstitious diviners, and sorcerers.

Curates and chaplains are furthermore to make lists of all their parishioners who have been excommunicated no matter by whom, and denounce them publicly on Sundays and feast days until they get written, sealed proof of their absolution. In the same spirit the statutes demand that everyone observe the reservation of cases.

> For we have learned that many priests, secular as well as regular, having no special faculty in this matter, do not respect in fact that they may not lawfully absolve in the cases reserved to us by law or custom, which holds sure peril for souls. For that reason we strictly order them to abstain from such practices in the future unless it is a case of imminent death. In that case they should enjoin those whom they absolve from such sins that, if it should happen that they recover from the sickness they now suffer from, they present themselves as soon as they can before us or our penitentiary to seek the grace (beneficium) of absolution for the said reserved cases.

The bishop wants a kind of control he thinks he cannot get through the normal functioning of the confessional. That seems to be the assumption, at any rate, that makes him eager to reinforce his limitations on the absolution of parish priests. Thus the statutes of Lisieux make it clear that the full range of disciplinary prerogatives—including reservations—must be observed in practice. They declare in no uncertain terms, moreover, that the forgiveness of the sacrament is not valid for reserved cases when they talk threateningly about "sure peril for souls." That parishioners may not plead ignorance, the statutes continue, pastors are ordered to explain *every Sunday in Lent* mortal sins, their aggravating circumstances, and reserved cases; and they should admonish those who feel culpable of any reserved sins to seek a proper remedy quickly.[17]

The statutes of Lisieux, in their tone and meaning, comport well with the spirit of the canon lawyers who simply and mechanically assert the law. Andreas de Escobar would have understood this language perfectly and probably have believed such regulations were really valuable in leading men to salvation by rooting out vices that were too serious to be left to the parish clergy.

Now it is true that not all the authorities on forgiveness support the practice of reservations with the determination of the Synod of Lisieux or the complacency of Andreas de Escobar. Some summas and manuals, for example, are content merely to enumerate the nine cases of Benedict XI. Nevertheless it is common to find authors in the position of Gerson, objecting to the current practice of reservations yet feeling obliged to defend the rights of the bishops. Thus even Antoninus of Florence, despite some hesitancy, accepts the legitimacy of the plethora of reservations.

The *Confessionale—Defecerunt* has a long discussion of the obligations and rights of the mendicants, and Antoninus is unmistakably sensitive to the dangers of keeping absolution of certain sins both from the mendicants and from ordinary parish priests. On the authority of Durandus, Antoninus insists that there are only two legitimate justifications for reserving sins: first, when certain priests are deprived of powers on account of their own conduct; second, when reserving a case will result in a benefit to the whole community. Nevertheless, Antoninus offers his readers an extensive list of sins commonly reserved to bishops. For in addition to the nine cases of Benedict XI, he gives an impressive variety of other sins, including some of Andreas de Escobar's more unusual examples.[18]

On the other hand, Antonius de Butrio, writing with the

[17] *Manuale secundum usum lexouiensem*, "1448 Precepta syn. Lexoviensis," A2b–A3a.

[18] Antoninus, *Confessionale—Defecerunt*, 3. The expanded version of the *Defecerunt* (Flach: Strasbourg, 1499) notes at the end of the discussion of the Sixth Commandment that synodal constitutions reserve sacrilege, incest, and sometimes sodomy and bestiality; confessors are accordingly advised to find out the custom of the diocese they are visiting.

"advice of modern wise men," has a somewhat bolder view of the extent of reservations. He, unlike Antoninus of Florence, gives a limited list and emphasizes throughout the public nature of the sins for which a confessor must send a penitent to a higher authority. De Butrio identifies "manifest" adulterers, murderers, and usurers, and those guilty of "public" blasphemy. Even in the case of sodomy, de Butrio thinks that an ordinary priest can absolve it if the vice is hidden. And only intentional, not accidental, abortion and infanticide are reserved to the bishop.[19] Thus with these simple yet uncompromising qualifications, Antonius de Butrio does much to meet the criticisms of Gerson. Indeed, de Butrio's manual is superior in this respect to the *Opus tripartitum*.

Godescalc Rosemondt also follows Gerson in his criticisms of the abuse of ecclesiastical authority. His discussion of papal and episcopal cases comes at the end of the section "On Excommunication," in which he attacks the "ill-advised and dangerous" multiplication of censures and invokes the authority of Gerson to call for the express revocation of all obsolete and harmful excommunications. He continues this protest against the abuse of ecclesiastical authority when he turns to reserved cases. For while he gives a fairly substantial list of episcopal reservations, based on the *Summa theologica* of Antoninus of Florence, he does not hesitate to express his real feelings about them. How many episcopal cases there are—and what they are—is entirely uncertain, he complains. And then he adds: "I am amazed at how easily and frequently men are ensnared by these censures."[20]

The last of the great summas for confessors, the *Sylvestrina*, also continues the protest of Gerson and defends in particular

---

[19] de Butrio, *Speculum de confessione*, 67, D2a.

[20] Rosemondt, *Confessionale*, 20, 9 and 23–24. In another passage Rosemondt explicitly notes the conflict between the function of discipline, which is expressed in reserved cases, and the function of consolation, which is expressed in the power of the ordinary priest to absolve. He begins by commenting on the consoling implications of a teaching on the reiteration of confession—"et ex hoc sequitur vnum notabile consolatorium dictum." He then explains that if someone confesses to a priest with powers to absolve reserved cases, including papal cases, and forgets a sin, any priest can subsequently absolve that forgotten sin even if it is a reserved case (if, Rosemondt adds, it is not convenient to return to the priest with special powers). Ibid., 7, 82. Rosemondt's insight that reservations hinder consolation is more explicitly argued by Sylvester (see below, n. 21 and text).

the rights of the mendicants. Sylvester begins by enumerating the nine cases of Benedict XI. But his real intentions are revealed when he considers whether the bishop can reserve cases "as he pleases." To this question Sylvester gives two answers. With respect to the Dominicans and Franciscans, and nowadays some other mendicant orders, a bishop may *not* reserve at will because of a bull of Clement V. With respect to other religious and curates, if a bishop reserves without good reason he commits a sin! In his discussion of the confessor, Sylvester explains his thought on this subject in greater detail. As for simple priests, although the doctors affirm the existence of many episcopal cases, curates may absolve all hidden sins that bishops have not explicitly reserved. But Sylvester does not want to give the impression that bishops may reserve sins as they please. They are justified in denying priests the power of absolving certain sins only in the two circumstances St. Antoninus had admitted: first to deprive guilty priests of their powers; second, for the common good. Furthermore, he has a simple judgment on how this teaching is to be understood: "It is not expedient for the common good (utilitati communi) to reserve so many cases; rather this puts a snare in the path of salvation." It is true that Sylvester does not like the degree of discretion the *Angelica* gives to priests. But he also thinks that the bishop who reserves sins without reasonable justification commits a serious sin himself.

As for the mendicants, Sylvester is, as we might expect, even more definite. In the first place, to allow a bishop to reserve whatever he wished would mean that the privileges of the friars, which come from the pope, could lawfully be violated. Then he offers a second reason why it is wrong to think that a bishop can restrict the friars' absolution as he pleases:

> that would totally annul and sweep away the arrangement of Clement's bull *Dudum*, and frustrate its intention, which is that the people might have their consolations in the Lord from confessing freely to the said friars; and that would not be possible if bishops could reserve cases to themselves as they pleased.[21]

[21] *Sylvestrina*, "Casus," qq. 2–5, par. 3–5; "Confessor 2," q. 5, par. 5; "Confessor 3," q. 1, par. 5 (italics added). Cf. above, n. 14. John Eck, like Godescalc Rosemondt, explicitly follows Gerson on episcopal reservations, although he is not sure how extensive is the abuse of penances that betray

The reserved cases of the bishops run headlong into the consolations of the friars, and Sylvester does not like it.

Those who follow Gerson, then, are clear on the issue: to reserve sins, to restrict the power of ordinary confessors, dangerously impedes the forgiveness of sins and the consolation of the sinner. Even those who protest, however, even those who warn that prelates who reserve cases without good reason are guilty of injustice, still respect the hierarchy's authority and its right to discipline the community of the faithful by restricting the efficacy of the Sacrament of Penance in the parishes.

IMPOSING PENANCES

According to the medieval theology of penance, a sinner must not only be absolved from his guilt but must also pay for his sins in the form of some kind of punishment. Purgatory is the middle place of destination for people who die absolved of guilt but with an outstanding debt of temporal punishment. Not until the expiatory fires of purgatory have "satisfied" this debt will they enter heaven.

Obviously absolution from guilt is far more important than remission of punishment. Nevertheless, indulgences, which are ways of reducing the punishment owed for sin, aroused controversy in the sixteenth century because Christians retained a lively interest in that intermediate suffering place and wanted to avoid its worst or, if possible, all of its pains. And that is one reason why penance—the work of "satisfaction" for sin that the priest assigns the penitent in confession—is vital to the practice of forgiveness. Logically considered, of course, purgatory is just as transitory as this life, and preachers of repentance were naturally led by this logic to stress absolution from guilt, not remission of

---

the sin of the penitent in his day (Schauerte, *Busslehre des Eck*, 175, 240–241). Michel Mollat thinks that the proliferation of *peccata majora* reserved to bishops from the middle of the fourteenth to the end of the fifteenth century is evidence of "l'immoralité élémentaire" of this period (*La Vie et pratique religieuses au XIVe siècle et dans la première partie du XVe, principalement en France*, 2 vols. [Paris, 1963–1965], II, 109). It seems more reasonable, however, to look on the issue as a struggle over authority between mendicants, parish clergy, prelates, and ecclesiastical reformers. Cf. Paul Guérin, *Les Conciles généraux et particuliers*, 3d ed., 3 vols. (Paris, 1868), III, 23, 67, 232, 308, 317–318; H. C. Lea, *History of Auricular Confession*, I, 312–319. The first example Lea finds of a case reserved to a bishop is in 1102, by the council of London, ibid., 313.

punishment. Remission of punishment remained, however, a theme of considerable prominence in the literature on the forgiveness of sin. And the penance imposed by the priest, which the penitent was to perform after he was absolved and sent away, is the source of some anomalous restrictions on the efficacy of the Sacrament of Penance.

Why did people not only fear this threat of punishment, but also look to the performance of ascetic acts to diminish it? The first and most obvious answer is to look at the historical roots of penitential exercises, in the theology of expiation of the ancient and early medieval church. There is a direct continuity between the institutions of public and private forgiveness, and one common element is the acceptance of ecclesiastical determination of the penance to be performed by individual sinners. There were, moreover, persistent demands that something of the old rigor of satisfaction for sin be preserved; and penances were the only area in which asceticism might fit with the modern theory of the working of the sacrament. In other words, the weight of tradition and the disciplinary authority of the clergy help to account for the continued interest in doing penance in the late middle ages.

But the simplest reason for doing penance on earth comes from Peter Lombard, who warns, in language anyone can understand, that suffering in purgatory is a lot more painful than the penitential exercises that effectively remit it during this life. As the Lombard puts it, if one dies without having satisfied the penalty owed for sin, "he will feel the fire of purgatory and he will be more harshly punished than if he had completed his penance here."[22]

Ideally penances were also remedies for sin, even in the late middle ages. This idea is also a carry-over from canonical penance and the penitentials, whose arduous and threatening penalties were meant to reform old sinners and discourage new ones. Thus the *Raymundina* offers commonplace advice when it encourages priests to impose penances with an eye to the correction of the sinner:

[22] Galtier, "Satisfaction," *DTC*, 14^1, 1189. Robert of Flamborough offers this severe warning, which the confessor is to give his penitent: "frater opportet te in hac vita puniri vel in purgatorio incomparabiliter autem gravior erit pena purgatorii quam aliqua in hac vita" (Dietterle, "Die Summae confessorum," *ZKG*, 24 [1903], 369–371). Cf. Rebello, *Fructus*, 49–50; [Poeniteas cito], *Confessionale pro scholasticis*, A5a–A6a; [Poeniteas cito], *Libellus de modo poenitendi*, C2b.

There are three kinds of satisfaction, namely prayer, fasting, and alms: and this triad is opposed to the nefarious triad of the devil, prayer against pride, fasting against carnal concupiscence, alms against avarice.

Raymond's advice seems reasonable and unexceptionable, and a variety of authorities repeat it.[23] Nevertheless Bartholomaeus de Chaimis, when he urges confessors to remember the remedial ends of penance, also warns that these antidotes are to be taken generally and not specifically. Bartholomaeus is concerned that the individual penitent be considered, and he notes that in some cases these rules are not helpful: take for example the possibility that one may have to give a penance to a poverty-stricken thief.[24]

Because penance was principally a way to reduce the temporal punishment owed for sin, however, authorities also suggest a variety of alternative and often highly ascetic forms of satisfaction. Among the ways to do penance and circumvent purgatory, according to Jodocus Winshemius, are intense contrition, observance of the evangelical counsels, good works, martyrdom, and profession of religious vows. Jacobus de Clusa praises—in addition to the traditional prayer, alms, and fasting—vigils, the hair shirt, and flagellation. He insists at the same time that the most excellent of all is entrance into a religious order. And such opinions are common and appropriate: for the ascetic tendencies of medieval religion make these higher demands perfectly consistent with the spirit of the theology of forgiveness, if not with its actual operation. Higher demands are a residue from the older practice. Thus when a commentary on the "Poeniteas cito" advises penitents to spurn pleasures, plays, public spectacles, and evil company, it is simply reasserting the desirability of returning to an age of discipline, when penance was a way of life with an element of heroic self-denial.[25] But the best example of this nos-

[23] *Raymundina*, III, 34, 34, pp. 467–468; Guido de Monte Rocherii, *Manipulus curatorum*, II, 4, 1; "Poeniteas cito," *PL*, 207, 1156, lines 85–91; [Poeniteas cito], *Libellus de modo poenitendi*, B5b–B6a; [Poeniteas cito], *Summa penitentie*, D5b–E1a; [Poeniteas cito], *Confessionale pro scholasticis*, A4B (cites John of Freiburg rather than the *Raymundina*); *Sylvestrina*, "Confessor 4," q. 3, par. 4 (cites the *Raymundina*). Cf. Thomas of Chobham, *Summa confessorum*, 232, n. 4, 240–241.

[24] Bartholomaeus de Chaimis, *Confessionale*, IV, 1, X3b–X4b.

[25] Winshemius, *Institutiones*, D4b–E1b; Jacobus de Clusa, *Confessionale*, cap. 24, B4b; [Poeniteas cito], *Libellus de modo poenitendi* (1495), A4a–b;

talgia for the days when discipline had teeth is the persistent reference to the "Penitential Canons." Irrelevant to modern practice —anachronistic and harsh beyond any hope of revival in the later middle ages—the Penitential Canons nevertheless found their way into the literature on the forgiveness of sins, to rest as a reminder that all was not what it once was, that there were times in history when the church expected penitents to demonstrate sorrow for their sins.

The two authors most responsible for the dissemination of the Penitential Canons—Astesanus of Asti and Andreas de Escobar—both invoke the authority of St. Augustine, to whom they attribute the judgment that whoever does not know the canons scarcely deserves to be called a priest. It is Astesanus, in fact, who introduces the canons to the summas and manuals for confessors, and it is his version that is accepted as a model.[26] Yet there is something puzzling about the importance of these rules to fifteenth and sixteenth century authorities, for penances had already become arbitrary by the twelfth century and sacramental and pastoral theology treats this fact as a commonplace. That the duration and severity of penance was up to the priest and the penitent was common doctrine among Astesanus's literary predecessors—Alain de Lille, Conrad of Germany, Robert of Flamborough, Raymond of Peñaforte, William of Rennes, and Monaldus di Capo d'Istria, to name a few, support this principle.[27]

Furthermore, when we analyze Raymond of Peñaforte and his glossator William of Rennes, we realize that pastoral theology

cf. ibid., A3a, where the commentary states the traditional distinction between *principal* forms of satisfaction—prayer, fasting, and alms—and *secondary*—pilgrimages, vigils, flagellation, and other ascetic acts.

[26] Dietterle, "Die Summae confessorum," *ZKG*, 26 (1905), 353–354; "Die 47 Canones poenitentiales desselben Buches [*Astesana*, V] (tit. 32) haben sich einer ausserordentlich Beliebtheit erfreut. Sie finden sich gewöhnlich dem *Dekrete* Gratians beigefügt, ferner als Anhang zum *Supplementum Summae Pisanae* . . . und zum römischen Pönitentialbuch (Venetiis 1584), auch im Auszuge mitegeteilt im *Lumen confessorum* des Andreas Didaci Hispanus." Astesanus seems to think that there is another way to achieve at least part of the knowledge conveyed in the penitential canons: "est autem alia discretio qua quis cognoscit per habitum acquisitum discernere inter perplexitatem peccatorum," *Astesana*, 5, 16, di.38. Cf. H. J. Schmitz, *Die Bussbücher*, II, 720ff.

[27] Alain de Lille, *Liber poenitentialis*, PL, 210, 294B, 297C–D; Dietterle, "Die Summae confessorum," *ZKG*, 24 (1903), 369–371, 528; *Raymundina*, III, 34, 41–49, pp. 472–480; *Monaldina*, fol. 174a, 176, 227.

had at its disposal authoritative opinions that more than justified ignoring the Penitential Canons. Raymond asks what length a penance ought to be and in reply first notes the familiar maxim that it ought to be arbitrary, the decision of the priest. But then he observes that "regularly seven years of penance are to be imposed for adultery, perjury, fornication, voluntary homicide, and other serious sins." These are the determinations of the Penitential Canons, he explains, and some say that conscientious priests may depart from them only for a good reason. "Others say truly that all penances are arbitrary without distinction. . . . And it seems that custom has sanctioned this last opinion. The first, however, is safer, although more difficult." William of Rennes comments more realistically on the word "custom," which, he says, "must be observed, because in fact today penances are arbitrary." Indeed, Raymond also admits later that it is not a good idea to impose a penance on an unwilling penitent. The confessor, Raymond says, must make sure the penitent is sorry for his sins and intends to give them up; but if the penitent is unwilling to undergo the rigor of the canons, the confessor, after attempting to persuade him to comply, should only impose a satisfaction he will willingly fulfill. When William of Rennes comments on this opinion, he makes the disposition of the penitent far more decisive: William speaks of imposing a penance that the penitent "wants to undergo spontaneously and without murmuring," and to avoid the possibility that the penitent will fail in his obligation he urges that nothing or very little be imposed as a requirement. Once again William is more lenient than Raymond. The concluding argument for leniency, however, is Raymond's. He invokes the example of our Lord, who never imposed heavy penances but only said, as in the case of the woman caught in adultery, "Go thy way and sin no more." Raymond then observes with a logic that seems irrefutable: "If the priest cannot rejoice at his entire purgation, at least he may rejoice that he might be able to send him, freed from hell, to purgatory."[28]

Against the trend toward lightening penances and making them arbitrary, the *Astesana*'s inclusion of forty-seven penitential canons represents a throwback to an older regime. We should not believe that the ancient asceticism of the canons was reintroduced. Indeed, there is every reason to believe it was not. We must take note of the Penitential Canons here, however, because

---

[28] *Raymundina*, III, 34, 41, pp. 472–473; 46, p. 473; 49, pp. 479–480.

some authorities on the forgiveness of sins seem to have wanted more than the memory of this rigor to persist; they apparently wanted to persuade confessors actually to give harsher penances. Such a reform could only have reinforced this restriction on the free working of sacramental forgiveness. Harsh penances inevitably create another opportunity for sinning, because the penitent is obliged to complete the penance he accepts (some thought the penitent had to complete his penance in the state of grace). Thus the attempt to establish longer and harder penances directly affects the practice of confession, even if it does not mean that the discipline of the ancient church was being literally revived.

Astesanus of Asti's opinions are not pure rigorism, probably because he realized that times had changed and fourteenth-century penitents were not about to go off and do seven years of penance for every serious sin. Indeed, his discussion of the "measure of satisfaction" begins with a reference to the medicinal purposes of penances and shows that the length of the penance is not directly proportional to the seriousness of the sin. Thus he notes that the canons tax fornication in a youth more heavily than in an aged man: the youth is less guilty, because of the greater degree of temptation, but he is also more likely to commit the sin, and therefore he is punished more heavily as a deterrent. Similarly, homicide by a layman is a greater sin than fornication by a priest; but the canons give the first seven years and the second ten years, again because it seems more likely that priests will fornicate than that laymen will murder.

When Astesanus turns to the problem of whether one must impose the letter of the Penitential Canons, he follows rather closely the opinions stated in the *Raymundina* and its gloss. Some say that penances are completely arbitrary, that it is left to the priest to fix them according to the special circumstances of the sin and the penitent. Others say that one may depart from them only with good reason and that the priest's "choice" consists only in deciding how he should diminish or increase what the canons set down. Like Raymond, Astesanus calls the second opinion "safer but more difficult"; the first he calls "more common," and, again in agreement with Raymond and William, notes that it is approved by custom and should be observed on the grounds that nowadays penances are truly arbitrary. He then concludes with advice that is familiar, but which reasserts for late medieval readers the suspicion that piety had fallen off and that something was wrong with religious observance. The priest is to tell his penitent how much penance he should do for each sin, warn him that he would not live long enough to complete it, and impose one penance for them all. No one should be forced to accept a penance he does not want or think he can complete, and Astesanus warns against overwhelming penitents. The example of Christ's simple admonition to the adulteress is again invoked to justify departures from the letter of the law. But despite these usual and certainly honest mitigations, Astesanus does end up by giving confessors a list of penances that are heavy. He talks as if he knows they are not being observed. And yet he offers the Penitential Canons as if they were relevant, as if, as he puts it at the beginning of his discussion of satisfaction, the conscientious priest will be familiar with them.[29]

Andreas de Escobar's thoughts on the Penitential Canons prove that some were still capable of resisting what must have seemed inevitable in the fifteenth century. He is clearly unhappy with the customary relaxations that Alain de Lille had faced with resignation in the twelfth century. Andreas wants confessors to remember the rigor of the law. He quotes the warning Astesanus had used, that the confessor who is ignorant of the Penitential Canons scarcely deserves to be called a priest. For Andreas the canons are in no sense a historical curiosity. He wants them publicized:

> Therefore I have placed—for the information of simple priests having the cure of souls—some canons for sins taxed by law, which every priestly curate is bound to know under pain of mortal sin.

A sample of the rigor for which Andreas was so nostalgic gives us some insight into a mentality that can with justice be called reactionary. A priest living openly with a concubine is to wear a hair shirt and fast on bread and water three months a year for seven years, and the same penalty is pronounced for notorious incest and adultery. Sexual intercourse with a nun is worth fifteen years, three years of which include periods of fast on bread and water. Intercourse with your wife on Sunday, a feast day, or in Lent is penalized with seven days penance. Sodomy and bestiality are worth fifteen years, five of them with bread and water fasts. Two weeks' penance is prescribed for having been "wan-

[29] *Astesana*, V, 31, 1–2, V, 32.

ton" (luxuriatus) with one's wife on Good Friday, and seven years for homicide, adultery, and fornication. Harsh as these are, Andreas defends the wisdom of the ancient church. The Penitential Canons ought to be observed literally, he urges, for notorious offences: ". . . if it is public and especially scandalous then certainly neither more nor less penance is to be given than that which the law expresses."

Of course even Andreas must bend with the times. There are a number of mitigating circumstances that allow for the diminution of penances, and they are given to the priest to determine. Nevertheless priests departing from the letter should tell a penitent what he deserves: ". . . and because he ought to do seven years' penance for every mortal sin; but because he could not fulfill that in this lifetime, he ought to give himself at least one Our Father for every day [of the penance]." A penitent's only alternative is seeking the indulgences and other benefits of the church. But above all, he must obviously choose his confessor well, because the penance can be greater, lesser, or equal to the sin (and Andreas obviously believes that the Penitential Canons offer some heavenly assurance that the prescribed penalty fits the crime). The alternative is suffering in purgatory, which clearly is a serious threat to Andreas. Thus it is an understatement to conclude, as one historian has put it, that Andreas betrays "his discomfort in accommodating himself to the customs of his age."[30] And while he admits the principle of arbitrary penances in the end, he popularizes, even more than did Astesanus, the Penitential Canons.

Andreas was not alone in his longing for a stricter satisfaction: Jacobus de Clusa may even have outdone him. Jacobus begins by advising the penitent to put himself in the hands of a good confessor, by which he means one who is guided by the Penitential Canons. Even if a confessor relaxes them—and he need not follow the letter of the law—he should not disregard them without reason. On the contrary, it would be positively dangerous for a priest who did not know the canons to hear confessions. His line is consistently hard: "Today," he complains, "we see many guilty, but few truly penitent." For one can hardly call them penitents

---

[30] Andreas de Escobar, *Canones penitentiales*, C3b–E2a; R. Stapper, "Das 'Lumen confessorum,'" *Römische Quartalschrift*, 11 (1897), 275–277. Stapper also says of him: ". . . er gehört zu den letzten Vorkämpfern für die Reste alter Strenge" (ibid., 276).

when they return to their old sins immediately; and it is certainly inadequate for the adulterer or fornicator to take a few Our Fathers or a few days' fasting as a fitting penance. They should rather fast for a certain number of days every week for years! If the penitent protests that this is beyond his powers, one need only reply, with St. Bernard, that no one wants to do adequate penance; but if one has found the strength to sin, why can one not find the strength to make satisfaction to God? The penitent should hope in God, ask for help, or else he will suffer the bitterest fire of purgatory. Once again Jacobus warns against bad confessors. People get the best physicians they can find for the cure of their bodies, but because they are unwilling to undergo a truly ascetic penance, they are willing to confess to any stupid or sinful itinerant priest. They shun a severe penance because, like Cain, they think their iniquities are too great for pardon. But they should rather model themselves on the submission of David, Noah, Abraham, Moses, John the Baptist, and St. Bernard. And to bring the story home, he tells a story of a dead monk who appears to his brothers and says mysteriously, "No one knows," three times. When asked what no one knows, the apparition replies: "How severely God judges and how harshly He punishes."[31]

Andreas de Escobar and Jacobus de Clusa are exemplars of rigid satisfaction. Nevertheless they also illustrate, in their rigorous way, the basic conflict between two principles that characterizes almost all thought on imposing penances: first, that priests should know and in some way use the Penitential Canons, which prescribe seven years' penance for each mortal sin; and second, that priests have the choice of departing from these rules, and that they should depart especially when the penitent is unwilling to endure an arduous penance. In discussing the imposition of penance, therefore, the authorities on the forgiveness of sin enunciated some common propositions and cited some commonplace

---

[31] Jacobus de Clusa, *Confessionale*, cap. 7, 25, and app. 2, A4b, Cia, C4b–Dib. Even John Eck lamented the disappearance of the fervor to do ascetic penances as Schauerte (*Die Busslehre des Eck*, 84) shows: "Eck vergleicht die strengen Bussbestimmungen der Vorzeit mit der milden Praxis seiner Tage, den früheren Eifer und Gehorsam mit dem späteren Widerwillen gegen Busswerke und singt ein bewegtes Klaglied von der Erkaltung des Busseifers und der Gottesliebe in seiner Zeit." This is the reason why numerous indulgences are needed today, "die an die Stelle der schweren Bussübungen getreten seien."

texts that are not wholly consistent but which express the basic dilemma of a genre that is trying to emphasize the consolation of absolution and at the same time preserve the discipline of satisfaction for sin. A brief summary of these propositions and commonplaces will give the best idea of the ordinary teaching among authorities who are less enthusiastic for rigidity than Andreas or Jacobus.

Because the Penitential Canons existed, because no ecclesiastical authority had officially declared them a dead letter, a surprising number of important authorities on forgiveness refer to them. Nicolaus de Ausimo, Guido de Monte Rocherii, Antoninus of Florence, Angelus de Clavasio, Bartholomaeus de Chaimis, and Sylvester Prierias all either cite the general rule of seven years for each mortal sin or else go even further and talk about the whole regime of the canons. Shorter works also subscribe to these rules. Thus, for example, the *Directoire des confesseurs*, *Manuale parrochialium sacerdotum*, *Tractatus de instructionibus confessorum*, the manuals of Jodocus Winshemius, Johannes Romming, the diocese of Albi, and a commentary on the "Poeniteas cito" either include the Penitential Canons, give the general rule of seven years for every mortal sin, or at least insist that penances ought to be proportional to the severity of the offense.[32] In other words, it is not only conservative clerics like Jacobus de Clusa and Andreas de Escobar who talk about rigorous penances; the *Sylvestrina, Manipulus curatorum, Confessionale—Defecerunt*, and even the "lax" *Angelica* offer these regulations to a wide public in the years before the Reformation.

Yet these same authorities knew very well that the contrary was true: penances were arbitrary, not fixed, and they were becoming increasingly lighter. It is instructive, therefore, to see how they got around the rigors of the Penitential Canons to which they referred, to make what they said correspond with what people were doing.

[32] *Supplementum*, "Penitentia 2," 1; Guido de Monte Rocherii, *Manipulus curatorum*, II, 4, 5; Antoninus, *Confessionale—Defecerunt*, 48; *Angelica*, "Confessio 6"; Bartholomaeus de Chaimis, *Confessionale*, "Canones penitentiales"; *Sylvestrina*, "Confessor 4," q. 2, par. 3; [Gerson?], *Directoire* R7a–b; *Manuale parrochialium sacerdotum*, V, B2a–b; *Tractatus de instructionibus confessorum*, E4a–E6b; Winshemius, *Institutiones*, D4b–E1b; Romming, *Penitentiarius*, c.54, E2b–E3a; [Poeniteas cito], *Confessionale pro scholasticis*, A5a; *Confessionale* (Albi), G5a.

One way out, the one most closely connected to the ancient penitential system and most familiar to students of the Reformation, was the use of indulgences. Now the temporal value assigned to an indulgence is nothing else than an equivalent to the duration of a penance done under the canons. An indulgence of seven years for making a pilgrimage, for example, means that the pilgrim's trip, because it enjoys the benefits of the treasury of merits, will shorten his temporal punishment due to sin by as much as if he had fasted for seven years under the old penitential discipline. Since many people, including historians, have been confused about the meaning of the temporal value of indulgences, it is worth examining the clear description of the *Sylvestrina*. Indulgences, Sylvester explains, are valid for the remission of punishment in the forum of the church as well as the forum of God, whether satisfaction has been demanded by a priest, or the Penitential Canons, or God. In answer to the question as to the meaning of the value of ten or one hundred days and the like, he says he follows the common doctrine on indulgences taught by the *Pisanella*, the Archdeacon, Albert, and Thomas:

> When it is said that they are worth as much as they sound (quod tantum valent quantum sonant), it is meant that if they are said to be one hundred days, they are not worth merely ninety but rather one hundred—as much for the remission of punishment as one hundred days of penance according to the taxation made by law or by the priest or by divine justice. For these days are not days of heaven or purgatory, but of the world.

Astesanus of Asti agrees with this—an indulgence of one year means a penitent will be punished so much less in purgatory as if he had done one year of penance in this life. Angelus de Clavasio seems to think that indulgences may not be as good as they sound, for while he explains that one who accepts an indulgence worth seven years is absolved of the obligation to do seven years of fasting as imposed by a priest, "nevertheless it would be better to do it and reserve the indulgence for the rest in purgatory, if the imposed penance was not fully worthy."[33] Still,

[33] *Sylvestrina*, "Indulgentia," q. 2, par. 5, and q. 4, par. 8, which reads: "Quarto quaeritur quomodo intelligendus sit iste valor decem aut centum dierum, vel huiusmodi? Et dico, quod secundum communem doctrinam, praecipue Alber & Pisa. & Archi. & est mens S. Thom. cum dicitur quod

Angelus fully agrees that the value of a penance is to be under-stood in terms of the canons.

When we consider the true meaning of indulgences, it becomes clear that far from representing a radical departure from the older discipline, they manage to preserve that mentality with some success. For indulgences are couched in the language of the Penitential Canons, and the assumption for all who gave and sought indulgences was that the fires of purgatory were waiting for those who did not adequately perform works of satisfaction for sin in this world. If you believe that each mortal sin requires seven years' penance to be remitted, then you will believe that most Christians will suffer severely in the next world. In other words, indulgences imply that the old discipline was accurate in its estimate of the bill of suffering to be paid for sin. Indeed, the same thing might be said of those who think that penances are "arbitrary" because they are up to the decision of the priest.[34] If

---

tantum valent quantum sonant, intelligitur, quod si dicuntur dies esse centum, non sunt tantum nonaginta, sed sunt centum valentes tantum ad remissionem poenae quantum centum dies poenitentiae *secundum taxationem factam a iure vel sacerdote vel iustitia diuina; quia isti dies non sunt dies coeli seu purgatorii, sed mundi*" (italics added). Angelus and Astesanus are quite as definite: *Angelica*, "Indulgentia," 1; *Astesana*, V, 40, a. 2, q. 1. Ac-cording to [Poeniteas cito], *Confessionale pro scholasticis*, A5a–b, both the shame of confessing and sacramental absolution (by virtue of the passion of Christ) remit much *poena*, and *cordis contritio* can be so great that it remits punishment fully; but one never knows, and since it is sure that the slight penances customarily imposed will leave much more than the penances prescribed in the canons, one is advised to lessen purgatorial suffering by taking advantage of the numerous indulgences it lists. Cf. H. C. Lea, *History of Confession*, II, 148–168, and John T. McNeill, *The Celtic Penitentials*, 192–199, whose summary judgment on indulgences (p. 199) bears the stamp of the era (1923) in which it was written: "Thus the rigours of penance were escaped through the superabundant merits of the faithful . . . . The scholastic teaching [on indulgences] is only the logical development of this general conception, under the influence of increased sacerdotal and centralizing tendencies . . . . *The evil genius of the Latin Church, having corrupted its discipline through the very guides to repentance, might long ago have ex-claimed in triumph*: 'Mischief, thou art afoot, / Take thou what course thou wilt!'" (italics added).

[34] Antonius de Butrio (*Speculum de confessione*, I, A3a–b) expresses this urge to subordinate penitent to priest in the determination of penances: "vnde ponat se penitens omnino in potestate & judicio sacerdotis, nihil sibi reseruans sui." See also Guido de Monte Rocherii, *Manipulus curatorum*, II,

one goes no further, this principle implies that the priest can change the penance for one reason or another, but that it is his responsibility to see that some fitting penance—that will somehow correspond to the gravity and number of the sins—will be imposed and performed. Needless to say, the realities of the observance of satisfaction in the late middle ages were far from the Penitential Canons. And consequently there were a host of more lenient principles that helped priests depart from the letter and even the mentality of the law.

Thus a priest who is determining the penance he now finds is arbitrary is told that public penances are for public sins only, and that in no circumstances should the penance betray the sin of the penitent.[35] Nor should the penance result in notable loss or inconvenience to someone else—you must not, for example, impose heavy alms on a poor man's wife, or send a servant on a pilgrimage.[36] Similarly there is concern that the penance take into account circumstances about the sinner as well as his sin—his social status, his occupation, his health and age, his contrition, and, above all, his disposition to do penance.[37] All of these circumstances allow softening; but the last one represents perfectly the change of focus in penance because it admits that the penitent's unwillingness to undergo arduous penance is not a bar to

---

4, 5; *Supplementum,* "Penitentia 2," 1; *Angelica,* "Confessio 6"; Bartholomaeus de Chaimis, *Confessionale,* IV, 1, X3b; [Poeniteas cito], *Confessionale pro scholasticis,* A5a; [Gerson?], *Directoire,* R7a–b; Winshemius, *Institutiones,* D4b–E1b.

[35] *Sylvestrina,* "Confessor 4," q. 4; "Nec pro occulto peccato poenitentia manifesta, id est, talis vnde possit oriri suspitio de peccato commisso." A few others: *Supplementum,* "Penitentia 2," 2; Antoninus, *Confessionale—Defecerunt,* 48; Gerson, *Opus tripartitum,* I, 17, Du Pin, I, 441A; de Schildis, *Speculum sacerdotum,* 166; *Manuale parrochialium sacerdotum,* V, C4b.

[36] Antoninus, *Confessionale—Defecerunt,* 48; *Sylvestrina,* "Confessor 4," q. 3, par. 4.

[37] Some typical examples of considerations in imposing penances: Guido de Monte Rocherii, *Manipulus curatorum,* II, 4, 5 (quality and quantity of sins, dignity, nature, age, and the like of the penitent; sickness or frailty); [Gerson?], *Directoire,* R7a–b (estate, age, strength, degree of contrition, and nature of sin); Bartholomaeus de Chaimis, *Confessionale,* IV, 1, X3b (condition, dignity, sex, office, poverty, disposition of the penitent, and others); Romming, *Penitentiarius,* c.54, E2b–E3a (contrition and disposition of the penitent); *Supplementum,* "Penitentia 2," 1 (especially the penitent's contrition). All versions of the "Poeniteas cito" emphasize the special treatment of the sick penitent when they repeat, gloss, or comment on *PL,* 207, 1153, lines 45–49.

forgiveness of guilt and the sacramental absolution of the priest. Whereas the ancient system had looked for assurance of contrition in willingness to perform penance, by the high middle ages this test was clearly no longer relevant. And despite the desire of some authorities to keep alive the old penance of expiation, particularly by those who kept talking about the Penitential Canons, reference to the willingness of the penitent made the death of that idea certain. Indeed, it is by asserting that confessors must make sure that their penitents are willing that authorities on the forgiveness of sins begin to construct a whole new mentality about penance: they assert that leniency is preferable to harshness. As the *Confessionale* of Albi puts it, the priest should give an appropriate and instructive penance, but it must be one that the penitent is willing to bear, "because it is better to be reproved for too much mercy than for too much justice." On this principle Sylvester enunciates the same degree of caution that we saw in William of Rennes. It is not merely a matter of bargaining a penitent down to something the priest can talk him into taking. Rather the penitent should only be given a penance he will do "without murmuring."[38] In a similar fashion some authorities instruct priests to keep the penance down not merely to what the penitent willingly will tolerate, but also to what the priest judges the penitent is capable of. The difference is not so subtle as it may seem, for in this case the confessor is responsible for judging or choosing; and it is conceivable that some penitents might be willing to accept more than they ought to.[39]

Leniency is better than severity for other reasons. We have already seen references to the example of our Lord, who told the

[38] *Confessionale* (Albi), G5a: ". . . quia melius redargui de nimia misericordia quam de nimia justicia"; Antoninus, *Confessionale—Defecerunt*, 48; *Sylvestrina*, "Confessio 1," q. 25, par. 27; ibid., "Confessor 4," q. 2, par. 3, q. 11, par. 15; Gerson, *Opus tripartitum*, I, 17, Du Pin, I, 441A; Rosemondt, *Confessionale*, 7, 77; [Gerson?], *Directoire*, S3a–b; *Supplementum*, "Penitentia 2," 2.

[39] Antoninus, *Confessionale—Defecerunt*, 48: "In penitentia iniungenda hec maxime attendas secundum omnes: ut talem des et iniungas: quam credas omnino quod implebit quantumcunque magnus sit peccator"; Guido de Monte Rocherii, *Manipulus curatorum*, II, 4, 5; Johannes von Freiburg, *Summa confessorum*, III, 34, 110; *Angelica*, "Confessio 6"; Rosemondt, *Confessionale*, 7, 77. Although these citations insist that the priest must take care to impose only what he thinks a penitent is willing to bear, the usual assumption is that penitents will be reluctant to do enough, not that they will overestimate their own powers of performance.

adulteress merely to go her way and sin no more (John 8:3–11). Other citations observe that He said He did not wish the death of a sinner (Ezechiel 33:11) and that He warned the lawyers against burdening the faithful (Luke 11:46; Matthew 23:4). The example of the treatment of the adulteress is cited in the *Raymundina*, as is the warning to the lawyers. Both are obvious places, and they enjoy a certain currency. Thus Romming's counsel that the degree of contrition and the willingness of the penitent should be taken into account in imposing a fitting penance concludes decisively: "Do not weigh him down with penance, [but follow] the example of the Lord, who never imposed a heavy penance although He thoroughly detested sin. Hence He says, 'Woe to you lawyers, who oppress men with burdens that they cannot carry.' "[40]

But the example of the Lord, who does not want the death of sinners, raises the most critical issue for penance and the most relevant one for a discussion of the limitation on the power of the keys. For the penitent is obligated to do his penance. If he does not, he faces three possibilities: having committed a serious sin; being forced to reiterate a confession now invalidated; and repeating the penance because he did not complete it in the state of grace. Because of these possibilities, the theology of satisfaction presented the gravest threats to the claims of the theory of forgiveness to console men. Many authorities realized that severe penances threatened to create new sins.

The *Directoire des confesseurs* offers a refreshingly ingenuous commentary on this fear. According to canon law, the *Directoire* begins, the ancient rule prescribed seven years' penance for each mortal sin, "in order to recover the seven gifts of the Holy Spirit which are lost through sin." In consideration of the charge of the Lord, "Nolo mortem peccatoris, etc.," and also because they wanted to remove the despair of the sinner, "the fathers and lords of the church" softened this regulation. The explanation is

[40] See above, n. 28 and text; Romming, *Penitentiarius*, c.54, E2b–E3a: "Neque eum poenitentia grauet exemplo domini qui nunquam grauem imposuit poenitentiam, at bene peccatum detestatus est. Hinc dicit. Vaeh vobis legisperitis qui oneratis homines oneribus quae portare non possunt [Luke 11:46; Matt., 23:4]." Cf. *Sylvestrina*, "Confessor 4," q. 3, par. 4. Similar in spirit is the assertion that leniency is better than severity because the degree of sorrow is more important than the duration of mortification and abstinence: [Poeniteas cito], *Confessionale pro scholasticis*, A5a; Dietterle, "Die Summae confessorum," *ZKG*, 27 (1906), 441–442.

most revealing. Many penitents, the *Directoire* recounts, became discouraged after three or four mortal sins and said, "I will never complete my penance in my lifetime, and I would rather be damned than do so much." And for reasons such as that it was necessary to find a remedy so that no one could excuse himself from doing penance and serving God and his salvation. That is why the holy fathers of the church left it up to confessors to measure out the penance according to their good discretion, taking into consideration the contrition of the penitent, the gravity and number of his sins, his estate, his age, and his strength. The penitent should be encouraged to stay away from sin (a much more important thing than abstinence from food and drink). He should be advised that what he does not satisfy here (as in the ancient church, seven years for each mortal sin), he will suffer for in purgatory (although penitential exercises and indulgences can diminish it). There are many possible penances (prayer, bare feet and hair shirt and so on), but the confessor should never impose a penance on an unwilling penitent. Rather than that, he should change it.[41] Thus the *Directoire* justifies current leniency as completely consistent with Christ's will and the history of the church, primarily because it defeats despair.

Lest sinners despair, leniency is better than severity. This argument is as common as it is logical if you want to preserve the consolations of the forgiveness of sins.

Sylvester argues that a penitent should never be sent away in despair: that priests should impose only what a penitent is absolutely willing to bear; that if telling a penitent what penance he deserves will cause despair, the priest should not even do that.[42] According to sacramental theology, leniency is manda-

---

[41] [Gerson?], *Directoire*, R7a–b: The section "De Penitence" gives the history of the mitigation of penances: ". . . Selon droit canon fut anciennement cause et iuge pour tous et pour ung chascun peche mortel sept ans de penitence pour recourer les vii. dons su sainct esprit / qui par peche mortel sont perdus: mais les peres et autres seigneurs de leglise en considerant ce que nostre seigneur dist: Nolo mortem peccatoris, etc. y ont voulu pourueoir. Et aussi pour oster la desperance du pecheur." Despair enters because many become discouraged after having committed three or four mortal sins and say: "Ie nauray pas acheue ma penitece en ma vie iameroye mieulx estre damne q la faire si grande." Cf. ibid. R7b–S3b.

[42] *Sylvestrina*, "Confessor 4," q. 2, par. 3; [Poeniteas cito], *Confessionale pro scholasticis*, A5a; Winshemius, *Institutiones*, D4b–E1b. The *Sylvestrina* (*loc.cit.*) argues that the man unwilling to do things necessary for forgiveness—such as avoidance of some sin—may not be absolved; but even he is

tory for similar reasons. Jean Gerson comments in at least four places on a remark of William of Paris, asserting that absolution is more important than satisfaction. It is better, the Consoling Doctor insists, to impose a light penance and leave something to be expiated in purgatory, than to impose a heavy one that, if it is not fulfilled, will implicate the penitent in mortal sin and possibly condemn him to hell.[43]

The force of this paradox—that the Sacrament of Penance could cause mortal guilt after it had forgiven it if the penance were omitted or not completed in the state of grace—led to a simple solution: the lightest penances imaginable.

One way to achieve a sort of compromise, with maximum leniency, is to give a penance in two parts: the first, obligatory penance should be extremely light; a second, optional set of penitential exercises can be more rigid. The *Tractatus de instructionibus confessorum* accepts this alternative. Satisfaction is worthless if completed in mortal sin, the *Tractatus* explains, and it is therefore essential to be prudent in the imposition of penance. Thus while the author repeats in general the rules of the Penitential Canons, he advises that confessors be cautious and use the letter of the canons only as a threat. Instead the confessor should suggest a light penance and add to it a heavier one that may hopefully but not necessarily be fulfilled. Antoninus of Florence's *Confessionale —Defecerunt* also proposes that solution. Antoninus recalls the advice of Chrysostom, who prefers mercy to justice, and urges flexibility. The priest should let a penitent know that if he misses a day of a penance, he can make it up the next day. If the confessor doubts that the penitent will complete a penance, he may give him an alternative—alms instead of fasting, for example. But if there is likelihood that the penitent will fall back into sin, then he can be given prayers for only a few days and alms and fasting for a longer period, because the latter need not be repeated if

---

to be given some good work to do, not as a penance with absolution, of course, but so that he may be saved from despair. See also *Manuale parrochialium sacerdotum*, V, B2a–b; and see above, "The Good, Complete Confession," n. 24 and text.

[43] Gerson, *Super Moderatione casuum reservandorum*, Du Pin, II, 416A; idem, *De Arte audiendi confessiones*, Du Pin, II, 452B; idem, *Super absolvendi potestate*, Du Pin, II, 414C; idem, *Regulae morales*, III, 103C; *Supplementum*, "Penitentia 2," 3; *Manuale parrochialium sacerdotum*, V, B2a–b.

they are done in mortal sin. Above all, however, the confessor must make sure that the penitent can perform the penance. If there is serious doubt, another penance should be imposed. To be sure, great sinners are to understand that they should be doing seven years' penance for each mortal sin. But they should also be told that they are being given a light penance not because their sins are light but so that they will not despair and neglect it; for, Antoninus explains, omission of penance is a mortal sin that requires reiteration of the confession.[44] Thus both the *Tractatus* and Antoninus solve this dangerous problem by advising confessors to preserve the sense of debt for sin by imposing a more severe but optional set of exercises while requiring only a light penance the confessor is sure will be observed.

Another solution, which can be used with the first, is safer and more radical: give a penance that can be completed immediately, before the penitent leaves the church, before he has a chance to fall back into sin. Angelus de Clavasio, Bartholomaeus de Chaimis, and Godescalc Rosemondt agree on this expedient and their arguments show that they understand the relationship between the imposition of penance and the consolation of the penitent in very much the same way.

The *Angelica* first broaches this solution when talking about a case of reiteration of confession—must someone tell all his sins again if he commits a mortal sin before having completed his penance? Angelus has a mild solution for this case: "I say that it is enough for him to complete the penance and only confess the commission [of the mortal sin]." But Angelus shows that there is no certainty among pastoral authorities on this question by adding the following advice:

> Nevertheless it would be more cautious if the confessor were to impose some penance that the penitent could do immediately and in the state of grace; and afterwards add another that he does not intend to impose as a sacramental penance but rather enjoins as some voluntary satisfaction such that it would suffice however he fulfills it, and even if he does not fulfill it he does not intend to bind him but to leave it up to him.

---

[44] *Tractatus de instructionibus confessorum*, E4a–E6b; Antoninus, *Confessionale—Defecerunt*, 48. According to Duns Scotus, however, satisfaction also works *ex opere operato*; and he thinks it is probably of value if completed after having fallen back into sin (Michel, "Pénitence," *DTC*, 12^1, 1030).

And to make sure the reader does not miss this advice Angelus repeats it, with even more strongly worded warnings against defeating the consoling purposes of the sacrament, at the end of the section on interrogations:

> After [the confession] impose on him as a sacramental penance one that he can fulfill immediately before falling back—and then another that he perceives the sinner is likely to do; whence he must beware lest he impose such a penance that he will not likely fulfill it, because that would amount to binding him rather than loosing him.[45]

To loose is to console, and that is Angelus's primary concern.

Bartholomaeus de Chaimis was a canonist, like Andreas de Escobar, but his advice to confessors on the imposition of penance conforms not to the rigor of Andreas, but rather to the mildness of the theologically oriented *Angelica* and *Sylvestrina*. Make sure the penitent will voluntarily receive the penance you give, Bartholomaeus urges, and then adds:

> And if the penitent wants to receive absolutely no penance imposed on him by the priest, but nevertheless says he has displeasure or contrition for the sin committed and a firm intention of not falling back, he is to be absolved lest he succumb to desperation (according to Scotus).

Indeed, Bartholomaeus is even more explicit than Angelus on the degree of permissiveness that should guide the confessor:

> It is sound advice of the doctors that, in order to avoid the ambiguity of repeating penance done in mortal sin, the con-

---

[45] *Angelica*, "Confessio sacramentalis," 19: "Cautius tamen esset quod confessor aliquam penitentiam iniungeret quam statim et in statu gratie penitens possit agere, et postea aliam adijcere quam non intendat pro penitentia sacramentali imponere: sed pro quandam voluntaria satisfactione iniungere: ita quod qualitercunque impleat sufficiat et etiam si non impleat non intendat illaqueare sed in suo arbitrio ponere"; and *op.cit.*, "Interrogationes": "postea imponat ei penitentiam talem quam statim possit complere ante recidiuationem pro sacramentali. & postea aliam quam videat quod peccator verisimiliter faciet. vnde caueat ne imponat penitentiam talem quam verisimiliter non implebit: quia esset potius illum illaqueare quam soluere." This may be the intention of the *Alphabetum sacerdotum*, A2b, which instructs the priest, after absolution, as follows: "Deinde dicat sacerdos Orate pro me et ego pro vobis. Hoc facto confitens peragat penitentiam si commode potest."

336

fessor ought to impose on every penitent *one Our Father* or some other brief satisfaction that can be performed immediately in the state of grace.

He may then add another, but he should make it clear whether that additional satisfaction must be repeated if it is done in mortal sin. Bartholomaeus also insists that someone who is contrite cannot be said to be in the state of mortal sin.[46] Bartholomaeus's desire to bolster the authority of the priest by advising a second penance appropriate to the sin is at first sight inconsistent with the lax counsel that only one Our Father is enough. But the emphasis remains on avoiding complications: Bartholomaeus is obviously urging that the additional penance be optional or else that one be specifically allowed to do it in the state of sin. Furthermore he wants to free penitents from the obligation to confess before they resume a penance whose performance has been interrupted by sin; and that is why he reminds his readers of the contritionist doctrine—that as soon as one becomes contrite he is forgiven and no longer is in the state of sin.

Godescalc Rosemondt represents still another voice for this mildest solution. Long penances are inappropriate, he states flatly, and urges that penances be of the sort that can be completed on the spot. Extra penitential works can be advised without making them obligatory; but he notes that Alexander of Hales, Thomas Aquinas, Bonaventure and some others think that

---

[46] Bartholomaeus de Chaimis, *Confessionale*, IV, 1, X3b–X4b: "Et si peccator omnino nullam penitentiam uelit accipere a sacerdote sibi impositam dicit tamen se habere disciplicentiam alias contritionem de peccato commisso & firmum propositum non recidiuandi absoluendus est ne cadat in desperationem secundum Scotum [*Quaestiones*, dis. 15, q. 1] . . . . Salubre etiam consilium doctorum est quod cuilibet confitenti ad uitandum ambiguitatem de iteranda penitentia facta in peccato mortali confessor *unum pater noster* uel aliquam aliam breuem satisfactionem *quam statim in statu gratie* exequatur iniungat. Et deinde ei declaret si contingat reliquam satisfactionem sibi per eum iniunctam agere in peccato mortali an debeat illam iterare uel non. non tamen dicitur in mortali qui contritus est" (italics added). Sylvester's advice is consistent with this position but he does not refer to the danger of falling back into sin before completion of the penance. Rather he argues that if the penitent is unwilling to accept the penance he deserves and can only bear a light one, then comply; never let him go away in despair— "deinde potius imponat ei vnum pater noster" or some other light penance he will do. *Sylvestrina*, "Confessor 4," q. 2, par. 3. Cf. Foresti, *Confessionale*, 67b, who also advises a light penance that can be done immediately before falling back into sin.

satisfaction knowingly performed outside the state of grace is use-less. In another place Godescalc repeats his admonition that con-fessors not be severe in the imposition of penances. If the confes-sor discerns that a penitent will not fulfill a difficult penance, he should give a light one—even for very serious sins. Indeed, Godescalc asserts that a penitent may properly refuse too harsh a penance and ask for another. Finally, he takes up the problem of forgotten penances. If the penitent had been so utterly distracted in confession that he has forgotten the penance given him, then he must repeat the confession. But if he forgets out of human neglectfulness, he need only confess that negligence at the next confession. At that next confession the priest does not need to hear all the sins because he could as easily impose a penance for one sin as for a thousand. *As a matter of fact, he could choose to impose no penance at all.* To Godescalc Rosemondt this mildness is the reasonable solution; others are dangerous:

> And in this respect many confessors err and are led by zeal through ignorance, certainly not according to knowledge, im-posing a yoke and great burdens that sinners cannot bear on their shoulders.[47]

The protagonists of mildness—who range from Gerson, An-toninus, Angelus, Sylvester, Godescalc Rosemondt, and other famous authorities on pastoral care, to Bartholomaeus and a number of anonymous manuals—probably were persuaded most by what penitents were doing. The assumption that people were not willing to perform the letter of the Penitential Canons was, in fact, the reason that rigorists like Andreas de Escobar and Jacobus de Clusa were complaining. This lack of ardor for long and harsh penances was reported in the twelfth and thirteenth centuries, and it is safe to assume that it was continuous there-after. In other words, the Penitential Canons, and anything else prescribing harsh penances, were utterly unreal. Yet none of the standard authorities on forgiveness completely freed themselves from a sense of obligation to that law. None ever approached the

---

[47] Rosemondt, *Confessionale*, 1, 1, and 7, 77–78. After asserting that the priest could choose to impose no penance at all, Rosemondt comments: "Et in ea parte multi confessores errant & zelo per ingorantiam quidem non secundum scientiam ducuntur iugum & magna onera quae peccatores ferre non valent humeris eorum imponentes" (ibid., 7, 78).

angry and contemptuous denunciation of Wessel Gansfort, who condemned in the most vehement language all attempts to require satisfaction for sin:

Therefore they would do better by good example of life, by correcting the habits of penitents, than by terrifying with strokes and lashes. For they do more against the liberty of the penitent and the generosity of a forgiving God, making His gift diminished and their confession scrupulous, entangling both falsely.

Wessel's final judgment is as logical as it is simple if one wants to free penitents from the archaic bonds of the ancient discipline:

Therefore every sentence of obligatory punishment after the remission of guilt is stupid.[48]

But the voice of Wessel, pleasing as it was to Luther, could never have ruled the late medieval church. Wessel was a radical who followed his theology to its logical conclusions whether tradition was tractable or not. In this case, practice had come to about the same conclusion as Wessel, but authorities on confession and forgiveness could not come out and say it. Practice and logic meant that the lightest penances were to be the rule. But those who believed that the true Church had preserved some kind of accurate measure of the divine economy of temporal punishment were sincerely disturbed by the laxity of contemporary discipline. If purgatory would pass away, it was nevertheless a painful place. A confessor did best when he steered his penitents straight to heaven. And that is why so many authorities preserved the utterly obsolete Penitential Canons—to "guide" the confessor and terrify the penitent. Nevertheless, the main job was steering penitents away from hell. Consequently, the most prudent authorities urged confessors to impose a penance that could be done immediately, such as one Our Father, before the

---

[48] Wessel Gansfort, *Farrago*, 58b–59a: "Melius ergo facerent bono exemplo uitae, confitentium mores corrigendo, quam uerberibus & flagris terrendo. Magis enim contra libertatem confitentis, & liberalitatem remittentis dei faciunt, diminutam illius donationem facientes, & scrupulosam istorum confessionem, utrumque falso implicantes. Infamatur deus non liberaliter et integre donare; terretur plectendus integre confiteri &c." Ibid., 62a: "Stulta igitur omnium sententia de poenali obligatione post remissam culpam."

penitent left the church, returned to his sins, and fell from the state of grace. But such prudent advisers could not, with Wessel Gansfort, call every penance "stupid" and reject it as a superfluous insult to the generosity of a forgiving God. Had they followed this radical line, authorities would have abolished for many penitents an additional way to commit sins. As it was, even more liberal theologians, conscious of the threat posed by severe penances, could talk about the Penitential Canons as if they said something about the religious world of the late middle ages. In so talking they kept alive a rigoristic mentality, and preserved for scrupulous priests and penitents another limitation on the free and universal action of the sacrament of the forgiveness of sins.

RESTITUTION

The last restriction on the power of the priest to forgive his penitent immediately and finally is restitution. This condition is at once the easiest to define, the most complicated to describe, and the most difficult to assess. It is like penance because it is a form of satisfaction. But it is far more rigid than penance because there is, theoretically, no room for bargaining. The debt is owed to a person harmed, and you can pay it back only to that person, in full, insofar as these conditions are humanly possible. Restitution is also like excommunication, because its conditions are carefully defined in canon law. Like excommunication, restitution has a double life: guilty parties are subject to its requirements in both the public forum and the forum of conscience. And if the sanctions of the public forum are not effective, conscience—guided by the confessor—stands ready to demand its due. As we shall see later, the history of the good bishop, Bartolomé de Las Casas, reveals how the confessor's right and duty to demand restitution was potentially a powerful coercive instrument. In theory, restitution provided sanctions that would affect particularly the consciences of rich, powerful, and violent men.

Because they are heavily influenced by canon law, and because they are encyclopedic source books, the summas for confessors treat most thoroughly the intricacies of restitution. The *Raymundina* defines it as the obligation to restore ill-gotten goods, but specifies arson and sacrilege along with simony, plunder, robbery, usury, and fraudulent commerce. Obviously it is the victim's loss as much as the sinner's gain that determines the nature of this obligation; and that consideration makes the category of restitution a broad one.[49]

Whereas the *Raymundina* has no special section devoted to restitution, the alphabetical summas have articles under "Restitutio" that run for thousands of words. The *Supplementum*, *Angelica*, and *Sylvestrina*, for example, have exhaustive discussions, with many subdivisions and separate questions, that fully exploit the implication that any kind of harm requires restitution if it is possible. The *Angelica* gives a good idea of the sweeping nature of this obligation. Its definition—"any satisfaction that must be done to someone else"—might cover anything, and this seems to be Angelus's intention. The obligation to make restitution ensnares someone who throws something into a public street from his house and harms the person or clothing of a passerby; the wives and children of robbers; a woman whose adultery leads to the displacement of legitimate heirs; a man who deflowers a virgin; or a confessor who absolves without proper powers. Angelus's long list of cross-references to other articles in his summa touches an enormous variety of professions and sins. One of the most interesting sections treated in the article itself is on homicide. The requirement of restitution by a murderer includes directions that the value of the victim's earnings, had he lived a normal lifetime, be calculated and restored to the survivors. Similarly, if one wounds or mutilates someone, one must pay for medical treatment and loss of earnings.[50]

Angelus's discussion of homicide stands between the cross-references to other articles and the five-column discussion of usury, and it gives a good idea of the important kind of moral issue that is raised under restitution and the precise way the casuist wanted to estimate it. Now it is of course true that the *Angelica*'s treatment of restitution could not be typical of the literature on forgiveness as a whole. The article is by itself longer than many manuals. Nevertheless the shorter works on confession recognize the obligation to make satisfaction and they treat it seriously either by discussing cases at some length or else by

---

[49] *Raymundina*, III, 34, 47, p. 478; ibid., II, 5–8, pp. 166–256; Tentler, "Summa for Confessors," *Pursuit of Holiness*, 119–122.

[50] *Angelica*, "Restitutio 1," "Homicidia," "Ledens," 1, "Raptor"; cross references to "Adultera," "Adultere filius," "Advocatus," "Alchimista," "Ambasiatores," "Beneficia ecclesiastica," "Clericus," and "Stuprans."

making it absolutely clear that it is a condition of forgiveness. The "Poeniteas cito" mentions restitution twice, and its most popular printed version asserts that even those who aid or favor unjust acquisitions must make satisfaction to the injured parties.[51] About one-third of the manual of Johann Nider and the longer version of the *Confessionale—Defecerunt* of Antoninus of Florence are devoted to the discussion of restitution. Antoninus directs priests not to absolve or give penances to penitents who are unwilling to make full restitution for any loss of reputation or property owing to their sins.[52] Foresti condemns those who send illegitimate offspring to hospitals—"out of shame or greed" —and argues that they are excommunicated and cannot be absolved until they have made full satisfaction.[53] The *Manual for Parish Priests* warns confessors not to allow alms-giving in place of honest restitution to injured persons.[54] Jean Gerson is sufficiently concerned in the *Opus tripartitum* about the fulfillment of restitution to direct penitents to consult higher authorities when there is a great amount of restitution and there is some doubt about to whom the restitution should be given.[55] And the *Directoire des confesseurs* puts it forcefully:

> For it would not be enough to have contrition and displeasure for one's sins and faults, confessing them devoutly to the priest, as we have said above, if [restitution, satisfaction, and penance] were not present. For this is the key of the sacrament of confession: restitution and satisfaction for everything one has done wrong.[56]

[51] *PL*, 207, 1153, line 5, and 1156, line 92; [Poeniteas cito], *Libellus de modo poenitendi*, A3a–b, B6a; [Poeniteas cito], *Summa penitentie*, A5a–b, D6a, E1a–b; [Poeniteas cito], *Confessionale pro scholasticis*, A1b, A5a; [Poeniteas cito], *Penitentionarius. de confessione*, A2a, A4b; [Poeniteas cito], *Penitencionarius* (Latin and German), 2a, 4b.

[52] Nider, *Manuale confessorum*, III, 1 (cf. *Confessionale* [Albi], G1b); Antoninus, *Confessionale—Defecerunt*, 48.

[53] Foresti, *Confessionale*, fol. 1b–2b: "Si filios ex damnato coitu susceptos ex verecundia vel avaricia ad hospitale misit: quia nisi satisfaciat in excommunicationem incidit: nec potest absolui: donec in integrum satisfaciat."

[54] *Manuale parrochialium sacerdotum*, V, B2a–b.

[55] Gerson, *Opus tripartitum*, II, Du Pin, I, 446B.

[56] [Gerson?], *Directoire*, Q8a: "car il ne suffiroit pas auoir contrition et desplaisance de ses pechez et deffaultes: de les confesser deuotement au prestre: cõme dessus est dit: si ces trois ny estoient. Car cest la clef du sacrement de confessiõ: que restitution et satisfaction de tout ce quon a meffait."

Restitution is a requirement of justice. It should not surprise or offend anyone to learn that the medieval church insisted that people guilty of libel, robbery, cheating, murder, or mutilation were held accountable for the damage they had caused—that, in fact, they had to make restoration to the very people who had been harmed. What we must stress here, however, is the role of the confessor in enforcing restitution. He is to determine whether the penitent owes restitution, and he is to make his absolution conditional on payment. No amount of sorrow can make up for this obligation. And although the sinner who is impecunious and therefore incapable of making full restitution is not held to do so, this exception is not meant to undermine the obligation. The authority of the confessor and the sanctions of conscience are powerfully asserted in this most onerous requirement for the efficacy of forgiveness.

CONCLUSION

Restrictions on the working of the Sacrament of Penance strengthened ecclesiastical discipline. They invested priests and prelates with the power of binding sinners and, in secular language, they enabled the clergy to control people, to change their behavior. Cases of excommunication *latae sententiae* and reservations invoke these controls by the very commission of some specifically proscribed act. The culpable penitent becomes incapable of being forgiven by an ordinary priest and must seek someone who has the power of lifting the excommunication or forgiving the reserved sin. In addition, the imposition of an obligatory penance means that the priest can bind the penitent with a series of exercises theoretically designed as expiations and deterrents. Penances may be refused, of course, but once accepted they must be performed; and we have seen that some authorities continued to urge that heavier penances be meted out. Finally, of all the conditions on forgiveness, restitution is undoubtedly the gravest. We have no evidence to show that sentences of satisfaction were frequently pronounced in the confessional and carried out in practice. Nevertheless we know for certain that authorities on the forgiveness of sins considered it absolutely necessary to require satisfaction to injured parties. The sanctions exist in conscience, but they are severe threats because they propose a clear obligation before absolution can be certainly valid.

In other words, the law placed conditions on the operation of divine grace. And even the most beneficent theories of forgiveness, the ones that make absolution easiest to obtain and believe it has been obtained, must contend with exceptions taken from ecclesiastical law. Once again, discipline and consolation cohabit, inseparably if not always peacefully.

Yet in one profound sense the theories of the working of the sacrament and the restrictions placed on its efficacy reveal an essential compatibility between discipline and consolation. For both the theory of how penance works, and the explanation of how it does not, focus on the authority of the sacramentally ordained and hierarchically governed priesthood. If a few contritionists dangerously suggest that forgiveness occurs outside of the Sacrament of Penance, prior to priestly absolution, they nevertheless insist that forgiveness is administered through an ecclesiastical sacrament. This truth is even more decisively asserted by those who believe that priestly absolution can raise imperfect to perfect sorrow; or forgive anyone who does not place an obstacle in its path; or imprint a spiritual adornment that can take effect retroactively; or operate so broadly that its ritual expression should be in simple, universal, declaratory language, "I absolve you," and nothing more. To assert the power of priests to forgive also makes it easier for the sacramental system to incorporate that tangle of archaisms and legalisms that constantly threatened to restrict the efficacy of the Sacrament of Penance. For that legal thicket was—just like the power of absolution—the sole preserve of priests. They controlled forgiveness: they dispensed its consolation to imperfectly contrite sinners; they withheld its consolation from those whom a legal system identified as in need of a special discipline. The heavenly road can be straight and smooth or crooked and rough. But in either case it begins on earth, where penitents obediently submit to priestly confessors.

CHAPTER VI

CONCLUSION

Discipline

IN theory and practice, sacramental confession provided a comprehensive and organized system of social control. Its first principle was the sacramentally ordained priest's dominance, which was expressed in a variety of ways. The necessity of confession to priests was founded on Scripture, canon law, reason, and common sense, and most effectively translated into the fear that one who neglected this indispensable ritual would remain guilty and suffer eternal damnation. Between four and six special cases of conscience helped to strengthen moralists' demands that penitents receive penance more frequently. In addition, the proper jurisdiction of priests was defined and protected, and their authority was emphatically guaranteed by a number of central doctrines. Only priests could absolve from serious sin—with the words "I absolve you"—and place the penitent in contact with the passion and merits of Christ. The position of the priest was also exalted by some theories that made him the unique dispenser of supernatural benefits that could rescue the penitent from his own defects and weaknesses. Thus in these theories, the faithful could see unmistakable advantages of confession to a priest—advantages that secured his preeminence.

In the actual conduct of confession, moreover, priestly superiority is symbolized by an etiquette of deference to the confessor. The interrogation of penitents is the practical counterpart of the supernatural power of the priest's keys in that it communicated in action the superior status of the confessor, who investigated as well as judged. The confessor's expertise bolstered this superior status, for he was provided with a huge store of technical information that helped him to master the situation. This image of the confessor's authority was not so important, however, that pastoral authorities would suffer serious error or incompetence to save the confessor's dignity. On the contrary, they advised a confessor to refer to learned books and wiser authorities if he found he did not have the requisite knowledge (although even in this instance it is the priest, not the penitent, who normally has access to this special knowledge).

Authorities wanted to ensure that confession was done correctly; and because they preferred to embarrass an ignorant confessor than allow improprieties, they not only advised that he admit it when he did not know how to deal with a certain problem, but they even gave some encouragement to the laity to judge their confessors. Thus we come to a second essential principle of discipline: the goal is to make people obey not only men, but morality and law. Here is the substance of this form of social control. Moral and legal norms—which medieval religious authorities were disposed to believe were in agreement—had to be obeyed. Thus sins were enumerated, classified, weighed, graded, and analyzed. Consent was defined. The border between mortal and venial sin was delineated, even for thoughts and desires. If the penitent was married, his sexual conduct—including its motivation—was liable to be judged by particularly harsh and meticulous norms. Other areas of life, other kinds and groups of people, were subject to similar scrutiny. In addition, all the legal technicalities limiting the choice of penitents and circumscribing the power of priests were expounded in detail. Thus the interests of a holy and impersonal law—promulgated and interpreted by hierarchical and scholarly authorities—were guaranteed against fallible curates and errant sinners. The exceptions and difficulties placed before penitents were designed to preserve the integrity of law and ensure that certain kinds of undesirable behavior fell under special kinds of sanctions. We should note that some technicalities seem to be preserved beyond their specific usefulness—they seem to persist only because they are symbols of the hierarchical distribution of power. When Gerson attacks reservations, for example, he appears so moderate and reasonable, and his allies so sensible and respectable, that it is difficult to see any reason, aside from the maintenance of traditional authority, why those abusive practices were not quickly abolished. That they persisted implies an interest in the preservation of authority for its own sake. And in this, as in other cases we have examined, the venerability of authority is not only represented by individual men but enshrined in a holy law; although, we should add, authoritative men and laws tend to be closely identified.

346

The third principle of the system is that its primary subject is the conscience of the individual. A penitent has many obligations to fulfill, but it is essential that he fulfill them conscientiously. He is not expected to remain contentedly in ignorance. He is supposed to know a great deal about sins, and he is definitely expected to be able to recognize when he has willfully committed serious sins. He must feel sorry—in one of a variety of possible ways—for those sins, and, displaying as many as sixteen different virtuous qualities, he must tell all of them he can remember to the priest. Completeness, like the rest of these obligations, is measured by conscience, by sincere intentions. The penitent must also receive absolution with some kind of confidence and be able to maintain that in some sense he does not intend to return to his sins. The penitent's obligations—which subject him to priesthood, hierarchy, morality, and positive law—are onerous. If he has sinned, he is supposed to feel guilty. If he has not fulfilled the requirements for forgiveness, he should continue to feel guilty. Indeed, sacramental confession can become an additional source of guilt, which may arise not only because one has sinned but also because one has not been able to meet adequately the requirements for forgiveness. The element of psychological guilt as a central sanction is vitally important. For while it is true that the encounter with the priest entails submission and shame, the heart of the system is reliance on internal feelings of guilt. If the system is working, sinners will feel guilty outside of confession; and confession will help insure that guilt is elicited independently of the presence of any other human being. The institutions of forgiveness belong most decidedly to a religion of conscience and a system of discipline primarily through guilt.

Consolation

There is no doubt, however, that the penitent is supposed to derive profound psychological benefits from sacramental confession, and authorities try to ensure that this forum offers consolation as well as discipline. We have already noted in many places the inherent tension between these two functions. Now it is appropriate to emphasize their compatibility within the system.

We must begin with a truism: if deviants are to be corrected, they must not be indefinitely isolated or alienated. They must obviously be reformed, reconciled, and reintegrated. To have a

347

method of condemnation without a way to forgive and restore would be self-defeating, unless one's goal were to establish an increasingly restrictive, purified, and smaller community through permanent excommunication. A relatively accessible and routine means of consolation, on the other hand, is compatible with the attempt to achieve conformity to law, especially if law and the community subject to that law are defined in universal terms. In this respect, there can be no doubt that the medieval church intended to be a universal church, not just a sect. Other institutions of discipline and social integration persist, and serve an almost innumerable variety of human groups and communities in Europe before the Reformation. But precisely because the universal obligations imposed by moral theology, canon law, and sacramental confession remain universal and rely on the inculcation of guilt as their major sanction, penance must cure guilt.

These two functions are compatible not only in their general goals, but in certain details. If, for example, the requirements for a good confession seem onerous, at least they are fairly specific. That means that the work prescribed is not vague and endless. Furthermore, there is an important body of opinion interested in maintaining some kind of moderation in describing the obligation of a good, complete confession. Thus penitents are advised to do their best and trust to the adequacy of that effort. In this connection, the authority of the priest can console as effectively as it can discipline. If ordination sets him indelibly apart, this very superiority can be invoked to assure the penitent that there is present—immanent—a spiritual power that will save as well as judge. Especially noteworthy here are those theories that exalt the keys. It is significant that of the six most authoritative or popular authors on confession—Guido de Monte Rocherii, Jean Gerson, Antoninus of Florence, Angelus de Clavasio, Sylvester Prierias, and Andreas de Escobar—only Andreas fails to mention the power of the keys to raise imperfect to perfect sorrow. The doctrine of the *obex*, or obstacle, although it is not universally accepted, is nevertheless widely held and represents a radical affirmation of the benefits of sacramental absolution. In an admittedly uncommon and even more exaggerated form, the same kind of benefits are offered in the doctrine of the ornament of the soul. Yet the benefits of the keys do not even depend on specific theological doctrines. The almost unanimous rejection of the notion that the priest "shows" someone absolved, the unanimous acceptance of a declaratory, indicative absolution, the very insistence on the necessity of confession, as well as the ancient tradition of confessing to priests, all add up to a convincing proof that ordained priests truly forgive and effectively console.

In practice, as in theory, discipline and consolation can be complementary. The etiquette that prescribes deference before the priest also ensures a more formal and less uncertain atmosphere for the penitent. If the penitent's obligations seem difficult and even dangerous, the equally serious obligations of the pastor of souls must be reassuring to the anxious penitent. And to anyone conscious of even a part of the maze of legal restrictions and technicalities encumbering the power to forgive sins, the confessor's expertise would be as comforting as it would be awe-inspiring. Thus without denying the tensions between consolation and discipline, it is evident that they also mesh. Social control and the cure of anxiety are accommodated in one institutional system.

But the accommodation could never be perfect. Sacramental confession had ambitious and not totally reconcilable goals. And it is best to look at the institution from that perspective when we examine the ways that sacramental confession was open to misunderstanding, suspicion, and reasoned attacks.

The Reformation's Attack on Sacramental Confession

The Protestant reformers of the sixteenth century did not agree on what institutions of discipline and consolation should replace medieval sacramental confession; but they agreed that it had to be replaced. Luther thought that to go to a minister of the word, unburden your conscience, and hear him pronounce absolution was a comfort essential to poor sinful Christians. He would never abolish that opportunity, he said, and he proved his sincerity by confessing to Bugenhagen frequently throughout his life.[1] Even Calvin was hesitant to abolish private confession

---

[1] Karl Binder, "Streiflichter zur Beichte und Eucharistie in katholischer und protestantischer Sicht," *Wissenschaft im Dienste des Glaubens. Festschrift für Abt Dr. Hermann Peichl O. S. B.*, ed. by Josef Kisser et al., Studien der Wiener katholischen Akademie, vol. 4 (Vienna, 1965), 67; Luther, "Von der Beichte," (1522), *WA*, 10, pt. 3, 61–64—"aber dannocht wil ich mir die heymliche beicht niemants lassen nemen und wolt sie nit umb der gantzen welt schatz geben. Dann ich weyss was trost und stercke sie mir gegeben hat" (p. 61); "Ein Sermon vom Sakrament der Busse"

immediately. Nevertheless, the reformed tradition in general had little sympathy for it and Calvin did not encourage it.[2] Zwingli, the most thorough opponent of the traditional penitential system, had so little use for private confession that he could scarcely suggest any circumstances in which he would recommend it.[3] Despite this range of opinion among the major reformers, however, they all found the same fundamental defects in the medieval institution, which we may say, without exaggeration, they detested.

(1519), *WA*, 2, 714–719; Erich Roth, *Die Privatbeichte und Schlüsselgewalt in der Theologie der Reformatoren* (Gütersloh, 1952), 31–42; E. Fischer, *Zur Geschichte der evangelischen Beichte: I. Die katholische Beichtpraxis bei Beginn der Reformation und Luthers Stellung dazu in den Anfängen seiner Wirksamkeit; II. Niedergang und Neubelung des Beichtinstituts in Wittenberg in den Anfängen der Reformation*, Studien zur Geschichte der Theologie und der Kirche, vol. 8, no. 2, and vol. 9, no. 4 (Leipzig, 1902–1903), I, 162–169, 175–185; Paul Althaus, *The Theology of Martin Luther*, tr. by Robert C. Schultz (Philadelphia, 1966), 316–318.

[2] John Calvin, *Institutes*, III, 4, 1–39; idem, *Ioannis Calvini Opera quae supersunt omnia*, 59 vols., Corpus Reformatorum, ed. by W. Baum, Eduard Cunitz, and Eduard Reus, vols. 29–87 (Brunswick, 1863–1900), letter to Farel (May, 1540), 9, 41: "I have often testified to you that it does not seem useful for the churches to abolish confession unless that which I have recently established is substituted in its place . . . . When the day of the Supper approaches I decree that those who desire to take communion present themselves to me first, and at the same time I direct them in that intention so that those who are unused to this and inexperienced in religion may be better prepared; also that those who have need of a special admonition may hear it; finally that, if there are any who are tormented by some disquiet of conscience, they may receive consolation. Because the danger is great, however, that the people (who do not distinguish sufficiently between the yoke of Christ and the tyranny of antichrist) may think themselves led back to a new servitude, I also attempt to cure this doubt. I not only state that the papal confession is rejected by me, but I openly show the reasons why it is displeasing; and then I pronounce in general that it is not only to be abhorred because of those superstitions in which it was involved, but that no law ought in any way to be suffered that binds consciences in snares. For Christ is our unique lawgiver, to whom we are debtors. Afterwards, I teach that there is nothing derogatory to our liberty here, since I impose nothing at all that Christ Himself has not ordained. For how shameless it would be not to deem it fitting to make good your faith to the church whose communion you seek, and how miserable will the condition of the church be if it is forced to receive into the participation of so great a mystery those whom it is utterly ignorant of, or whom it strongly suspects." See also, Roth, *Privatbeichte*, 133–161; Binder, "Streiflichter," 70–71.

[3] Roth, *Privatbeichte*, 102–104.

They were not obsessed with the ignorance, greed, lechery, or scarcity of confessors. They were not protesting the failure of bad men to make available their essentially wholesome truths. On the contrary, the reformers condemned what we have examined: the theory and practice of sacramental confession as it was supposed to be, according to the common teaching of irreproachably Catholic authorities. On certain points they may have focused on the particular doctrines of particular scholastic theologians. But on the whole, they were talking about the ordinary habits and assumptions that even simple manuals taught. Even Luther, who was most willing to renew rather than destroy, so transformed the doctrine and behavior of confessing that it became unrecognizable as the descendant of the obligatory, *ex opere operato* sacrament of purification he had experienced. Indeed, it was Luther who first stated the arguments that more radical reformers would use to eliminate private confession entirely. Thus it is Luther, ironically, who must take primary responsibility for the situation in modern Christianity that allows a theologian to assert, by way of definition, "a Protestant doesn't confess." Most importantly, the emotional center of the sixteenth-century campaign was the reformers' denunciation of sacramental confession because it tormented rather than consoled. They proclaimed a different teaching and observance and guaranteed that it would console.[4]

Perhaps Luther's best known criticism of the medieval institution is his denunciation of the theory that accepts sorrow based purely on fear—the famous "gallows sorrow" experienced by the thief, about to face execution, who hates his punishment but not his crime.[5] Luther's attack on this "hypocrisy" is an integral part of his own theory of justification, it is true. But as a criticism

[4] Binder, "Streiflichter," 66; Roth, *Privatbeichte*, 144–148; Spykman, *Attrition and Contrition*, 257. Calvin asserts explicitly that confession is intolerable not because of its abuses but because of its essence: "Au reste il n'a pas esté question d'abolir la confesse Papale entre nous, pour les abus qui s'y commettent: mais pource que c'est en sa propre substance, origine, et integrité, une corruption insupportable" (*Reformation contre Antoine Cathelan, Opera*, 9, 132).

[5] Luther, *Grund und Ursach aller Artikel D. Martin Luthers so durch römische Bulle unrechtlich verdammt sind* (1521), *WA*, 7, 364; cf. *Luther's Works, American Edition*, 55 vols., 1–30, ed. by Jaroslav Pelikan, 31–55, ed. by Helmut T. Lehmann (Philadelphia and St. Louis, 1955—), vol. 32, pp. 34–43, hereafter cited as *LW*; *WA*, 1, 99; Roth, *Privatbeichte*, 22–23, 66–67.

of existing theory and practice, this was one of Luther's least significant and least relevant objections. As we have seen, "fear sorrow" was not a popular idea at the end of the middle ages, even among proponents of the adequacy of imperfect sorrow or attrition. Moreover, Luther mounted a campaign that went far beyond the condemnation of hypocritical contrition. For he struck at the most basic assumptions of medieval confession.

Luther completely undermined the necessity of confession to priests, an indispensable element in the medieval system. He rejected the pope's right to command yearly confession and insisted, on the contrary, that confession must always be the freely willed choice of the penitent. Christ did not make us one another's slaves, and thus no one can be compelled to confess. Only the realization that one needs to confess should compel a Christian, and even preparation for the Lord's Supper does not require it.[6]

Examination of conscience according to the variety of categories we have studied also disappears from Lutheran practice. Luther severely condemns this fundamental part of the medieval institution, as he insists that only the distinction between man's and God's commands is important. A penitent should again respond primarily to the urgings of his conscience and concentrate on those sins that particularly trouble him. In addition, Luther reduces the importance of the examination of conscience by insisting that the penitent should focus his attention on a new life rather than on past sins.[7]

[6] Luther, *Von der Beichte, ob die der Papst Macht habe zu gebieten* (1521), *WA*, 8, 156-157, 164ff; Roth, *Privatbeichte*, 45–47. For a different emphasis, on the persistence of "obligatory" confession in spite of Luther's condemnation of papal compulsion, see Leonhard Fendt, "Luthers Reformation der Beichte," *Luther: Mitteilungen der Luthergesellschaft*, 24, no. 3 (1953), 121–137; and Ernst Kinder, "Beichte und Absolution nach den lutherischen Bekenntnisschriften," *Theologische Literaturzeitung*, 77 (1952), nr. 2, 543–550. But while Fendt, Binder, and Roth point out the persistence of old practices (which Fendt greatly deplores), they confirm the essential importance of the breaks with the medieval tradition; see, for example, Fendt, 123; Kinder, 544; Roth, 144–148.

[7] Luther, *Decem praecepta Wittenbergensi praedicata populo* (1518), *WA*, 443, 516ff.; idem, "Ein Sermon D. M. Luthers am Gründonnerstag" (1523), *WA*, 12, 492–493; "Ein Sermon von der Beicht und dem Sacrament" (1524), *WA*, 489; Roth, *Privatbeichte*, 47–49; Fischer, *Geschichte der evangelischen Beichte*, I, 49, 130.

But the elimination of the detailed examination of conscience is subsidiary to Luther's most damaging criticism of medieval practice: his denial that a complete confession is necessary or even possible. Already in 1518, before he fully developed his campaign against the Catholic confessional, he had emphasized the hidden sinfulness of man; the sinfulness even of good works; and the inevitability of secret sins, such as sexual desire. Luther then accepts the principle that only sins that entail full consent to the deed and are universally recognized as serious sins should be confessed; and the examples he gives are murder, lying, stealing, and adultery. In the place of casuistic determinations to ensure that all mortal sins are confessed, Luther suggests some general statement be made, such as, "Behold, all that I am, my life, all that I do and say, is such that it is mortal and damnable."[8] By 1524, Luther offers a simple rule to free penitents from a burden he considered intolerable: confession, he asserts, should be short.[9]

Luther's attack on accepted theories of how the Sacrament of Penance works entailed a rejection of ordinary assumptions about contrition and absolution. Contrition remained an essential step in the Lutheran view of justification. But it was no longer an act or habit of the penitent, aroused for each sin, or for each sin occurring to him, or for all sins recollected collectively. In a line of argument consistent with his condemnation of gallows sorrow, Luther openly spoke in strict disciplinary terms of a contrition that is true if it bears fruit in a changed heart, spirit, disposition, and life, so that one sins no more. True penance, he declared, lasts for a lifetime, not just the space of a confession.[10] In other

---

[8] Luther, "Sermo de poenitentia" (1518), *WA*, 1, 322–323; idem, *Defense and Explanation of all the Articles* (1521), *LW*, 32, 42–44; "Pro veritate inquirenda et timoratis conscientiis consolandis conclusiones" (1518), *WA*, 1, 623–633 (esp. conclusions 46 and 47); "Ein Sermon vom Sakrament der Busse" (1518), *WA*, 2, 715, 721: "Ein Sermon von der Beicht und dem Sacrament" (1524), *WA*, 15, 489; Fischer, *Geschichte der evangelischen Beichte*, I, 135–137, 145, 211–214.

[9] Luther, "Ein Sermon von der Beicht und dem Sacrament" (1524), *WA*, 15, 489.

[10] Luther, "Sermo de poenitentia," *WA*, 1, 319, 322; *Grund und Ursach aller Artikel*, *WA*, 7, 361; "denn wo die rew recht angaht, durch gottis gnadenn, da wirt zugleich der mensch gewandelt ynn eyn ander mensch, herz, mut, synn, und lebenn, und das heysz ich nymmer thun und eyn new leben"; cf. *LW*, 32, 38–42.

words, he followed the tradition of Lombardist contritionism, which we have consistently identified with discipline, not consolation.

But Luther's teaching goes far beyond medieval contritionism, and ends up by undermining the disciplinary function of contrition in penance more completely than even the Scotists could have done. For Luther makes his contrition a purely passive sorrow, and defines it in terms of the terrors of conscience he had himself experienced. This fear and trembling, a necessary prelude to justification, contains the truth of justification in a hidden form. But passive contrition is the penitent's work only in the sense that he admits his impotence and worthlessness in the face of an all-powerful and all-just God. Only the recognition that one can do nothing on one's own is a part of contrition that might be described as a work of the penitent. Certainly there is no room for discussions of the quality, intensity, or perfection of the penitent's sorrow. The contrite man need do only one thing: believe the promise of forgiveness, for that belief constitutes forgiveness itself.[11]

And that is the heart of Luther's consoling doctrine, which thoroughly negates the medieval system and its promise of consolation. Luther used contritionist language to undermine contritionism itself and to build a new institution of forgiveness. God's forgiveness comes first, he declares in 1518, but it is hidden in the form of wrath so that one cannot be certain of it. Then the priest pronounces absolution and causes peace, and we become capable of recognizing the fact of forgiveness.[12] In this explana-

[11] Luther, "Sermo de poenitentia," *WA*, 1, 322: "Contritio vera non est ex nobis, sed ex gratia dei: ideo desperandum de nobis et ad misericordiam eius confugiendum"; ibid., 323: "Secundum vide, ne ullo modo te confidas absolvi propter tuam contritionem (Sic enim super te et tua opera confides, id est, pessime praesumes): sed propter verbum Christi, qui dixit Petro: Quodcunque solveris super terram, solutum erit et in caelis. Hic, inquam, confide, si sacerdotis obtineuris solutionem, et crede fortiter te absolutum, et absolutus vere eris, quia ille non mentitur, quicquid sit de tua contritione. Nam sic non crederes sententiae pronunciatae super te a deo, qui mentiri non postest, ac sic te veracem et ipsum mendacem faceres." See Althaus, *Theology of Luther*, 173–178, 248–269, and Roth, *Privatbeichte*, 35–42, for many citations.

[12] Luther, *Resolutiones disputationum de indulgentiarum virtute* (1518), *WA*, 1, 540 lines 8–12: "Quando deus incipit hominem justificare, prius eum damnat, et quem vult aedificare, destruit, quem vult sanare, percutit, quem vivificare, occidit." Ibid., lines 30–38; "Hoc autem facti quando hominem conterit et in sui suorumque peccatorum cognitionem humiliat ac tremefacit.

tion, however, neither a sufficient sorrow nor the priest and his formula cause anything. The priest merely declares the forgiveness of Christ. And the peaceful conscience, which is a product of the firm belief that one is forgiven, is a prerequisite of forgiveness. One of Luther's favorite ways of dramatizing this paradox was to insist that if we do not believe we are forgiven—if we do not find peace in the promise of forgiveness—we make God a liar. But we can appreciate the full impact of that assertion only if we contrast it with the medieval sacrament's promises of peace from its traditional sources: from the adequacy of confession, and particularly its completeness; from the adequacy of sorrow for sin; and from the power of a sacramentally ordained priest's absolution, perhaps most clearly evident in its ability to raise attrition to contrition. Luther's salvation by faith not only asserts the necessity of trusting belief in the promise of forgiveness; it also rejects unequivocally all the requirements of sacramental confession. In other words, Luther cut every traditional element of discipline out of the theory of justification and made it as purely a theory of consolation as he could. A logical consequence of this doctrine is the abolition of reservations, the jurisdiction of one's own priest, and the canon law meaning of excommunication. A compatible corollary is the rejection of the whole structure of satisfaction for sin—penances, indulgences, and purgatory itself.

. . . Verum tunc adeo ignorat homo sui iustificationem, ut sese proximum putet damnationi, nec infusionem gratiae, sed effusionem irae dei super se hanc putet esse. . . . Stante autem hac misera suae conscientiae confusione, non habet pacem neque consolationem, nisi ad potestatem ecclesiae confugiat suisque peccatis et miseriis per confessionem detectis postulet solatium et remedium; neque enim suo consilio vel auxilio sese poterit pacare, immo absorberetur tandem tristicia in desperationem." Ibid., 541, lines 15–22, "Ex istis nunc patet, quod supra quaerebatur, scilicet quod licet remissio culpae fiat per infusionem gratiae ante remissionem sacerdotis, talis tamen est infusio gratiae et ita sub forma irae abscondita . . . ut homo incertior sit de gratia, cum fuerit ipsa praesens, quam cum est absens, ideo ordine generali non est nobis certa remissio culpae nisi per iudicium sacerdotis, nec per ipsum quidem nisi credas Christo promittenti: Quodcunque solveris etc." Ibid., 542, lines 7–18: "Igitur remissio dei gratiam operatur, sed remissio sacerdotis pacem, quae et ipsa est gratia et donum dei, quia fides remissionis et gratiae praesentis. . . . Non ergo prius solvit Petrus quam Christus, sed declarat et ostendit solutionem. Cui qui crediderit cum fiducia, vere obtinuit pacem et remissionem apud deum (id est, certus fit se esse absolutum) non rei sed fidei certitudine propter infallibilem misericorditer promittentis sermonem: Quodcunque solveris etc."

Luther's pastoral instruction makes the consequences of this teaching easy to understand. The 1531 *Small Catechism*'s formulas for the use of penitents in confession represent the distillation of his doctrine of penance. They renounce the medieval tradition's detailed examination of conscience and good, complete confession. They prescribe, on the contrary, a general avowal of sinfulness, provide an opportunity for confessing some particular sins—offenses that are open, serious, or especially troublesome—and direct the energies of the penitent away from guilt and the awareness of these sins to belief in forgiveness outside himself. Before God, the *Small Catechism* declares, Christians should acknowledge their guilt for sins they do not even realize, as the Lord's Prayer bids them to do. "But in the presence of the father confessor," it adds, "we should confess only those sins we know and feel in our hearts." The *Catechism* defines these in a list that reveals agreement with medieval ethics on the names of sins, but which breaks with traditional institutional methods of controlling sin:

> Here consider your calling according to the Ten Commandments, namely, whether you are a father or mother, a son or daughter, a master, mistress, or servant, if you have been disobedient, unfaithful, slothful, angry, unchaste, or quarrelsome, if you have injured any one by words, or deeds, if you have stolen, neglected, or wasted aught, or done any other evil.[13]

The two specific models of confession offered—one for servants and the other for a master or mistress—express those general classes of sins in similarly general (and familiar) formulaic recitations. Thus the master is directed to say, "I did not guide my children, wife, and servants to the honor of God (das ich mein kind und gesind, weib nicht trewlich gezogen hab zu Gottes ehren)," or, "I have cursed, given a bad example with vulgar words and deeds, hurt and slandered my neighbor, sold at too much profit, given poor or underweight merchandise"; and he may add anything else he has done against the laws of God and his own calling. To ensure that this is not an occasion for scrupulosity, however, the instructions contain this emphatic paragraph:

[13] Luther, "How One Should Teach Common Folk to Shrive Themselves" (1531), *LW*, 53, 119–120; *WA*, 30^1, 384.

But if someone should not be bothered by such or still greater sins, let him not try to find or feign other sins and thus make confession a torment. Let him tell one or two sins that he knows, e.g., especially do I confess that I once cursed, once I was inconsiderate in my words, once I neglected this N., etc. And let it remain at that.

Obviously Luther did not abolish the sense of sin that arises from the personal admission of a list of transgressions. No matter how general these formulas remain, they clearly retain the idea of sin as specific wrong acts. Indeed, Luther is openly skeptical in his instructions about sinners who cannot find anything specific to say:

But if you know of no sin at all (*which seems almost impossible*), don't confess any particular one, but receive forgiveness upon the general confession, which you make to the father confessor before God.

Yet even when Luther points to sins, he is aware of dangers: this paragraph is designed to protect confession from ruminating penitents and interrogating priests. In other words, it is designed to guarantee consolation, even at the expense of discipline. The logic of salvation by faith—which asserts peremptorily that Christ's promise is true and must be believed—requires that consolation take precedence over discipline in the institutions of forgiveness. Thus the formula of absolution begins with Matthew 8:13: "As thou believest, so be it done unto thee." And the declaration of forgiveness is as positive as it can be: "And I, by the command of Jesus Christ our Lord, forgive thee all thy sin." The pastoral office is chiefly to comfort.[14]

The balance in favor of consolation was already evident in 1518. It is true that the *Ten Commandments Preached to the People of Wittenberg* and *Instruction for the Confession of Sins* retain, in summary form, the medieval manuals' basic strategy of control by identifying sins. And while Luther's treatment of sins avoids in these works multiple categorizations and excessive casuistic detail, we can only say that in this respect Luther is a reformer in the spirit of Gerson.[15] But no medieval authority—

[14] *LW*, 53, 120–121; *WA*, 30¹, 385–387.
[15] Luther, *Decem praecepta*, *WA*, 1, 394–521, esp. 394, 516–521; idem, *Instructio pro confessione peccatorum* (1518), *WA*, 1, 257–265. While the

not even Gerson—would have dared give this version of how the sacrament works:

> Beware of the great error of those who approach the Sacrament of the Eucharist leaning on that frail reed—that they have confessed, that they are not conscious of mortal sin, or that they have sent ahead of them their own prayers and preparations. All those eat and drink judgment to themselves, for by these things they do not become worthy and pure, but rather they become defiled through that trust in their purity. But if they believe and trust that they will obtain grace there, this faith alone makes them pure and worthy, a faith that does not rely on those works, but on the purest, most holy, most firm word of Christ, Who says, "Come to me all you who labor. . . ."

The context—an instruction on confessing—makes these favorite themes of Luther all the more startling. The practical application of his teaching, already clearly in opposition to the old practice, becomes even more explicit as he goes on to attack the search for sins as an occasion for "fear and anguish of conscience," which drive people away from the Sacrament of the Altar. Tests of worthiness are rejected. The only disposition necessary for communion is the desire for grace, belief in its possibility, and awareness of one's weakness and corruption. This sacrament demands only that you hunger and thirst for it.[16]

Compare these instructions with the manuals and summas for confessors. Place Luther's emphasis on general sinfulness against the directions to investigate sins in the *Angelica, Sylvestrina, Confessionale—Defecerunt, Opus tripartitum*, or *Peycht Spigel*. Consider some of the obsessions of this literature that must inevitably disappear, such as sinful thoughts, nocturnal emission, or the motivation and position of the marital act.[17] Recall the con-

---

Decem praecepta retains much of the medieval manual for confessors' treatment of sins, it directly attacks the elaboration of categories as burdensome and already urges that confession should be short: "Ex ignorantia docentium iste tumultus confessionum natus est, cum confessio debeat esse brevis et aperta, ut cito possit expedire uterque," *WA*, 1, 517.

[16] *Instructio, WA*, 1, 264.

[17] Cf. *Decem praecepta, WA*, 1, 482–499, where Luther still deals with sins of lust in a traditional way, with a gradation of sexual sins—fornication, promiscuity, deflowering, abduction, adultery (simple and double), incest, and sacrilege (483); a discussion of the sin "ardentior amator"—but noting

ditions of a good confession and the circumstances a sincere penitent or confessor must keep in mind. By 1518, Luther has begun to eliminate the core of discipline from the practice of confession. In addition, he has denied that confession is a purifying rite, which, if performed correctly, justifies one in receiving the Sacrament of the Altar. There could be no doubt in 1518 that no matter how much Luther admired confessing, his reforms would be fundamental for religious practice. For they directly changed the areas and mechanisms of control by the clergy.

But the campaign was waged in the name of consolation. When Luther talks about "the word" and "the promise," he means consolation. And he generally makes the connection between theological justification and psychological peace whenever he talks about the forgiveness of sins. That connection was already clear in 1518; and perhaps never did he express it more beautifully than in a brief tract of that year, *Conclusions for Inquiring into the Truth and Consoling Terrified Consciences*. It is about salvation by faith—as its summary conclusion asserts. But that only means that it is about contrition, confession, absolution, and consolation. And in every phase of his argument—the role of the priest, the meaning of absolution, the requirements imposed on the penitent to confess and be contrite—Luther returns to his basic theme, that forgiveness is given unconditionally to those who have the faith that Christ has forgiven them as He promised. One paradoxical conclusion deserves our attention, because when we place it against the traditional beliefs about sacramental confession we can appreciate the radical nature of Luther's innovations. If it were possible, Luther's fortieth conclusion states, to conceive of a man who was not contrite and yet believed himself absolved, we would have to conclude that such a man is truly

---

"difficile est . . . regulam tradere" (483, 489); unnatural vices—but very briefly (489); involuntary pollution (489–490); sinful words (490–494); and signs (494–498). Without claiming that Luther revolutionized sexual ethics, we can note the dramatic change in pastoral instruction on sexual sins; see for example, *Katechismuspredigten* (1528), *WA*, 30^1, 7–8, 75–77; *Deudsch Catechismus* (*Der Grosse Katechismus*) (1529), *WA*, 30^1, 160–163; and *Der kleine Catechismus, WA*, 30^1, 286–287, 332–335. Similarly Calvin, *Institutes*, II, viii, 41–44 (vol. 1, pp. 405–408) has a very general treatment of sexual sins, which only mentions the man who is an adulterer with his own wife. See also André Biéler, *L'Homme et la femme dans la doctrine de Calvin* (Geneva, 1963), 60–63; Ronald S. Wallace, *Calvin's Doctrine of the Christian Life* (Edinburgh and London, 1959), 174–176.

absolved: "Finge casum (per impossibile), sit absolvendus non contritus, credens sese absolvi, hic est vere absolutus."[18] That proposition is paradoxical for Luther, because he thought of the faithful Christian as someone who realizes he needs absolution because he is contrite, which means that he has experienced the enormity of his sinfulness and the terrors of judgment. Luther did not conceive of a penitent who truly believed himself absolved, but had achieved that certainty by deceiving himself about his impotence, iniquity, and fear. Nevertheless, the hypothetical case is instructive, for it expresses succinctly two of the Reformation's most radical contributions to the theology of forgiveness.

First, absolution is an objectively unconditional offer of forgiveness. It requires nothing for its validity beyond what has already been given in the sacrifice of the cross and the promise attached to it. Failures of confessors cannot impede its efficacy. It does not depend on the power of priests whose ordination makes them the unique dispensers of forgiveness; or on priests whose jurisdiction is specially defined; or on the wording of the formula pronounced over the penitent; or on any knowledge, talent, or skill of the pastor of souls. A confessor can be ignorant, or even joking, and absolution will remain valid. Such inadequate priests will find it difficult to communicate the promise of forgiveness that is absolution, it is true. Nevertheless, absolution remains unconditional objectively, because it is guaranteed outside of the temporal, visible church, by the cross and the promise.

Second, absolution is subjectively certain. No matter how you get it—from reading the promise in the Gospel, or hearing it in a sermon, or recalling its conferral through Baptism, or receiving it in the Eucharist, or having a minister of the word pronounce it after private confession—absolution works if you believe it works. Failures of penitents cannot impede its efficacy —excepting only the failure of unbelief. Indeed, the penitent's inadequacy turns out to be his advantage: for recognition of one's

[18] Luther, "Pro veritate inquirenda et timoratis conscientiis consolandis conclusiones" (1518), *WA*, 1, 629–633; conclusion 40. Cf. "Sermo de poenitentia," *WA*, 1, 323–324, where belief makes absolution valid even if the priest is joking: *Grund und Ursach aller Artikel*, *WA*, 7, 379–380; (*LW*, 32, 49–50).

impotence and corruption is the first step to justifying faith. Thus the penitent need only accept his defects, not fear them. For once again, there are no conditions or prerequisites. His forgiveness does not depend on the thoroughness of his examination of conscience; the completeness of his confession; the quality of his contrition; or the performance of his penance. There is only one condition—one prerequisite, one *facere quod in se est*—by which a man merits forgiveness: unquestioning faith that one's own sins have been forgiven.

Luther establishes this unconditional and certain absolution by asserting that its source is outside of us. To begin with, it exists beyond the visible church. For while it is true that Luther emphatically retained a visible community—the place where the promise was effectively preached—he nevertheless safeguards that promise from the fallibility of human institutions. Ultimately, it is not the church's absolution but Christ's absolution, independent of persons, times, and places. In addition, it exists totally separate from the penitent. In a variety of metaphors, Luther teaches sinners that the cause of forgiveness is not internal—in human virtues and performances—but external, in Christ alone, Who becomes, as it were, physically interposed between us and the righteousness of God. Because God looks at Christ's righteousness, not our sinfulness, if only we believe it, He always certainly forgives.[19]

The correct word is forgive, not purify. For it is essential to this new system of consolation that all traces of the psychology of merit be eliminated. Sinners remain sinners—with all their corruption and weakness. But their sins are not counted against them because they have believed. In the consciousness of consolation they become free to do good works; but they do not become free of the condition of man, which is sinfulness. Yet the consequence of this sinfulness is not a renewal of the disciplinary

[19] Luther, *Defense and Explanation of All the Articles*, LW, 32, 28: "Meanwhile the righteousness of Christ must be our cover. His perfect godliness must be our shield and defense." Idem, *Lectures on Galatians*, 1535, LW, 26, 232: "Thus we live under the curtain of the flesh of Christ (Heb. 10:20). He is our 'pillar of cloud by day and pillar of fire by night' (Ex. 13:21), to keep God from seeing our sin." These examples express metaphorically the rejection—implied in the theological doctrines of imputed righteousness, non-imputation of sinfulness, *simul justus et peccator*, and *justitia Christi extra nos*—of purification through sacramental confession.

functions of the confessional, but a more urgent affirmation of an unconditional and certain absolution.[20]

Thus Luther's radical doctrine of consolation undermined the traditional institution's discipline. The Fathers of Trent knew that, and they reaffirmed the goodness of uncertainty and the need to retain confession's disciplinary aspects, right down to reserved cases. It was only logical that they should condemn the vain presumption of the heretics' claim to certitude as well.[21]

The Swiss reform merely took Luther's attack further. If Calvin united justification and sanctification in a way that many have suspected as a return to the old legalism, he nevertheless reaffirmed the truth of the certitude of forgiveness solely through the sacrifice of Christ. He attacked the same elements of sacramental confession that Luther had attacked: its definition, scriptural foundation, necessity, compulsion, conduct, legal regulation, and pretensions to monopolize forgiveness. His original contribution was to attack them more thoroughly. Calvin did not, like Luther, find it a consoling treasure that he could not do without. On the contrary, he called it butchery. Zwingli was even more hostile.[22] And all who rejected it, did so in the name of consolation.[23]

They were not impractical men who did not understand the need for institutions of social control. But they agreed that this use of social control placed too great a burden on the Christian conscience. Consequently they invoked Christian liberty to effect the transformation and eventual abolition of sacramental confession, just as Gerson had invoked Christian liberty before them to

[20] Luther, *Lectures on Galatians, 1519, LW*, 27, 231: "Accordingly, Job is both righteous and a sinner [simul iustus, simul peccator]." See also, Althaus, *Theology of Luther*, 242–250, and above, n. 12 and n. 19.

[21] *Canons and Decrees of the Council of Trent. Original Text with English Translation*, tr. by H. J. Schroeder (St. Louis and London, 1941), 6th Session, ch. 9, "Canons Concerning Justification," 12–14, pp. 35, 43–44, 314, 322; 14th Session, "Sacrament of Penance," ch. 7, pp. 96, 371–372; Spykman, *Attrition and Contrition*, 144–230.

[22] Calvin, *Institutes*, III, 4, esp. 3 and 17, and IV, 10, 1; Spykman, *Attrition and Contrition*, 230–258. For Calvin's use of "carnificina" to describe various aspects of confession, see *Opera*, 1, 158, 707; 2, 469; 6, 495; 7, 467. Spykman, 8, refers to Calvin's labeling confession a "laniena conscientiarum"; Roth, *Privatbeichte*, 15–16, 101–104, 109–112, 114–115, 119–132.

[23] Cf. Steven E. Ozment, *The Reformation in the Cities. The Appeal of Protestantism to Sixteenth-Century Germany and Switzerland* (New Haven and London, 1975), esp. pp. 15–56.

protect the consolations of sacramental confession from the flagellants. The reformers turned discipline over to other institutions—with what success we cannot speculate here—in the name of theologies of consolation.

Judging Sacramental Confession

The criticisms of the reformers recall many of the themes we have touched on in the course of this study, and lead naturally to the attempt to make some final evaluation of sacramental confession on the eve of the Reformation.

Was there no system at all—was there nothing but confusion, as H. C. Lea suggests? The differences of opinion we have noted among late medieval authorities make that a conceivable conclusion, but one that cannot be sustained. Explicit agreement among authorities on what is sinful, how a penitent makes a good confession, how and why church law must be obeyed, even why a priest is necessary, is more extensive and profound than the disputes. Beyond these explicit areas of agreement, moreover, we have discerned inner compatibilities between discipline and consolation that are further evidence that confession was complex but not confused. Accepting that there was a system, therefore, and keeping in mind its complexities, we can better evaluate some other criticisms.

Was sacramental confession "Pelagian," the natural product of a religion of works? The heavy emphasis on the benefits of submission to the keys indicates, rather, that special powers are necessary to supplement weak human beings precisely because they lack those Pelagian powers to achieve justifying contrition on their own. Was it then a magical ritual? On the contrary, it demanded the most rationalistic and conscientious effort on the part of the faithful penitent, whose purification certainly depended on his own intentions. Was it a purely legalistic and externalized religious ritual? For similar reasons that charge ignores the obvious: because authorities on confession expected obedience in the depths of conscience, an inner guilt at transgression, and a willing acceptance of personal spiritual obligations. Was its moral and sacramental theology decadent and excessively lax? Such a conclusion would surely have to overlook plain facts: that it always defined moral regulations in detail, imputed guilt to sinners individually, asserted the necessity of sincere cooperation with sacramental grace, and taught in sensitive areas of human conduct a harsh moral code. Did it heedlessly create scrupulous consciences? One would have to ignore the explicit attempts of some of the best and most prestigious authorities to prevent and cure scruples of conscience to hold that view. Was it a clerical tyranny? That charge cannot make sense if we recall that priests were also subject to the guilt of conscience and restricted to this institution for its cure. Indeed, if priests could establish their separateness and superiority through regulations on sexuality, they also had to conform to sexual regulations that were much harder than those imposed on the laity. Priests did not author a conspiracy; they participated in a system.

Yet if we take these questions and switch around the answers, we see that every accusation is founded on the institutional reality we have studied. Sacramental confession could be considered Pelagian because it was rationalistic, and because it constantly defined the requirements for forgiveness in the language of human effort and merit. Its formulaic absolution—with the curious worrying that the wrong words might render absolution ineffective—certainly looks like magic. Its mazes of sins, excommunications, restitutions, reservations, jurisdictions, irregularities, impediments, and casuistic distinctions more than suggest legalism. Any number of moral and sacramental doctrines were purposefully "lax," especially when measured by the standards of medieval asceticism and evangelical perfection. Indeed, some can appear lax when judged by modern standards. Finally, priests certainly participated in and were subject to this system, but these male celibates also dominated it, while hierarchical and scholarly authorities articulated the rules that guaranteed that dominance.

In short, the meaning of every judgment of sacramental confession—favorable or unfavorable—depends on what evidence you choose, what part of the institution you pay attention to. But if we stand back from these judgments and view the institution as a whole, we can see why they have arisen, in what ways they express something actual, and how they miss equally real phenomena. The institution cannot be divorced from its historical setting. It was not created by a council of theologians or bishops, it developed over time. Because it was the product of historical evolution, it was complex. Yes, sacramental confession was legalistic and evangelical, Pelagian and Augustinian, laxist and rigorist, magical and rationalistic. To understand these paradoxes is to begin to understand our own preconceptions and more accurately assess the importance of sacramental confession in the Reformation.

It is true that a plausible case might be made for ignoring this complexity and identifying sacramental confession as an independent and direct cause of the Reformation. Such an explanation would begin with the despair and alienation that the institution caused in Luther, Calvin, and Zwingli and look for evidence that these reactions were widespread. The heart of such an argument would be to demonstrate that the church in the later middle ages successfully imposed a stricter observance of confession on the laity of western Europe. In support of this contention we might cite direct legislative action by the hierarchy; the increasing influence of the mendicants; spiritual and institutional reform movements aimed at internal "purification"; and the publicization and standardization of religious norms through printed books. The result of this activity would be to generalize the anxiety and alienation experienced by members of the spiritual elite and create the conditions on which a movement might be built. A basic assumption throughout this argument would be that the reformers were correct; that confession was legalistic, Pelagian, rationalistic, and alternatively hypocritical in its laxity and tyrannical in its rigor, but primarily the latter.

That case looks particularly plausible because the values of a secularistic and pluralistic society dispose us to approve of Luther's and Calvin's critiques. We respond sympathetically to what appears to be a defense of a more modern conception of freedom of conscience—freedom from external authority, scrupulosity, and legalism. We think we understand Luther and Calvin. And perhaps we do. Certainly recent changes in the practice of penance in the Roman Catholic Church suggest that the reformers were in fact pointing in a direction that all western Christianity would eventually follow.

But, disregarding the inadequacy of the evidence for a decisive change in the practice of confession at the end of the middle ages, we must still conclude that such an argument would be at best half true. For even if a case for more extensive observance of confession were proven; even if we could show that change to be a forerunner of protest and reform; we are not likely to find patterns that exactly duplicate those of Luther's Saxony and

Calvin's Geneva. Indeed, we need only point to the extremely important institutional differences between reformed and evangelical Christianity to suggest that different processes are at work. In spite of agreement on the basic abuses of the old religion, solutions to the problems of justification, excommunication, and reconciliation are not identical. Neither are answers to difficult questions about conscience, responsibility, and, above all, ecclesiastical authority. The wide differences in remedies indicate that the reformers saw many different defects to be cured. There is no simple pattern. As a cause of reformation, Protestant or Catholic, sacramental confession must be interpreted in its specific context. And if we were to investigate the variety of structures of discipline and consolation that emerge in the late sixteenth and seventeenth centuries, we would find clues to the meaning of many sixteenth-century struggles over the institutions of forgiveness. And the persistence of dominant themes should not allow us to ignore elements that do not fit.

On more substantial grounds we must reject the view that Luther and Calvin simply articulated the reactions of sensitive Christians throughout Europe because this ignores too many sensitive Christians. The balance that this study has tried to maintain is justified, even in the face of the temptation to assert that the reformers' criticisms were persuasive because they were accurate. On the contrary, many Europeans liked Roman Catholic sacramental confession and retained it. And in opposition to the assumption that only the reformers spoke for modern moral sensibilities, we can also see that sacramental confession could be valued for reasons that are still compelling. Two brief counterexamples may express concretely the plausibility—to the sixteenth century and to us—of claims that confession actually consoled and properly disciplined.

If Luther saw sacramental confession as a source of torment, Ignatius Loyola most decidedly did not. In the popular imagination Jesuit confessors are associated with the authoritarian values of submission and duplicity. It would be much more historically accurate, however, to dwell on their emphasis on the consoling power of sacramental confession. Ignatius's own biography demonstrates this clearly. When tempted to despair of his forgiveness, Loyola looked for comfort not in limitations on the Sacrament of Penance, but in a more intensive reliance on confession. Early in the history of the society the Bishop of Salamanca forbade him and his followers to define the line between venially and mortally sinful thoughts. Loyola's disappointment is revealing, as he admits that he "found great difficulty in remaining in Salamanca, because this prohibition against defining mortal and venial sin seemed to close the door to his helping souls."[24] In subsequent years Jesuit casuistry and sacramental theology continued to exalt the consolations of sacramental confession. In doing so they drew on the best traditions of medieval pastoral theology; kept faith with the original spirit of the order; and responded to needs that modern society continued to generate.

Similarly, we should not believe that our almost automatic sympathy for the reformers' extirpation of the tangle of laws entrammeling Christian liberty justifies a total condemnation of the disciplinary function. Even from the perspective of a pluralistic society we can find examples of the exercise of ecclesiastical authority to admire. The career of Bartolomé de Las Casas provides just such an example.

Bartolomé's conversion from an *encomendero*—an exploiter of unfree Indian labor—to an apostle of Indian liberation began in the confessional. The refusal of a Dominican to hear Bartolomé's confession because he held unfree Indians was an important event in this dramatic story. While Bishop of Chiapa, in 1546, Las Casas wrote a manual for confessors to be used by priests in his diocese. It deals with only one subject: the strictest and most absolute requirement of restitution by all who enjoy ill-gotten gain by conquest. To Las Casas it is an extremely populous category of sinners; and he is uncompromising as he defends the rights and obligations of confessors to demand full restitution as a condition of absolution. He even spells out procedures for drawing up and notarizing contracts by which penitents surrender the lands and persons they hold contrary to God's law. It is impossible not to admire the goals. The means Las Casas chooses are the most rigid application of the disciplinary weapons of sacramental confession. His arguments are based on law—canon and moral. He cites everything from the decretals to the gospels, including such familiar authorities as Antonius de Butrio and the *Summa confessorum* of John of Freiburg. They are hard words, Bartolomé admits. But he is merciless and relentless.[25]

[24] Ignatius Loyola, *St. Ignatius' Own Story, As Told to Luis González de Cámara, With a Sampling of His Letters* (Chicago, 1956), 49–51; James Brodrick, *Saint Ignatius Loyola. The Pilgrim Years* (London, 1956), 97–102.

[25] Bartolomé de Las Casas, *Obras escogidas*, vol. 5, *Opusculos, cartas y*

This study has emphasized, I think correctly, the dangers of rigorism and unrealistic demands in sacramental confession. But in the case of Las Casas we do not deal with clerical control over marital sexual behavior. We deal with a campaign against exploitation, slavery, and, it is no exaggeration to say, crimes against humanity. In such a context it is difficult to disapprove of the means or to complain about clerical tyranny. The tragedy was that the bishop was not more powerful.

These two counter-examples are only meant to suggest the dangers of oversimplification and easy value judgments. The development of Jesuit moral and sacramental theology should make us hesitate to assert that Calvin and Luther were best qualified to deliver consolation to everyone, as their theologies claimed. And the instructions for confessors of Bartolomé de Las Casas should cause us to reflect on some complicated reasons why not all enlightened Christians rushed to expunge the disciplinary power given to pastors of souls.

Sacramental confession, then, played a complex role in the social and intellectual revolutions of the sixteenth century. The institutions of forgiveness had changed dramatically from the time of the Fathers, and an increasing awareness of that change stimulated the attack of the reformers. The controversy, nevertheless, was more than a matter of correct history and theology. It was a matter of social and psychological experience. Thus for one party, sacramental confession would represent an unchristian instrument of torment and an encouragement to hypocrisy—leaving people proud, licentious, and unrepentant; utterly failing to comfort them; and leading ultimately to eternal damnation. For another party it would remain the highest pastoral art, a just and certain discipline; making essential but possible demands on Christian consciences; preserving the divine order in Christ's Church; and assuring, as well as anything in this world could, the consoling gift of eternal salvation. Both parties in the struggle were talking about the same institution, with its assumptions about the nature of sin and human responsibility; its principles of authority; its methods of securing obedience; and its methods of curing anxiety.

Inevitably the debate was angry. If the reformers were to

---

memoriales, Biblioteca de autores españoles, vol. 110 (Madrid, 1958), 235–249; idem, *Bartolomé de Las Casas. A Selection of His Writings,* tr. and ed. by George Sanderlin (New York, 1971), 7, 13–21, 87–88, 182–185.

"justify" any fundamental changes in the church, they would need an ideology that put justification, in every sense of the word, on a new basis. For the practical center of justification in medieval theology was sacramental confession, which entailed, as we have seen, a massive structure of discipline. That system of discipline stood ready to condemn, in the forum of penance and conscience, any deviation from legitimate authority. Consequently the reformers had to deny the legitimacy of the men and institutions that threatened them; and their theology therefore opposed, with increasing determination, the medieval system of sacramental confession. For the reformers, destruction of sacramental confession was an essential *means* to all of their goals. The leaders of the Counter-Reformation, on the other hand, reaffirmed sacramental confession with fervent devotion because they saw in its preservation a necessary condition of survival for the whole ecclesiastical order.

At the same time, however, Protestant reformers saw the destruction of sacramental confession as a primary and essential *goal*, just as the defenders of the traditional faith believed with conviction that it had to be preserved for its own sake. In this debate the clash was not merely over discipline and authority: it expressed itself most passionately in the claims of every religious system to console. "The truth of punishment causes contrition, and the truth of the promise causes consolation," Luther proclaims in the *Babylonian Captivity of the Church*, "if it is believed; and by this faith a man merits the forgiveness of sins." Faith, not sacramental confession, is the key: "Once faith is possessed, contrition and consolation will come as the inevitable and spontaneous consequence."[26] As if in direct response, the *Catechism of the Council of Trent* teaches that Christ instituted the Sacrament of Penance and priestly absolution so that men would not remain in "anxious suspense" over the forgiveness of their sins. The faithful are admonished to believe firmly this consoling teaching:

[26] Luther, *De captivitate Babylonica ecclesiae praeludium* (1520), *WA*, 6, 545: "Magna res est cor contritum, nec nisi ardentis in promissionem et comminationem divinam fidei, quae veritatem dei immobilem intuita tremefacit, exterret et sic conterit conscientiam, rursus exaltat et solatur servatque contritam, ut veritas comminationis sit causa contritionis, veritas promissionis sit solacii, si credatur, et hac fide homo mereatur peccatorum remissionem. Proinde fides ante omnia docenda et provocanda est, fide autem obtenta contritio et consolatio inevitabili sequela sua sponte venient."

If the sinner have recourse to the tribunal of penance with a sincere sorrow for his sins, and a firm resolution of avoiding them in future, although he bring not with him that contrition which may be sufficient of itself to obtain the pardon of sin; his sins are forgiven by the minister of religion, through the power of the keys. Justly, then, do the Holy Fathers proclaim, that by the keys of the Church, the gate of heaven is thrown open.[27]

Fully understanding the late medieval heritage, the reformers and counter-reformers agreed that discipline and consolation were the central issues in the debates on justification, sanctification, and sacramental confession. They knew that beneath theological abstractions lay ordinary social and psychological problems. That common ground made their conflicting solutions all the more immediate and irreconcilable.

[27] *Catechism of the Council of Trent for Parish Priests. Issued by Order of Pius V*, tr. with notes by John A. McHugh and C. J. Callan, 10th printing (New York and London, 1947), "On the Sacrament of Penance," 190.

Bibliography

Abbreviations

Angelica   Angelus [Carletus] de Clavasio. *Summa de casibus conscientiae.* Lyon, 1500.

Angelica (1534) Angelus [Carletus] de Clavasio, *Prima pars summae Angelicae cum commento.* Lyon, 1534.

Astesana   Astesanus de Ast. *Summa de casibus conscientiae.* Lyon, 1519.

BCN   *Bibliotheca Catholica Neerlandica, Impressa 1500–1727.* The Hague, 1954.

BMC XVth   British Museum, Department of Printed Books. *Catalogue of Books Printed in the XVth Century Now in the British Museum.* 10 vols. London, 1908–1971.

Campbell   Marinus Frederick A. G. Campbell. *Annales de la typographie néerlandaise au XVe siècle,* with 4 *Suppléments.* The Hague, 1874–1890.

Copinger   Walter Arthur Copinger. *Supplement to Hain's Repertorium bibliographicum.* 2 pts. in 3 vols. London, 1895–1902.

Dagens   Jean Dagens. *Bibliographie chronologique de la littérature de spiritualité et de ses sources, 1501–1610.* Paris, 1952.

DTC   *Dictionnaire de théologie catholique.* Ed. by Alfred Vacant and E. Mangenot. 15 vols. Paris, 1909–1950.

Du Pin   Jean Gerson. *Opera omnia.* Ed. by Ellies Du Pin. 7 vols. Antwerp, 1706.

GKW   *Gesamtkatalog der Wiegendrucke.* 7 vols. ("Abano" to "Eigenschaften.") Leipzig, 1925–1938.

Glorieux   Jean Gerson. *Oeuvres complètes.* Ed. by Palémon Glorieux. 7 vols. Paris, Tournai, Rome, and New York, 1960— .

Goff   Frederick R. Goff. *Incunabula in American Libraries, A Third Census* . . . New York, 1964.

Hain   Ludwig Hain. *Repertorium bibliographicum in quo libri omnes ab arte typographica inventa usque ad annum MD typis expressi ordine alphabetico vel simpliciter enumberantur vel adcuratius recensentur.* 2 vols. Stuttgart, 1826–1838.

Kronenberg Maria E. Kronenberg. *Campbell's Annales . . . Contributions to a New Edition.* The Hague, 1956.
      ———. "More Contributions to a New Campbell Edition." *Het Boek,* 36 (1964), 129–139.

LW   Martin Luther. *Luther's Works. American Edition.* 55 vols.: 1–30, ed. by Jaroslav Pelikan; 31–55, ed. by Helmut T. Lehman. Philadelphia and St. Louis, 1955— .

Monaldina Joannes Monaldus di Capo d'Istria. *Summa in vtroque iure tam ciuili quam canonici fundata.* Lyon, [1516].

Pell.   Marie Pellechet. *Catalogue générale des incunables des bibliothèques publiques de France.* 26 vols. Reprint. Nendeln, Liechtenstein, 1970.

PL   Jacques Paul Migne, ed. *Patrologiae cursus completus . . . Series latina.* Paris, 1844–1890.

Raymundina Raymond of Peñaforte. *Summa sancti Raymundi de Peniafort . . . de poenitentia et matrimonio cum glossis Ioannis de Friburgo.* Rome, 1603; reprint, Farnborough, England, 1967.

Reichling Dietrich Reichling. *Appendices ad Hainii-Copingeri Repertorium bibliographicum.* 7 vols. Munich, 1905–1911.

Sylvestrina Sylvester Prierias Mazzolini. *Summa summarum, que Sylvestrina dicitur.* Bologna, 1515.

WA   Martin Luther. *D. Martin Luthers Werke. Kritische Gesamtausgabe.* Weimar, 1883— .

ZKG   *Zeitschrift für Kirchengeschichte.*
ZkTh   *Zeitschrift für katholische Theologie.*

PRIMARY SOURCES

Alain de Lille. *Liber poenitentialis. PL*, 210, 279–304.

Albert d'Aix. *Alberti Aquensis Historia Hierosolymitana. Recueil des historiens des croisades. Historiens occidentaux*, vol. 4. Paris, 1879. Pp. 265–273.

Albertus Magnus. *Commentarii in IV Sententiarum. Opera omnia*, vol. 30. Paris, 1894.

Alphabetum sacerdotum. [Paris], 1500?

Andreas de Escobar. *Modus confitendi . . . . Interrogationes . . . . Canones penitentiales . . . . Casus papales et episcopales*. Nuremberg, 1508.

Angelus [Carletus] de Clavasio. *Summa de casibus conscientiae*. Lyon, 1500.

———. *Prima pars summae Angelicae cum commento. Summa Angelica de casibus conscientialibus . . . cum additionibus . . . Iacobi Ungarelli patauini . . . necnon et a venerabile P. F. Augustino patauino*. Lyon, 1534.

Antoninus of Florence. *Summa theologica*. 4 vols. Basel, 1485.

———. *Summula confessionis* [*Confessionale—Defecerunt*]. Strasbourg, 1499.

———. *Tractatus de institutione confessorum*. Brescia, 1473?

Astesanus de Ast. *Summa de casibus conscientiae*. Lyon, 1519.

Augustine. "De poenitentibus." *PL*, 39, 1713–1715.

Berthold von Freiburg. *Summa Johannis, deutsch*. Augsburg, 1472.

Burchard of Worms. *Decretorum libri XX. PL*, 140, 538–1058.

Butrio, Antonius de. *Directorium ad confitendum. Modus confitendi*. Rome, c. 1474.

———. *Speculum de confessione*. Louvain, n.d.

Calvin, John. *Institutes of the Christian Religion*. 2 vols. Tr. by Ford Lewis Battles; ed. by John T. McNeill. Library of Christian Classics, 20 and 21. 7th printing. Philadelphia, 1975.

———. *Ioannis Calvini Opera quae supersunt omnia*. 59 vols. Corpus Reformatorum, ed. by W. Baum, Eduard Cunitz, and Eduard Reus, 29–87. Brunswick, 1863–1900.

Canons and Decrees of the Council of Trent. Original Text with English Translation. Tr. by H. J. Schroeder. St. Louis and London, 1941.

Capreolus, Johannes. *Defensiones theologiae divi Thomae Aquinatis....* 7 vols. Turin, 1900–1908.

Caracciolus, Robertus. *Sermones prestantissimi viri Roberti de Litio.... De quadragesima: de penitentia ...* Lyon, 1513.

Catechism of the Council of Trent for Parish Priests. Issued by Order of Pope Pius V. Tr. with notes by John A. McHugh and Charles J. Callan. 10th printing. New York and London, 1947.

Chaimis, Bartholomaeus de. *Interrogatorium siue Confessionale.* Milan, 1474.

Chaucer, Geoffrey. *The Complete Works of Geoffrey Chaucer.* Ed. by Fred N. Robinson. Boston and New York, 1933.

Columbi, Jehan. *Confession generale auec certaines reigles au commencement tresutile: tant a confesseurs que a penitens.* N.p., 1520?

Compendium theologiae. Du Pin, I, 233–422.

Confessio generalis breuis et vtilis tam confessori quam confitenti. Vienne, n.d.

Confessionale ad usum Albiensis diocesis. Lyon, 1499.

Dambach, Johannes von. *Consolatio theologiae.* Strasbourg, c. 1478.

Dandolo, Fantinus. *Compendium pro catholicae fidei instructione.* Antwerp, 1490?

Denis the Carthusian. *Speculum conuersionis peccatorum.* Alost, 1473.

Duns Scotus, Joannes. *Quaestiones in librum quartum sententiarum. Opera omnia,* vol. 18. Paris, 1894.

Eruditorium penitentiale. Paris, 1490?

Falk, Franz, ed. *Drei Beichtbüchlein nach den zehn Geboten aus der Frühzeit der Buchdruckerkunst.* Reformationsgeschichtliche Studien und Texte, ed. by J. Greving. Vol. 2. Münster, 1907.

———, ed. *Die pfarramtlichen Aufzeichungen (Liber consuetudinum) des Florentius Diel zu St. Christoph in Mainz (1491–1518).* Erläuterungen und Ergänzungen zu Janssens Geschichte des deutschen Volkes, ed. by Ludwig Pastor, vol. 4, no. 3. Freiburg im Breisgau, 1904.

Faren, Antoine. *La Pratique de soy bien confesser.* Lyon, 1485?

FitzRalph, Richard. *Defensorium curatorum contra eos qui priuilegiatos se dicunt.* . . . Lyon, 1496.

Foresti, Jacobus Philippus (Bergomense). *Confessionale seu Interrogatorium.* Venice, 1497.

Galbert of Bruges. *The Murder of Charles the Good, Count of Flanders.* Tr. and ed. by James Bruce Ross. Records of Civilization, Sources and Studies, ed. by W. T. H. Jackson. Rev. ed., New York, Evanston, Ill., and London, 1967.

Geiler von Kaisersberg, Johann. *Navicula penitentie.* Augsburg, 1511.

[Gerson?, Jean Charlier de]. *La Confession de maistre iehan iarson.* Paris, c. 1491.

[Gerson?, Jean Charlier de]. *Le Confessional aultrement appelle le Directoire des confesseurs . . . de nouuel mis de la langue latine en langue francoyse.* Paris, 1547.

Gerson, Jean Charlier de. *LInstruction des curez pour instruire le simple peuple . . . . Opusculum tripartitum.* Paris?, 1510?

————. *Oeuvres complètes.* Ed. by Palémon Glorieux. 7 vols. Paris, Tournai, Rome, and New York, 1960— .

————. *Opera omnia.* Ed. by Ellies Du Pin. 7 vols. Antwerp, 1706.

Götz, Johann B. *Das Pfarrbuch des Stephan May in Hilpolstein vom Jahre 1511. Ein Beitrag zum Verständnis der kirchlichen Verhältnisse Deutschlands am Vorabend der Reformation.* Reformationsgeschichtliche Studien und Texte, ed. by J. Greving. Vols. 47–48. Münster, 1926.

La Grant confession de pasques. Paris, c. 1492.

Gratian. *Decretum. Tractatus de peonitentia.* PL, 187, 1519–1644.

Guido de Monte Rocherii. *Manipulus curatorum.* Paris, 1489/90.

Hortulus anime. Nuremberg, 1511.

Hefele, Charles Joseph, and H. Leclerq. *Histoire des conciles.* 8 vols. Paris, 1907–1916.

Jacobus de Clusa. *Confessionale compendiosum et utilissimum.* Nuremberg, 1520.

375

Jacobus de Gruytroede. *Speculum aureum anime peccatricis.* Paris, 1480.

Johannes von Freiburg. *Summa confessorum.* Lyon, 1518.

Joinville, Jean de. *The Life of St. Louis.* In Joinville and Villehardouin, *Chronicles of the Crusades*, tr. by M. R. B. Shaw. Baltimore, 1963.

à Kempis, Thomas. *The Imitation of Christ.* Tr. by Leo Sherley-Price. Baltimore, 1952.

Kunhofer, Engelhardus. *Confessionale continens tractatum decem preceptorum.* Nuremberg, 1502.

Laporte, Jean, ed. *Le Pénitentiel de saint Colomban. Introduction et édition critique.* Monumenta Christiana Selecta, ed. by J. C. Didier, vol. 4. Tournai, Paris, Rome, and New York, 1958.

Las Casas, Bartolomé de. *Obras escogidas*, vol. 5: *Opusculos, cartas y memoriales.* Biblioteca de autores españoles, vol. 110. Madrid, 1958.

––––––. *Bartolomé de Las Casas: A Selection of His Writings.* Tr. and ed. by George Sanderlin. New York, 1971.

Le Roy, François. *Le Mirouer de penitence tres devot et . . . proffitable à toutes personnes et specialement à gens de religion desirans de leurs meurs faire conversion. . . .* 2 vols. Paris, 1507–1511.

Loyola, Ignatius. *St. Ignatius' Own Story, As Told to Luis González de Cámara, With a Sampling of His Letters.* Tr. by William J. Young. Chicago, 1956.

Lupi Rebello, Jacobus. *Tractatus fructus sacramenti penitentie.* Paris, 14[9]4.

Luther, Martin. *D. Martin Luthers Werke. Kritische Gesamtausgabe.* Weimar, 1883–.

––––––. *Luther's Works. American Edition.* 55 vols.: 1–30, ed. by Jaroslav Pelikan; 31–55, ed. by Helmut T. Lehman. Philadelphia and St. Louis, 1955– .

Maillard, Olivier. *La Confession de frere Olivier Maillard.* Paris, 1481.

––––––. *La Confession generale de frere oliuier maillart.* Lyon, 1485?

––––––. *Oeuvres françaises—sermons et poésies.* Ed. by Arthur de la Borderie. Nantes, 1877.

Manuale parrochialium sacerdotum. Nuremberg, 1512.

Manuale secundum usum lexouiensem. Rouen, [1523].

Matthew of Cracow. *Confessionale seu . . . De modo confitendi et de puritate conscientie.* Paris, n.d.

————. *Incitatio ad digne suscipiendum corpus Christi.* Du Pin, III, 310–323.

Mauburnus, Joannes (or Jean Mombaer). *Rosetum exercitiorum spiritualium.* Basel, 1504.

Mazzolini, Sylvester Prierias. *Summa summarum, que Sylvestrina dicitur.* Bologna, 1515.

Mehring, Gebhard, ed. *Stift Lorch. Quellen zur Geschichte einer Pfarrkirche.* Württembergische Gesichtsquellen, vol. 12. Stuttgart, 1911.

Methodius. *The Symposium. A Treatise on Chastity.* Tr. and annotated by Herbert Musurillo. Ancient Christian Writers. The Works of the Fathers in Translation, ed. by Johannes Quasten and J. C. Plumpe, no. 27. London and Westminster, Md., 1958.

Monaldus di Capo d'Istria, Joannes. *Summa in vtroque iure tam ciuili quam canonici fundata.* Lyon, [1516].

Nicolaus de Ausimo. *Supplementum summae pisanellae.* Venice, 1489.

Nicolaus de Saliceto. *Antidotarius anime.* Paris, 1552.

Nider, Johannes. *Consolatorium timoratae conscientiae.* Paris, 1478.

————. *Expositio preceptorum decalogi.* Paris, 1482.

————. *Manuale confessorum. De lepra morali.* Paris, 1479.

Odo of Sully. *Synodicae constitutiones.* PL, 212, 58–68.

Officiarium curatorum insignis ecclesiae Eduensis. Paris, 1503.

Peycht Spigel der sünder. Nuremberg, 1510.

"Poeniteas cito." *PL,* 207, 1153–1156 [here attributed to Peter of Blois].

[Poeniteas cito]. *Confessionale pro scholasticis et aliis.* Cologne, 1490?

[Poeniteas cito]. *Libellus de modo poenitendi et confitendi.* Paris, 1495.

[Poeniteas cito]. *Penitencionarius.* Leipzig, 1490?

[Poeniteas cito]. *Penitentionarius de confessione.* Strasbourg, c. 1497.

[Poeniteas cito]. *Penitentiarius magistri iohannis de galandia.* Paris, 1499?

[Poeniteas cito]. *Summa penitentie.* Nuremberg, 1490?

Pseudo-Methodius. *The Bygynnyng of the World and the Ende of Worldes.* Ed. by Aaron J. Perry. Early English Text Society, Original Series, 167. London, 1925.

Quentin, Jean. *Examen de conscience pour soy cognoistre et bien se confesser.* Paris, 1500?

Raymond of Peñaforte. *Summa sancti Raymundi de Peniafort . . . de poenitentia et matrimonio cum glossis Ioannis de Friburgo* [i.e., William of Rennes]. Rome, 1603; reprint, Farnborough, England, 1967.

Raulin, Jean. *Itinerarium paridisi . . . complectens sermones de penitentia, . . . de matrimonio ac viduitate.* Paris, 1519.

Robert of Flamborough. *Liber Poenitentialis. A Critical Edition with Introduction and Notes.* Ed. by J. J. Francis Firth. Pontifical Institute of Medieval Studies, Studies and Texts, 18. Toronto, 1971.

Romming, Johannes. *Penitentiarius, in tres parteis, contritionem, confessionem, et satifactionem discretus . . . Nuremberg,* 1522?

Rosemondt, Godescalc. *Confessionale.* Antwerp, 1518.

Schildis, Hermannus de. *Speculum sacerdotum de tribus sacramentis principalibus.* Speier, c. 1479.

Statuta synodalia lexouiensia. Paris, c. 1483.

Stella clericorum. Deventer, 1490.

Stephan Lanzkranna (or von Landskron). *Himelstrass. im latin genant Scala celi.* Augsburg, 1510.

Summa rudium. Reutlingen, 1487.

Summula Raymundi. Cologne, 1506.

Surgant, Joannes. *Manuale curatorum predicandi.* [Basel], 1503.

Thomas Aquinas. *Commentum in quartum librum sententiarum. Opera omnia.* Vol. 11. Paris, 1894.

Thomas of Chobham. *Summa confessorum.* Ed. by F. Broomfield. Analecta mediaevalia Namurcensia, 25. Louvain and Paris, 1968.

Tibus, Adolph. *Die Jakobipfarre in Münster von 1508–1523. Ein Beitrag zur Sittengeschichte Münsters.* Münster, 1885.

Tractatus de instructionibus confessorum. Erfurt, 1483?

Vio, Thomas de. *Summula peccatorum*. N. p., 1526.

Vivaldus, Joannes Ludovicus. *Aureum opus de veritate contritionis*. Saluzzo, 1503.

Wessel Gansfort, Joannes. *Farrago rerum theologicarum uberrima*, Basel, 1522.

Winshemius, Jodocus. *Institutiones succincte in rite faciendam ... confessionem sacramentalem*. Erfurt, 1516.

Wolff, Johannes. *Beichtbüchlein des Magisters Johannes Wolff (Lupis), ersten Pfarrers an der St. Peterskirche zu Frankfurt a. M. 1453–68. (1478)*. Tr. and ed. by F. W. Battenberg. Giessen, 1907.

Secondary Works

Althaus, Paul. *The Theology of Martin Luther*. Tr. by Robert C. Schultz. Philadelphia, 1966.

Amann, E. "Pénitence—Repentir," *DTC*, 12¹, 722–748; "Pénitence—Sacrement," *DTC*, 12¹ 748–948.

Anciaux, Paul. *La Théologie du sacrement de pénitence au XIIe siècle*, Universitas Catholica Louvaniensis. Dissertationes ad gradum magistri in Facultate Theologica vel in Facultate Iuris Canonici, ser. 2, vol. 41: Louvain and Gembloux, 1949.

Appel, Helmut. *Anfechtung und Trost im Spätmittelalter und bei Luther*. Schriften des Vereins für Reformationsgeschichte, vol. 165. Leipzig, 1938.

Auer, Albert. *Johann von Dambach und die Trostbücher vom 11. bis zum 16. Jahrhundert*. Beiträge zur Geschichte der Philosophie und Theologie des Mittelalters, vol. 27, no. 1/2. Münster, 1928.

Barth, Medard. "Beicht und Kommunionen im mittelalterlichen Elsass; Ein Durchblick." *Freiburger Diözesanarchiv*, 74 (1954), 88–99.

Baudrier, J. *Bibliographie lyonnaise*. 14 vols. Lyon, 1895–1921, 1950–1963.

Bibliotheca catholica neerlandica impressa 1500–1727. The Hague, 1954.

Biéler, André. *L'Homme et la femme dans la doctrine de Calvin.*

La Doctrine réformée sur l'amour, le mariage, le célibat, le divorce, l'adultère et la prostitution, considérée dans son cadre historique. Geneva, 1963.

Binder, Karl. "Streiflichter zur Beichte und Eucharistie in katholischer und protestantischer Sicht." *Wissenschaft im Dienste des Glaubens. Festschrift für Abt Dr. Hermann Peichl O. S. B.* Ed. by Josef Kisser et al. Studien der Wiener katholischen Akademie, vol. 4. Vienna, 1965. Pp. 65–122.

Binz, Louis. *Vie religieuse et réforme ecclésiastique dans le diocèse de Genève pendant le grand schisme et la crise conciliaire (1378–1450).* Vol. 1: "Mémoires et Documents" publiés par la Société d'histoire et d'archéologie de Genève, vol. 46. Geneva, 1973.

Bloomfield, Morton W. "A Preliminary List of Incipits of Latin Works on the Virtues and Vices, Mainly of the 13th, 14th, and 15th Centuries." *Traditio*, 11 (1955), 259–379.

———. *The Seven Deadly Sins.* Lansing, Mich., 1952.

Boyle, Leonard E. "The Oculus sacerdotis and Some Other Works of William of Pagula." *Transactions of the Royal Historical Society*, 5 ser., 5 (1955), 81–110.

———. "The Summa for Confessors as a Genre, and Its Religious Intent." In *The Pursuit of Holiness in Late Medieval and Renaissance Religion. Papers from the University of Michigan Conference*, ed. by Charles Trinkaus, with Heiko A. Oberman. Leiden, 1974. Pp. 126–130.

Braeckmans, L. *Confession et communion au moyen âge et au Concile de Trente.* Gembloux, 1971.

Brandl, Leopold. *Die Sexualethik des heiligen Albertus Magnus. Eine moralgeschichtliche Untersuchung.* Studien zur Geschichte der katholischen Moraltheologie, ed. by Michael Müller, vol. 2. Regensburg, 1955.

Bride, A. "Réserve. Cas réservés." *DTC*, 13², 2441–2461.

British Museum. *Catalogue of Books Printed in the XVth Century Now in the British Museum.* 10 vols. London, 1908–1971.

Brodrick, James. *St. Ignatius Loyola. The Pilgrim Years.* London, 1956.

Browe, Peter. *Beiträge zur Sexualethik des Mittelalters.* Breslauer Studien zur historischen Theologie, ed. by. F. X. Seppelt et al., vol. 23. Breslau, 1932.

———. *Die häufige Kommunion im Mittelalter.* Münster, 1938.

————. "Die Kommunionvorbereitung im Mittelalter." *ZkTh*, 56 (1932), 375–415.

————. "Die Pflichtbeichte im Mittelalter." *ZkTh*, 57 (1933), 335–383.

————. *Zur Geschichte der Entmannung. Eine religions- und rechtsgeschichtliche Studie.* Breslauer Studien zur historischen Theologie, N.S., vol. 1. Breslau, 1936.

Bürck, Franz J. "Die Lehre vom Gewissen nach dem hl. Antonin." *Der Katholik*, 39 (1909), 17–37, 81–99.

Campbell, Marinus Frederick A. G. *Annales de la typographie néerlandaise au XVe siècle*, with 4 *Suppléments*. The Hague, 1874–1890.

Chevalier, Cyr Ulysse Joseph. *Répertoire des sources historiques du Moyen Age. Bio-bibliographie.* Rev. ed., reprint. New York, 1960.

Copinger, Walter A. *Supplement to Hain's Repertorium bibliographicum.* 2 pts. in 3 vols. London, 1895–1902.

Dagens, Jean. *Bibliographie chronologique de la littérature de spiritualité et de ses sources, 1501–1610.* Paris, 1952.

Dargin, Edward V. *Reserved Cases According to the Code of Canon Law.* Catholic University of America, Dissertation in Canon Law. Washington, D.C., 1924.

Delaruelle, E., E.-R. Labande, and Paul Ourliac. *L'Eglise au temps du grand schisme et de la crise conciliaire*, Histoire de l'église depuis les origines jusqu'à nos jours, ed. by Augustin Fliche and Victor Martin. Vol. 14. Paris, 1964.

De Roover, Raymond A. *La Pensée économique des scolastiques. Doctrines et méthodes.* Conférence Albert-le-Grand 1970. Montreal and Paris, 1971.

————. *San Bernardino of Siena and Sant' Antonio of Florence: The Two Great Economic Thinkers of the Middle Ages.* Kress Library of Business and Economics, 19. Boston, 1967.

Dictionnaire de biographie française. Ed. by J. Balteau et al. 13 vols. Paris, 1933—

Dictionnaire de spiritualité, ascetique, et mystique, doctrine et histoire. Ed. by Marcel Viller et al. 7 vols. Paris, 1932—

Dietterle, Johannes. "Die Summae confessorum (sive de casibus conscientiae)—von ihren Anfängen an bis zu Silvester Prierias

—unter besonderer Berücksichtigung ihrer Bestimmungen über den Ablass." *ZKG*, 24 (1903), 353–374, 520–548; 25 (1904), 248–272; 26 (1905), 59–81, 350–362; 27 (1906), 70–83, 166–188, 296–310, 433–442; 28 (1907), 401–431.

Doherty, Dennis. *The Sexual Doctrine of Cardinal Cajetan.* Studien zur Geschichte der katholischen Moraltheologie, ed. by M. Müller, vol. 12. Regensburg, 1966.

Douglass, E. Jane Dempsey. *Justification in Late Medieval Preaching. A Study of John Geiler of Keisersberg.* Studies in Medieval and Reformation Thought, ed. by Heiko A. Oberman, vol. 1. Leiden, 1966.

Eckermann, Willigis. "Busse is besser als Ablass. Ein Brief Gottschalk Hollens, O. E. S. A. (d. 1481), an Lubertus Langen, Can. Reg." *Analecta Augustiniana.* 32 (1969), 323–366.

Eisenstein, Elizabeth. "L'Avènement de l'imprimerie et la Réforme. Une nouvelle approche au problème du démembrement de la chrétienté occidentale." *Annales: économies, sociétés, civilisations*, 26, no. 6 (November-December, 1971), 1335–1382.

Falk, Franz. *Die Druckkunst im Dienste der Kirche zunächst in Deutschland bis zum Jahre 1520.* Schriften der Görres-Gesellschaft zur Pflege der Wissenschaft im katholischen Deutschland. Cologne, 1879.

Febvre, Lucien and Henri-Jean Martin. *L'Apparition du livre.* L'Évolution de l'humanité, vol. 49. Paris, 1958.

Fendt, Leonhard. "Luthers Reformation der Beichte." *Luther; Mitteilungen der Luthergesellschaft*, 24, no. 3 (1953), 121–137.

Firth, J. J. Francis. "The *Poenitentiale* of Robert of Flamborough." *Traditio*, 16 (1960), 541–556.

Fischer, E. *Zur Geschichte der evangelischen Beichte: I. Die katholische Beichtpraxis bei Beginn der Reformation und Luthers Stellung dazu in den Anfängen seiner Wirksamkeit; II. Niedergang und Neubelung des Beichtinstituts in Wittenberg in den Anfängen der Reformation.* Studien zur Geschichte der Theologie und der Kirche, vol. 8, no. 2, and vol. 9, no. 4. Leipzig, 1902–1903.

Fritz, Joseph. "Zwei unbekannte Bearbeitungen des Modus confitendi von Andreas Hispanus." *Der Katholik*, 4th ser., 10 (1912), 57–64.

Fuchs, Josef. *Die Sexualethik des heiligen Thomas von Aquin.* Cologne, 1949.

Galtier, P. "Satisfaction." *DTC*, 14¹, 1130–1210.

Geffken, Johannes. *Der Bildercatechismus des funfzehnten Jahrhunderts und die catechetischen Hauptstücke in dieser Zeit bis auf Luther.* Leipzig, 1855.

Gesamtkatalog der Wiegendrucke. 7 vols. Leipzig, 1925–1938.

Goff, Frederick R. *Incunabula in American Libraries. A Third Census.* . . . New York, 1964.

Göttler, Joseph. *Der heilige Thomas von Aquin und die vortridentinischen Thomisten über die Wirkungen des Busssakramentes.* Freiburg im Breisgau, 1904.

Gründel, Johannes. *Die Lehre von den Umständen der menschlichen Handlung im Mittelalter.* Beiträge zur Geschichte der Philosophie und Theologie des Mittelalters, vol. 39, no. 5. Münster, 1963.

Guérin, Paul. *Les Conciles généraux et particuliers.* 3 vols. 3d ed. Paris, 1868.

Gwynn, Aubrey. "Richard FitzRalph, Archbishop of Armagh." In *Studies. An Irish Quarterly Review*, 22 (1933), 389–405, 591–607; 23 (1934), 395–411; 24 (1935), 25–42, 558–572; 25 (1936), 81–96; 26 (1937), 50–67.

———. "The Sermon-Diary of Richard FitzRalph, Archbishop of Armagh." In *Proceedings of the Royal Irish Academy*, 44 (1937–1938), 1–57.

Hain, Ludwig. *Repertorium bibliographicum in quo libri omnes ab arte typographica inventa usque ad annum MD typis expressi, ordine alphabetico vel simpliciter enumerantur vel adcuratius recensentur.* 2 vols. Stuttgart, 1826–1838.

Hammerich, L. L. *The Beginning of the Strife Between Richard FitzRalph and the Mendicants. With an Edition of His Autobiographical Prayer and His Proposition Unusquisque.* Det Kgl. Danske Videnskabernes Selskab., Historisk-filologiske Meddelelser, 26, 3. Copenhagen, 1938.

Harnack, Adolf. "Medicinisches aus der ältesten Kirchengeschichte." *Texte und Untersuchungen zur Geschichte der altchristlichen Literatur*, ed. by Oscar von Gebhardt and Adolf Harnack, vol. 8, no. 4. Leipzig, 1892. Pp. 37–147.

Hellinga, L., and W. Hellinga. "Additions and Notes to Campbell's Annales and GW." *Beiträge zur Inkunabelkunde*, ser. 3, no. 1 (1965), 76–86.

Hill, Rosalind. "Public Penance: Some Problems of a Thirteenth-Century Bishop." *History*, n.s. 36 (1951), 213–226.

Hödl, Ludwig. *Die Geschichte der scholastischen Literatur und der Theologie der Schlüsselgewalt.* Vol. 1: . . . *bis zur Summa Aurea.* Beiträge zur Geschichte der Philosophie und Theologie des Mittelalters, vol. 38, no. 4. Münster, i.W., 1960

Hurter, Hugo. *Nomenclator litterarius theologiae catholicae theologos exhibitens aetate, natione disciplinis distinctos.* 5 vols. Reprint, New York, 1962.

Jungmann, Josef A. *The Mass of the Roman Rite: Its Origins and Development (Missarum Solemnia).* Tr. by F. A. Brunner. 2 vols. New York, 1951–1955.

Kinder, Ernst. "Beichte und Absolution nach den lutherischen Bekenntnisschriften." *Theologische Literaturzeitung*, 77, No. 2 (1952), 543–550.

Klomps, Heinrich. *Ehemoral und Jansenismus. Ein Beitrag zur Überwindung des sexualethischen Rigorismus.* Cologne, 1964.

Kronenberg, Maria Elizabeth. *Campbell's Annales . . . Contributions to a New Edition.* The Hague, 1956.

———. "More Contributions to a New Campbell Edition." *Het Boek*, 36 (1964), 129–139.

Kurtscheid, B. *A History of the Seal of Confession.* Tr. by F. A. Marks. Ed. by Arthur Preuss. St. Louis and London, 1927.

Le Bras, Gabriel. *Les Institutions ecclésiastiques de la Chrétienté médiévale.* 2 pts. Histoire de l'Eglise depuis les origines jusqu'à nos jours, ed. by Augustin Fliche and V. Martin, vol. 12. Paris, 1964–1965.

Lea, Henry Charles. *A History of Auricular Confession and Indulgences in the Latin Church.* 3 vols. Philadelphia, 1896.

Mausbach, Joseph. "Historisches und Apologetisches zur scholastischen Reuelehre." *Der Katholik*, 15 (1897), 48–65, 97–115.

———. "Katholische Katechismen von 1400–1700 über die zum Busssakramente erforderliche Reue." *Der Katholik*, 16 (1897), 37–49, 109–122.

McNeill, John T. *The Celtic Penitentials and Their Influence on Continental Christianity*. Chicago University Dissertation in Church History. Paris, 1923.

————. *A History of the Cure of Souls*. New York, 1951.

————, and Helena M. Gamer. *Medieval Handbooks of Penance: A Translation of the Principal Libri Poenitentiales and Selections from Related Documents*. Columbia Records of Civilization: Sources and Studies, no. 29. Reprint of 1938 edn., New York, 1965.

Michaud-Quantin, Pierre. *Sommes de casuistique et manuels de confession au moyen âge (XII-XVI siècles)*. Analecta Mediaevalia Namurcensia, 13. Louvain, Lille, and Montreal, 1962.

Michel, A. "Pénitence, du IVe Concile du Latran . . . à nos jours." *DTC*, 12¹, 948–1127.

Molien, A. "Pain bénit." *DTC*, 11², 1731–1733.

Mollat, Michel. *La Vie et pratique religieuses au XIVe siècle et dans la première partie du XVe, principalement en France*. 2 vols. Centre de documentation universitaire. Paris, 1963–1965.

Moorman, John. *A History of the Franciscan Order from Its Origins to the Year 1517*. Oxford, 1968.

Morey, Adrian. *Bartholomew of Exeter, Bishop and Canonist. A Study of the Twelfth Century, With the Text of Bartholomew's Penitential*. Cambridge, 1937.

Morin, Jean. *De Contritione et attritione. Exercitatio historicotheologica*. In *Thesaurus theologicus*. Vol. 11: *Tractatus II de Sacramentis*. Venice, 1762.

Müller, Michael. *Die Lehre des hl. Augustinus von der Paradiesesehe und ihre Auswirkung in die Sexualethik des 12. und 13. Jahrhunderts bis Thomas von Aquin*. Studien zur Geschichte der katholischen Moraltheologie, ed. by Michael Müller, vol. 1. Regensburg, 1954.

Nelson, Benjamin N. *The Idea of Usury. From Tribal Brotherhood to Universal Otherhood*. Princeton, N.J., 1949.

Nock, Arthur Darby. *Early Gentile Christianity and Its Hellenistic Background*. New York, 1964.

Noonan, John T. *Contraception. A History of Its Treatment by the Catholic Theologians and Canonists*. Cambridge, Mass., 1965; paper edn., New York and Toronto, 1967.

————. *The Scholastic Analysis of Usury*. Cambridge, Mass., 1957.

Oberman, Heiko. *The Harvest of Medieval Theology. Gabriel Biel and Late Medieval Nominalism.* Cambridge, Mass., 1963.

Ortolan, T. "Censures ecclésiastiques." *DTC*, 2², 2113–2136.

Ott, Ludwig. "Das Opusculum des hl. Thomas von Aquin *De forma absolutionis* in dogmengeschichtlicher Betrachtung." In Martin Grabmann and K. Hoffmann, eds., *Festschrift Eduard Eichmann.* Paderborn, 1940. Pp. 99–135.

Paetow, Louis J., ed. *Morale scholarium of John of Garland (Johannes de Garlandia).* Memoirs of the University of California, vol. 4, no. 2. Berkeley, Calif., 1927.

Palmer, Paul F., ed. *Sacraments and Forgiveness. History and Doctrinal Development of Penance, Extreme Unction and Indulgences.* Sources of Christian Theology, vol. 2. London and Westminster, Md., 1959.

Patton, Hugh. *The Efficacy of Putative Attrition in the Doctrine of Theologians of the XVI and XVII Centuries.* Dissertatio ad Lauriam in Facultate Theologica Pontificiae Universitatis Gregorianae. Rome, 1966.

Paulus, Nikolaus. "Ein Beichtbüchlein für Erfurter Studenten aus dem 16. Jahrhundert." *Der Katholik*, 19 (1899), 92–96.

———. "Die Beichtbüchlein des Jodocus von Windsheim." *Der Katholik*, 19 (1899), 382–384.

———. "Johann Romming und dessen Beichtbüchlein für die Nürnberger Schuljugend." *Der Katholik*, 21 (1900), 570–575.

———. "Noch einmal das Erfurter Beichtbüchlein des Jodocus Morder von Windsheim." *Der Katholik*, 20 (1899), 94–96.

———. "Die Reue in den deutschen Beichtschriften des ausgehenden Mittelalters." *ZkTh*, 28 (1904), 1–36.

———. "Die Reue in den deutschen Erbauungsschriften des ausgehenden Mittelalters." *ZkTh*, 28 (1904), 449–485.

———. "Die Reue in den deutschen Sterbebüchlein des ausgehenden Mittelalters." *ZkTh*, 28 (1904), 682–698.

Peddie, Robert A. *Conspectus incunabulorum.* 2 pts. London, 1910–1914.

Pellechet, Marie. *Catalogue général des incunables des bibliothèques publiques de France.* 26 vols. Reprint, Nendeln, Liechtenstein, 1970.

Périnelle, Joseph. *L'Attrition d'après le Concile de Trente et d'après Saint Thomas d'Aquin.* Bibliothèque Thomiste, vol. 10. Le Saulchoir, 1927.

Pettazzoni, Raffaele. "La Confession des péchés dans l'histoire des religions." *Mélanges Franz Cumont* (vol. 4 of *Annuaire de l'Institut de philologie et d'histoire orientales et slaves*). 2 vols. Brussels, 1936. Vol. II, 893–901.

Plöchl, Willibald M. *Geschichte des Kirchenrechts. Band II. Das Kirchenrecht der abendländischen Christenheit 1055 bis 1517*. Vienna and Munich, 1955.

Poschmann, Bernhard. *Die abendländische Kirchenbusse im Ausgang des christlichen Altertums*. Münchener Studien zur historischen Theologie, ed. by E. Eichmann, M. Grabmann et al., no. 7. Munich, 1928.

————. *Die abendländische Kirchenbusse im frühen Mittelalter*. Breslauer Studien zur historischen Theologie, ed. by F. X. Seppelt, F. Maier, and B. Altaner. Vol. 16. Breslau, 1930.

————. *Penance and the Anointing of the Sick*. Tr. and rev. by Francis Courtney. The Herder History of Dogma. Freiburg and London, 1964.

Rahner, Karl. *Theological Investigations*. Vol. II. *Man in the Church*. Tr. by Cornelius Ernst. Baltimore, 1963.

Reeves, Marjorie. *The Influence of Prophecy in the Later Middle Ages. A Study in Joachimism*. Oxford, 1969.

Reichling, Dietrich. *Appendices ad Hainii-Copingeri Repertorium bibliographicum*. 7 vols. Munich, 1905–1911.

Rhodes, Dennis E. "A Problem in the Liturgical Bibliography of Normandy." *Gutenberg-Jahrbuch*, 1968, 188–190.

Riley, Lawrence Joseph. *The History, Nature and Use of EPIKEIA in Moral Theology*. Catholic University of America Studies in Sacred Theology, 2d ser., no. 17. Washington, 1948.

Robertson, D. W. "A Note on the Classical Origin of 'Circumstances' in the Medieval Confessional." *Studies in Philology*, 43 (1946), 6–14.

Roth, Erich. *Die Privatbeichte und Schlüsselgewalt in der Theologie der Reformatoren*. Gütersloh, 1952.

Sackur, Ernst. *Sibyllinische Texte und Forschungen. Pseudo-Methodius, Adso, und die tiburtinische Sibylle*. Halle, 1898.

Schauerte, Heinrich. *Die Busslehre des Johannes Eck*. Reformationsgeschichtliche Studien und Texte, ed. by J. Greving, vols. 38–39. Münster, 1919.

Schmitz, Hermann Joseph. *Die Bussbücher und die Bussdisciplin der Kirche, nach handschriftlichen Quellen dargestellt.* 2 vols. Mainz and Düsseldorf, 1883.

Schulte, Johann Friedrich von. *Die Geschichte der Quellen und Literatur des Canonischen Rechts von Gratian bis auf die Gegenwart.* 3 vols. Stuttgart, 1875–1880.

Spykman, Gordon J. *Attrition and Contrition at the Council of Trent.* Kampen, 1955.

Stanka, Rudolf. *Die Summa des Berthold von Freiburg. Eine rechtsgeschichtliche Untersuchung.* Theologische Studien der Österreichischen Leo-Gesellschaft, vol. 36. Vienna, 1937.

Stapper, Richard. "Das 'Lumen Confessorum' des Andreas Didaci." *Römische Quartalschrift für christliche Alterthumskunde und für Kirchengeschichte,* 11 (1897), 271–285.

Teetaert, Amédée. *La Confession aux laïques dans l'église latine depuis le VIIIe jusqu'au XIVe siècle.* Universitas Catholica Lovaniensis. Dissertationes ad gradum magistri in Facultate Theologica vel in Facultate Iuris Canonici, ser. 2, vol. 17. Paris, Wetteren, and Bruges, 1926.

———. "La Doctrine pénitentielle de saint Raymond de Penyafort, O. P." *Analecta Sacra Tarraconensia,* 4 (1928), 121–182.

Tentler, Thomas N. "The Summa for Confessors as an Instrument of Social Control," with "Response and *Retractatio.*" In *The Pursuit of Holiness in Late Medieval and Renaissance Religion,* ed. by Charles Trinkaus with Heiko Oberman. Leiden, 1974. Pp. 101–126, 131–137.

Thomassin, Louis. *Ancienne et nouvelle discipline de l'église touchant les bénéfices et les bénéficiers.* 3 vols. Paris, 1725.

Thomson, Samuel Harrison. *The Writings of Robert Grosseteste, Bishop of Lincoln, 1235–1253.* Cambridge, 1940.

Toussaert, Jacques. *Le Sentiment religieux en Flandre à la fin du moyen âge.* Paris, 1963.

Valton, E. "Excommunication." *DTC,* 5², 1734–1744.

Vogel, Cyrille. *La Discipline pénitentielle en Gaule des origines à la fin du VIIe siècle.* Paris, 1952.

Wallace, Ronald S. *Calvin's Doctrine of the Christian Life.* Edinburgh and London, 1959.

Watkins, Oscar D. *A History of Penance.* 2 vols. London, 1920,

Wenzel, Siegfried. *The Sin of Sloth: Acedia in Medieval Thought and Literature*. Chapel Hill, N.C., 1960.

Wilms, Hieronymus. "Das Confessionale 'Defecerunt' des hl. Antonin." *Divus Thomas*, 3d ser., 24 (1946), 99–108.

Ziegler, Josef Georg. *Die Ehelehre der Pönitentialsummen von 1200–1350. Eine Untersuchung zur Geschichte der Moral- und Pastoraltheologie*. Studien zur Geschichte der katholischen Moraltheologie, ed. by Michael Müller, vol. 4. Regensberg, 1956.

Zimmermann, Charlotte. *Die deutsche Beichte vom 9 Jahrhundert bis zur Reformation*. University of Leipzig Dissertation. Weida i. Thür., 1934.

Addendum to Bibliography

Bossy, John. "The Social History of Confession in the Age of the Reformation." *Transactions of the Royal Historical Society*, 5 ser., 25 (1975) 21–38.

Boyle, Leonard E. "The *Summa confessorum* of John of Freiburg and the Popularization of the Moral Teaching of St. Thomas and of Some of His Contemporaries." In Armand A. Maurer, Etienne Gilson et al., eds. *St. Thomas Aquinas. 1274–1974. Commemorative Studies*, 2 vols. Toronto, 1974. Vol. I, 245–268.

Ozment, Steven E. *The Reformation in the Cities. The Appeal of Protestantism to Sixteenth-Century Germany and Switzerland*. New Haven and London, 1975.

Index

Abelard, 16, 19, 20, 167

absolution, 3, 22–27, 56–57, 65–68, 96–97, 123–124, 233, 263–300, 344, 345, 347–349, 357, 360–361

Adrian of Utrecht, 38, 261

Alain de Lille, 17, 19, 129, 321

Albert the Great, 30, 36, 167, 170, 173, 187–191, 195, 197, 199, 202–204, 215, 216, 224, 228, 328

Albi (manual), 225, 289, 327, 331

Alcuin, 20

Alexander of Hales, 195, 337

Aliquando, 198–199, 207

Ambrose, 4, 243

Andrea, Johannes, 223

Andreas de Escobar, 30, 39–42, 49, 67, 84–86, 112–113, 115, 123, 128, 272, 305–307, 315, 321, 324–327, 336, 338, 348

Angelica, 34–37, 39, 41, 51, 83, 86, 106, 118, 120, 123, 348; proper confessor, 64–68; confession necessary, 66; confession apostolic, 69; interrogations, 90; key of knowledge, 126–127; marital ethic, 173, 181, 183–184, 186, 188; *nimis ardenter*, 177n, 179; *contra naturam*, 198–202, 206–207; menstruation, 209; holy times, places, 213–214, 218–219; conjugal act meritorious, 224n; *causa sanitatis*, 226n; attrition—contrition, 253–255; absolution, 292–294; 298; easiest forgiveness, 269–273; reserved cases, 317, 341; indulgences, 328–329; penances, 327–329, 335–336, 338; laxism, 36, 162, 198, 232; and Luther, 35

Anselm, 247

Antoninus, 39, 41, 49, 106, 119, 127; interrogations, 88–89, 91, 164, 185; key of knowledge, 98, 124; shame, 83; scrupulosity, 76–77;

casuistry, 147; economic sins, 223; marital ethic, 172–173, 181, 212; *nimis ardenter*, 180; *contra naturam*, 197–198, 207; menstruation, 209; attrition—contrition, 256; absolution, 264, 270, 273, 290, 348; reiteration, 123–124; reserved cases, 305, 315–316; penances, 327, 331n, 334–345; restitution, 342

Antonius de Butrio, 44, 82–84, 89, 123, 127, 176, 178, 189, 315–316, 329n, 367

Archdeacon, 202, 328

Aristotle, 153, 185n, 224, 229, 248

Astesana, 34, 35, 39, 49n, 58–59, 65, 86–87, 117, 118, 123, 158n, 191–192, 200, 214, 217, 229, 237, 239, 258–259, 266–267, 270, 273, 290, 321–325, 328

attrition, *see* contrition

Augustine, 8–10, 129, 140, 143, 168–170, 174, 228–232, 296, 298, 321, 364

Autun (manual), 95

Bartholomaeus de Chaimis, 44, 123, 178, 204n, 266–267, 290, 305, 320, 327, 330n, 335–338

Benedict XI, 313, 315, 317

Bernard of Clairvaux, 114, 326

Bernard of Gannat, 274–279, 283

Berthold of Freiburg, 34, 39, 171–172, 178n, 191, 211–212, 218, 224n, 244n

Biel, 243n, 265, 292

Binz, 39n

blessed bread, 79–80

Boccaccio, 103

Boethius, 118

Bonaventure, 32, 173, 240, 255, 276, 337

Bossy, 162n

Library of Congress Cataloging in Publication Data

Tentler, Thomas N.   1932–
  Sin and confession on the eve of the Reformation.

  Bibliography: p.
  Includes index.
  1. Penance—History. I. Title.
BV840.T43   234'.166   76-3022
ISBN 0-691-07219-1